Women in Culture and Politics

WOMEN IN CULTURE AND POLITICS: A CENTURY OF CHANGE

EDITED BY

JUDITH FRIEDLANDER

BLANCHE WIESEN COOK

ALICE KESSLER-HARRIS

CARROLL SMITH-ROSENBERG

INDIANA UNIVERSITY PRESS • BLOOMINGTON

Library of Congress Cataloging-in-Publication Data

[Stratégies des femmes. English]
Women in culture and politics.

Translation of: Stratégies des femmes.
Based on papers presented at three meetings of the
New Family and New Woman Research Planning Group held
in France in 1979 and 1980 and in the United States in
1982.
1. Women—Europe—Addresses, essays, lectures.
2. Women—United States—Addresses, essays, lectures.
3. Feminism—Europe—Addresses, essays, lectures.
4. Feminism—United States—Addresses, essays, lectures.
I. Friedlander, Judith. II. New Family and New Woman
Research Planning Group.
III. Title.
HQ1208.S7713   1986   305.4'094   85-45098

ISBN 0-253-31328-7
ISBN 0-253-20375-9 (pbk.)

1 2 3 4 5   90 89 88 87 86

CONTENTS

Women and Culture

Women and Politics

**Political Theory: Socialist Feminism, a
Critique from Within**

ACKNOWLEDGMENTS

We would like to express our heartfelt appreciation to a number of people and institutions for their support of the New Family and New Woman Research Planning Group and for the publication in French and English of our papers.

First, we cannot thank enough Ioannis Sinanoglou, Executive Director of the Council for European Studies at Columbia University. Since 1979 Dr. Sinanoglou has enthusiastically and patiently helped us prepare our applications to the Rockefeller Foundation and has administered the grants we received. His help and encouragement have been invaluable. We are also very appreciative of Marion Kaplan, previous Executive Director of the Council, who assisted us in the initial stages with the original application.

We are sincerely grateful for the continuing support of the Rockefeller Foundation, which has awarded us three grants. The Foundation made it possible for us to hold two meetings in France and one in the United States and to pay the translation costs in preparation of the English language version of our book. At Rockefeller, we especially want to thank Alberta Arthurs and Kathleen McCarthy (formerly with the Foundation) for their guidance.

We also appreciate the additional financial assistance of the National Endowment for the Humanities and the American Council of Learned Societies as well as the generosity of the University of Paris VII and the University of Pennsylvania for agreeing to serve as sponsoring institutions.

We thank Louise Tilly for inviting us to organize several panels for the International Conference of Europeanists in 1982. Her kind support throughout the history of the Research Planning Group made this entire project a reality.

We appreciate the help of Regula Noetzli of the Charlotte Sheedy Literary Agency, Françoise Pasquier of Editions Tierce, and Indiana University Press for making it possible to have both a French- and an English-language edition of our papers.

We thank as well Maurice Pons and Suzanne Lipinska, at the Moulin d'Andé in Normandy, and Ingram Paperny, at the Inn at Shaker Mill in upstate New York, for providing us with excellent facilities, superb food, and gracious hospitality during our three meetings.

Turning to the group, we gratefully acknowledge Lillian Robinson for helping us make local arrangements in France for the first meeting. We thank Rosalind Greenstein and Marianne Sirgent for their extremely capable and intelligent simultaneous interpreting during our three conferences. The job they did in both English and French was nothing less than extraordinary. We appreciate as well the hard work of all the translators in France and the United States who created French and English versions of our multilingual texts. Since their names appear on the articles they translated, we will not repeat them here. Let us only single out Naomi Holoch for special thanks. The excellent work she did for us does not appear on these pages.

Finally, we would like to thank those scholars from Europe and the United States who presented papers at one or more of our meetings, but whose articles are not in this volume:

England—Sue Bruley, Jill Liddington, Jean Radford
France—Christine Delphy, Christianne Dufrancatel, Liliane Kandel, Michelle Perrot
Germany—Barbara Duden, Elisabeth Meyer-Renschhansen
Italy—Marina D'Amelia, Paola DiCori, Simone Piconne Stella
Netherlands—Selma Leydesdorff, Marjan Schwegman
United States—Estelle Freedman, Sandra Gilbert, Susan Gubar, Esther Newton, Annete Niemtzow, Gayle Rubin, Cynthia Secor, Carroll Smith-Rosenberg

FOREWORD TO THE
UNITED STATES EDITION

This book began as part of a dream to bring together feminist scholars from the United States and Europe. When we first made plans in the late 1970s, few international conferences for women had taken place. Few feminist works had been translated. We in the United States knew but a handful of researchers in France, Germany, or Italy. More familiar with England, we were entirely ignorant of the Netherlands. Although most of us working in the United States had already recognized the importance of doing interdisciplinary research, few seemed interested in a comparative approach. Too much thinking was still going on in national isolation.

And so we sought to construct an international network of feminist scholars, representing six countries—England, France, Germany, Italy, the Netherlands, the United States—and a variety of disciplines—history, literary criticism, philosophy, political science, anthropology, sociology. In 1978 we adopted a model suggested by the Council for European Studies at Columbia University, that of a research planning group. We would hold a series of working conferences, compare patterns across national lines, and attempt to decipher some of the forces that had created the contemporary woman, her economic options, her creative forms, her definition of self.

Known as the New Family and the New Woman Research Planning Group, we met twice in France (1979 and 1980) and once in the United States (1982). By the third meeting, we were ready to prepare our papers for publication.

The history of this book mirrors the changing perspectives and developing theoretical and methodological approaches to women's scholarship over the past six years. We began with quite concrete goals: to seek phenomena common to all six countries and to trace their impact upon women's lives and women's "culture." The original funding proposal, submitted in the summer of 1978, explained that the research planning group would focus on two main themes:

> the impact of those paradigmatic crises of the twentieth century—war, depression and political upheaval—on women's roles in Western Europe and the United States . . . [and] women's culture—both the high

xi

culture of such creative giants as Stein, Woolf, Colette and Kollowitz
and the more pervasive traditional culture of working-class women.

By the time we first met in France in June 1979, those members of
the United States delegation who had written the proposal had expanded the suggested period of study to consider related issues in the
nineteenth century and the years following the Second World War.
Despite this change, many in the group felt that a clear conception of
the project was still lacking, for it placed too much emphasis on the
social and cultural. A large number of European scholars and an
outspoken minority of United States participants considered politics
of equal critical concern: How had women organized politically? Were
similar or different patterns espoused by women of the left and right?
How did women's political movements compare and contrast with
men's movements? Our British colleagues, especially, felt that we had
not given sufficient weight to class issues in general or to the working
class in particular.

Slowly, over the next few years, planning group members broadened their perspectives, seeking to define commonly shared scholarly
interests, to trace patterns that crossed national boundaries, and to
look for themes that would encourage comparative research. By the
time we met in the United States in 1982, we had influenced one
another considerably. Our work treated similar problems, whether we
were writing about women in political parties, religious organizations,
or the theatre. All too often, we observed, women's political work was
called "auxiliary": their labor devalued, their opportunities to gain
recognition in art limited.

We were the researchers as well as the subjects of our studies and we
believed we had a historical mandate to identify new domains, create
new institutions, or try to carve out places for ourselves in areas that
had previously excluded, devalued, and ignored us. We focused on
the imaginary, on how women were represented by men and on how
we saw ourselves. Much of our work necessarily dealt with questions
about cultural elaborations of biological differences. As we worked
together over the years, building on each other's insights, developing
our work too in the context of our specific national, intellectual, and
political worlds, many of our ideas reinforced each other's, enabling
us to challenge traditional research in our fields with greater strength
and understanding.

The years spanned in the planning and development of this volume
were among the most productive of new theoretical perspectives and
methodological approaches in the history of women's studies. The
field today is radically different from what it was in 1978. One of the

most basic changes involved a fundamental reshaping of the questions we asked. Students of women had initially focused on the ways society constructed gender, distributed power along gender and class lines, and so affected our lives as women. Society was both active and male. Daughter of the women's movement of the 1960s and 1970s, women's studies had first sought to trace women's present invisibility, powerlessness, and economic exploitation, back into the past, searching for the roots of our oppression in a world dominated by male social, political, and economic directives. But this definition of the problem, seemingly so correct, was, in fact, limiting and distorting. By asking, as we did in the research planning group, how "paradigmatic crises" had affected women, we made men the central actors in women's social and political dramas.

In order to represent women more adequately, the contributors to this volume began to reconstruct women's experiences and visions through women's own words. The more we learned, the more completely we realized how traditional marxist, literary, and anthropological theories concerning class and culture had restricted our research. As our approaches to the study of women changed, we saw, for example, that women both reflected and transcended class distinctions. But we were still not ready to recognize the extent of our own cultural and ethnic bias; our group was entirely white and, consequently, lacked perspective on a whole range of issues. Nevertheless, as the conferences progressed, we confronted our own racism and the prevailing racism and anti-Semitism in our dominant cultures.

In 1982, just before our last meeting, Editions Tierce, which specializes in books about women, expressed interest in bringing out a French version of our collected papers; and the volume entitled *Stratégies des femmes* was published in 1984. In 1983 Indiana University Press agreed to publish the English-language text. We have included the Foreword to the French edition in the pages that follow.

The papers in this volume have been divided into four parts: Women in Historical Context, Women and Culture, Women and Politics, and Political Theory. Despite our having drawn together over the years, the articles here still represent many different points of view and perspectives. Each section covers a wide range of subjects and approaches. As the French Foreword suggests, a strength of the book is the challenge it makes to those who want to impose one dominant theory, a single idea. But for all the variety, there is a theme which runs through the vast majority of these papers: sexuality, the battle over the female body.

In one article the subject is marriage strategies in nineteenth-century London among the laboring classes; in two others it is the

utopian dreams of the Russian theorist and activist Alexandra Kollontai. There are discussions of Catholic and Protestant conservative
women's organizations in France, the Netherlands, and Germany in
the twentieth century and the invention of the New Woman in England, Germany, and the United States in the same period. Other
papers raise the problems of "family planning" in Nazi Germany and
contemporary Italy; of surviving as a Jewish woman in Poland during
the Second World War and as a German woman just after the war. But
in all of them, a central concern is the social, cultural, and political
control of women's bodies. Sometimes these issues are raised at the
expense of themes more frequently developed by scholars of the
Second World War. Even those articles devoted to philosophical and
political questions about equality, the defeat or assimilation of difference, the emancipation of women, and the challenges facing socialist women or those papers concerned more concretely with the
economic choices women could (had to) make in the United States
and Europe raise the problem of female sexuality and the control of
the female body. The literary critics represented here who look at
attempts to create and elaborate a woman's culture in literature and
the theatre reflect as well, at least metaphorically, on the subject of
what one of the authors has suggestively called Female Insubordination and the Text.

   While we invite the reader to enjoy the multiplicity of ideas and the
many different case histories, we hope s/he will come away from this
book with a notion of where this international group of feminist
scholars has located the struggles of women. Our coming together was
a call for action which we hope will continue. We have joined others in
the attempt to redefine the social, cultural, and political roles of
women and in doing so offer bold, sometimes transgressive, visions of
the future, of a time fast approaching when the academy and its
ancillary cultural pillars will no longer dream of establishing rules for
acceptable scholarship and works of art, in Western Europe or the
United States, which exclude the perspectives of women.

                                        The U.S. Editorial Committee
                                        February 1985

FOREWORD TO THE FRENCH EDITION

This collection is the result of the collaborative efforts of women from several countries during three meetings which took place first in France, then in the United States, in 1979, 1980, and 1982. The purpose of these meetings was to enable us to discover some palpable cohesiveness in our actions and our thinking at the very heart of our irreducible diversity.

Feminism has brought us together. Yet this is not to be understood as a kind of universal feminism that might have united us in some abstract way from the very beginning in terms of definitions, issues, analytical methods, indeed through any systematic approach based upon consensus. We would not claim our efforts to be either exhaustive or unanimous; still less do we entertain the illusion that we could devise for future use any *single* feminist issue with universal application. Our group—representing only six countries, all of them Western—could not consider itself as a unit of the whole. We were unable to speak authoritatively for every culture, for every discipline, for every aspect of a subject of investigation that is being approached from so many overlapping points of view, nor for a single theory that could account for multiple fields of research. Any strategy inclined toward an overall response to an overall problem had to be rejected. Instead, we decided to take our chances on preserving the freedom to formulate new questions concerning any single point, as concretely as possible; specifically, the kinds of questions that unsettle old habits of categorizing and conventional thinking, including our own categories and our own thoughts. In the end, it may be the very notion of *belonging* to a category that we are challenging by our experience.

This will be apparent from the panorama presented by this book, which makes any simple categorization of women impossible. We do not discuss the "working-class woman" as if this were a perfectly acceptable term, but we do discuss working-class women coping with foundling homes in England, or young Jewish women factory workers on strike in New York, or still others in the factories of northern France who have found themselves temporarily outflanked by a right-wing Catholic organization. Nor, for that matter, will the reader find confirmation of the "Jewish woman," the "Communist woman," the "bourgeois woman," the "Catholic woman," the "lesbian," the "woman writer" (whom some of us prefer to call the "writer")* or the "feminist." What is clear from the multifold experiences of these different women, from how they see themselves, from their ideas and their struggles, are the facets of a history which cannot be rendered in monolithic form. A more fitting image might be that of a kaleidoscope, with its infinite possibilities for transformation, starting from a certain number of finite components. It seemed to us that the lives, the accounts, the thoughts of these women were also made up of disparate pieces: some fragments being common to all of them, or almost all, others not; some fragments shared with men, others not; and some, finally, being merely bits of colorless glass.

Still, it appears that a certain consistency, previously hidden below the surface, is now becoming more distinct, without ever becoming standard. Moving from one essay to another, the reader will find that certain historical interludes or countries persistently reappear more than others, that certain questions will repeat themselves, certain hypotheses will answer each other either by reinforcement or contradiction. Little by little, upon reading them, one discovers that real women, in the diversity of their practical experience and quite contrary to conventional thinking, show themselves to be sometimes passive, sometimes active, sometimes both at once. We are concerned here with real women within the context of a complex power network, whether or not these powers are hierarchic, but linked, as power always is, to material or symbolic structures, or to both at the same time. In this framework, one finds various forms of power reinforcing each other, sometimes contradicting each other, or sometimes so diffused that it is difficult to define power in terms of ordinarily oppressive institutions, of established ideologies, of exploitative structures. Case by case, one also sees how these powers are forced to adjust to the strategies of women who, consciously or unconsciously, are playing their own game, either according to the recognized and accepted rules of the game or outside the game.

Lastly, these essays indicate that it is sexual identity above all which refuses to be categorized. Codified by necessity in order to buttress the societies in which we live, nevertheless (as is clear in many of the concrete situations revealed by these essays) sexual identity may be more or less oblique, more or less unsure, more or less transgressed.

---

*It is possible to "feminize" certain nouns in French merely by adding a final *e:* thus, in this text, *écrivain* (writer) becomes *écrivaine* (woman writer). However, since *écrivain* has traditionally *not* been one of the nouns subject to gender transformation, the writing— and pronunciation—of *écrivaine* amounts to a radical transformation of the French lexicon. This "difference," much more subtle than in English, cannot be properly conveyed in translation.

One sees the persistence with which women are attempting to legitimize their individual and collective differences from men and their claim to equality. One sees them (and with them, their writings) trying to spring the trap in which some, even today, would like to bury feminists, and women in general: the trap of having to choose between citizenship, the claim to universal rights which are tied to a deceptive assimilation on one hand and, on the other, the recognition of our right to be different, including the realities of our experience, which are always taken by society as proof of the inferiority of one sex in comparison to the other. By questioning the stake we have in our sexual identity, which plays a crucial part in deciding our total identity, we are perhaps at last displacing something in the immutable system which subjects us all to hierarchy and exclusion.

French Editorial Committee:
MARIE-CLAIRE PASQUIER
MARCELLE MARINI
FRANÇOISE DUCROCQ
GENEVIÈVE FRAISSE
ANNE-MARIE SOHN
Translated by Carol Barko

Women in Historical Context

What is the role of female sexuality and/or marriage and mating customs in the historical experience? What is the relationship between women's perception of their places in the world and their capacity to change that world? The papers in this section address these questions from a variety of perspectives. Building on a series of discrete and disparate historical circumstances, all attempt to confront a recurring contradiction: how women can reconcile their own sense of what is right or good or customary with the changing demands of insistent social policies that are often designed to fit women into the needs of the state or the community.

These papers are about the role that sexuality and its regulation and control play in the struggle for economic and physical survival. Taken together, they capture something of what is imposed on women in terms of sexuality and marital expectation, in the context of what women themselves exact as a price.

The subtle role of ideology and the nature of social expectation play significant roles in shaping what women want and how they perceive the world around them. This is evident in Kessler-Harris's exploration of how socialized notions of *virtue* simultaneously undermine women's economic freedom and enhance traditional family roles. The close relationship between sexuality and economics is more precisely illustrated in Gittins's study of nineteenth-century Devon. There, a shifting occupational structure increased women's job possibilities at the same time it limited their marital options. But Devon's women were lucky compared to the London women studied by Ducrocq. For when the economy demanded male mobility, women's attempts to enforce customary expectations of marriage and support were stymied by the state, leaving women without protection and frequently without adequate means of support.

Women's attempts to regulate their own sexuality and to achieve a degree of control over their lives are also tied closely to the engines of the state, and by the twentieth century to mass culture and consumption, which are its instruments. Rapp and Ross explore the fragility of a 1920s feminist movement that participates in but neither confronts

1

nor controls the new sexual freedom of that decade. This perspective is enriched by the view of Grossmann that sexual openness has two aspects. While one suggests the possibility of freedom, the other places restraints on behavior in the hands of the state and the social reformers who become its agents.

The wrenching discovery that sexual truths are not universal emerges from the pain of those who survived by consciously violating the sexual prescriptions of their own culture. Friedlander suggests that M.'s use of the sexual metaphor protected her from discovery as a Jew at the cost of a separation from her own identity that may have been too heavy a price to pay, even for survival. Tröger comments that German women who saved themselves from rape, and their families from starvation, by seeking male protectors, lived afterwards in the perpetual denial of male weakness.

What then are we to make of this? The cross-national and -chronological scope of these papers, ranging as they do from the United States to England, Poland, Germany, and France and from the mid-nineteenth to the mid-twentieth centuries, suggests that female sexuality is an active agent in this historical process. Its use and manipulation by the state and by agents of industrialism need to be understood. At the same time, the active use by women of sexuality in the interest of their own survival requires further exploration.

INDEPENDENCE AND VIRTUE IN THE LIVES OF WAGE-EARNING WOMEN

THE UNITED STATES, 1870–1930

Alice Kessler-Harris

Whatever the differences of race or class among women, a common ideological bond puts them in a relation to the labor force that has historically differed from that of men. For men, a sense of self has typically come from job-related skill, security, success, or achievement—or the lack thereof. But these are qualities not suited to home roles. Conversely, patterns of behavior and expectations ideally suited to family roles are not necessarily conducive to achievement in the male world of labor. The disparity between male and female expectations limits the validity of any analysis of women's labor that focuses only on such issues as occupational mobility, job consciousness, and even unionization, worker control, and resistance. Instead it opens another kind of analysis that originates in the kinds of self images that have formed the historical boundaries of women's labor market behavior and experience.

Women's decisions to engage in wage work are deeply connected to "real-life" constraints that have historically emerged from women's roles in families. The number of babies, organization of the household and its income level, rural or urban settings, and ethnic or community approval all play a part in the varied patterns of women's work-force participation. These constraints have bred a series of ideological rationalizations that, in self-reinforcing fashion, both maintain the original behavior patterns and roles and inhibit alternative modes of solving life situations. In the United States, ideas about what

a women should be have historically bred opposition to such notions
as collective living, communal child care, and shared kitchens, and
they have diverted us from questions about the naturally ordained
nature of sex roles. The whole is of course sustained and reinforced
by economic pressures that have changed over time.

If we explain women's ability to participate in the labor market in
terms of the impact of real-life constraints on their historical choices,
we are soon caught in the morass of differing experiences, each
equally valid for the particular group to which it applies. Such a
method teaches us little about what is common to gender, though it is
useful for analyzing particular socio-historical situations. But if we
acknowledge that the same network of culture and socialization that
affirms real-life choices operates as well *inside* the labor market and
continues to influence women's behavior as wage earners in ways that
sustain their social roles, we can perhaps reach a common ground
from which to view the particular motivations and drives of female
wage earners.

I would argue that, whether married or single, women's self-images
begin in their relationships to home and motherhood, and I have
labeled them *virtue*—a shorthand, if you will, for conceptions of self
that capture women's sense of being as it emerges from her "naturally" prescribed roles. *Virtue* manifests itself in a number of ways:
attachment to the home, being a good mother, exhibiting genteel or
"ladylike," that is "feminine," behavior. In a society that rewards
economic success, often achieved by means of aggression and self-
assertion, women's instincts historically have been channeled
elsewhere. But for those who engage in wage work, *independence*—my
label for women's attempt to achieve without regard for family constraints—constitutes a more or less powerful pull. Notions of virtue
have historically limited women's capacity to seek independence, so
the relationship between the two notions can tell us much about
women's work lives. The tension they create provides a framework for
analyzing women's conceptions of their goals, their ambitions, and
their own and societal expectations. The lack of such an analysis
stymies our attempts to come to terms with some of the major problems we have faced in explaining women's consistently poor labor-
market position.

We know that virtue or attachment to the home has sometimes been
rejected by individual women; yet even when individual women flout
the conventional notion of virtue, it remains central to their decision-
making processes. And we know that, as ideologies do, the components of virtue have altered with changes in the family and in the
labor process and with labor-market needs. We now accept that ideas

and their manifestations are relative to particular ethnic, racial, and class groups. But that is all part of what we need to explore. Only by understanding the ways in which definitions of female virtue change over time can we identify the historical experience of female wage earners. And I would go a step further to suggest that so constant has been the importance of women's familial connection (in its varied forms) that it is precisely because the current women's movement challenges the ideas on which the connection rests that some find it so threatening.

I would like to make a case for looking at women's wage work this way—that is outside the structural patterns imposed by male categories—by illustrating briefly what happens when we do so in three areas. I want to look first at some expressed motivations for women's wage work among women who were cut off from male support in the 1860s and seventies, reaching into the eighties. Second, I want to examine self-imposed labor-market constraints in the period from the 1890s to about 1910. Finally, I want to explore the period from 1910 until 1930, when the notion of ambition emerged for women.

In the first period, women tended to justify their wage work in terms of the absence of male support. By the second, unmarried women had carved out a series of "proper" and appropriate jobs, and those who were married had developed elaborate rationales for job holding. Both of these periods reflect a notion of virtue that is emphatically determined by women's roles at home. In the third period, after 1910, that notion of virtue changed to encompass economic support for the home, making room for women to declare their own job-related ambitions. In its full flower in the 1920s, and among some women, socially ordained roles at home gave way for the first time to an unapologetic notion of work for individual satisfaction. Virtue had produced its own contradiction.

These changes reflect abstract movements of ideas less than they suggest a trade-off between the needs of the family and shifts in the labor process. While the work women did and the numbers of women working for wages changed dramatically over time, women's wage work, as these illustrations indicate, remained conceptually unaltered. Throughout the period, wage work affirmed virtue only in so far as it contributed to present and future family life. Independent women, in short, lacked virtue in society's eyes until the twenties, when their roles as wage earners began to be seen as a more permanent part of the family economy.

The result of family-bound conceptions of virtue was such that even women who were in fact independent defended their positions as though they wished they were not. It was perhaps the conviction of

their own virtue that enabled women to act politically. In the Civil War
and immediate postwar period, for example, women played on the
absence of male support, at first crudely, pleading for help because
they were the widows, sisters, and daughters of people who had fallen
on the battlefield. This argument underlay the militance of sewing
women in 1863 who organized themselves into protective unions in
response to visibly deteriorating conditions. And it was used by 1865
as a rationale for women to move into new fields of employment.
"How inhuman," wrote a seamstress to a labor paper, "to refuse
employment to women on the pretext that possibly they may marry.
Many women now asking for employment gave up their husbands to
die for the country."[1]

One suspects that the argument persisted because it worked, gar-
nering public sympathy and inserting opening wedges in trade-union
doors. It was the basis of successful petitions to President Lincoln in
which women asked for direct access to arsenal work without the
intervention of middlemen. It was picked up by the labor press—
Fincher's Trades Review, for example, printing petition after petition
that urged higher wages for women whose husbands, fathers, and
brothers had died in the war. And we can gauge its success to some
extent because it was accompanied by a simultaneous excoriation of
women "who are not in indigent circumstances, but who find time to
earn the means of freer expenditures for dress or some other darling
object of ambition."[2]

The reforming and middle classes who addressed problems of low
pay and a glutted labor market offered solutions that ranged from the
hope that women would marry to the suggestion of forced emigration
to the West. A few feminists proposed to solve the problem by training
women for decent jobs. But by and large it was thought that women
with husbands would not seek paid work and that men with sufficient
incomes would keep their wives at home.

For many women, that solution held no promise. The New York
Times estimated in 1869 that about a quarter of a million young
women in the eastern-seaboard states could never look forward to any
matrimonial alliance because they outnumbered men by that much.[3]
The surplus population of women contributed to a rising tide available for work, depressing wages to the lowest possible level and
contributing to anxiety about wage competition.

If husbands were not to be obtained in the centers of population,
there was always the possibility of westward migration. The editor of
Boston's *Daily Evening Voice* proposed state intervention to this end in
1865. He knew, he said, "of no more useful object" to which the
commonwealth could lend its aid than that of opening "the door of

emigration to young women who are wanted for teachers, and for every other appropriate as well as domestic employment in the remote West, but who are leading anxious and useless lives in New England."[4]

Wage-earning women had different solutions. They agreed, at least on paper, that those who married should withdraw from the labor market in order to reduce wage competition. Some opted for organization, searching for allies among male trade unionists. But to do so, they had to struggle against a labor movement that accepted social notions of virtue. The labor press, reflecting the opinions of a tiny though influential group of skilled craftsmen, bewailed the misfortune that permitted "sisters and daughters . . . to leave home, even for congenial employment in workshops and factories." "We shall spare no effort," proclaimed *Finchers Trades Review,* "to check this most irrational invasion of our fireside by which the order of nature is reversed." The *Workingmans Advocate* concurred. "Man is and should be head in his own department, in the management of his business for the support of his family. Woman should be head in her department, in the management of household affairs, and in the care and government of the children." To sustain this division of roles, the editors suggested that woman should be "sympathetic, tender, soft-voiced with faith, hope and charity templed in her soul." Her strength lay "in the very weakness of her slighter nature and more delicate frame, and the charm, subtle and sure, of a feminine manner, is a more potent spell than enchanter wove."[5]

Women who wished to assert their independence—to organize—could expect little help there. And yet, despite these rigid conceptions of women's roles, the labor press recognized the need for women without husbands to seek jobs. "No one hesitates to give employment to a young man," Boston's *Daily Evening Voice* argued,

> because of the probabilities of his entering the army. It is not so much a fear that business will suffer, as a determination to keep women in the track of domestic duties, that leads to this cruel ignoring of her necessities.[6]

Under these circumstances, women sometimes resorted to more devious means for protecting themselves. Denying their desire to flout convention, they played what was perhaps a tongue-in-cheek role. This is best captured by a group of Boston sewing women in April 1869. Meeting in convention, they petitioned the Massachusetts state legislature to give them homes. After years of suffering through the declining real wages of the Civil War, they asked for relief. While they protested their ignorance and weakness and appealed tearfully for care, these women had developed a comprehensive and well-thought-out scheme for public housing that would free them from economic dependence. They worked constantly, they argued. They were deprived of honorable society and religion, and even reduced to "ruinous" avocations in order to make ends meet. They prayed the legislators to "think for us, care for us, and take counsel from your ever kind hearts to do for us better than we know how to ask." Then they presented their proposal.

> we ask that an opportunity be given us to make homes. We pray your honorable body to cause to be purchased in the neighborhood of Boston, a tract of good cultivated land; and to lay out the same in suitable lots. . . . It is our desire that these lots should be let on lease to poor working women of Boston, to whom the state would be willing to furnish rations, tools, seeds and instructions in gardening, until such time as the women would be able to raise their own food, or otherwise become self-supporting.[7]

It was not their fault, they argued in justification, that they had no husbands. Women far outnumbered men in Massachusetts. Nor was it strength that led them to ask for "a separate existence." That was evidence only of "a great distress." Women "collected together in a separate village" would, they claimed, be no danger to the community. Rather, they would "exercise a moral influence on each other." And to prove their good intentions, they declared their willingness to withdraw their petition entirely if the legislature would "give us good and kind husbands and suitable homes, make our conditions something distantly approximate to that of your own wives." With more references to their weakness and humility, the petition closed.

Predictably, the Massachusetts legislature did nothing. Yet these women brilliantly captured the core of tension: a restraining ideology rooted in revered familial relationships forbade effective solutions to the dilemma facing female wage workers. Having been placed outside bounds, through no fault of their own, they had been denied women's traditional protections and left to fend for themselves. Even before the Civil War, such women had become a visible "underclass." Had the Civil War not exacerbated the problem by reducing the numbers of potential husbands and creating poor widows of otherwise respectable wives, they might have remained so indefinitely. As it was, the march of economic events revealed their predicament in its starkest light. In exposing women's real economic conditions and removing the possibility of self-blame it gave women license to protest and unionize. And it gave well-intentioned men, as well as those who feared competition, the opportunity to admit women into their organizations.

Arguments for jobs for the husbandless left notions of women's roles unchallenged without hindering those in need from working for wages. At the same time, they conditioned women's decisions to engage in wage work, structuring the choice of jobs and the jobs available to them. As the labor market expanded, there followed, in the late nineteenth century, a discussion as to what jobs were appropriate for women to do—that is, which would be the least harmful to their home roles.

In the reforming and middle classes, this debate focused on whether the harsh conditions of work and the temptations to which women were exposed would forever inhibit them from becoming good wives and mothers. And it particularly emphasized sexual morality (which explains the boarding houses and working girls clubs of that period, as well as some early support for vocational education). But that form is not visible among wage-earning women themselves. Rather, wage-earning women eagerly took advantage of jobs in newly restructured areas in order to benefit from the rise in real wages current in the period and where the continuing subdivision of labor enabled them to take jobs formerly held by men. They were inhibited by their own notions of home needs—notions that differed among immigrant, black, and native-born women. Though gender was sometimes less important than class and race in decisions as to *whether* to work, internal notions of virtue influenced choices about *where* to work. The visible manifestation of the decision-making process is in the expression of propriety. Important job shifts in potteries, in textiles, and, beginning in the 1880s, in offices reflected both greater opportunity for women and fewer inhibitions among those seeking jobs. And a simultaneous and complementary rise in home work— apparently chosen by many women—confirms the sense that internal standards were operating among those able to choose among jobs.

In a broad sense, these notions of propriety served as the organizational principles for women's work-force participation. They created a reciprocally confirming system in which successful job experiences for women were defined in terms of values appropriate to future home life: neatness, morality, cleanliness, sex segregation, and clean language all defined appropriate women's jobs. Men's jobs, in contrast, reflected ambition, competition, aggression, and the search for increased income. Such definitions confirmed women's places at home, even while they engaged in wage labor, and legitimized their restricted roles despite visible evidence that the choices available to women often left them in indefensible poverty. Not incidentally, such restrictions also served to order the labor market in ways that benefited employers. They acted as devices to divide the wage-labor force, enabling employers to exercise greater control in a period of flux.

For women, internal standards emerged in terms of self-imposed hierarchies in jobs, in terms of self-exclusion from inappropriate jobs, and in notions of "ladylike behavior." These self-imposed standards seem to be most visible between about 1890 and 1910; the years of the great expansion in the United States of the so-called "new immigration." Women entered the labor force in jobs that reflected their class and ethnic positions. They worked for material necessities, choosing their jobs from the options offered by their particular ethnic and class reference groups. Since the job market denied women self-directed ambitions toward upward mobility and cultural attitudes affirmed motivation to marriage and children, women were encouraged to adopt those forms of thought and behavior that would yield eventual marriage.[8]

Women talked about taking jobs because they attracted a "nice class of girls." Conversely, they remembered being warned away from other jobs. "Factory girls were immoral" was the advice given by an old neighbor to Mary Kenney when she went to Chicago to seek work.[9] Clean jobs within factories were more desirable than those that made hands dirty. And where they had choices, women refused jobs that required them to wear old or dirty clothes in the streets. Agnes Nestor, later a trade-union leader, described the women who worked on fine leather gloves in her factory as "looking down" on those who worked on coarser hides. Factory workers felt superior to menial domestic workers. A Cohoes, New York, newspaper reported in 1881 that operatives felt "they take a higher place in the social scale than is accorded them when they do housework."[10]

But factories took second place to what were then called mercantile houses—department stores. Department stores offered extremely long hours, low wages, and close supervision. Leonora O'Reilly remarked in 1899, "Department store women have a caste feeling about their work and think that persons working in a mercantile establishment are a little higher in society than the women who work in a factory."[11] Rose Schneiderman, later to become a Women's Trade Union League president, reported that when she quit her job as a department store clerk to become a sewing machine operator at twice her former salary, her mother was "far from happy. She thought working in a store much more genteel than working in a factory."[12] The feeling of social superiority was reflected in different living styles. Despite low wages, shop workers tended to sacrifice food in order to dress well. Perhaps because their sexual morality was so often in question, they tended to live in better neighborhoods than factory workers with comparable wages. Factory workers, in contrast, ate better, at the sacrifice of the other amenities.[13]

What women gave up in ambition or independence on the job, they compensated for in the home-related virtue that was thought to attach to particular kinds of work. High wages and promotion, though desirable, were not the measure of virtue for them. Just as department store women willingly acquiesced to low wages because their jobs seemed to offer gentility, those who chose wages above "virtue" faced social censure. While waitresses often earned more than the ordinary factory operative, social disgrace attended the public character of their job. They were said to be "more free and easy in manner and speech" than other wage-earning women. Among waitresses, many disapproved of those who worked in restaurants that served liquor despite the significantly larger tips offered in these places.[14]

How any particular woman dealt with these issues in her own life reflected the tensions imposed by the constraints of her particular ethnic or racial group and the realities of the job market. For black women, faced with discrimination that confined them to the bottom of the labor-market pool and lacking social contraints against wage labor, gender disappeared as the primary operative category in work choice. Race was paramount. And virtue, having dictated the need to work, coerced most black women into accepting what was available. Other ethnic groups exercised their own constraints. Jewish women whose culture validated economic contributions to family life tended to take advantage of vocational training more rapidly than any other immigrant group. Like Italians, the unskilled among them worked together in their own ethnic group. Italians concentrated in New York City's garment industry (where 52 percent of all working Italian women were employed in 1910) and in candy making and artifical flowers, partly out of a desire to remain under the protection of kin, rather than as the result of free labor-market choice. Native-born white women most commonly emphasized nice surroundings. For them, one mark of genteel employment was the absence of immigrant work mates. Observers noted that "native born girls of Anglo-Saxon stock prefer [red] when possible to choose an occupation socially superior to factory work,"[15] ranking jobs with the greatest percentage of "American-born" girls highest.

In its most virulent, self-imposed form this notion of propriety probably lasted until the First World War. At that point one might want to argue that it had in some way become embedded into the behavior patterns adopted by immigrant women who wanted to be "Americanized." Among Jewish immigrant women in New York, efforts to emulate "ladylike" behavior ranged from attempts to dress like ladies to flat contradictions of an old-world culture that reinforced economic roles for women. It stirred trouble between mothers and daughters, emerging particularly in the generation that went to school in America. One immigrant offered the following description of what she learned about manners in night school: "We wore long skirts . . . and of course we were not allowed to lift it too high, only allow a little bit of the shoe to be seen. And [the teacher] used that as an example of our behavior in life. That we should be careful not to get any moderness."[16]

In the prewar years, less privileged women ordinarily assumed not that marriage meant giving up work but that their continued wage work would depend on family needs. Those who put wage work first did so at the cost of family life. Rose Schneiderman, a frequently cited example, went to work at thirteen. The daughter of a widowed immigrant mother, she chose trade unionism as a career knowing that it would lead to a life without marriage. Anzia Yezierska, poverty-stricken child immigrant to America, learned English so that she could satisfy her burning passion to write. She abandoned a husband and gave up custody of her only daughter so that she could, in the words of her fiction, "make herself for a person."

Among the more affluent and those with some education, intimations of ambition existed in the period before the war. There had, of course, always been numbers of women who had chosen not to marry—whose restless energy had turned toward social settlements or the YWCA or found outlets in Greenwich Village rebellion. While the very talented, the very rich, and the hardy had long been able to mold the minds of Wellesley girls or pioneer their way into medical school, there was a sense after the war that marriage and satisfying work need not be mutually exclusive alternatives. Charlotte Perkins Gilman's *Women and Economics* offers the most articulate theoretical statement of possibility in the United States. Crystal Eastman and her group of New Women before World War I offer the most dramatic examples. These women acted on the assumption that they were entitled to pursue careers and to marry.

But it was not until after the war that these attempts at independence became compatible with a measure of virtue. Changing definitions of virtue introduced into the labor market a kind of woman who had not earlier been seen there and for whom community and ethnic values carried less weight than they had for the poor women who early-on constituted the bulk of the female labor force. Labor process shifts contributed to removing ideological constraints by creating the illusion of a technological imperative which necessitated training and the introduction of a tightly organized hierarchy to control the shop floor. To sustain that system required the introduction of incentives, in which women, as workers, had to be encouraged to participate. New organization forms in manufacturing and offices that emerged in the twenties began to break down one of the major barriers to women's conception of themselves as full participants in the labor force, opening the door to work-related ambitions. Ironically this happened first among middle-class women who had discouraged immigrant wives from making direct contributions to household income. Ambition crept into their vocabulary, producing what at first seemed like an irreconcilable conflict. To aspire, to achieve, not merely to do the least offensive job became at least a possibility for daughters as well as for sons.

Advice on how to "make it" flowed freely. "There is no such thing as limitation of opportunity in business," an audience of office workers heard in 1915. "The only limitation is the limitation we set ourselves."[17] Young girls still in high school were advised to sell life insurance as the "surest as well as most convenient means of providing for an independent old age." In 1916, the Boston Bureau of Vocational Information, set up by college-educated women for women, sponsored a series of lectures. "If you expect to get to the top, believe that you can get there, and then climb with all your might and main." Eliminate all thought of marriage: "If you have in mind that you . . . are going to do this for . . . years, perhaps all your life, you will be more likely to succeed."[18]

Paradoxically, perhaps ambition among the middle class legitimized the right for less privileged women to work. Defensiveness disappeared as former household workers found jobs in candy factories, while candy dippers told their daughters not to "come with me to learn dipping," but to go to work in an office or department store where the work was more certain and the pay steady.[19] Southern mill families urged their daughters to take "business courses."[20] Teaching jobs opened as possibilities for Colorado miners' daughters like Alice Smedley and immigrant children like Anzia Yezierska. Secretaries interviewed in the early part of the 1920s reported that though they liked their jobs, they were discouraged about not being able to "get ahead" in them. So great appeared the desire for promotion among secretaries and stenographers that a barrage of literature attempted to persuade them that secretarial work was a satisfactory occupation in itself.

But the influence of old notions of virtue had not disappeared. They continued to affirm personality patterns and social roles consistent with the home, reinforcing the occupational stereotypes that divided administrative and professional networks into those that threatened to negate home roles and those that did not. Women's mobility in the office and business world remained stringently limited. In contrast, careers in nursing, libraries, teaching, and social work drew on years of socialization and a consciousness bred to serve. They fitted the demand for personal satisfaction, yet met the criteria for women's work. They were careers in the sense that they paid relatively steady salaries instead of poor and intermittent wages, but they offered only limited possibilities for advancement and therefore helped to curtail whatever ambition a young woman might have had.

The cycle was self-reinforcing, rewarding personality traits considered feminine and punishing others. One employment manager put it this way: "Select a woman who you think could be married at any time if she chose, but just for some reason does not."[21] Successful women often achieved their positions by utilizing their feminine characteristics. College women, for example, could do better in banks if they helped homemakers deal with savings, budget, and family problems that affected financial stability.[22]

Viewed from the perspective of a constraining ideology, the changing labor-force participation of married women seemed especially threatening. The new kinds of jobs women were entering tended to sustain or create gender-free illusions of mobility—illusions that had little to do with family lives and could best exist parallel to, but not in support of, their primary family roles. For it was in the jobs that hinted at upward mobility that the dangerous potential of an ambitious womanhood posed the greatest threat.

As a result, married women who had escaped or transcended the prevailing social constraints drew mixed admiration and doubt. The press emphasized their dual roles. "Woman President of Bank Does Housework in Her Home" trumpeted one headline.[23] Another paper captioned a photograph of the woman who invented tea bags: "Gertrude Ford proves that it is possible to maintain a house, Be a Devoted Mother *and* conduct a Successful Business."[24] Women could play two roles, but if the press were to be believed, success at work ought to be buttressed by a satisfying home life. A New York *Herald* reporter described the ascent of a young Scottish immigrant girl to an executive post at Western Union: "In spite of her sustained contact with the business world, the reporter noted, "she remains conspicuously feminine in dress and demeanor and believes in marriage and children for the average woman above all the rewards of the business world."[25]

Women did not "make it" in the 1920s. Married women of all classes faced persistent job discrimination. The labor market maintained, and in most areas rigidified, traditional patterns of job segmentation.

Yet the attitudes with which women went to work in 1925 would have been unrecognizable in 1875. In the 1870s wage-earning women demanded higher wages and better working conditions. By the 1920s, no longer content with doing better where they were, women asked for different jobs, upward mobility, and economically secure careers—all demands that had historically been associated with men and that reflected the changing composition of the female labor force as well as the tempting new jobs available. Virtue still inhered in woman's ability to sustain family life. What had changed were conceptions of what families needed. One could speculate that the mobility aspirations that isolated working-class men into individualistic job consciousness had a different impact on working-class women. Among some groups—garment workers in the teens, for example, or southern textile workers in the twenties—the freedom to boldly assert the right to work led women to identify as workers—an identification that made trade-union organization feasible, though it did not remove the real constraints against successful unionization.

My sense of what happened is that the changing labor process produced its own dilemma—creating for some women jobs that enabled them to see the possibilities for more satisfying wage work and for less educated women jobs that held the potential for combining wage and household work. For the better off, possibilities were restrained in the thirties by depression, manipulated in the forties by war, and rigidly channeled in the 1950s by a heavy dose of home and motherhood idcology, as well as by the incentives of household consumption. By the 1960s, they could no longer be contained, releasing in that decade a generation of repressed ambition.

Two opposing conceptions of wage labor inform women's current attempts to enter into work. One asserts women's new freedom from the family and claims the power to be as ambitious and success-oriented as men. The other insists that women must carry into wage labor some of the best of women's own "morality and virtue" and, by struggle, alter the conception of work for men and women. At the same time, we face the dilemma of how to organize reproduction and family life in a world that holds paid labor as virtuous for women as it is for men. That is our battle, but it would have drawn empathy from a young seamstress who asked in 1874, "Why is it can a woman *not* be virtuous if she does mingle with the toilers?"

Notes

1. *Daily Evening Voice*, June 12, 1865.
2. *Daily Evening Voice*, April 7, 1865.

3. New York *Times,* October 17, 1869, p. 3. The *World* estimated the number at 300,000, December 1, 1863, p. 4.

4. *Daily Evening Voice,* January 7, 1865, p. 2.

5. *Fincher's Trades Review,* June 6, 1863, p. 2; "Two Heads or One," *Workingman's Advocate,* May 7, 1870, p. 4; *Workingman's Advocate,* April 9, 1870, p. 1; in the same paper, see also "A Wife's Power," March 11, 1876, p. 1; November 13, 1869, p. 4; and "A Perfect Wife," March 19, 1870, p. 1.

6. Ellen Butler, "Women and Work," *Daily Evening Voice,* January 12, 1865, p. 1.

7. "The Wail of the Women," *Workingman's Advocate,* April 24, 1869, p. 1.

8. See Leslie Tentler, *Wage Earning Women* (New York: Oxford, 1979), on this point. Carolyn Dall, *Women's Right to Labor* (Boston: Walker, Wise, & Co., 1860), 72, provides a particularly clear statement. "How we rate an idle boy! How we bear with a dawdling girl! That father grows impatient whose son does not rise early, or show some desire for employment; but the same man keeps his daughters in Berlin wool and yellow novels, and looks to marriage as their salvation, even when he blushes to be told of it."

9. Mary Van Kleeck, *Artificial Flower Makers* (New York: Survey Associates, 1913), 38; Mary Kenney O'Sullivan, "autobiography," in O'Sullivan papers, Schlesinger library, 28.

10. Quoted in Daniel Walkowitz, "Working Class Women in the Gilded Age: Factory, Community and Family Life among Cohoes, N.Y. Cotton Workers," *Journal of Social History* (Summer 1972): 476.

11. Clippings from the Utica *Daily Press,* March 29, 1899, in O'Reilly collection, Schlesinger, Box 8, file 85.

12. Rose Schneiderman with Lucy Goldthwaite, *All for One* (New York: Paul Erickson, 1967), 43.

13. *Wage Earning Women in Stores and Factories,* Vol. 5 of the Report on Women and Child Wage Earners, 134–35.

14. Ibid., 193, 199.

15. Elizabeth Butler, *Saleswomen in Mercantile Stores,* Baltimore, 1909 (New York: Russell Sage, 1912), 144, 121.

16. Ella Wolff interview, typescript in Amerikaner Yiddish Geshichte Belpe, December 27, 1963, p. 3.

17. Eleanor Gilbert, lecture manuscript, "Office work as Training for Executive Positions," October 25, 1915, in Bureau of Vocational Information, Box 1, file 7, Schlesinger.

18. Edward Woods, "Selling Life Insurance: A Vocation for Girls," *The Scholastic* (February 9, 1924): 9. See also Ida White Parker, "Women in the Insurance Fields," *The Businesswoman* (January 1923): 17–18; Eugenia Wallace, "Filing, a Stepping Stone," *The Spotlight* (February 1918): 4; clipping from the New York *Times,* dated February 29, 1924, in file 63, Box 4, BVI, Schlesinger; Mrs. Crocker, "Women in Civil Service," March 28, 1916, in file 23, Box 1, BVI.

19. Interviews of February 11, 1919, and February 27, 1919, in Philadelphia Candy Study Home Visits, Box 40, Women's Bureau papers, National Archives.

20. Interview, November 28, 1921, South Carolina Home Visits, Box 43, Women's Bureau, National Archives.

21. Ella V. Price of the Narrow Fabric Company, Reading, Pennsylvania, April 12, 1918, file 179, Box 14, BVI.

22. "Training Women for a New Occupation," *School Life,* 1922, clipping in

file 63, Box 4, BVI. "For example," the article continued, "the withdrawal of an account gives indication of possible distress in a household. In such a case, the home service director may investigate the circumstances, and often she can suggest methods of retrenchment that will enable the family to continue saving."

23. Clipping from unidentified paper, dated March 20, 1923, in file 23, Box 1, BVI, Schlesinger about Mrs. E. M. Abernethy of Lexington, Oklahoma.

24. Unidentified clipping dated March 9, 1925, in file 69, Box 4, BVI.

25. New York *Herald,* July 3, 1925, p. 3.

BETWEEN THE DEVIL AND THE DEEP BLUE SEA

THE MARRIAGE AND LABOR MARKETS IN NINETEENTH-CENTURY ENGLAND

Diana Gittins

There has been increasing recognition[1] that to understand women's situation properly it is necessary to consider *both* their relation within the labor market *and* the domestic economy. The relative importance of one or the other, however, is variable and depends on the person's age and the fluctuations of a marriage market. Historians, like other social scientists, have been guilty of assuming that because at some point the majority of a population marries, it is irrelevant to examine groups other than the married or to consider in more detail the nature of the marriage market. This approach has enhanced the notion that marriage is "normal," "natural," and constant. It is not. Rather, it is an important socio-economic and political transaction which many enter, some do not, and many leave by various means. This paper represents an attempt to consider the relative and changing importance of the marriage and labor markets in a small Devon textile town during a period of rapid economic change.

Devon was one of the main centers of the woolen industry until the eighteenth century and was dominated largely by wage labor from the sixteenth century. Production was organized on a protoindustrial basis:[2] it expanded by an increase in the number of producing units rather than by any dramatic change in technology or shift in the scale of production.[3] From the eighteenth century onward the woolen industry in Devon began a rapid decline as a result of competition from Yorkshire. Devon became increasingly dependent on agriculture, which was characterized by a mixture of family-run smallholdings and more capitalistic medium-sized holdings.

In contrast with the county as a whole, the area around Buckfastleigh continued throughout the nineteenth, and into the twentieth, centuries as a small but quite prosperous enclave of the woolen industry. It managed to survive largely because of easy access to a local supply of wool. The industry was characterized by a number of small masters (woolstaplers) operating in small workshops in, or near to, their homes and reliant on laborers in the surrounding countryside to carry out spinning (invariably done by women and children in family farming) and town laborers—either at home or in workshops—to carry out the other major processes of sorting (women), combing (men), and weaving (men and women). The "urban" and "rural" were not sharply differentiated; one person often moved back and forth between agricultural and industrial work, and households frequently contained a mixture of members involved in both sectors.

During the course of the nineteenth century the woolen industry became increasingly mechanized, but protoindustry based on small workshops and households continued to exist alongside the expanding factories. The demise of protoindustry in the town was greatly accelerated by the mechanization of woolcombing around 1850. From then on, capital became increasingly separate, and by 1871 we can speak of a final proletarianization of the work force, in the sense that workers were not only separated from the ownership of the means of production but had also lost all control over the labor process itself.[4] We need to ask at this point exactly *who* was proletarianized and, more specifically, what were the effects of these marked changes in the labor market on the marriage market and how in turn were these mediated through households and living arrangements.

First consider the overall occupational structure of the town:

The whole labor force expanded somewhat, but more noticeable is the expansion in the number of women (though this may simply indicate their increased "visibility" with the demise of protoindustry). Although the actual proportion of men in the property-owning sector remained constant, there were marked changes in the woolen industry. In 1851 there were twenty-five woolstaplers, but by 1871 there were only four, and only two of these owned large enterprises. Legal documents for the largest firm revealed how a farmer bought a tannery in 1806 where he and his sons set up business. In 1842 they rented a mill for hand combing, then in 1846 bought it. Here they mechanized the woolcombing process. By 1851 the father had retired and his sons carried out the related trades of serge manufacture, tanning, and farming. The woolen mill employed eighty-three women, thirty-seven men, four boys, and eight girls; by 1861 it is recorded as employing 270 women and children (although it seems

Occupational Structure of Buckfastleigh, 1851 and 1871

| | Men | | Women | |
	1851	*1871*	*1851*	*1871*
Private Income	11	14	31	29
Professional, business	50	49	11	12
Farmers	16	32	1	—
Shopkeepers	38	35	23	24
Artisans/ skilled workers	152	193	64	61
Servants	22	33	53	65
Woolcombers	247	37	—	1
Weavers, Woolsorters	2	23	167	210
Miners, quarrymen	28	71	—	5
Agricultural laborers	110	148	—	—
Laborers	12	68	14	51
Domestic	—	—	16	23
	688	703	380	481

Total, 1851 = 1068 (36% women)
Total, 1871 = 1184 (41% women)

likely at least a few men were employed in select jobs). During the course of the century the firm, Hamlyn Brothers, continued buying workshops, land, and houses; and their consolidation of capital by the end of the century is striking.

While there was a general increase in the number of laborers, the expansion of the woolen industry was achieved first and foremost through female labor. The mechanization of woolcombing effectively ousted men (though not boys) from the industry. Woolcombing had been a highly skilled, well-paid, and well-organized craft that was entirely male dominated. Its collapse through mechanization and the parallel exploitation of cheap female labor were the chief factors enabling the growth and consolidation of capital in the local woolen industry. At a rough estimate, approximately half of the 247 men listed as woolcombers in 1852 simply left the area to search for suitable work elsewhere. The relative ease with which men, as opposed to women, could travel about in search of work had at least two important implications. On the one hand, it meant a man had a greater chance of retaining his class and status position by seeking equivalent work elsewhere. On the other hand, it meant that women left at home were at the mercy of the local labor market and offered aspiring capitalists a pool of cheap, and often desperate, labor. In this instance at least, mechanization was a highly successful means of profit-making and capital accumulation because it cheapened labor costs by *feminizing* the labor force as well as proletarianizing it. The two were not quite synonymous, but were nevertheless inextricably linked.

Notice the increase of male artisans between the two years, particularly when viewed in conjunction with the female labor force. For while the number of women in wage labor increased, the number in the property-owning sector and in skilled work in fact *decreased*. Apparently, consolidation of capital and proletarianization affected women far more adversely than men. Or rather, the consolidation of capital was in fact *made possible* through a proletarianization of women.

While obviously there were men who became proletarianized, they nevertheless had distinct advantages over women. On the one hand men had greater possibilities for geographical and social mobility made possible largely through a patriarchal ideology which allowed them the acceptability of sleeping outdoors, traveling alone, staying in inns and taverns, having access to lodging and help organized by their craft. Women's mobility was far more severely limited, operating basically through female kin networks. Women moved to and from other households as domestic servants or else fell into prostitution or parish relief.

The other option for men was to cushion the effects of proletarianization within families. Even if a father became proletarianized, his standard of living and his sons' chances of mobility were retained largely through the use of unmarried daughters' labor power. Unmarried daughters in the parental home were exploited twice, by the economic system *and* by their families as a means of increasing their standard of living and also to promote sons' chances of mobility.

To explore some of these themes further, let us consider the circumstances of unmarried children who were still living at home over the age of twenty-five:

Although the numbers are obviously small, the difference between sons and daughters living with a single mother is striking in both years. It is interesting to note the fairly high numbers living with both parents where the father alone works, and in particular to note the increase of sons in this situation between the two years. Why, however, were so many women living with their mothers—was it a case of daughterly love and support (a manifestation of Shorter's increase in

**Unmarried Men and Women, 25 or Over, Living with Parent(s)—
Domestic Situations, 1851 and 1871.**

Living with:

	Mother	Father	Parents both work	Parents father works
1851				
Women	22	3	6	20
Men	8	—	5	8
1871				
Women	16	5	3	16
Men	5	4	3	19

"love" as a result of "modernization"?), or did the daughters (and sons) have something to gain from this arrangement in a more calculative way (as Anderson would argue)?

**Mothers' Economic Situation: Unmarried Men and Women over 25
Living with Single Mothers, 1851 and 1871**

	Professional, (business) farming	Private income	Pauper/ no occ.	Wage (laborer)
1851				
Women	6	9	7	—
Men	4	—	2	2
1871				
Women	1	2	11	2
Men	—	—	3	2

In 1851 the majority of the mothers of unmarried daughters were in an economic situation involving some ownership of property, however small, and one may assume that for most of these daughters there was a high chance of inheriting their mother's property upon her death. There were thus real economic advantages to these women remaining unmarried, often probably in exchange for providing help of one sort or another to their mothers. While fifteen of these women were in this position, seven of them were not and were apparently supporting their mothers (one daughter was also a pauper, and all the rest were weavers) in conditions of severe poverty. Moreover, they were all in their thirties and forties. Why, one wonders, had they chosen to eke out a subsistence supporting their mothers instead of getting married? This may reflect the somewhat unbalanced sex ratio of the town (a surplus of women); it may also reflect what seems to have been a fairly widely accepted expectation that the youngest child (preferably a daughter) was responsible for looking after her parent(s) in old age and thereby foregoing marriage, or women may have simply preferred to live this way.

Between 1851 and 1871, however, there is virtually a reversal of the situation with eleven of the mothers now paupers offering no hope of inheritance to their daughters. Five of the daughters, however, had illegitimate children at home; it seems likely that some sort of a "bargain" was struck where mother looked after the home and the illegitimate child while the daughter went out to work. But there were other forces at work which also need to be considered.

First, the operation of state policy through the Poor Law was increasingly shifting the responsibility of the poor, aged, and infirmed on to kin—and on to female kin in particular. Second, the majority of men, when widowed, remained in a strong position in the marriage market until at least the age of sixty, as well as having a stronger position in the labor market. Women's eligibility in the marriage market, however, deteriorated rapidly after the age of thirty-five. Single, widowed or abandoned by husbands who left them to search for work elsewhere, women over thirty-five became even more reliant than they had been before on the labor market, other kin, other women in a similar situation, and, in the last resort, on parish relief. If state policies did not deliberately and consciously set out to oppress women, their effects, given the conditions of both the labor and marriage markets, were to do just that.

The rise in illegitimacy which occurred between these years[5] is another indicator of the generally weakening position of women in the marriage market. In contrast with Shorter's thesis that illegitimacy was an indicator of new attitudes to love and sex, others[6] have shown how rising illegitimacy was more a result of socioeconomic changes affecting the ability to marry. Specifically, the increased amount of men's geographical mobility in search of work meant many marriages were "frustrated." This is by far the most cogent explanation in the case of Buckfastleigh.

Illegitimacy had been perceived as a problem since at least Elizabethan times; the overriding concern was that children should not be a financial burden on the parish. Various measures were enacted by law[7] and reinforced ideologically in terms of "morality" to try and ensure that the mother and alleged father were economically responsible, rather than the parish. Originally the laws were somewhat biased in women's favor, as they could name the father and seek his marriage or financial support. But the increase in men's mobility, among other factors, made the laws increasingly difficult to enforce. Illegitimacy remained a pressing economic problem for state policy.

The Commissioners of the New Poor Law, in their attempt to rationalize poor relief and cut expenditure, placed the onus of illegitimacy entirely on the woman, arguing that bastardy would never decline until it was "what Providence appears to have ordained that it should be, a burden on its mother, and, where she cannot maintain it, on her parents."[8]

The Poor Law Bastardy Act of 1832, containing some of the most violently misogynist phrases imaginable, provoked a great deal of controversy; much of it was eventually revoked.

Premarital intercourse and pregnancy had been common in Western Europe for a long time. These traditions had not changed. Increased male mobility and misogynist state policy, however, now made pregnancy a much riskier and more precarious tactic for women in the marriage market. Pregnancy no longer guaranteed either marriage or economic support. Moreover, the knowledge by men that this was the case greatly enhanced their ability to exploit women sexually with little fear of the consequences. State policy, although amended, in this case is a very clear instance of strengthening the position of men at the expense of women, as well as reducing parish costs!

Under the new conditions, if a woman became pregnant outside marriage, her economic survival was far more dependent on her participation in the labor market and/or her dependence on other female kin. It was only if both were lacking that a woman could seek parish relief in the workhouse. Women's weakened position in the marriage market therefore resulted in greater reliance on what the labor market had to offer: a situation, once again, which worked very much to the advantage of capitalists such as Hamlyns.

Very few unmarried men and women lived with their single fathers (three women, no men in 1851; five women, four men in 1871).

Of those daughters who did, however, they were all recorded as "housekeepers," presumably temporarily taking over the domestic work until their father could make a suitable remarriage. Of the sons in this situation, each one was engaged in his father's business or trade and was probably waiting to inherit his property, having, therefore, a rational economic motive for remaining at home and postponing marriage.

What the daughters' benefits were is hard to assess—possibly, the promise of some inheritance plus present economic support, or they may have been given no choice, with fathers refusing any offers of marriage to their daughters and thereby enforcing their staying at home if they were to maintain their class position. C. Hall summarizes the position of such families in the period 1780–1850:

> In general boys would receive an education and training to enter a business or profession and then would be given either a share in the existing family business or capital to invest in another business. . . . Daughters, on the other hand, would either be given a lump sum as a marriage settlement (though it would be noted they were sometimes not allowed to marry because of the impossibility of removing capital from the business), or they would be left money in trust, usually under the aegis of a male relative to provide an income for them together with their widowed mothers. The money in trust would then often be available for the male relatives to invest as they pleased.[9]

Let us take as an example the family of William Berry, a farmer who was aged fifty-six in 1851, and married to Alice, aged forty-seven. They farmed 168 acres, had one live-in servant (male) aged thirteen, and a live-in apprentice (male) aged seventeen. The oldest son, John, was twenty-three, then came three daughters aged twenty-two, twenty and seventeen, a son aged ten, a daughter of five, and a son of three. The four oldest children were listed as "farmer's sons or daughters," and Alice was listed as a "farmer's wife," from which we can reasonably assume the farm was very much a family business.

By 1861 the Berrys were farming 240 acres and again had two live-in male servants, aged twelve and seventeen. Of the seven children present in 1851, only one had left (Caroline, aged twenty-nine, married John Tooley in 1860; they lived with John's mother, a farmer of 50 acres, and one male farm servant). The other six were all active on the farm. By 1871 William was widowed, but now farming 410 acres. The two eldest sons, aged forty-three and thirty, neither married, remained on the farm waiting, presumably, to inherit it. The next-to-youngest daughter, Elizabeth, was now thirty-seven and the only remaining daughter. She was described as housekeeper, and there were now two female domestic servants and one male farm servant. William died in 1874; what Elizabeth did thereafter is unknown. Presumably one, or both, sons, took over the farm; Elizabeth may or may not have kept house for them. The Berrys appear to have been a sort of peasant farming family who, through extensive use of family labor, ended up quite prosperous. Initially it would seem the one who lost more than she gained in this arrangement was Elizabeth, possibly forbidden to marry by a father needing a housekeeper. However, not long ago I discovered her tomb; she is buried with another woman, Alice Silly. Both were single and lived into their sixties. The tomb was erected by Alice (not by Elizabeth's family), who survived longest.

Arguably, then, housekeeping for a parent and foregoing marriage was an alternative strategy which eventually led to greater independence. To what extent there was a real degree of choice is difficult to surmise.

This type of situation differed in certain ways from that of working-class women who, while probably losing some income if they left home and stayed single, could band together with other women (kin or nonkin) and survive economically (at a much earlier age than women like Elizabeth Berry) without any great drop in standard of living or loss of status—which middle-class women would encounter if they undertook wage labor. For example, Mary Tozer was twenty-three in 1851, unmarried, and worked as a woolsorter. She was born in Buckfastleigh but lodged with Eliza Furneaux, fifty-two, an unmarried weaver. Next door lived Mary's family of orientation: her father, fifty-five, was a master shoemaker; her mother was fifty-four, her brother Samuel, twenty-two, single and also a shoemaker; her sister Eleanor, eighteen, with no occupation listed; a niece of eleven months; and an apprentice shoemaker.

Whether Mary made the decision herself to move in with Eliza and Phyllis is impossible to know although the cottages in this street are very small and there may have been pressure to move out. In 1861, however, Mary was still unmarried but now lived with Phyllis, who had married Thomas Churchward, a fundholder. Mary was listed as their servant. Her father was dead and her brother Samuel was the master shoemaker; their mother lived with him, as did her unmarried sister Eleanor (now twenty-nine), her niece, and another niece not listed in 1851. Eliza Furneaux, still an unmarried weaver, now lived with Samuel and was listed as his aunt; the original ménage, then, had certain kinship links not obvious in 1851.

In 1871 Mary was still unmarried and lived with Phyllis and her husband. She was still listed as their servant although it was unusual for a servant to stay so long with one family and there were probably close ties of either friendship and/or kinship between the two women. The use of the term *servant* may simply indicate the enumerator's lack of understanding of the nature of the relationship. Samuel was now married and had two children; their mother and Eliza were both dead. The unmarried sister, Eleanor, now lived next door to Samuel with her daughter (the niece present in 1851 and 1861, illegitimate); she and her daughter were both listed as dressmakers.

Eleanor remained part of the family and was able to keep her illegitimate child until her brother married; by the time she moved next door she was thirty-eight and presumably "out" of the marriage market (like Elizabeth Berry), having to rely on her own and her daughter's labor power to survive. Mary, possibly out of the marriage market more by deliberate choice, survived by working as a servant in another household. Or it may have been that Phyllis and Mary were only able to retain their friendship and cohabit by one of them marrying and the other describing herself as their "servant."

These examples suggest that both working-class and middle-class women were under a more or less rigid system of kin control: "pre-marital coresidence of parents with marriageable children must be regarded as one of the major preconditions for the continuation of kin control."[10] Middle-class women, however, were under stricter control involving careful consideration of property and status of potential husbands. Working-class women had more independence from their parents, given their greater accessibility to the labor market (though living alone on a woman's wage was almost impossible), while trying to enter the marriage market could easily result in being left with an illegitimate child, as in Eleanor Tozer's case.

Yet consider that in 1851 18 percent of all households were headed by women (and 50 percent of these were "all-women" households). Other research suggests that Buckfastleigh was not atypical in this respect. L. Davidoff found a comparable figure of 20 percent for Colchester in 1851,[11] and M. Ryan, discussing Oneida County, New York, at about the same time says: "At any given moment at least one in four of the adult women of Utica was either a spinster or a widow."[12] By 1871, 20 percent of all households in Buckfastleigh were headed by women, and 47 percent of these were all-women households. Kin control was not *that* all-pervasive! Many of these women were, of course, widows. For the female population as a whole there was an early peek of widowhood in their thirties which remained relatively constant until their fifties, when it rose again sharply. Widowhood for men was insignificant until their fifties. While many widows in 1851 still remarried, this was far less common by 1871, suggesting again a weakening position for women in the marriage market. Other women were left to fend as best they could, with or without dependent children, while their husbands went elsewhere in search of work. Many never returned, although some did. Illegitimacy, widowhood, and separation were all facets of the same process: an unstable marriage market which was particularly disadvantageous to women. Its very instability was a source of cheap labor for entrepreneurs.

Between 1851 and 1871 the number of female lodgers more than doubled, and over half of them were single. To what extent lodging was an escape from kin control (the majority were local) is hard to assess, but the situations of those with whom they lived suggests that more women were deliberately choosing to live more independent lives.

Female Lodgers, 1851 and 1871:
Occupations and Sex of Those with Whom They Lodge

	1851	*1871*
	No.	No.
Male-Headed Households		
Woolcombers	10	0
Woolstaplers	1	0
Shoemakers	1	0
Agricultural laborers	1	4
Masons	0	2
Carpenters	0	1
Millwrights	0	1
Mine laborers	0	1
	13	9
	1851	*1871*
Female-Headed Households		
Weavers	1*	7*(3)
Woolsorters	0	1*
Spinners	0	1
Laborers	0	1*
Charwomen	0	3
Grocers	0	1
Innkeepers	0	1
Landowners	0	1
Paupers	1*	2*
	2	18

* = Occupation of lodger and landlady identical

The change is striking: above all, in 1871 there is a large increase in female lodgers living in all-women households *and* a large proportion living with other women of the same occupation. The lodgers of 1851 look more like unpaid domestic helpers in a subservient position to a male head of household, while those of 1871 would seem to have chosen (and had the ability to choose) a more independent arrangement in which to live.

There does seem to be some substantiation for Anderson's exchange model here, with the difference that some women decided that living with other *women* in similar circumstances was a pleasanter arrangement than marriage or residing with kin. Apparently the reverse was true for men: only *one* male lodger in 1871 was in an all-male household. This also suggests a strong network system becoming stronger during this period. Presumably under the protoindustrial system women were more dependent on marriage or living with parent(s) for economic survival and, similarly, more dependent on husband or father and under his closer scrutiny and control. Proletarianization made women somewhat less dependent on marriage for survival (and marriage itself had become less secure). But it also made them more dependent on the labor market; wages were poor, and as single women their chances of ever rising above the status of laborer were almost nil.

To examine the apparent weakening of working-class women's position in the marriage market, consider as an example the domestic situations of unmarried weavers over the age of twenty-five:

**Domestic Arrangements of Unmarried Weavers
over the Age of 25**

Live with/as:	*1851*	*1871*
Both parents	24	41
Widowed father	1	5
Widowed mother	6	9
Unmarried mother	—	2
Married male kin	1	2
Unmarried female kin	—	3
Lodgers	4	3
With other women (nonkin)	3	5
Total	39	70

Of those who lived with parent(s) in 1851, the households also contained 24 dependent and 62 employed siblings; in 1871 there were 107 dependent siblings and 114 who were employed. Of those siblings who were employed, in 1851 26 were male and 36 were female, while in 1871 37 were male and 87 were female. Where both parents were in the household, with only a few exceptions the wife was *not* employed. Moreover, of the male siblings who were employed, most were in skilled occupations. A typical example would be that of Thomas Churchward's family in 1871. Thomas was forty-eight, married, and listed as a woolcomber; his wife, Elizabeth, forty-seven, had no listed

occupation. Seven children lived with them: Elizabeth, twenty, unmarried, was a woolsorter, as were her sisters Harriett, eighteen, and
Eliza, thirteen. Frederick, fifteen, was a miller, while the three remaining children, aged ten, seven, and two, were outside the labor force.

This suggests that the economic changes occurring had important
effects on working-class family structure. In particular, it suggests
that the father/husband was able, even when himself in a poorly paid
laboring occupation, to maintain the family's standard of living and
his status by (1) keeping the wife/mother at home doing unpaid
domestic work and (2) giving a son or sons the chance of upward or
outward mobility by means of using his daughters' ability to sell their
labor power. The more unmarried working daughters a family could
retain the higher their chances of a reasonable standard of living and
the better the chances for sons to become socially and/or geograph-
ically mobile. The weakening of working-class women's position in the
marriage market and the increased demand for them in the labor
market (*but* at such low rates of pay as to make independence of the
parental family difficult, though not impossible) gave working-class
families a means to survive the effects of proletarianization.

It was undoubtedly women who suffered most as a result of these
changes: exploited by parents *and* by capitalists in the labor market,
increasingly cut off from any chance of owning their own property,
and placed in a weaker and more vulnerable position in the marriage
market. There were, however, what appear to have been certain
alternative strategies of resistance. Those who did marry might eventually attain a higher standard of living when their children—and
daughters in particular—started earning. Some, like Elizabeth Berry,
could serve as housekeepers to male kin until the latter died and they
could finally choose their own living arrangements. Others, like Mary
Tozer, could survive without marriage through wage labor and living
with other women or, again, like her sister Eleanor, could remain
unmarried, work as wage laborers, and live with kin until their own
illegitimate children could help them to survive.

Whereas previously the marriage market was a woman's main
means of access to economic security, involving her in production and
domestic work within the home, with a reasonable degree of security
in the event of widowhood, the combined forces of capital consolidation, proletarianization, and increasingly misogynistic state policies
put her in a position of dual dependence on *two* markets. In both her
position was weak. Economic survival was precarious whether, and
when, she entered one or both. There *was* some element of choice,
but to a large extent it was a choice between the Devil and the Deep
Blue Sea.

Notes

1. See, for instance, Kate Young, Carol Wolkowitz, Roslyn McCullagh, eds., *Of Marriage and the Market: Women's Subordination in International Perspective* (London: CSE Books, 1981).

2. For a discussion of protoindustrialization, see Hans Medick, "The Proto-Industrial Family Economy," *Social History* No. 1 (1976).

3. Charles C. Tilly, "The Historical Study of Vital Processes," in C. Tilly, ed., *Historical Studies of Changing Fertility* (Princeton: Princeton University Press, 1978).

4. David Levine, *Family Formation in an Age of Nascent Capitalism* (New York: Academic Press, 1977).

5. Illegitimate baptisms as a percentage of all baptisms were 4.3 percent, 1841–50; 6.3 percent, 1851–60; 10.8 percent, 1861–70.

6. U. Henriques, "Bastard and the New Poor Law," in *Past and Present* No. 37 (July 1967); Cissie Fairchilds, "Female Sexual Attitudes and the Rise of Illegitimacy: A Case Study" in *Journal of Interdisciplinary History* 8:4 (Spring 1978); D. Levine, *Family Formation;* F. Ducrocq, in this volume.

7. See Henriques, *"Bastard and the New Poor Law,",* and Ducrocq, in this volume, for a full discussion of this.

8. Henriques, "Bastard and the New Poor Law," 109.

9. Catherine Hall, "Gender Divisions and Class Formations in the Birmingham Middle Class, 1780–1850" in R. Sanwel, ed., *People's History and Socialist Theory* (London: Rutledge Kegan Paul, 1981).

10. B. Ankarloo, "Marriage and Family Formation" in T. Hareven, *Transitions: The Family and the Life Course in Historical Perspective* (New York: Academic Press, 1978), 114.

11. Leonore Davidoff, "The Separation of Home and Work? Landladies and Lodgers in 19th and 20th Century England" in S. Burman, ed., *Fit Work for Women* (London: Croom Helm, 1979).

12. M. Ryan, *The Cradle of the Middle Class: The Family Oneida County, New York, 1790–1865* (Cambridge: Cambridge University Press, 1981).

FROM POOR LAW TO JUNGLE LAW

SEXUAL RELATIONS AND MARITAL
STRATEGIES (LONDON, 1850–1870)

Françoise Ducrocq
Translated by Helene J. F. de Aguilar

Many scholars have discussed and analyzed the economic, social, and ideological consequences of capitalism and capitalist modes of production. Few, however, have focused directly on the role and position of women during the course of this socioeconomic revolution. Rarer still are those who have devoted their research to working-class women.

Marx and Engels were delighted to see women enter the capitalist production market and stressed the liberating nature of the move,[1] while at the same time they deplored the resultant upheaval in sex-bound divisions of labor.[2] Their position made it possible to retain the idea of progress and link the new opportunities available to women to the ideas of an evolutionary shift in customs and a greater measure of autonomy for women within patriarchal-capitalist institutions such as marriage and the family. Once released from the yoke of traditional agrarian society—no longer fettered by the requirements of patrimonial inheritance—men and women would, it was thought, inevitably have a more equal relationship to one another, even in sexual matters. Widespread prostitution might indeed attest to the double standard and the exploitation of working women by upper-class men, but this development did not contradict women's lessened alienation

I would like to thank Eric J. Hobsbawn and John Gillis for having alerted me to the existence of the Thomas Coram Foundling Hospital material. I am also very appreciative of the generous criticisms and encouragement I received from Pat Thane and Martha Vicinus.

within the confines of the working class itself. As it happens, history has vindicated these theorists. A certain economic, or material, independence *does* underlie the evolution of the feminist struggle,[3] effectively permitting certain women to achieve a different social and interpersonal status. This phenomenon, however, at least in England, was delayed until the turn of the century when the demand for equal rights emerged for all people, whatever their class, age, or sex.[4]

Recent feminist research on the nineteenth century has barely recognized the anachronistic character of ideologies defending progress. In fact, scholars of women have seen in the idea of progress a way to support their interest in giving back to women an active role in history. Subversion, rebellion, and revolt have been the foci of this new inquiry. The historian's challenge lies in deciding to what degree women managed to consolidate some form of power within civil, albeit not political, society, even though sexual discrimination continued to exist and now constituted a scheme of systematized inferiority and dispossession. The actual possibilities for individual emancipation were exaggerated so as to mask the structural constraints of the system.

My aim in this essay is to demonstrate that during the nineteenth century the new ideological imperatives, both economic and social, did not permit the evolution of social power for women, but, on the contrary, restricted the sexual freedom they previously enjoyed. Unquestionably, under particular conditions, especially in regions of intensive industrial development, where salaries were higher,[5] employment steadier, and information about contraception easier to come by, women did derive various benefits from the modification of work relations. Elsewhere, however, in London for instance, power relations between the sexes became increasingly unfavorable to women as working-class patterns of morality were gradually codified and rationalized.

Methodological problems have also led to erroneous interpretations of the ideological effects of socio-economic changes on women. The majority of our sources on the subject of sexual relations are partial in both senses of the word. They are provided by observers whose language and viewpoint were profoundly affected by their sex, class, and motives. Extensive and invaluable documentation exists, from philanthropic societies, parliamentary commissions, health officials, street songs and music hall renditions, novels and "popular" plays, and investigations by sociologists or by journalists who were seeking sensational material. The problem with this data is that even when the observers tried to transcribe exactly the "testimony" of lower-class women, they inevitably distorted it according to their own social,

moral, or sexual identity. Only rare exceptions—the autobiographies
of Hannah Mitchell, for example, or of the women of the Cooperative
Guild[6]—escape this major flaw, but these accounts remain extremely
reticent on the topic of sex. I do not mean to discard any of these
sources as irrelevant; I merely point out their limitations.

At the present time, researchers in the field have located at least one
collection of direct testimony dictated by lower-class women concerning their own sexual experience: the records of the Thomas
Coram's Foundling Hospital. This institution, which assumed responsibility for the offspring of unwed mothers, required the latter to
explain how they had been seduced and abandoned. The responses of
these women constitute an extraordinary set of documents which,
although they cannot inform us on every aspect of women's sexual
behavior, do allow us to assess more accurately the situation of working women as regards premarital sex in London during the second
half of the nineteenth century.

Among the laboring classes, the high rate of illegitimate births[7] on
the one hand and of prenuptial pregnancies on the other attest,
along with other indices, to a special sort of sexual moral code regulating premarital liaisons. This code diverged from that prevalent in the
middle class, which viewed sexuality as wholly restricted to the institution of marriage. Whatever controversies surround the spectacular
rise in illegitimate births between 1750 and 1850,[8] historians generally
concur that premarital sex was by and large tolerated in preindustrial
society. As Laslett has shown,[9] this acceptance applied to two types of
situations: either the partners legitimized an undesired pregnancy by
the marriage ceremoney, or the sexual act served in fact to seal a
promise of marriage. These rules of sexual conduct were still in force
in the nineteenth century. According to William Acton, "The 'keeping
company' of the labouring classes, accompanied by illicit intercourse,
as often as not leads to marriage."[10] Mayhew, discussing the first half
of the century and Booth, writing on the second, likewise emphasized
this basic characteristic of the moral code in certain subgroups of the
working class. Premarital sexual relations were not, of course, accepted by the family or the community unless, in accordance with the
traditional moral code, they were sanctioned by marriage or by the
man's formal recognition of the progeny. Otherwise, society os-
tracized mothers abandoned by their seducers. Despite numerous
accidents along the way, as the high rate of illegitimacy indicates, the
prevailing moral code did, in general, tolerate premarital sex.

In nineteenth-century London, three factors disrupted the delicate
social balance in which this attitude was rooted: the reform of the Poor
Law; the unique economic situation of the metropolis within an indus-

trial urban society; and, finally, the demographic anomalies of sex distribution.

Beginning in 1834, premarital sex would be regarded in terms of a new legal context. Since the first part of the seventeenth century, women had been granted both the right and the obligation to prosecute the man they claimed had fathered their child, to have his goods confiscated should he refuse them support, and to send him to jail if he had no goods to confiscate (laws of 1662 and 1733). The man was otherwise required to marry the woman who held him accountable for her pregnancy.[11] In 1834 the passage of the New Poor Law gave shape to a different concept of public assistance and abolished the older schemes. The clause on bastardy, for example, removed all legal aid to abandoned single mothers and all material aid outside the workhouse on the pretext that both forms of assistance constituted an incitement to illicit sex. As Pat Thane remarks, the preparatory commission's findings recommended that "a bastard should be what providence appears to have ordained that it should be, a burden on its mother and where she cannot maintain it on her parents."[12] By 1844 widespread dissatisfaction with the new provisions of the Poor Law had forced the partial elimination of this clause. But henceforth, few women had recourse to the earlier procedure: its cost was relatively high and its implementation difficult. After 1834, then, a woman's ability to interest a man in the practical outcome of premarital sex was reduced by new legal precedents.

Victorian moralists made the situation worse. Blinded by the spectacle of a break with their dominant moral code—a break they confused with an absence of moral sense—moralists reenforced the breach between lower-class sexual codes and the altered material conditions of poor women. Their capacity to do this emerged from the fact that London women in the latter half of the nineteenth century faced an urban crisis of industrial development which severely curtailed their traditional autonomy.[13]

London at this time did not really mirror the level of national development. Its previously flourishing industries—silk weaving, ship building, mechanical apparatuses, semi-finished products—now lagged behind other enterprises of capitalism. The city's distance from the great coal mines raised the price of energy while the high cost of land virtually prohibited the establishment of large industrial complexes within the city limits. The peculiar circumstances of London's industrial development produced, among other things, a special organizational system—the "sweating system"—which isolated male from female workers and exacerbated their dependency upon market fluctuations. Employment was rendered still more precarious by the cyclical crises of recession and, in London specifically, by the seasonal nature of the many occupations subject to the variables of climate and the "fashionable season." Women composed a sizable portion of the "casual labour"[14] force and occupied three major areas: 22.79 percent of all women worked in domestic service; 10.04 percent worked in garments and footwear and 1.6 percent in piecework. The low status of women's work in London, a result of the oversupply of workers and its consequent poor remuneration and insecurity, made some alliance with a man mandatory if a woman were to improve the material conditions of her life and, sometimes, even to survive. Illegitimate offspring intensified the gravity of the situation and were especially problematic for domestics, who could reconcile neither maternity nor marriage with their employment.[15]

Thus, contrary to the views espoused by writers such as Edward Shorter, a woman's working outside the family unit was not, in London, especially liberating. To a greater extent than in the past, working-class women found their wage-earning activities forcibly restricted by the financial structure of their families or their mates. Within an economic framework which was difficult for both sexes, breaches of promises to marry became common. In a big city like London, moreover, although geographic, social, and vocational mobility were more limited than generally imagined, one had only to change neighborhoods to disappear forever. In contrast with comparatively stable rural or village communities, where the weight of family and neighbors could exert decisive moral or physical pressure, control mechanisms in the city were far more lax and facilitated the breaking of verbal agreements between sexual partners.[16]

Demographically as well women were at a disadvantage in London, where the nationwide imbalance in the distribution of the sexes[17] was accentuated by the need for many female domestics. This state of affairs further reduced women's choices and interfered with their judgment, while it placed men in a stronger position: they could easily find another partner, and at the same time they enjoyed relative impunity at the social and legal level.

The new configuration of elements obliged the poorest women to compound risky premarital ties in a broader and more serious social gamble. With the contemporary "givens," economic and communal, coexisted the tenacious old custom which approved sexual relations provided they were subsequently ratified by the male's acknowledgment of paternity and proof of his readiness to assume responsibility for the mother, in most cases through marriage. This old custom proved to be injurious to women when, as was now the case, they lacked the power to enforce its terms.

An analysis of the Thomas Coram's Foundling Hospital records, comprising the statements of hundreds of women, provides a cogent illustration of the sexual situation of working-class women. These records significantly modify the wide variety of preconceptions held about them.

Since the end of the eighteenth century, the Foundling Hospital had represented a "second chance" for "deserving" unwed mothers abandoned by their lovers. I have selected only a fraction of the 454 petitions made to the Committee of Governors between 1851 and 1878.[18] These petitions, hand-written by the petitioner or else by the official who took down her deposition, were an essential preliminary for the hospital's adoption of any child. An interviewee was then charged with verification of the testimony through multiple inter-rogations and counterinterrogations with all interested (or otherwise associated) parties. This procedure, on which we would elaborate if space were available, guaranteed the accuracy—if not the details, at least the contours—of these life histories. These depositions, then, provide a rare instance of first-hand documentation, quantitatively meaningful, produced by lower-class women themselves about their own sexuality. The texts can obviously not be regarded as autobiogra-phies *stricto sensu*, for they took shape around the questions asked by the committee.[19] However, the entrance conditions were sufficiently vague and the amount of information sufficiently extensive for us to discern certain general outlines. We must make allowances, needless to say, for the emotional tenor of the interviews—the humiliation, the timidity, the trauma of suffering relived—and for any resultant distor-tion of reality.

Given the terms for adoption the cases in the sample are relatively uniform. The unwed mother had to prove that she or her family was financially incapable of supporting the infant. Above all, she had to demonstrate her respectability. This had to be her *first* child[20] and she had to show that she was a *victim*, be it of financial mishap (death, unemployment) or of a man's duplicity or faithlessness. The socio-economic background of the petitioners was, as a result, quite homog-eneous.

Predictably, 53.3 percent of the women were drawn from the lower rungs of domestic service. The next important group consisted of artisans, 13.65 percent. These percentages are perfectly representa-tive of the female labor force in London. The majority of the artisans worked in the garment industry as seamstresses, hosiers, milliners, and needle workers of various sorts. The rest were laundresses, press-ers, upholsterers, bookbinders, and chair caners. These occupations were by and large unskilled, paid by the piece and exceptionally precarious. A significant proportion of women (15.20 percent) lived with their families at home. Theirs was hardly a life of leisure. They were all active as household assistants, family helpers, and dress-makers, remaining at home because of temporary unemployment or in response to the family's economic needs. Since they had no inde-pendent income, their pregnancy, more than that of other women, amounted to an economic and family tragedy.

Whatever the occupational category to which they belonged, the petitioners all came from households unable to offer them sustained financial aid.[21] Their relatives were semiskilled or unskilled workers, often old and ill or crushed by dependents. Many of the women were orphans. [22]

The socio-economic origins of the men involved was somewhat different: 16.28 percent belonged to a higher social class. They were "gentlemen," office workers, students, or teachers. The majority, how-ever, worked in semiskilled or unskilled jobs; they owned or were employed by small businesses, or they might occupy low positions in the domestic-service hierarchy. A sizable minority of sailors and sol-diers, whose professions placed them in a peculiar situation vis à vis any impending marriage, was also present.

What is striking is that on the whole these couples were a priori situated in ways compatible with matrimony. The potential husbands appeared to offer the women the prospect of a socially honorable resolution. Household skills, plus the possible accumulation of some savings, gave female domestic servants an extra edge on the marriage market because the husband might anticipate a well-run home and some subsidy for his own endeavors. In sum, we can assume that these petitions reflect with fair accuracy the nature of seduction and sexual behavior under normal, working-class conditions.

Recurrent themes in the evidence strongly suggest that women from the strata of the working class reported upon earlier viewed sex as inseparable from marriage, an institution which involves a biolog-ical function (reproduction) and a social grouping (the family and kinship unit). What is remarkable, in fact, is the discrepancy between the steps taken by women to ensure that everything would turn out all right, that the love affair which provoked premarital sex would finally integrate itself into the *ideal* institutional plan, and their subsequent experiences. The determination of the women to conform to the rules of marriage is confirmed by the elaborate precautions they took so that an amorous encounter would not end in a brief affair but would culminate instead in marriage. They struggled to compensate for the absence of judicial, communal, or familial guardrails by another pro-tective strategy which varied very little from case to case.

To begin with, sexual relations were, as we have seen, initiated with partners whose social status promised a "happy ending." Moreover, the lover was in most cases part of the same occupational or domestic milieu and nearly all meetings happened through mutual acquaintances: couples came together in reassuring familiar surroundings. In the case of domestic workers, for example, 76.4 percent of the introductions were arranged through friends, relatives, or contacts at work. Friends and relations were felt to be safe intermediaries: a twenty-eight-year-old women whose lover was a stone setter in Edgware Road states:

> When first acquainted with the Father, I was living with my sister, earning a livelihood as a dressmaker. The Father worked for my brother-in-law and lived in the house. We knew one another for 18 months. Father courted and promised me marriage which was known to my sister and brother-in-law. [23]

Here, as in many other cases, the lover's professional identity and his place of residence strengthened the sense of security. Such symbolic certification was sometimes provided by fellow employees or the employers:

> When first acquainted with the Father I was living with Captain G. of Hammersmith as housemaid. This was 18 months ago. The Father was an acquaintance of the cook at Captain G.'s and hence arose an intimacy between us. . . . His visits were known to my master and mistress.

Lodgers or landlords might also serve this purpose:

> When first acquainted with the Father I was working and lodging as a dressmaker and milliner with Mrs. T. of 29 Shaftesbury Place. The Father lodged in the same house. After he had lodged there 4 weeks he paid me attention and for seven months courted me with a view of marriage known to Mrs. T.

Similarly, the fact that meetings occurred on the very premises where both parties were employed seems to have constituted in and of itself a kind of guarantee:

> When first acquainted with the Father I was living with Mrs. F. . . . as kitchenmaid. This was six years ago. The Father was a footman and we lived together three years during which time he courted me.

When, on the other hand, the first encounter occurred some Sunday in the park, in a music hall, during a day off on the Brighton or

the Windsor train, among friends, at the Great Exhibition, perhaps in
the church pew or quite simply on the street, it was unusual for the
boyfriend not to be introduced at once to family and friends:

> When first acquainted with the Father I was living with my mother at
> Milton Street . . . earning my livelihood as a dressmaker . . . I met the
> Father in Kensington in January last when he accosted me and we met
> several times in the same manner. He promised me marriage. A
> fortnight after I introduced him to my mother and my sister and he
> visited me accordingly.

Needless to say, these protective devices were illusory. They do,
however, attest to a certain degree of caution on the part of the
women.

In the same way, and contrary to the imaginings of Victorian moralists—bent in their purifying zeal upon closing down a variety of music
halls, pubs, and fairgrounds [24]—courtship was as public as possible;
the sexual act, of necessity private, was carried out in the vast majority
of cases within a working or family setting, as if without design, at
home.

Dinah S., for example, twenty-six years old, housemaid, described
as follows her experience with William S., a carpenter:

> The Father accosted me and agreed to visit me which he was in the
> habit of doing with the knowledge of Mr. and Mrs. P. . . . The Father
> seduced me about 15 months ago at my mistress' house. It was not
> exactly with my consent. It occurred in the kitchen.

The "seduction" sometimes happened at a friend's home or in the
lover's room:

> I knew his sister Mrs. N. now Mrs. N. of Clapham . . . hence our
> acquaintance. He courted me till June . . . when he seduced me at his
> sister's.

Meetings in a park or hotel were less frequent.[25] Eliza H. was living
with her mother in Clerkenwell when Vincent D., a commercial traveler, paid attention to her:

> we met frequently afterwards for 6 weeks, at the end of this time he
> took me to Greenwich for a holiday and there at a Coffee House,
> seduction took place with my consent.

One additional fact corroborates the ritualistic quality of premarital
sex; intercourse hardly ever occurred save within the context of an

ongoing relationship, usually of at least six months' duration. The sex act thus took place in most cases after a protracted courtship; the relationship continued throughout the pregnancy and even after the birth of the child. Elizabeth V. was a housemaid for Mrs. C., whose husband ran a pub in Ball Pond, Islington. There she met her lover, a laborer who worked on the docks:

> He paid me attention, courted and promised me marriage which was known to my mistress. We used to walk together, after 12 months acquaintance he seduced me on a Sunday morning when the family was absent. He called accidentally. Crim. Con. was repeated twice only . . . The father continued to visit, but not criminally.

Paradoxically, sexual intercourse gave further insurances. This method of holding on to a fiancé carried obvious risks which did not escape the notice of all petitioners. Some, in fact, claimed that coitus had been achieved against their will or by force (locked doors, seduction under the influence of alcohol, blackmail), and there are many reasons for taking these protestations seriously rather than viewing them as artful self-justifications before the Foundling Hospital's interviewers. But the immense majority of women stressed their willingness, complete or partial, or else they indicated that despite initial reluctance sexual relations were repeated many times over many months.

The women state: "It was not against my consent"; "He seduced me at my mistress' with my consent"; or "The Father effected his purpose partly by persuasion, partly by force"; "It was not with my consent, that is only partly so"; "He seduced me against my consent. It was repeated." These varying shades of acquiescence conform, of course, to prescribed rites of sexual conquest which, given the established rules for male-female relations, compelled the woman to remain passive; she was the pursued, not the pursuer. Direct, immediate consent, on the other hand, represented more than a tactical move; it had to do with sexual desire. "I gave way to him because I was fond of him," proclaimed Georgina. By analyzing the past history of these women with great zeal, we might easily overdo things and forget how much of life eludes rationality, especially as regards love and sex. To overlook the nonrational dimension would be absurd.

**Reactions given by women, according to occupation,
to having sexual intecourse**

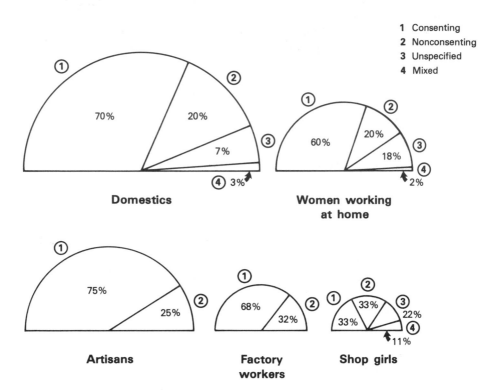

1 Consenting
2 Nonconsenting
3 Unspecified
4 Mixed

Domestics

70%   20%   7%   ④ 3%

**Women working
at home**

60%   20%   18%   2%

Artisans

75%   25%

**Factory
workers**

68%   32%

Shop girls

33%   33%   22%   11%

At a certain level, then, the psychological and social placement of women and their traditional position in the partriarchal order conditioned their approach to sex. The intimate act also *made the affair real* and, in conformity with old customs, accelerated the real marriage. The perfectly amenable reaction of most families toward illegitimate pregnancies indicates that intercourse was not considered proof of weakness or immorality but rather as one more preliminary to marriage, rightly set in place.

The definitive component of this matrimonial strategy was the "promise of marriage." It was this formal proposal alone, entailing as it traditionally did the man's honor, that authorized premarital sex. The real dividing line between acceptable and improper behavior was drawn on the basis of the existence or nonexistence of this pledge. If everything proceeded smoothly, the banns were published shortly thereafter. For this reason it was preferable that the proposal be made before witnesses; then the finacé was presented to the parents or their substitutes, or to the employers, and was granted formally the right to woo the young woman—to "keep company" with her and pay her visits. Such great symbolic importance was attached to this promise that once extended in private, by letter or merely orally—even following sexual intercourse—it constituted in the eyes of women a socially binding oath. William R. wrote:

> Dear Prudence, I now write you these few lines in respecting of our getting married we Promise that we would get married on April that is next month and I hope it will be so.

Edward H., a house painter, concluded his letter with a reminder:

> I love you so dearly that I don't wish for rows. Dear Fan I shall be waiting anxiously to see you at one but not after so I must conclude with my best love to you
> I am your accepted husband

Often this promise was renewed, even several months after the birth of the child:

> if i had not the kindst love towards you i should never of asked you to be married . . . what i have promised you i shall keep.

All the petitioners of the Foundling Hospital were adamant about the existence of such a promise and many regarded it explicitly as the turning point: "Under this promise I yielded to him." Equally, when it appeared that the marriage promise was only a trick, sexual relations became reprehensible and ceased at once: "and then after she discovered that he would not marry her, she steadily refused his solicitations to renew that intercourse."[26]

The whole configuration, in structure and in tone, shows that love relations were conducted by standards analogous to those of preindustrial England's moral code. As in the past, marriage determined the attitudes toward premarital sex among London's working women. Marriage alone could regulate love and passion, reproduction, and the material conditions of life.

Such, at least, was the original claim. In certain working-class sectors, of course, when all other possibilities had been eliminated, or in the case of a second union after widowhood or separation, long-term extramarital relations were fully accepted. For that matter, even among the petitioners some women had no hesitations: they preferred an illegitimate pregnancy, whatever its hazards, for their social and economic status, to marriage with a man they scorned or hated.

For these women, as for the others, everything revolved around marriage—but everything was not subordinated to it.

Yet one must not confuse the initial expectations with the arrangements dictated by practical realities. The moral code of the working classes differed from the dominant code: it was neither a reversal nor an imitation. It was simply bound up in a radically different material, ideological, and psychological reality. Women had to navigate carefully between complex motivations—love and the desire to marry—which pushed them not to alienate an ardent lover, to take the risk of becoming pregnant in the absence of effective means of contraception, and to accept the custom of their class, which tolerated sexual relations as a preliminary to marriage.

Despite all measures taken to transform an affair into marriage, premarital sex during the second half of the nineteenth century turned out to be an extremely dangerous social gamble. A whole series of events could cause the matrimonial strategy to fail and provoke ruin. The man might meet another woman, or his feelings might just change. Thus, in a letter to the future mother of his child, George R., a footman, wrote somewhat cynically:

> I cannot think how or by who you came in the family way being quite sure it was not by me. I am going to be married shortly to a very nice young woman.

Sometimes relatives and employers intervened for the worse, speeding the lover's departure, the relatives through clumsy threats against him, the employers through dismissing him for "bad conduct." But in the vast majority of cases, economic factors peculiar to London's working classes played the decisive role. A number of professional activities committed men to certain mobility—they had perhaps to follow their masters or to serve in the army or navy. The man would promise to write, then vanish altogether, sometimes ignorant of his fiancée's plight. In a second scenario, unemployment, underemployment, or accumulated debts led to a change of neighborhood, city, or for that matter country.

The prospect of assuming the responsibility for supporting a family could also intimidate the lover. Examples abound. After his fiancée informed him of her pregnancy, John R., mason, reassured her with a promise of imminent matrimony. She received the following letter several months later:

> I write to you these few lines to let you know that I am now on the road for Gloster I shall stay there all winter if all is well. Do not make yourself unhappy there is plenty of nice young men in holloway it is not in my power to make you happy if I was ever so willing.

Similarly, Thomas F., unemployed servant-butler, wrote:

> It is no use to say that I come to any terms for I cannot get a place . . .
> I do not know where I can go to I cannot make money anymore than
> you . . .

Then, there was the case of John F., gardener:

> The Father and I were friends and he courted me and promised
> marriage. The Andrews knew this. Courtship continued for 12 months
> before he seduced me, it was repeated. When I found myself pregnant,
> he said he could not be married as he had no sufficient means.

William K., carpenter:

> The Father promised to . . . publish the Banns on the following
> Sunday but he wrote to say he was out of work and was going to leave
> London.

Joseph J., milkman:

> When pregnant I told the Father and he said he was out of employ-
> ment.

Frederick J., carpenter:

> As soon as I found myself pregnant I told him when he said his
> circumstances would not permit him then to marry me.

Some chose to enlist. Once they were soliders men were no longer
bound to respect their promise of marriage:

> The Banns were published at St. Olaves' near London Bridge Octo'
> 70. I found afterwards that the Father enlisted in the Artillery.

Others went abroad, to India, America, Australia, New Zealand,
Canada, or decamped without any explanation:

> The Banns were published. He deserted me on the morning of the
> marriage.
> He called upon me on 19th nov. 1861 at Mrs. S. and said he would
> marry me and was going to the Registrar Office. Since whilst I have not
> seen him.
> When pregnant I told him and he said he did not believe it. He
> afterwards left for New York.

Still others rudely admitted that better opportunities had arisen or
that the right time for marriage had not yet arrived:

> You must try and forget me because it can never result in anything.
> You will think me cruel no doubt but many things are turning out too
> serious for me.

All this did not transpire without some pangs of conscience. Many
men broke off their engagements only on the eve of the birth. Some
provided meager financial aid or counseled abortion. Robert G., man-
servant, wrote to Caroline H., housemaid:

> My dear Carry I wish you would do what I telle you and not be so
> stupid but go to the Chemist and get something . . .

Thomas McP. to Jane P., assistant to housemaid:

> He told me to go to the Doctor who would put a stop to it.

What is obvious is the basic contradiction between the economic and
social outlook on the one hand and the cost of maintaining a family on
the other. As John Gillis observed:

> The very characteristics which made the skilled labourer respectable
> in his own eyes and in those of society, that is to say his ambition,
> flexibility, and his will to resist the temptations of immediate pleasures
> which could compromise the promise of the future, implied the need
> to postpone marriage until, frequently, the regrettable result was an
> illegitimate birth.[27]

The geographic and professional mobility of men was thus in direct
opposition to the most traditional mindset of women.

This observation, nevertheless, cannot wholly account for the profound shift in power relations between the sexes in the wake of the
reform of the Poor Law. However specific to the second half of the
nineteenth century these circumstances may be, they were not essentially new. Couples in the preindustrial era likewise faced considerable
difficulties, as is evident from the late age of marriage. The high rate
of illegitimacy also followed a more or less regular ascending curve
from the beginning of the eighteenth century onward. The outstanding feature from the ethical and social point of view, after 1834, was
the depenalization of male irresponsibility in cases of illegitimate
births. This male exemption placed an unbearable financial burden
on women since there was no other form of relief. And, above all, it
eventually delegitimized premarital sex. Vestiges of the old order
persisted, leading the majority of women and their families to track
down the fathers or to seek redress from them, but these efforts now
most often proved futile:

> When I said I should swear the child to him, he said he would go
> away.

In fact, ideologically, the new legislative provisions of the bastardy
clause reactivated—reintroduced—a retroactive freedom-of-choice
for the male sex.

Certain men clearly envisioned their breach of promise and departure as a temporary abandonment. Matthews H., a footman, wrote to
Ellen R., a nursemaid:

> As I find that I cannot get work to do in either England or Ireland I
> am now going to emigrate to Australia and I hope to be able to send
> you something to keep you with Gods help you must forgive the past as
> soon as I will have enough to take you out you shall have it . . . I am
> sorry not to sent you more but my passage money took every fraction I
> had you must do the best for a few months.

And on two occasions the petitions under analysis reveal that the
father subsequently reclaimed the child from the Foundling Hospital.
John H., a Spitalfield carpenter, wrote: "and with your kind permission I should like to clame my child." Similarly John D., valet, came to
look for his daughter five years later. But the majority decided quite
simply to forget the irritating episode and rejected the women bru-
tally:

> He told me to drown myself. My father subsequently saw him when
> he denied paternity and said he could do nothing for me.

The Foundling Hospital petitions suggest that we seek explanations
that do more than simply underline the oppression and estrangement
women and men have both experienced through the crises brought
on by urban development and the internal contradictions of the
capitalist system. They also signal a strengthening of patriarchal beliefs on sexuality, which are based on the double standard and on the
assumption that women should be held responsible when sexual intercourse leads to pregnancy. In the name of the "struggle against vice
and immorality" among the lower classes, men found restored to
them an escape route from the consequences of the sex act. Although
certain individuals might have been sincerely conscience-stricken, or
felt themselves forced to make drastic professional changes in order
to shirk their responsibilities, the fact remains that the male pursuit of
amorous and erotic pleasure was once again undertaken at the expense of women.

Women were most assuredly the *victims* of this new balance of power. Their pathetic panoply of ploys, designed at once to protect them and to assuage sexual desire, served exclusively to proclaim their "respectability" and to prevail upon a few institutions to take charge of their children, lest they mortgage irremediably their lives and their survival. In the long run, indeed, the emotional mortgage would never be paid in full; this is evident in the maternal grief expressed at the moment of separation as well as in the numerous letters from mothers who year after year sought news of their children. Remarks of the following sort, from the pen of a Foundling Hospital investigator, are not unusual:

> The Petitioner is deeply distressed at the thought of parting with her child and declares she has put off, from month to month, her application to the Institution in the hope of being able to support her child but her declining health renders her incapable.

Working-class women would be able to elude the practical and social consequences of premarital sex only with the establishment of the Welfare State together with a measure of access to contraceptives. This did not, however, release them from their economic and ideological dependence on the institution of marriage. In fact, our concern in this essay is not solely to analyze one particular turn of fortune in women's history but rather to underscore the paradoxical nature of our connection with institutions, in the political-social and political-moral sense. Marriage, especially, is susceptible to many simultaneous levels of interpretation: a kind of protection, a former of attitudes, and a source of alienation.

In this particular case, by examining the Poor Law, we can observe very clearly how external constraints actually facilitated a wider range of libidinal choices. The economic contradictions of the patriarchal order allowed what its morality condemned, so that women at this period fulfilled only imperfectly the role of moral regulator assigned to them by those who promoted the idea that it was in women's nature to play such a role. During the second half of the nineteenth century, patriarchal-capitalist morality had, nevertheless, joined forces with economic regulations to establish a coherent system the effect of which would foster conformity with the rules of the dominant ideology and bar all sexual expression outside the institutional framework.

By means of this study, we can see the extent to which we must analyze the exact role institutions play in fixing historical, social, and cultural parameters. If for some time women regarded their revolt only in relation to legal-political institutions, since the 1960s they have assigned greater importance to the struggle within the private sphere.

Is it not time now to reconsider women's ties to institutions and political society? Sexual conduct occupies precisely the intersection between these two spheres. The recent debates on abortion in France, Great Britain, and the United States, to mention only these three countries, should remind those who have forgotten that the sexual revolution is a myth. For while the institution of marriage is no longer in every case an absolute prerequisite for social respectability, it still constitutes for most women a kind of economic coercion. The ethical system created by members of the masculine sex assumes equality and universality, but it has perpetuated a system of inequality of the sexes when it comes procreation.

Thus in order to consider any possible transformation of the patriarchal-capitalist system in our time, we must evaluate correctly the methods and strategies of women to modify and simultaneously to utilize, on an institutional level, the contradictions within the system itself.

Notes

1. Friedrich Engels, *The Origin of the Family, Private Property and the State* (New York: International Publishers, 1942 [1891]).

2. Friedrich Engels, *The Condition of the Working Class in England* (London: Panther Press, 1974 [1892]).

3. Ivy Pinchbeck, *Women Workers and the Industrial Revolution* (London: Frank Cass, 1977 [1930]).

4. Legislative reforms granting the right to vote to all citizens, including women, and likewise granting women the right to own property whether inherited or acquired.

5. On this subject see Jill Liddington and Jill Norris, *One Hand Tied Behind Us* (London: Virago Press, 1977).

6. Hannah Mitchell, *The Hard Way Up* (London: Virago Press, 1977) and Margaret Llewelyn Davies, ed., *Life as We Have Known It* (London: Virago Press, 1977).

7. Reaching 10 to 20 percent of the births in some regions.

8. Edward Shorter, *The Making of the Modern Family* (Huntington, N.Y.: Fontana, 1975).

9. Peter Laslett, *Family Life and Illicit Love in Earlier Generations* (London: Cambridge University Press, 1977). See also Joan Scott and Louise Tilly, "Women's Work and the Family in Nineteenth Century Europe," *Comparative Studies in Society and History* 17 (1975): 36–64; Louise Tilly, Joan Scott, and Miriam Cohen, "Women's Work and European Fertility Patterns," *Journal of Interdisciplinary History* 6:3 (Winter 1976): 447–76; and Cissie Fairchilds, "Female Sexual Attitudes and the Rise of Illegitimacy: A Case Study," *Journal of Interdisciplinary History* 8:4 (Spring 1978): 627–67.

10. William Acton, "Prostitution," in N. Longmate, *The Workhouse* (New York: St. Martin's Press, 1975), 32.

11. As U. R. Henriques notes in his article "Bastardy and the New Poor Law," *Past and Present* no. 37 (July 1967): 104, "More important, by the provisions of 6 George 11 chapter 31 and 49 George 111 chapter 68, if a single woman declared herself pregnant and charged a man with being the father of the child-to-be, any Justice, on the application of the overseers or of a substantial householder, could issue a warrant for his arrest and committal to gaol, unless he could either give security to indemnify the parish or enter into a recognizance with sufficient surety to appear at next Quarter Sessions and perform the order then to be made."

The article by Diana Gittins in this volume also discusses the impact of the Poor Laws.

12. Pat Thane, "Women and the Poor Law in Victorian and Edwardian England, *History Workshop* Issue 6 (Autumn 1978): 32.

13. For a study on this autonomy in Europe, see Michelle Perrot, "La Femme rebelle," in *L'Histoire sans qualités* (Paris: Galilée, 1979).

14. Sally Alexander, "Women's Work in Nineteenth Century London," in *The Rights and Wrongs of Women* (London: Penguin, 1976).

15. The average salary of a seamstress in the East End was 3s 2d per week; that of a domestic around 8s; the cost of a wet nurse from 5 to 7 s per week.

16. Aware of the importance of this social problem the Salvation Army began toward the end of the century to provide specialized assistance in the search of vanished seducers.

17. As U. R. Q. Henriques notes, the censuses of 1801, 1821, and 1841 all indicated a "surplus" of 500,000 to 600,000 adult women.

18. These 454 petitions were selected out of 550. I have not included women who resided outside greater London or the few petitions of women belonging by birth or occupation to the petty bourgeoisie: governesses, teachers, etc. See note 22 for details about the location today of the records from the Foundling Hospital.

19. The questionnaire was reproduced in the same form at each interview under the guise of a free exchange; its object was to elicit particular responses however they might come out. This procedure, once studied, allowed first for a listing of the typical array of questions at the interview. A table then permitted their classification on the basis of the answers obtained to each question. Next these answers were studied on a graph, mapping out certain variables. The social environment was considered insofar as it exerted influence over the petitioner. This method, here briefly described, has the advantage of reducing to bare essentials the reports which followed the interviews: a series of fixed questions to which a certain number of answers corresponded, which can be logged and ordered. The treatment of these data quantitatively (i.e., general analysis of the reports) as well as qualitatively will be processed according to the SSPS program.

20. The report of a doctor or midwife always accompanied the petition.

21. By "family" we mean parents or extended family (grandparents, brothers, sisters, uncles, and aunts) who in the petitions are referred to as "friends."

22. To give an idea, of the 454 petitions, 250 women gave information concerning their families. Over half of these had lost one or both parents.

23. It is impossible to provide the usual reference data for these quotations. Each petition consists of a small, faded blue folder containing a two-page application along with testimonial letters and other assorted confirmatory papers giving proof of the petitioner's morals. This folder is folded lengthwise in three and then bound up with additional letters in bundles of ten or

twelve, tied with red calico ribbon. There are several "bundles" for each year, stored in boxes. Every petition bears a number indicating the order of its arrival and, of course, the name of the father and mother, their child's birth date, etc. This information is in my possession. Publication of it is nevertheless prohibited, for the current administration of the Thomas Coram Foundation for Children "is firmly committed to protecting the privacy of the adopted children's descendants." That is why I have only given the initials of the people mentioned in these documents.

In 1953 the name of the Foundling Hospital was changed to the Thomas Coram Foundation for Children, the Headquarters of which are located at 40 Brunswick Square, London, WC 1. The archives of the Foundation are at the Greater London Record Office. I first gained authorization to consult the material in 1975.

24. "The Society for the Suppression of Vice" and later the "London City Mission" closed down a number of taverns and prohibited the great London fairs.

25. Especially where the man belonged to the petty bourgeoisie (mainly office workers) or the army.

26. Retranscription of the petitioner's "statement" by a witness.

27. John Gillis, "Servants, Sexual Elations and the Risks of Illegitimacy in London, 1801–1900," *Feminist Studies* 5:1 (Spring 1979): 163.

THE 1920S

FEMINISM, CONSUMERISM, AND POLITICAL BACKLASH IN THE UNITED STATES

Rayna Rapp and Ellen Ross

> Polygamy, free love and the disruption of the home are to follow in the wake of human suffrage. There is no difference between woman suffrage, socialism, and the present feminist movement.
>
> *Woman's Protest,* May 1914

> Who and what is behind the anti-family movement? (Paul) Weyrich lists the major ones as those who do not believe in God, hardcore socialists, economic opportunists eager to make a buck from pornography, abortion, etc., and women's libbers who want a different political and cultural order.
>
> RICHARD A. VIGUERIE
> *The New Right: We're Ready to Lead,* 1980

Almost seventy years separate these antifeminist tirades, but the link they make between profeminist legislation and a threat to the family

We would like to thank Elsa Dixler for her help on the history of the 1920s and Ellen Dubois and Alice Kessler-Harris, who both provided thoughtful and thorough criticism of this paper. This paper is a revised and condensed version of "The Twenties Backlash: Compulsory Heterosexuality, the Consumer Family and the Waning of Feminism," in Amy Swerdlow and Hannah Lessinger, eds., *Race, Class and Sex, the Dynamics of Control* (Boston: G. K. Hall, 1983).

is all too familiar. The first wave of American feminism, culminating in the winning of suffrage in 1920, generated a strong political opposition in the decade that followed, just as our own generation's feminism is facing a powerful right-wing backlash. As feminist "survivalists" intent on defending the movement we've built since the late sixties, we turned to the 1920s to learn whether history must inevitably repeat itself. The earlier decline of feminism provides some sobering lessons, and there are indeed some parallels with our own era. But much also separates the twenties from the eighties and some of those differences suggest new and hopeful strategies for today's movement.

In the early twenties, the feminist movement still seemed powerful, and suffragists and anti-suffragists alike agreed that women had won a great victory. To consolidate their new-won power, a broad-based coalition of women's organizations came together under the umbrella of the Women's Joint Congressional Committee (WJCC) to lobby in Washington. The WJCC's strength lay in its diversity. Its members included everyone from the National League of Women Voters to the Women's Christian Temperance Union; from the National Women's Trade Union League (NWTUL) to the YWCA and even, temporarily, the DAR. The gains of the early twenties seemed to portend still greater victories to come. Women quickly won civil rights as political office holders and jurors, pushed a Constitutional amendment outlawing child labor through an intimidated Congress, and won the Sheppard-Towner Bill, which provided a very modest amount of money for maternal and infant health clinics. The AMA, which opposed the bill, thought that women had become "one of the strongest lobbies that has ever been seen in Washington."[1]

But by mid-decade, American politics had shifted well to the right, and the coalition's programs met a series of roadblocks. In 1923, the Supreme Court ruled against the concept of a minimum wage protecting women and many states that had already passed such laws began repealing them. Like our own ERA, a child labor amendment, which initially seemed popular, was blocked in key states by anti-ratification campaigns. The Catholic Church, defending the "traditional" family against government "intrusion," and the manufacturers' associations which still depended on child labor in textiles orchestrated the opposition.[2]

The tide of anti-Bolshevism and antipacifism that swept over the United States beginning about 1917 engulfed not only socialists but feminists as well. Feminist groups and causes were targeted as "subversive," "Bolshevik," or "antifamily"; the National Women's Trade

Union League was called a Communist organization, and even the
U.S. Women's Bureau was charged with trying to "Bolshevise" America by destroying the family through the Sheppard-Towner Act. An
outraged DAR revoked Jane Addams's honorary membership. Feminism was particularly suspect in the War Department, which produced the "Spider Web" chart in 1922. Linking feminist and women's
organizations, the chart demonstrated the imminence of a Bolshevik
takeover and named Florence Watkins, head of the PTA, as the connecting link.[3]

Feminist activists recognized how destructive this red-baiting was. It
not only defeated their legislation, but diverted endless energy in
rebuttals and defensive campaigns. It also undermined the feminism
and progressivism of some members of the WJCC. Some of the delegates at the League of Women Voters' 1921 convention believed, for
instance, that the Communist International was indeed behind the
Sheppard-Towner Act. And there was a 1923 campaign within the
National Federation of Business and Professional Women's Clubs to
prevent any association with the NWUTL because it was supposedly
Communist-run. Even the League of Women Voters adopted a more
timid method of taking stands on national issues.[4]

Confronted by such opposition, the feminist movement also suffered from a problem we would today call burnout. As the NWTUL's
Florence Kelley graphically described it, "Truly we are like a semi-
paralyzed centipede with its legs all moving at different rates of speed,
if at all, and how few legs moving!"[5] Confusing and bitter splits about
strategy also divided the movement. When the Women's Party reorganized around a platform of total sexual equality in 1921, the basis
for a major division was laid. In 1923, Representative Daniel Anthony,
Susan B. Anthony's nephew, introduced the ERA in Congress on their
behalf, but most feminists opposed it. They felt that the ERA would
undermine their longstanding strategy of seeking protective legislation for working women. Feminists lined up on opposite sides in state-
level campaigns for protective laws like the eight-hour day in New
York in the early twenties and in California and Indiana later on.[6]

In the inhospitable political and cultural climate of the twenties, a
"generation gap" began to emerge within feminism. The League of
Women Voters, successor to the National American Women's Suffrage
Party, complained of difficulty in recruiting younger members. The
membership of the Association of Women for the Prevention of
Lynching, an extremely effective organization of southern white
women, had an average age of forty-eight by the early 1930s. And as
one ex-suffragist remarked in 1928, "The feminist movement just isn't
all that smart among the juniors."[7]

However, something more intangible created the most powerful barrier to the continuation of feminism as a mass movement. A dramatic transformation of American culture, fusing sex, love, and consumerism, made the all-female organizations of the feminists seem stodgy and outmoded. Not only the winning of suffrage but the rapid expansion of the economy and new educational and cultural possibilities held out enormous promises for women, promises in which feminists also believed. Paradoxically, while some women benefited from an opening up of new "life-styles," the net effect of the new culture was to demobilize and destroy the old one within which feminism had thrived for several generations.

The "roaring twenties" were fueled by a huge expansion in corporate wealth and a doubling of industrial production. Assembly-line mass production had developed rapidly, but for business the problem was how to sell what they were so efficiently producing. Foreign markets, installment buying, and advertising were all expanded to create new buyers. By the end of the decade, there were 25 million cars registered in America, 70 percent of them bought on credit. A new system of credit-fixed monthly mortgage payments helped spur the home building industry. A growing advertising industry set about "effecting a self-conscious change in the psychic economy" as historian Stuart Ewen puts it, creating new needs for "prestige," "glamour," or "sex appeal," new fears of looking old or having "halitosis," and new pressures on families.[8]

Modern families engaged in new kinds of consumption. During the twenties 70 percent of American homes got electricity, and sales of domestic appliances boomed. Power companies not only advertised appliances, they also extended consumer credit and repaired what they sold for free. Seventy percent of gas stoves and 90 percent of washing and sewing machines were purchased on credit. The packaged food industry also flourished: during the decade, Campbell, Kellogg, and Quaker Oats became household words. Most Americans also switched to store-bought, ready-made clothing purchased from mail-order houses and department stores. American businesses soon learned that 80 percent of domestic funds were spent by women; in home economics courses, buying, not frugality, became defined as the civic duty of young girls.[9]

When, in the 1920s, the General Confederation of Women's Clubs offered their membership lists for use in both consumer and sexual surveys, the fusion of the two topics was anything but accidental. *The Ladies' Home Journal* had labeled the twenties the decade of the "cosmetics revolution," and mass-circulation pulp journals full of Avon, Pond's, and Woodbury ads created home markets for products that sold feminine attractiveness. By the late 1920s, *True Romance* had a circulation of two million, and like *The Ladies' Home Journal* and *Good Housekeeping,* it mingled sex and sales. By the end of the decade, beauty pageants had taken on a standardized, popular format: women had been trained not only to do the consuming but to be consumed as well.[10]

Promoted by psychologists and other social service professionals, what we have come to think of as the "heterosexual revolution" was indeed an important element of the consumer culture of the twenties. The rise of companionate marriage as an ideal and the labeling of female-centered sociability as lesbian and deviant—two main themes of the heterosexual revolution—indirectly undermined organized feminism by labeling the intense friendship networks on which feminist organizations were based as stodgy and old-fashioned.[11]

Earlier generations of women had internalized notions of sexual difference and distance between women and men, and prescriptive literature viewed sex as a wife's duty. But the writings of the new sexual modernists—Havelock Ellis, G. Stanley Hall, and later Freud and such disciples as Helene Deutsch and Marie Bonaparte—transformed the image of the female. In the new psychological discourse, women were sexual, and orgasm was defined as a natural imperative for both sexes. Victorian marriage, repressive and formal, was criticized by modernists in favor of a union in which partners became friends and lovers. Heterosexuality, its problems and pitfalls, became a topic of concern among a broad spectrum of social reformers, health activists, and educators. New marital and sexual practices were debated and publicized, and movements for trial marriage, serial marriage, and divorce as solutions to sexual incompatability gained popularity. The twenties marked the height of the struggle for birth control, and by this time, a large majority of middle-class women used contraception. By the thirties, a growing proportion of working-class women would use it as well. The Victorian image defining maternity as women's ultimate fulfillment was being replaced by attention to their sexual partnership with men.[12]

Many of the sexual modernists who expressed such sympathetic interest in women's heterosexual liberation also pinned punitive labels on those who could not, or would not, conform to the new prescriptions. Women's lack of orgasm with males was attributed to their resistance to "fully adult" sexuality; "frigid" women were labeled immature, even masculine. Psychologists routinely labeled feminists as neurotic, sublimating sadists and saw their homosocial liaisons as "compensations" for their lack of heteroerotic success.

The heterosexual revolution was thus a double-edged sword.

Women undoubtedly benefited from the more open discussion of female-male sexuality and its frustrations. But they also lost the diffuse homosocial and homosexual milieu within which earlier generations of women had operated. Sexual surveys revealed that college-educated women had had rich experiences in homoeroticism. And those women who continued to keep their social distance from men— who lived in what was popularly known as "the Boston marriage"— were seen as obstacles to the growth of heterosexual relationships.

The negative image of lesbians that appeared in sexologists' writings centered on their dangerous, "intermediate" sexuality, and lesbianism served as a focus for a cultural discourse concerning proper degrees of gender dichotomization in a period when *womanhood* and *manhood* were being redefined. Carroll Smith-Rosenberg and Esther Newton have analyzed the evolution of "mannish women" in the 1920s and the image's implications for lesbian self-definition. Though lesbianism as a category was partly created by sexologists, some women eagerly claimed it as their own, for it provided a sphere in which women could both assert their social independence from men and develop a woman-created eroticism. Thus the creation of a specifically lesbian subculture, built out of the dismantling of a formerly diffuse, homosocial sphere, was intensified in this era.[13]

Simultaneously, prior homosocial institutions, so important to feminist organizing and consciousness, lost much of their legitimacy. The proportion of single-sex colleges declined continuously from the 1870s on as co-education became more and more popular. Settlement houses lost social and financial importance for white women, as social work became a profession rather than a live-in vocation and restrictive immigration quotas diminished the pool of prospective clients.[14] Settlement work by black women, however, did not diminish in this period, nor did the antilynching campaigns in which so many participated.

Above all, consumer revolution reorganized the most prevalent of all homosocial institutions—the family itself. Generations of Americans had relied on close ties among same-sexed kin and kinlike friendships to transmit a variety of skills and cultural practices. But the rise of domestic science in settlement houses and public schools provided a compelling version of family life which competed with the knowledge immigrant mothers could pass on to their Americanizing daughters. As Jane Addams wrote, "An Italian girl who had had lessons in cooking at the public school will help her mother to connect the entire family with American food and household habits."[15] The rise of boys' clubs, sports clubs, and the Boy Scouts can also be viewed as replacements for skills no longer transmitted from father to son under conditions of expanding urban capitalism. As the power of parent-to-child networks decreased, adolescent peer culture grew with its emphasis on preparation for heterosexuality. The public schools, settlement houses, dance halls, and street life made claims on immigrant daughters and sons that separated them from the worlds of their parents.[16]

The rise of an adolescent peer culture occurred as public education expanded dramatically. By the end of the twenties, half the nation's youth were attending high school. When the Lynds conducted their now-classic study of Middletown, a city of 35,000, in 1925, there were fourteen girls' clubs to sponsor dances around high school events and dozens of boys' clubs promoting athletics. Mass mobilization and hysteria surrounded the endless cycle of basketball, football, and baseball games, accompanied by cheerleading and boosterism. Car ownership also came to play a role in adolescent culture. "If you want to know all that's changing in Middletown, it's spelled A-U-T-O," one local commented. By 1923, four million cars were being manufactured in America, and there were two of them for every three families in Middletown. The auto created a social upheaval. Use of the car caused family disputes among Middletown's teenagers, and the majority of what juvenile court handled as girls' "sex crimes" took place in automobiles.[17]

In the same period, the growth of the movie industry produced a mass culture consumed across the continent. In Middletown, programs changed frequently. Three hundred different screenings could be viewed in a single year, and teens reported attending up to three times a week. Although "wild West" films were popular, "society romances" were tops. With titles like *Married Flirts, The Daring Years, Flaming Youth, Old Wives for New,* and *Why Change Your Wife,* the movies presented a revised social anatomy of heterosexuality. Girls reported to survey researchers that they learned the details of making love in movies, such as what to do with both pairs of arms while embracing. As one seventeen-year-old put it, "No wonder girls of the older days, before movies, were so modest and bashful. They never saw Clara Bow and William Haines . . . if we did not see such examples . . . where would we get the idea of being 'hot'? We wouldn't." As Elizabeth Ewen points out, such films had a major impact on the Americanization of urban immigrant girls, whose assimilation linked bourgeois fantasy, consumption, and heterosexual romance, all experiences to be had outside of their families.[18]

Sold on celluloid, male-oriented images of glamour, young women were no longer recruitable to what appeared as outmoded "causes."

The new commercial culture of the twenties was not so much directly antifeminist as it was co-optive of feminist issues and concerns. By the late twenties, much that passed for feminist thought dealt with individual choices and personal fulfillment—life-style feminism supplanted its activist predecessor. Ruth Pickering, one of "those modern women" whose stories were printed in the *Nation* in the twenties, wrote, "I have traded my sense of exhilarating defiance (shall we call it feminism?) for an assurance of free and unimpeded self-expression (or shall we call that feminism?). In other words, I have grown up." Confessions from "Feminists—New Style" who had given up employment for domestic life expressed their choice in articles like "I Gave up My Law Books for a Cook Book" or "You May Have My Job, a Feminist Discovers Her Home." Such articles focused on the enormous difficulties involved in women's double shift at home and at work or the obstacles even professional women faced on the job. Themes of female independence, even militancy, were thoroughly co-opted, resurfacing in advertising, the most impressive example of which was staged in 1929 by advertising consultant Edward Bernays, Freud's nephew. In that year's Easter Parade, accompanied by enormous publicity, Bernays organized a contingent of smoking women in formations aping the suffrage demonstrations of an earlier decade. "Why not a parade of women lighting torches of freedom—smoking cigarettes?" he had suggested to George W. Will, owner of the American Tobacco Company.[19] We had indeed come a long way.

Looking at the twenties, we were struck by the contrast between the opening up of lifestyle opportunities for some women and the weakening of feminism as an organized, political movement to transform all of "woman's condition." Today's life-style feminism, "dressing for success," "getting yours," assertiveness training, may likewise benefit women as individuals but is no substitute for a vigorous political movement. Without a continued struggle for public and humane child care, reproductive and sexual freedom, equal pay, shelter from domestic violence, and all the benefits of legal equality, no individual woman's life-style is secure.

The organizations and institutions feminists established in the seventies deserve our zealous defense. Not only explicitly political groups but feminist health centers, women's centers, rape crisis groups, battered women's shelters, and women's studies programs have established a power base wider than the one that won the vote in 1920, and its political scope is broader and more varied. We need to maintain these institutions not only for their vital services, but as a lifeline to the next generation. Women's studies programs, for example, are still packing classrooms with young and enthusiastic women whose "conversion experience" is essential to our future.

A great difference between the twenties and today is the high and increasing proportion of women who are in the workplace to stay. Today's female labor force represents a true cross section of American womanhood. At a time when labor unions are under attack, their "female sector" is growing fast. As "women's issues" like day care, job segregation, and reproductive rights become matters of contract negotiation, we have the possibility of coalitions that unite women across racial, regional, religious, and ethnic barriers. The influx of organized female workers has the potential not only to transform labor unions, but to make an impact on national politics as well. As members of anti-Reagan coalitions that include unions, feminists have it in our power to make the depth of the twenties' backlash impossible to recreate today.

Notes

1. J. Stanley Lemons, *The Woman Citizen: Social Feminism in the 1920's* (Urbana: University of Illinois Press, 1975); William H. Chafe, *The American Woman. Her Changing Social, Economic and Political Role, 1920–1970* (London and New York: Oxford University Press, 1972); and Sheila M. Rothman, *Woman's Proper Place* (New York: Basic Books, 1978), are three excellent sources on this period. The quotation from Chafe, *The American Woman*, 28.

2. Clarke A. Chambers, "The Campaign for Women's Rights in the 1920's" in *Our American Sisters: Women in American Life and Thought*, ed. Jean E. Friedman and William G. Shade, 2nd ed. (Boston: Allyn & Bacon, 1976), 323–44; Lemons, *Woman Citizen*, 219–33.

3. Lemons, *Woman Citizen*, 210, 214–17, 218.

4. Ibid., 213–14, 222–23.

5. Quoted in Chambers, "The Campaign for Women's Rights in the 1920's," 334.

6. William L. O'Neill, *Everyone Was Brave* (New York: Quadrangle Books, 1971), 277–78; Lemons, *Woman Citizen*, 87.

7. Jacquelyn Dowd Hall, "'A Truly Subversive Affair': Women against Lynching in the Twentieth-Century South" in *Women of America: A History*, ed. Carol R. Berkin and Mary Beth Norton (Boston: Houghton Mifflin, 1979), 360–88; O'Neill, *Everyone Was Brave*, 307.

8. William E. Leuchtenburg, *The Perils of Prosperity, 1914–1932* (Chicago: University of Chicago Press, 1958), 179; Stuart Ewen, *Captains of Consciousness: Advertising and the Social Roots of the Consumer Culture* (New York: McGraw-Hill, 1976), 32, 167.

9. Joan Greenbaum, "Out of the Frying Pan: The Kitchen as Commodity and Culture," unpublished manuscript (1981), 6; Mary Ryan, *Womanhood in*

America: From Colonial Times to the Present, 2nd ed. (New York: Franklin Watts, 1979), 180; Heidi I. Hartmann, "Capitalism and Women's Work in the Home, 1900–1930," (Ph.D. dissertation, Yale University, 1974).

10. Ryan, *Womanhood in America,* 177–82.

11. Christina Simmons, "Companionate Marriage and the Lesbian Threat," *Frontiers* 4:3 (Fall 1979): 54–59.

12. Ryan, *Womanhood in America,* 151–82.

13. See Carroll Smith-Rosenberg, *Disorderly Conduct: Visions of Gender in Victorian America* (New York: Alfred A. Knopf, 1985), 245–96 and Esther Newton, "The Mythic Mannish Lesbian," *Signs* 9 (Fall 1984), 557–75.

14. Allen F. Davis, *Spearheads for Reform: The Social Settlements and the Progressive Movement 1890–1914* (New York: Oxford University Press), 228–35; Rothman, *Woman's Proper Place,* chapters 3, 4, 5. See also Blanch Wiesen Cook, *Women and Supplementary Networks* (New York: Out & Out Books, 1979).

15. Quoted in Barbara Ehrenreich and Deidre English, "The Manufacture of Housework," *Socialist Revolution* 5:4 (October–December 1975): 5–40, 30.

16. Elizabeth Ewen, "City Lights: Immigrant Women and the Rise of the Movies," *Signs* 5:3 suppl. (Spring 1980): S45–S65.

17. Robert S. Lynd and Helen Merell Lynd, *Middletown,* paperback ed. (New York: Harvest Books, 1956). Two other good studies of youth culture in the American twenties are Paula S. Fass, *The Damned and the Beautiful: American Youth in the 1920's* (Oxford and New York: Oxford University Press) and Lewis Ehrenberg, *Steppin' Out: New York Nightlife and the Transformation of American Culture, 1890–1930* (Westport, Conn.: Greenwood Press, 1981).

18. Mary P. Ryan, "The Projection of a New Womanhood: The Movie Moderns in the 1920's" in *Our American Sisters,* 36–84; Ewen, "City Lights," S55–S58.

19. Elaine Showalter, ed., *These Modern Women: Autobiographical Essays from the Twenties,* 16; Frank Stricker, "Cookbooks and Law Books: the Hidden History of Career Women in Twentieth-Century America," in *A Heritage of Her Own,* ed. Nancy F. Cott and Elizabeth H. Pleck (New York: Simon and Schuster, 1979), 476–98, 291; Ewen, *Captains of Consciousness,* 160.

GIRLKULTUR OR THOROUGHLY RATIONALIZED FEMALE
A NEW WOMAN IN WEIMAR GERMANY?

Atina Grossmann

> Housewife, mother and working woman.
> The synthesis of these three life styles is the
> problem of the age.[1]

This statement from a 1930 issue of the fashion magazine *Die Neue Linie* (The New Line) expresses the dilemma that the figure of the New Woman posed for German reformers throughout the years of the Weimar Republic. During a period of intense political upheaval and polarization, a Sex Reform movement brought together diverse viewpoints and affiliations in the name of a commitment to health, efficiency, and productivity in everyday life. Weimar sex reformers formed a consensus around the necessity of rationalization in both production and reproduction. A regulation of working women's sexual and procreative behavior, and a fascination with the new woman as a social and cultural phenomenon, were the crucial factors in that consensus. Inspired by a model of Bolshevik productivity—in goods and births—which was in turn not clearly differentiated from American efficiency, Sex Reform attacked capitalist disorder in the name of socialist and eugenic order.

I am grateful to Jane Caplan, Victoria de Grazia, Miriam Hansen, and Sally Stein for their comments.

Sex Reform and the New Woman

Sex Reform was a mass movement with ties both to the working-class movement and parts of the medical profession. Claiming up to 150,000 adherents at its height during the Depression, the movement built its own network of institutions and media: counseling centers, clinics, organizations, meetings, seminars, sex manuals, journals, garden plots, and hiking trips. It functioned as an integral part both of the working-class subculture and movement and of the emerging professional specialties of social medicine, family planning, and sexology. The umbrella movement brought together doctors, social workers, and lay people, many of them associated with working-class political parties. Fascinated by and celebratory of the New Woman, the sex reformers also sought to channel and control her. The regulation of abortion and female sexuality were central to an intense debate about the changing nature of women and the family in a new technologized world.[2]

Sex Reform sought to address real needs for reliable birth control and household management in a period of extreme economic instability. It also aimed to bring a certain order, regularity, and discipline into working-class lives. Women and women's bodies were the medium for this rationalization. While professionals wanted to impose this discipline in order to ensure a more efficient and reliable work force in the era of the assembly line, the working-class and women's movement—and working-class women themselves—also actively pursued and demanded such discipline in order to better manage the multiple burdens of home and work. The Sex Reform movement therefore was both response to and expression of the New Woman in post–World War I Germany. Sex Reform aimed to redomesticate a putative New Woman—independent and sexy—back to an identity that would accommodate marriage and family as well as wage labor and active sexuality. Sex Reform posited a New Woman who was no longer either an angel in the home nor a working drudge, but a thoroughly rationalized female: the efficient juggler of the double burden.

Sex Reform took as its propaganda icon the "old woman"—Käthe Kollwitz's "woman in need"—the exhausted proletarian housewife, mother of a large brood, eternally pregnant and long suffering. In fact, such families were becoming a statistical rarity, and sex reformers were really much more concerned with younger women who built the new smaller family and carried the double burden. For Weimar sex reformers, the New Woman was neither a Bolshevized worker comrade nor an Americanized flighty flapper, but a young working woman, either married or single. By *new* I do not mean to imply a "better" or more "liberated," but simply different, cause for anxiety.

A picture of this New Woman emerges from a wealth of material, all of it admittedly mediated through the lens of social workers, sociologists, government officials, political organizers, and physicians and focused on large cities, especially Berlin. In particular, the sources include the studies conducted by the Frankfurt Institute for Social Research and the German Academy for Women's Work; investigations of living and working conditions by trade unions, often complete with personal essays by members; reports, questionnaires, and interviews gathered by the emerging social work and social science professions. This type of documentation—home visits, participant observer field work, counseling center visits, interviews, questionnaires, and essay contests—was itself a result of newly rationalized techniques of information gathering and surveillance. The very quantity of material available, and the fact that much of it was gathered by older women about younger women, speaks to the significance attached to the New Woman and to the salience of intragender generational issues for our discussion.

This New Woman was not merely a media myth or a demographer's paranoid fantasy, but a social reality that can be researched and documented. She existed in office and factory, bedroom and kitchen, just as surely as in café, cabaret, and film. I think it is important that we begin to look at the New Woman as producer and not only consumer, as an agent constructing a new identity which was then marketed in mass culture, even as mass culture helped to form that identity; as a spur to Sex Reform even as Sex Reform helped to further that process.

We now need to revise the "revisionist" reading of Weimar women's history which forcefully punctured the myth of the "emancipated woman of the roaring twenties."[3] Looking back, social historians can dismiss the perceptions of "marriage crisis, fiasco of monogamy, birth strike" as hysteria or propaganda, but the fact remains that the particular cohort of young women who entered the labor force after the war were a worrisome unknown quantity. Despite our present understanding of the continuities of "patriarchy" and capitalism in Weimar, contemporaries—on the right and left—were struck by how much had changed—and how fast—since 1914. We should take seriously that perception of change and rupture and recapture some of its intensity. Furthermore we must analyze why so much of that sense was conceptualized and interpreted in terms of a New Woman.

Jugglers of the Double Burden

The New Woman of the 1920s had existed as a Bohemian or professional rarity and literary convention before the First World War. Afterwards she suddenly entered the public space and popular imagination as a mass phenomenon. Almost 11.5 million women—35.8 percent of the total labor force—worked for a living according to the 1925 census. About a third were married; many had young children or were of childbearing age.[4]

The New Woman was a result of the "great divide" of the First World War, the collapse of Empire and the establishment of a Republic with socialist aspirations. Young women workers, both white collar and blue collar, from both middle-class and working-class backgrounds, who had entered the work force straight from school increasingly shared consumption and leisure patterns and ambivalent attitudes toward family and the workplace. They had perhaps more in common with each other than with an older generation of women workers which had entered the industrial labor force from agriculture and domestic service and was still accustomed to thinking of women's wage labor as an episodic emergency measure rather than as a permanent condition of the rationalized sex-segmented labor market. Even as the growth of the service sector increased job opportunities for the young and unmarried, the introduction of the assembly line in consumer industry also required the long-term industrial labor of married women. Moreover, after the experience of the war and inflation, even bourgeois families could no longer assume that their daughters would never have to work or that husbands could be found to support them.[5] Indeed, wage-earning women in the Weimar period may have been more significantly divided by a generation gap than a white-collar/blue-collar gap, a circumstance too often obscured by the image of the New Woman as white-collar consumer.

Rationalization of production and the work process—the assembly line; scientific management; new standards of speed, efficiency, and productivity—fundamentally transformed German economic life after World War I. Taking off in the mid 1920s, fueled by American investment and the Dawes Plan and modeled on Henry Ford's "Americanist" plan for increased productivity without social conflict, rationalization was intended to facilitate a recovery and reordering of the German nation after the ravages of war, rebellion, and inflation. The rationalization of the economy contributed to restructuring the labor market and institutionalizing sex segregation at the same time it undermined traditional hierarchies based on skills. Restructuring caused tensions between the sexes around employment issues which manifested themselves in anxiety about the future of family life.

Most German women, in fact, still worked at traditional tasks, either as unpaid workers within the family and household or within family enterprises. Despite the widespread concern about young unskilled female workers replacing experienced, skilled male workers, women only rarely displaced men. In fact, far from precipitating a female invasion of male labor preserves, rationalization tightened, indeed institutionalized, the modern sexual division of labor.[6] However, rationalized work and family patterns affected even those women who did not directly work in the new sectors of the economy. While not significantly increasing the proportion of women in the labor force, rationalization reorganized it in such a way that women stood at the forefront: in assembly-line factories; in mechanized offices with typewriters, filing cabinets, and switchboards; behind the sales counters of chain stores; and in the expanded social-service bureaucracies of a Social Democratic–minded Germany.

For many, the invigorating tempo of the city—Berlin of the Golden Twenties was a "City of Women"—was also wholly merged with the accelerated tempo of the modern workplace. Women therefore experienced the crisis of rationalization (and later of the Depression) differently and perhaps more intensely than men. To the burden of endless unpaid labor at home were added the twin pressures of nerve-racking new work processes and the traditional wage differential between male and female workers. Women became the quintessential rationalized workers; they earned little and were extremely productive.

Rationalized industry was thought to depend on, and aimed to create, rationalized workers both at work and at home. Gramsci, in his essay on "Americanism and Fordism", put this in extreme form referring to sexuality:

> The exaltation of passion cannot be reconciled with the timed movements of productive motions connected with the most perfect automatism.[7] . . . The truth is that the new type of man demanded by the rationalization of production and work cannot be developed until the sexual instinct has been suitably regulated and until it too has been rationalised.[8]

If the new economy required a new type of man, it also and most especially required a new type of woman and family. In Germany, the rationalization of everyday life, including the rationalization of housework and finally of sexuality and procreation (birth control, sexual technique, and a properly small nuclear family) was primarily intended to serve not the full-time housewife, but the juggler of the double burden. Even as it drew more married women into industry and disrupted family life, rationalization supposedly also produced new labor and time-saving consumer goods, which could also help to organize work in the household.

Young Unmarried Women: *Girlkultur* and Potential Working Mothers

Many of the reports and documents marking the emergence of this New Woman were compiled by women professionals. An older generation of New Women, whether they had identified with the bourgeois or proletarian women's movement, was not itself consigned to being traditional and old-fashioned. Older women observed among their daughters and younger sisters the "urge to break away" *(Drang nach Draussen)*[9] into the world of "free time" *(Freizeit)* and urban culture, and away from work and family. Peter Gay has located a problematic of Weimar culture in the revolt of the sons against the fathers;[10] but we might also look to the generational conflicts among women. On many levels, the New Woman was a challenge to the "old woman." She rejected both the fate of the "old" proletarian mother of a large family and of the "old" single committed women's rights activist.

Significantly, the reports and complaints about young working women were virtually identical for white-collar and blue-collar employees. The impact of rationalization was seen as more similar than different: in both cases, observers worried about the tempo and haste in young women's lives; the lack of time for reflection, political involvement, or family; and the potential for sexual danger in the frantic pursuit of recreation as a respite from stressful monotonous wage labor. If some particularly worried about the romantic and sexual fantasies of typists and salesgirls (sitting too long could be overly stimulating, like horseback riding!), others worried about the eroticization (literally *Erotisierung*) of the factory atmosphere in much the same terms.

A fascinating survey conducted by Erich Fromm in 1929 among left-leaning workers and employees revealed that socialists shared these concerns with the older generation of feminists. Those surveyed generally defended women's right to contraception and abortion and accepted short bobbed hair (the *Bubikopf*) as a practical and hygienic innovation. Yet there was almost universal disapproval of women using makeup.[11] Erna Barschak's 1926 Women's Academy study of female apprentices—in factories as well as hairdressing salons—de-

scribed them "on the loose" in the big city *(Grosstadt)* in terms generally associated with white-collar workers:

> If the money will stretch, the young girls usually spend Sunday after
> Sunday and also often a weekday's evening in musty cinemas in the old
> city or the blue collar district where a world is opened up to them so
> different from the grey monotony of their own existence and work,
> where they discover an exciting, multi-faceted and colorful world en-
> ticingly filled with elegant young ladies dressed in the latest fashion,
> often not older than themselves, who drive cars, go to dances and the
> theatre, and are admired and courted by equally elegant young gen-
> tlemen.[12]

Few seemed to worry that women would not take their work seriously and try to get married as quickly as possible. Rather, observers
were concerned that women sought sexual adventures and urban
diversions that would make marriage and family seem virtually as
boring and unattractive as work in the office or factory. Contrary to
popular image, most young women workers did not live on their own
(sturmfreie Buden) but continued to live at home with parents and
siblings, often under crowded conditions and with enormous family
tensions. Young women workers resented the imposition of the double burden before they were even married. They were keenly conscious that their working brothers were not expected to take on the
same level of family responsibilities. Family conflicts about everything
from wearing a *Bubikopf* to the time spent with a boyfriend increased
young women's need to get away, out from under the family authority:

> And now sexual adventure is often looked for in a mere me-too
> attitude, out of sheer curiosity and sometimes even motivated by the
> wish to brag, to "show off." But also domestic troubles and unhap-
> piness at home, the feeling of being unloved and not understood are
> dangerous allies on the road to sexual temptation and early inter-
> course.[13]

Lisbeth Franzen-Hellersberg, a social worker of more *Völkisch* sym-
pathies than either the liberal feminist Barschak or the socialist
Fromm expressed the same concerns in her 1932 study of *Die
jugendliche Arbeiterin* (The Young Woman Worker). Her informants
were also desperate to escape from the domestic obligations and cares
of their working-class families. They preferred to stay out late rather
than return home to wait on fathers and brothers.[14] Most were
cynically disillusioned with the prospects of marriage and housework;
two-thirds of the young women interviewed rejected the possibility of

marriage! They focused on obtaining reliable birth control information and products, rather than on the traditional concerns of the proper young working-class or petit-bourgeois girl such as the household and hygiene education that the middle-class women's movement was eager to provide.[15]

Low paid as they were, these young women had reordered their spending and consumption priorities. Money that might earlier have gone into preparing a trousseau was now redirected towards body and health care, transportation, entertainment, and tobacco.[16] A physician responding to the Frankfurt Institute's Survey on Sexual Morality complained, "Emancipated women adopt more readily the bad habits of men than their good ones"[17]; and another remarked that women "have been seized by an amorous (non-marital) flurry."[18] On the other hand, despite, or perhaps because of, their willingness to engage in sexual experimentation, young women reported experiencing men as unreliable, often brutal and alcoholic; hardly an image to give hope to those worried about birth rate and the quality of modern marriages. If some women seem to have seized an extraordinary amount of sexual space, they also appeared to be applying standards of sober objectivity *(Sachlichkeit)* to, and keeping a somewhat cynical distance from, their sexual escapades.

The statistical reality that the vast majority of these young women would in fact go on to get married and have at least one child did not change the perception of marriage and family crisis. The demographic and social future was unknown. Women, it seemed, had assimilated the lessons of war and inflation: neither could they depend on men to provide for them materially, nor could they depend on them for emotional support. Would such young working women, white- or blue-collar, ever make fit wives and mothers for a society that desperately needed the soothing and stabilizing influence of maternal self-sacrifice and talent for coping?

The unease about young women's sexual activity and rejection of commitment to marriage and family was apparently confirmed by the declining birth rate and the smaller size of the working-class family. Women's sexuality was threatening because it might make women less willing to accept a humdrum housewife's existence; women's wage labor was threatening not only because of the financial resources it offered, but because of the time and commitment it took from family responsibilities. The two were intimately connected: precisely the young working girl needed the moral guidance of an attentive mother, and that attention would not be forthcoming if the mother were preoccupied with the double burden.

In 1930, organized women textile workers wrote descriptions of

Mein Arbeitstag, Mein Wochenende (My Work Day, My Weekend) for an essay contest sponsored by their union. These 150 detailed reports provide an extraordinarily rich insight into working women's daily lives. As politically active women, their leisure-time interests tended more toward hiking in the woods than fantasy in darkened movie theatres, but they too spoke of the need to get out and away: "Our bodies just scream for air."[19]

They too were keenly aware of the hardships of married life; hardly any unmarried women indicated any longing to exchange their single existence for the supposed security of married life. They cherished the extra time and freedom that being single and above all childless offered.

> I wished everyone of my co-workers could find a way to counterbalance the stresses of the job by sensible use of her leisure time. Unfortunately however, as a rule no one but single working women will succeed in this. Their married colleagues are hampered by household duties and children. . . . For a married working woman it is hardly possible any more to find a moment of quiet and feel like her own person.[20]

"It is impossible for a married woman to be her own person." Such sentiments articulated by working-class women who had traditionally carried the burden of reproducing the labor force were apt to strike a certain terror into the hearts of population and social-policy experts on both the left and the right.

Young women clearly perceived the endless chores of housework and mothering as work, obliterating for married women the distinction between work and leisure (workday and weekend). Such a life, rather than being understood as a fulfillment of female identity, was rejected, at least for the moment, as a hindrance to freedom and personal autonomy. Contrary to the common wisdom, which held that tens of thousands of German women were mourning the lack of available husbands after the war, studies indicated that these young women relished their relative freedom and were not eager to exchange it for wifely and maternal duties.

Married Women Workers and Their "Longest Day"

Even married women—proper housewives—expressed a certain thankfulness at not being mothers: "When I have finished (cleaning up from dinner), we go for a walk. If I had children, no doubt I would have to stay home."[21] Whereas young single women felt that they could not afford to be sentimental about their lovers and clearly recognized the hardships endured by the working mother, married working women could not afford to spend time and effort (the labors of love) creating comfortable domesticity.

Women's wage labor therefore raised fears more profound than the specter of competition at the workplace or a "sterile" Germany. Other terrors lurked behind the worry about the birth rate, or economic competition and double earners. The major problems, the most wrenching changes for both men and women, were not on the job, but at home where one was expected to recover from such stresses and changes. Women who worked in rationalized time- and motion-studied workplaces brought home with them new techniques for domestic labor and time management. Rationalization both demanded married women's wage labor and then proposed new methods and goods to facilitate that process.

The organized married women textile workers documenting their daily lives in *Mein Arbeitstag, Mein Wochende,* for example, proudly described their housework in the time-motion terms they had assimilated in the factory. They spoke of daily life (the private, the personal) in machine images, counting the minutes and hand motions required for specific tasks. They were acutely conscious of the time ticking away and in fact complained that they lacked the technical labor-saving devices that would help them make their housework as rational as their work in the factory! They could not yet afford vacuum cleaners or washing machines but they had already internalized the procedures and attitudes that would make them eager and efficient consumers when the appliances did become affordable: the new woman consumer was created ideologically before she was materially possible.

Clearly, advertising and the growth of mass circulation media to present that advertising, as well as the numerous state-sponsored exhibitions of new household and health technology, played a major role in introducing women to their new consumer tasks.[22] Nevertheless, a considerable number of German women gained an aptitude for, and awareness of, rationalized homemaking skills—keeping schedules, making lists, trying out labor-saving products, organizing time and space—at the workplace. Distinctions between home and work blurred and shifted as housework techniques reinforced work discipline and vice versa.

Politically influenced by the working-class parties (Social Democratic and to a much lesser degree the Communist Party) as well as disciplined by the nature of their work, the women textile workers were proud of their self-management techniques. They apparently believed, along with Lenin and Frederick Winslow Taylor, that technology could relieve the drudgery and "slavery" of housework.[23] They shared in the general progressive enthusiasm for new housing projects funded by the trade unions and Social Democratic municipal governments. They supported the new domestic culture of efficient "Frankfurt kitchens" and sleek easy-to-clean furniture which was informed by *Bauhaus* principles of functional architecture.[24] Many Social Democrats and Communists were willing to embrace the rationalization of industry as a form of increasing output and wealth and did not fully understand the extent to which rationalization depended on increased exploitation of the working class.[25] In a similar vein, and unlike conservatives who mourned the loss of "organic human values" in the home, most progressives welcomed—though with ambivalence—the introduction of housework technology.

Nevertheless, for the women speaking in *Mein Arbeitstag, Mein Wochenende,* rationalized housework was a survival technique, albeit applied under primitive conditions. They spoke the language of *Bauhaus* and factory; without benefit of modern machinery or collective labor, they shared in a hegemonic value system where daily life was divided into time sequences and work units. These women's breathless accounts of the split-second acrobatics of their daily regimen, reveal the degree to which their lives were informed by their working and the particular nature of their work. In painfully detailed descriptions, every moment was accounted for, every step considered. A married woman worker recorded her workday, begun with the ring of the alarm clock and certainly not finished with the screech of the factory bell:

> The alarm clock rings, sleepily I open my eyes, five A.M.! Only a little longer. Cozily I stretch in bed and close my eyes again. Immediately I am asleep once more. Terrified I start up again. A quarter to six! Out, out of bed on the double. Quickly I put something on, carefully I open the door to the kitchen, put my head under the faucet to wipe the sleep fully from my face, now the hair has to be brushed and combed, the dress thrown on and I already put on my apron. Water for the soup is put on the gas stove. The potatoes which I had peeled and cut the night before go into the pot. Meanwhile I walk over to the staircase window to polish the shoes and then return to the kitchen to add the necessary ingredients to the soup, potatoes and soup are cooking, the gas is turned to "low." Now I go into the garden next to the house to fetch some lettuce and at the same time empty out the ashbin from the stove and take along any other garbage that has accumulated. In a few minutes I am back to check the pots. The lettuce will be trimmed and washed and placed into fresh water. The kitchen will be wet-mopped and swept clean. And so must be the stairs. Soup and potatoes are done

and ready to be put aside for cooling off. Now I prepare the morning cocoa and the sandwiches to be taken along for lunch and place the cups on the table, it is almost 6:30.

And all that three-quarters of an hour activity occurred before the so-called "working day" even began! The report continues:

> I exchange my slippers for walking shoes, take off my apron, and already there sounds the long drawn-out, shrill and ugly tone of the factory siren. It is 6:45. Quickly I shut all the windows, one last glance into the mirror, once more with the comb through the hair, teeth brushed. Otto [her husband] has meanwhile gone downstairs with Robert who, as long as he has vacation and we are in the shop, is staying with my parents who live next door. Now I rush downstairs and over to my mother's to deposit the milk-pot. In a few minutes I am at the factory gate. Another three minutes' walk to the weavers' room. Quickly I run towards my looms, right after 7:00 a.m. they come to check if everybody is there.[26]

Other women echo the desperate need to keep everything tightly organized if the basics of family life and housework were to function at all:

> Every minute counts . . .[27] The practical *Bubikopf* haircut saves time. Everything must be done in a hurry, every movement spaced, because the train will not wait.[28]

The women seemed to operate on an internal time clock where every minute and action was measured and planned as though the factory inspector were keeping track. Such women were the best kind of workers: they internalized the discipline.

> I organize things in the morning in such a way that I make the same movements every day almost automatically.[29]

In the process they also disciplined their families, especially their children:

> Constantly I have to keep the clock in sight, admonish them to hurry up.[30]

As they were driven, so they were forced to drive others. Often they were then blamed for having destroyed the comfortable restfulness of the home they were seeking to preserve. The essays communicate a pervasive atmosphere of controlled chaos and nerve-racking speed-up:

A constant hurry and flurry.[31]

Sociologists and social workers observed and encouraged this hectic
rationalization of family life. They mourned the loss of preindustrial
rhythms with their time for common meals and recreation that had
supposedly been provided, even in the industrialized era, by the
working-class housewife. But they also reinforced the process by
giving academic shape to the new housework patterns. Just as sex
reformers would chart human sexual response in curves and graphs,
domestic-science advocates provided graphs delineating the rhythms
of housework, imposing a regularity by the very act of dividing up
time and motion. Married women's labor required careful reorgan-
ization of housework lest the entire family degenerate into chaos.

In the contemporary studies, both the wage-earning housewives
themselves and the household experts who advocated the profession-
alization of housework to make it more hygienic and rational ex-
hibited an acute consciousness of housework as real work.[32] The
popular journals of the working-class movement attempted to respond to the needs of a new generation of women workers with family
responsibilities. Their pages were filled with tips for quick, nutritious
recipes and time- and labor-saving techniques and appliances.[33] But
all these advice columns ignored the basic point that as long as working women remained primarily responsible for the maintenance of
the household and as long as the sexual division of labor within the
family was not fundamentally challenged, women would find it difficult to meet the new scientific standards of healthful and efficient
living in body care, nutrition, or housework.

Female social scientists and social workers were particularly eager to
approach housework in a more rational and scientific manner.
Women—the researchers and the researched—broke through the
sentimentality and mystification that had traditionally characterized
the treatment of housework by both leftist and conservative observers.
Klaus Neukrantz's proletarian novel of community and "cell" life in
Berlin observed for example:

> Kurt put his elbows on the table and watched how fast Anna got
> through with all the pots and pans. He was too tired to talk, but it was
> good to just sit quietly and watch her movements. How quickly and
> deftly she handled it all.[34]

More and more observers who looked closely—not only the researchers of the Academy for Women's Work but also the new corps
of social welfare professionals and officials in various ministries and
parliamentary committees—sensed the exhausting labor behind

"quick deft" housework, and feared that women might no longer be able or willing to shoulder that burden. The catalog for a major exhibition called "The Woman" held in Berlin from March through April 1933, but which had been written just prior to the Nazi takeover, put the problem succinctly:

> The strength to do joyfully all the repetitive little daily tasks springs from this special source—can only be understood by it—the concept of mother love and goodness. Because what man would be ready to take on, every day, without complaint and fatigue, the endless chores the housewife has to face.[35]

Iron discipline, good health, and ability to apply the principles of rationalization, like that evinced by the women writing in *Mein Arbeitstag, Mein Wochenende,* as well as the readiness to relinquish the excitement of 1920s urban *Girlkultur,* was required to keep a family (and society as a whole) going. The necessity of transforming young single women into thoroughly rationalized married New Women constituted one of the central contradictions of Weimar culture.

Some Questions about Fascism

Jessica Benjamin, in writing about Max Weber's concept of instrumental rationality *(Zweckrationalitat),* has noted this "process of disenchantment through which means rationality becomes a generalized form of social life."[36] The rationalization of labor, in particular of women's work, and thereby the creation of a new rationalized woman was stylized into a fitting metaphor for the generally unsettling impact of the new technology and work patterns. Women's presence in public spaces—at the workplace or in politics—seemed only commensurate with a generalized scientifization and bureaucratization which the industrial psychologist Fritz Giese termed the "neutralization of modern life through technology."[37]

Women caused particular concern in this process of "disenchantment"—the introduction of the "new objectivity" *(Neue Sachlichkeit)*—into daily life. Women, after all, had traditionally been understood as the embodiment of the irrational. They were thought to resist discipline, organization, and instrumental rationality and to remain need-oriented in the service of human needs.[38] The new rationalized woman seemed particularly threatening at the same time she was absolutely necessary if women could continue to fulfill their womanly and maternal duties in the new age. But if New Women learned to practice the speed and utilitarian values of rationalization in their own homes, who would provide the home to succor and replenish workers from the rigors of rationalized industry? The New Woman therefore expressed in dramatic form the discontents of civilization and the discomfort of industrialized mechanized society. She embodied within her dual identity the conflicts aroused by rationalization and the ambivalence of modernity. She represented both danger and salvation: if women's domesticity could somehow be reconciled with wage labor, if rationalization could be made functional for marriage and motherhood, then the restructured economy need not be a disaster for social life, indeed could provide the leisure and consumer goods to improve it. If, on the other hand, women, who were supposed to nurture the "haven in a heartless world" and offer respite from the fragmentation caused by the relentless demands of work, themselves began to adapt to that rhythm and therefore reject traditional more organic and womanly roles, then the insecurity of modern existence could become intolerable. Social scientists and sex reformers intervened to regulate precisely that conflict: to construct a New Woman who could efficiently and lovingly manage the tasks of housework, mothering, sexuality, and wage-earning. She would be thoroughly rationalized and thoroughly womanly, the sought-after synthesis of housewife, mother, and working woman.

Such a solution, however, required a massive intervention of state support services in health and social welfare, as the Weimar Republic halfheartedly attempted and then dismantled during the Depression. Given that failure, it may well be that fascist antifeminism grew as much out of the fear of not being able to maintain a certain type of female nurturance and comfort as out of the need, for example, to repress female sexuality or control population. On the other hand, fascist women's policy cannot be explained simply as a reaction against the New Woman.[39]

The question of transition to National Socialism becomes inescapable. What happened to these new working women? What happened to their younger sisters? The issue of generation is crucial: it makes a world of difference if a young woman came of age in 1925 during a period of relative economic stabilization and social innovation or in 1932 during the Depression—a generational speed-up along with all the other speed-ups of the era. It seems to me that National Socialism was not only an attempt to roll back the clock, a reaction against the New Woman, but also a continuation in a different and more politicized form.

It may well be that fascism appealed to young women because in fact it also celebrated their competence, their ability to manage in a new and modern world, and indeed offered mass political activity and mobilization as an escape from the restrictions of both wage labor and domesticity. Young women in the 1920s and early 1930s did not simply yearn for the security (and respectability) of the family as an escape from boring, alienating, and underpaid work, thus becoming more susceptible to the *Kinder, Küche, Kirche* appeal of fascism. They dreamed of freedom from both. The questions must be more complex, reaching beyond the dichotomy of home and job and beyond the trap of judging the New Woman as liberated or co-opted, married or single. Obviously these conclusions are highly preliminary and require much further research. We need to know much more about what the young women themselves thought, perceived, dreamed, and did, and how that in turn changed with age and occupation.

Finally, I propose that this kind of analysis of the New Woman of the interwar period has a particular relevance for us today, at a time when the demise of yet another generation of "brave new women" is being trumpeted through the media, when headlines and surveys suggest the emergence of "postfeminism" or the continuing dilemmas of "careers versus the lure of motherhood" and as we ourselves attempt our own precarious balancing acts and feats of rationalized time and motion organization.

Notes

1. *Die Neue Linie* 1: 6 (March 1930).

2. For further detail, see Atina Grossmann, "The New Woman and the Rationalization of Sexuality in Weimar Germany," in Stansell, Snitow, Thompson, eds., *Powers of Desire: The Politics of Sexuality* (New York: Monthly Review Press, 1983), 153–71; idem, "Satisfaction is Domestic Happiness: Mass Working Class Sex Reform Organizations in the Weimar Republic," in Dobkowski and Wallimann, eds., *Towards the Holocaust: The Social and Economic Collapse of the Weimar Republic* (Westport, Conn.: Greenwood Press, 1983), 265–93; idem, "Abortion and Economic Crisis: The 1931 Campaign Against Paragraph 218" in Bridenthal, Grossmann, Kaplan, eds., *When Biology Became Destiny: Women in Weimar and Nazi Germany* (New York: Monthly Review Press, 1984), 66–86.

3. Renate Bridenthal and Claudia Koonz, "Beyond "Kinder, Küche, Kirche': Weimar Women in Politics and Work," in *Liberating Women's History*, ed. Berenice A. Carroll (Urbana, Ill.: University of Illinois Press, 1976), 310–15; see also Bridenthal, Grossmann, Kaplan, eds., *When Biology Became Destiny.*

4. Among the many sources on women's, especially married women's, employment, see Helen Boak, "Women in Weimar Germany: The 'Frauenfrage and the Female Vote'," in *Social Change and Political Development in Weimar Germany*, eds. Richard J. Bessel and Edgar J. Feuchtwanger (Totowa, N.J.: Barnes and Noble, 1981), 161–62, 171 (footnote 45); Bridenthal and

Koonz, "Beyond 'Kinder, Küche, Kirche'"; Clifford Kirkpatrick, *Nazi Germany: Its Women and Family Life* (Indianapolis, New York: The Bobbs-Merill Press, 1938), 204; Tim Mason, "Women in Germany 1925–1940: Family, Welfare and Work, Part I," *History Workshop* 1 (Summer 1976): 77–78, 93; Annemarie Niemeyer, *Zur Struktur der Familie. Statistische Materialien* (Berlin: F. A. Herbig Verlagsbuchhandlung, 1931), 109; *Volks-, Berufs- und Betriebszählung vom 16.Juni 1925*, in *Statistik des Deutschen Reiches*, vol. 408: *Die berufliche und soziale Gliederung des deutschen Volkes* (Berlin: 1925), 189; Marguerite Thibert, "The Economic Depression and the Employment of Women," *International Labor Review* 27: 5 (May 1933): 626; Gabrielle Wellner, "Industriearbeiterinnen in der Weimarer Republik: Arbeitsmarkt, Arbeit und Privatleben 1919–1933," *Geschichte und Gesellschaft* 7:3/4 (1981): 550.

5. Anne Siemsen, "Berufswahl," in *Das Reich des Kindes*, ed. Adele Schreiber (Berlin: Deutsche Buch-Gemeinschaft, 1930), 220; she says that 30 percent of all married women were working.

6. See Renate Bridenthal, "Beyond 'Kinder, Küche, Kirche': Weimar Women at Work," *Central European History* 6:1 2 (1973): 148–66; Dörte Winkler, *Frauenarbeit im "Dritten Reich"* (Hamburg: Hoffmann und Campe, 1977), 20–23; Annemarie Tröger, "The Creation of a Female Assembly-Line Proletariat," in *When Biology Became Destiny*, pp. 237–70; and especially Thibert, "The Economic Depression"; and Judith Grunfeld, "Rationalization and the Employment and Wages of Women in Germany," *International Labor Review* 29: 5 (1934).

7. Antonio Gramsci, "Americanism and Fordism," in *Selections from the Prison Notebooks* (New York: International, 1971), 305.

8. Ibid., 297.

9. Maria Kahle, *Akkordarbeiterin. Aus meinem Tagebuch* (Gladbach-Rheydt: Volksverein Verlag, 1929), 28.

10. Peter Gay, *Weimar Culture. The Outsider as Insider* (New York: Harper and Row, 1968), especially 114–18.

11. Erich Fromm, *Arbeiter und Angestellte am Vorabend des Dritten Reiches. Eine sozialpsychologische Untersuchung*, ed. and trans. Wolfgang Bonss (Stuttgart: Deutsche Verlags-Anstalt, 1980), 168–99. Also Helgard Kramer, "Veränderungen in der Frauenrolle in der Weimarer Republik," *Beiträge zur feministischen theorie und praxis* 5 (1981): 20–24.

12. Erna Barschak, *Die Schüler in der Berufsschule und ihre Umwelt* (Berlin: F. A. Herbig Verlagsbuchhandlung, 1926), 21. Barschak investigated 1,200 *Berufsschülerinnen*. On women as film spectators, see Miriam Hansen, "Early Silent Cinema: Whose Public Sphere?" *New German Critique* No. 29 (Spring–Summer 1983), esp. 173–84; and Siegfried Kracauer, "Die kleinen Ladenmädchen gehen ins Kino," in *Das Ornament der Masse* (Frankfurt/M.: Suhrkamp, 1977), 279–94.

13. Ibid., 20.

14. Lisbeth Franzen-Hellersberg, *Die jugendliche Arbeiterin, ihre Arbeitsweise und Lebensform. Ein Versuch sozialpolitischer Forschung zum Zwecke der Umwertung proletarischer Tatbestände* (Tubingen: Mohr, 1932), 46.

15. Ibid., 74–75.

16. Susanna Dammer and Carola Sachse, "Nationalsozialistische Frauenpolitik und weibliche Arbeitskraft," *Beiträge zur feministischen theorie und praxis* 5 (1981): 109. See also Siegfried Kracauer, *Die Angestellten* (Frankfurt/M.: Suhrkamp, 1971), 92.

17. "Erhebung über Sexualmoral," in Max Horckheimer, ed., *Studien über Autoritat und Familie* (Paris: F. Alcan, 1936), 277.

18. Ibid., 280. On the supposed decline of prostitution and the rise of "free love," see the whole survey, 272–85. See also the government health reports *(Denkschrift über die gesundheitlichen Verhältnisse des deutschen Volkes)*, in *(Bundesarchiv (BA) Koblenz)*, R 86/931(7–15) [1916–1932]. For a somewhat different view, see *Materialien über die Lage der arbeitenden Jugend, 1930*, in BA Koblenz NS 26/816.

19. *Mein Arbeitstag, Mein Wochenende. 150 Berichte von Textilarbeiterinnen*, ed. by Deutscher Textilarbeiterverband (Berlin: 1930), 11.

20. Ibid., 26; on scepticism toward marriage among young working-class women, see also Alice Rühle-Gerstel in *Die Aufklärung* 11/12 (1929), especially 185–95. See also idem, *Die Frau und der Kapitalismus, Das Frauenproblem der Gegenwart, Eine psychologische Bilanz* (Leipzig: Verlag von S. Hirzel, 1932).

21. *Mein Arbeitstag, Mein Wochenende* 80.

22. See *Bundesarchiv Koblenz* R86/881(1–2), /885(1), /886(1–2), /888(1–2), /908, /937 for material on state-sponsored exhibitions.

23. See Clara Zetkin, "My Recollection of Lenin: An Interview on the Women Question," in *Feminism. The Essential Historical Writings*, ed. Miriam Schneir (New York: Random House, 1972), 340–41.

24. See Gisela Stahl, "Von der Hauswirtschaft zum Haushalt oder wie man vom Haus zur Wohnung kommt—Die Ökonomie des ganzen Hauses und die Ökonomisierung der Hausfrau," in *Wem gehört die Welt* (Berlin: Neue Gesellschaft für Bildende Kunst, 1977), 87–108; and Günther Uhlig, *Kollektivmodell "Einfamilienhaus." Wohnform und Architekturdebatte zwischen Frauenbewegung und Funktionalismus 1900–1933* (Giessen: anabas, 1981). See also the pioneering essay by Rosalyn Baxandall, Elisabeth Ewen, and Linda Gordon, "The Working Class Has Two Sexes," *Monthly Review* 28: 3 (July–August 1976); especially 6–8; see also Siegfried Giedion, *Mechanization Takes Command* (New York: W. W. Norton & Co., 1975), "Mechanization Encounters the Household," 512–627, also 41–45, 480–511.

25. See Molly Nolan, "Capital, Labor and the State: The Politics of Rationalization in Weimar Germany," paper presented at the American Historical Association, Los Angeles, Calif., December 1981.

26. *Mein Arbeitstag, Mein Wochenende*, 88.

27. Ibid., 90.

28. Ibid., 106.

29. Ibid., 95.

30. Ibid., 154.

31. Ibid., 88.

32. See, for example, Marie Baum and Alix Westerkamp, *Rythmus des Familienlebens. Das von einer Familie täglich zu leistende Arbeitspensum* (Berlin: F. A. Herbig Verlagsbuchhandlung, 1931).

33. See especially *Arbeiter Illustrierte Zeitung (AIZ)* 4–11 (1924/5–1932); *Der Weg der Frau* 1–3 (1931–1933), both associated with the Communist Party, and the Social Democratic *Die Frauenwelt* 1–10 (1924–1933).

34. Klaus Neukrantz, *Barrikaden am Wedding. Der Roman einer Strasse aus den Berliner Maitagen 1929* (reprint ed. Berlin: Oberbaumverlag, 1970), 5.

35. *Die Frau in Familie, Haus und Beruf. Amtlicher Katalog und Führer der Ausstellung Berlin 1933* (Berlin: 1933), 36. An example of how seriously women's work was taken and how it was made visible was the accounting on

26–27 of thirty years of labor by women agricultural workers in Thuringia—23,400 loaves of bread baked, etc.

36. Jessica Benjamin, "Authority and the Family Revisited: Or, A World without Fathers?" *New German Critique* 13 (Winter 1978): 36–37.

37. Fritz Giese, "Die Wiedergeburt des Köurpers und das technische Zeitalter," in *Das Reich des Kindes,* ed. Adele Schreiber-Krieger (Berlin: Deutsche Buch-Gemeinschaft, 1930), 387.

38. Ulrike Prokop, *Weiblicher Lebenszusammenhang. Von der Beschränktheit der Strategien und der Unangemessenheit der Wünsche* (Frankfurt/M.: Suhrkamp, 1976); also Christopher Lasch, *Haven in a Heartless World. The Family Besieged* (New York: Basic, 1977).

39. On Nazi women's policy see for example Claudia Koonz, "The Competition for a Women's *Lebensraum,* 1928–1934," in *When Biology Became Destiny,* 199–236.

THE ANTI-SEMITE AND THE SECOND SEX

A CULTURAL READING OF SARTRE AND BEAUVOIR

Judith Friedlander

> I chanced to read a comment by Isaac
> Bashevis Singer in one of his novels about
> survivors. A single statement of his
> suddenly clarified matters for me. In
> reference to his own difficulties in writing
> about victims, he remarked, "Although I did
> not have the privilege of going through the
> Hitler holocaust," . . . In the end, the only
> acceptable answer I could find to the
> question "Am I qualified to write this book?"
> was that my membership and my affection
> were my qualifications. When I judge these
> people, I judge myself.
>
> BARBARA MYERHOFF[1]

During the final months of World War II, M. hid out in a small Polish village under a gentile name. She had but one valuable possession: a set of false identity papers. Otherwise she was desperately poor, with little to eat, rags for clothing, a hovel for shelter, and a few burlap bags to cover her at night. Times, to be sure, were difficult for everyone, but only a Jew escaped from the ghetto could have lived as miserably as this. To invite people over was a risk she dared not take.

One day there was a knock at the door. It was the mayor. "You

Research for this chapter was funded by the Wenner-Gren Foundation for Anthropological Research and the SUNY Research Foundation.

know," he threatened, "rumor has it that you are a Jew." To answer, "Who, me? I'm not a Jew," would have given her away as quickly as if she were a drunk who denied she touched liquor. Instead, she looked him straight in the eyes and replied, "Where I come from, they say Jewish women are built with slits running horizontally." The mayor howled with laughter, and the questioning stopped. No Jewish woman could have said a thing like that.

Blond, tall, intelligent, determined to live, M. managed to survive in a world that was systematically annihilating the Jews. She did so by passing as a Pole. Maybe she could have come through the war as a Jew; certainly some did. But when she had the opportunity, M. dissociated her fate from that of her people. Husband murdered, the Wilno ghetto liquidated, M. avoided the last roundup and escaped the walled quarter, leaving her baby with peasants in one village and making it on her own in another.

We met in Paris in 1979, thirty-four years after the war, and M. was still running. As she told me her story, she began to cry, requesting we stop, promising to return, but she never did. In a way I was relieved, for anger and shame had crept over both of us. M. could not forgive herself for some of the choices she made, and I, to my surprise, was having difficulty as well.

I did not mean to be intrusive, but M. felt exposed. By the end, she was no longer really talking to me, but bitterly criticizing the lawyer she saw in the 1940s who insisted on learning every painful detail to prepare his brief for the reparations hearing. The nightmare of the war years, her personal losses, became a commodity whose value was based on the sum of money an attorney could win in exchange for these few morbid tales. Now I too was grabbing at her past and she fled, leaving me to imagine the part of the story she did not tell.

I interviewed over twenty individuals, Jewish women and men, all from the same part of Eastern Europe as M., many the victims of far greater hardships than she. Still it is M.'s story that haunts me the most. Courageous and humiliating, it illustrates with excruciating clarity how difficult it is to choose to be yourself when born into a group that is persecuted for being different. Obviously we do not need the Holocaust to see this dilemma, but the force of those circumstances dramatizes the more general problem faced by minorities in Europe and the United States.

M. grew up in Poland between the two wars, in a country newly constituted by the League of Nations and strongly influenced, on the Right and on the Left, by the conflicting ideals of Western European democracy: freedom, civil rights, nationalism, and assimilation. By the time the Germans invaded Wilno, M. knew well the practical value of being just like everybody else. True, the ideological landscape in Poland during those years did not lead every Jew to try to pass as a Pole. Many joined the partisans, and an even greater number bowed to Jewish destiny and ended their lives in concentration camps. There were people who spent the war in cellars and some fortunate enough to have left Europe in time. Thus, given the wide range of experiences, why focus on this one case?

M.'s account is important because it is troubling in ways that the others are not. In contrast to people who remained Jews to themselves and before the world, M. chose to resist by lying to the enemy. Challenging fascism on its own terms, M. denigrated herself as a Jew and a woman. Her triumph was not in the preservation of personal integrity, but in the satisfaction of proving that the fascists were wrong: the Jewish woman in her was invisible. Inviting the mayor to see for himself, M. privately evoked the progressive voices of European history, who, since the eighteenth century, have maintained that everybody is virtually the same. According to this view, freedom for the individual can best be achieved by minimizing differences.

With the help of Jean-Paul Sartre and Simone de Beauvoir, I wish to examine the implications of the principle of universality—the idea that we are basically the same—for two groups who have been identified as different and then return to M.'s story in a wider historical context to trace the various stages of cultural and ideological development that she went through before making her final choice. M.'s decision to pass as a Pole is logical, if distressing, and it raises questions for us that go beyond Holocaust studies. I call upon Sartre and Beauvoir, not as a committed existentialist, rather as an anthropologist who sees in their work a culturally significant contribution to a long-debated political and philosophical problem in Western democracies: must we choose between defending the rights of individuals and those of clearly differentiated racial/socio-cultural/gender-specific groups? As we shall see, even as they criticize democracies for discriminating against "others" and propose a socialist vision for the new society, they remain unable to resolve the problem, at least for the cases they treat, and finally cast their votes with the individual at the expense of the group.

Sartre and Beauvoir

Writing immediately after the war, Jean-Paul Sartre and Simone de Beauvoir analyze the meaning of freedom for Jews and women. In separate books, they base their discussions on Sartre's major philo-

sophical treatment of freedom, *Being and Nothingness*,[2] a curious starting point, actually, for studies of subjugated peoples. Sartre's original
description looks at the individual, not groups. What is more, he
recognizes bad faith, not oppression. Then, while rejecting the idea of
human nature, he still begins by posing the individual in terms reminiscent of the nineteenth century democratic idea of the universal
man:[3] a person stripped of all those unique characteristics that might
come from within and separate one from the other. The important
differences found among people are not inherent in the individuals
themselves, Sartre argues, but emerge from the outside, the external
situations in which they find themselves and from the choices they
freely make in those situations.[4] Man, we learn, is condemned to
freedom. Within the limits of a situation, he is free to make choices,
and, depending on how he exercises that freedom, he does so authentically or inauthentically.[5]

Authenticity, Sartre explains, "consists in having a true, lucid consciousness of the situation, in assuming the responsibilities and risks
that it involves, in accepting it in pride or in humiliation, sometimes in
horror and hate."[6] For the Jew, the same rules apply: "Authenticity for
him [the Jew] is to live in the full his condition as a Jew: inauthenticity
is to deny it or attempt to escape it."[7]

While existentialist morality should not be confused with religious
ethics, Sartre condemns inauthentic choices in preacherlike tones.
One should have the courage to be true to oneself and to the world.
Yet to be authentic as a Jew, says Sartre, is to choose to be faithful to
virtually nothing. There is no common core of traditions, no one
material experience, that *all* Jews share. Since the nineteenth century,
some Jews have been religious and others not. They belong to every
socio-economic class; they live in many different countries. Jews have
no single history,[8] no one land. Jews are Jews "because they have in
common the situation which takes them for Jews."[9]

According to this argument, Christians created modern Jews. Originally persecuted for supposedly having killed Jesus, then further
degraded by being assigned a despised, but vital economic function,
Jews survived dispersion and persecution as Jews thanks to non-Jews
who kept them apart. The choice to isolate Jews has its roots in history,
but there is no specifically Jewish history that explains the existence of
the Jewish people today. The Jew as we know him does not play a
historical role, but an ontological one: he is the object of the Christian
subject. If the Jew had not existed, the anti-Semite would have invented him.[10]

"The category of *other* is as primordial as consciousness itself," says
Beauvoir.[11] Borrowing from Hegel, she explains that in consciousness

there is "a fundamental hostility toward every other consciousness; the subject can be posed only in being opposed to the other, the inessential object."[12] Beauvoir describes *otherness* as the condition of women and Sartre as that of the Jews. Together they condemn the objectification of all peoples and call for the creation of a new society in which individual subjects can meet each other equally and choose freely to participate in all social activities as subjects. Forced to continue in this still imperfect world, Sartre and Beauvoir examine the possibilities for those treated as objects to assume their "otherness" and live—or die—authentically. Defending the right to be different with one hand, they take great pains to show how easily assimilable *their* Jews and women are with the other. Given the chance, they could be just like anybody else, for you are not born a Jew or a woman, you become one.

Sartre challenges the notion that there exists a cultural, social, economic, or even racial reality which encompasses all Jews. Beauvoir, however, cannot do the same and recognizes the indisputable biological differences that separate women from men. Still true to existentialist convictions, she belittles these facts, claiming that woman is not "determined by her hormones or by mysterious instincts,"[13] but by her situation. Like that of the Jew, the situation of woman is alienating. She sees herself as the subject sees her: "Woman sees herself and makes choices not in accordance with her true nature in itself, but as man defines her."[14]

There are important differences between the situation of women and that of the Jews, but these two groups are similar in interesting ways. Jews as *Jews* and women as *women* are forgotten in a universalistic scheme which, by definition, does not recognize the value of preserving collective diversity. What is more, they are inadequately represented by the particularistic design of history. Even to a greater extent than Jews, women have no common land, no common traditions, no common experience. Both groups conform neither to Hegelian principles of history nor to Marxist categories of class. By defying the analytical frameworks commonly used in social and cultural discourse, Jews and women lead Sartre and Beauvoir to what are often considered to be unsatisfactory conclusions. Both groups have two main choices: fight for the right to assimilate, thereby furthering the demise of what little specificity they might possess; or live by the male/gentile definition of their femaleness/Jewishness positively, in a state that has no authochthonous core.

Unlike other oppressed peoples—the proletariat, for example, or members of a persecuted religious sect—Jews and women are deeply divided, the argument goes, for they are tied to different economic interests and ideological persuasions. Having no common heritage, they share little more than the situation of being Jews and/or women. Their very identities are the negative imposition of the dominant society.

The nationalist who unites a people through their race, land, and language or the socialist who calls for solidarity among those who share class interests cannot speak effectively to Jews and women. Such visions do not provide us with the necessary analytical tools with which to understand these two groups. While we might, therefore, disagree with Sartre and Beauvoir, their descriptions clearly expose the limitations of two classical approaches. Neither a nation nor a class, it is misguided to look at Jews and women as if they were just like any other minority and to seek political solutions for them in conventional terms.

Socialists who use a philosophy that poses emancipation in individualistic terms, Sartre and Beauvoir let us see the inadequacies of contemporary explanations, but are unable to escape them. In spite of themselves, they end up promoting assimilation. As Michèle Le Doeuff puts it, "In *The Second Sex,* everything happens as though from the moment a minute gap is opened in the cage, it becomes the duty of the woman benefiting from it to make use of the escape to the maximum extent so as to posit herself as a subject condemned to be free."[15] Sartre, for his part, is a bit more ambivalent than Beauvoir, but he too finally concludes that the Jew should accept what the democrat has to offer. In his "abstract liberalism" the democrat is the Jew's best friend,[16] even though he protects only the man, not the Jew: "He [the democrat] affirms that Jews, Chinese, Negroes ought to have the same rights as other members of society, but he demands these rights for them as men, not as concrete individual products of history."[17] Yet since Sartre believes that Jews have no history or tradition anyway, they might as well enjoy the universal rights of man and, if permitted, lose the emptiness of their specificity caused only by their situation.

While Jews, more than women, have soundly rejected this view of themselves, many, with the possible exception of some orthodox sects, have tried to define their Jewish identity in Hegelian or Marxian terms. Having done so, consciously or not, they lend credibility to Sartre's argument. Sartre, it is true, based his analysis on a very limited sample of highly assimilated French Jews. However, even if he had known more about Eastern European Jews, for example, he would not have had to change his mind. The major political and cultural movements there, beginning with the Haskalah (the Jewish Enlightenment), applied the ideals and strategies of European nationalist movements and class struggles to solve the so-called Jewish problem, thereby undermining Jewish specificity. Forcing themselves to fit into categories that did not describe their situation, in order to prepare themselves for social and political emancipation, the secularizing Jews in the East—just like their counterparts in the West—did indeed lose their Jewish center.[18]

Even though Sartre was ignorant about Judaism, he correctly identified the confusion existing among Jews about what it means to be different. Thus, not only did he convincingly destroy the position of the anti-Semite, he also raised important questions for those of us supporting more progressive ideas about the "other." What is true for the Jew is in part true for the woman, and as we look over history from the perspective of the 1980s, we see that Sartre and Beauvoir have successfully unveiled some of the contradictions inherent in the cultural principles of democracy, nationalism, and socialism for Jews and women who want to remain different.

As we return to M.'s story, we should keep in mind the history of nationalist ideas and movements in Europe during the nineteenth and twentieth centuries, especially as they influenced national minorities in Eastern Europe. The problem of identity that interested Sartre and Beauvoir was a critical issue during the First World War, a period when people to the East fought to gain national autonomy on the Western European nation-state model, struggling for what they believed was the right to be different. Furthermore, we should recall the role played by the Versailles Treaty and the place it gave to national minorities in Eastern Europe, most particularly to those Jewish cultural movements which participated in the wider nationalist trends that swept across Europe. The choices M. made as a Jew and a woman cannot be understood without considering how Western European ideals about democracy influenced the political and cultural life in countries like Poland during the years between the two wars.

The Story of M.

In a little village near Brest-Litovsk, M. was born in 1916, into a comfortable middle-class family. She was the third of eight children—seven girls and a boy. While her parents were observant Hasidic Jews, they were lenient with their daughters and son and did not insist that the young respect the dietary laws or any other traditional restriction outside the house. M.'s father himself spent a lot of time away from home, for he earned his living as a forestry engineer and was not always as careful as he wanted to be.

Before Poland claimed it in 1921, M.'s village was ruled by Russia and the language used with non-Jews was that of the tsar. M.'s two older sisters went to Russian primary school where they learned the language well, but her parents and the rest of the family spoke it poorly, managing only to communicate minimally to conduct business affairs. By the time M. was ready for school, the obligatory idiom changed to Polish, and M., together with her younger siblings, studied that language, which they came to speak without an accent. At home, both before and after the First World War, the family spoke Yiddish among themselves.

In M.'s village, the young were receptive to the major political and cultural trends emanating from nearby cities. Many, for example, sympathized with the Left, and a considerable number of them, including one sister, joined the Communist Party. Others became Zionists, and some of them, like those in M.'s family, emigrated to Palestine before the Second World War. While the Jewish Socialist Bund was not strong, the Jewish community did take advantage of the Minorities Treaties and opened a Yiddish primary school.

Even though the family was well off, it was taken for granted that the children would work. M.'s oldest sister, the Communist, led the way for the girls by enrolling in the Yiddish Teachers' Seminary in Wilno in order to be certified to teach in the village's Yiddish school. In 1929 M. too went to the Wilno seminary. Not only was she seeking a diploma, M. explained, but she wanted to learn literary Yiddish well and prepare herself to educate a new generation of Jews in one of the two competing national Jewish cultures existing in Poland at that time.

In 1936, M.'s father died. Upon hearing the news, M.'s second older sister, who was already settled in Palestine by that time, returned to Poland and moved their mother and other siblings to the Promised Land. It was thanks to this sister that M.'s mother, sisters, and brother all left Poland in time and were spared the fate of most of the extended family—aunts, uncles, and cousins—who died in the Holocaust.

Recalling those years, M. bitterly concluded that what the Zionists argued in the 1920s and early thirties was borne out shortly thereafter. Cultural autonomy (so-called) could only be protected within Jewish national borders. If they did not become a people like everybody else, the Jews would be wiped off the face of the earth.

M., as we know, stayed behind. In 1936, that same decisive year for her family, she married G., a Wilno man and a cellist who came from a family of musicians. Both husband and father-in-law played in the Wilno Symphony Orchestra. After the wedding, M. gave up teaching and accompanied G. on trips throughout Poland as he toured with the city's orchestra.

M. and G. were representative of their generation. They identified *nationally*, not traditionally, as Jews. When I asked if she kept a kosher home, M. laughed and replied: "I did not eat kosher and my husband, that 'goy', he didn't either." As an expression of his Jewish identity, G. was a member of the Labor Zionist Party (Poale Zion). M., on the other hand, belonged to no particular party, and once she stopped teaching in a Yiddish school, her active participation in organized national Jewish activities was limited to joining her husband on social occasions. Finally, while most of her friends were Jewish, M. and G. did not live in the Jewish quarter of the city, but in the center of Wilno, near the beautiful Church of Saint Anne, which, M. noted with pride, Napoleon loved so much that he wanted to take it back to Paris.

In 1939 M. gave birth to a little girl and the Germans invaded Poland. The Polish army drafted G. immediately, but he was gone only a few days. As the soldiers retreated, their country was divided between Germany and Russia. Fortunately, Wilno came under Soviet rule and the Jews there gained a couple of more years.

The Russians did not discriminate against Jews. Even when they issued new passports stamped "Nationality: Jewish," M. and G. did not think to worry, for Jews were not singled out any more than other national minorities living in Soviet-controlled territories. The difficulties they endured were caused by the generally repressive economic policies imposed on Poland, not by ethnic persecution.

Soon after they took over Wilno, the Russians transferred all that was valuable, said M., onto Soviet soil. Entire factories were dismantled and reassembled in Russian cities. Even the Wilno Orchestra was moved to Minsk. While M. missed Wilno terribly, she admitted having enjoyed aspects of the orchestra's tour through the Soviet Union, particularly her visit to Moscow for Stalin's tenth anniversary celebration, during which every major orchestra in the country performed.

In 1941 Wilno was annexed to the Soviet Republic of Lithuania. The city's new status gave M. and G. the right to return home, and they came back at the end of May. The Germans, however, arrived a month later.

Unable to find a place of their own, the young couple and baby daughter moved in with G.'s parents. Located in the fashionable center of Wilno, there were many Poles in the apartment building, and everybody knew who the Jewish families were. As relations between gentile and Jew were traditionally strained, M. knew that the

Polish neighbors would have denounced them had the family dared disobey German orders and not register with the Kehilah (the Jewish City Council).

Jews were required to wear yellow stars on the front of their coats,[19] to walk in the gutters instead of on sidewalks, to go to the back of food lines, and to keep off the streets entirely between 5 P.M. and 5 A.M. They were allowed out again at such an early hour because they had to report for hard labor at that time. First the Germans called only the men, but soon the women had to present themselves as well.

Predictably enough, G. was drafted for work duty almost immediately. He had only been serving for a few days when a neighbor came to the door and announced that G. had been arrested and sent off to the city's prison. As M. reconstructed it, her husband must have been stopped by Poles or Lithuanians when he was on his way to work.

By the end of the first month of German occupation, M.'s husband had been killed, she herself had been drafted to help build a small airfield on the outskirts of Wilno, and the entire Jewish community— what was left of it, that is—had been moved into the Wilno Ghetto. To make room for those Jews who were living in various sections of the city, the Germans simply emptied out the old Jewish quarter.

M. did not know what was happening until it was too late. In defense of her ignorance, she reminded me that from 5 A.M. to 5 P.M. she was working at the airport outside the city. The rest of the time, she was a prisoner in her home. Most importantly, the Germans moved fast, building the walled city with their ample Jewish labor in less than twenty-four hours.

M. went to the ghetto with her daughter, her in-laws, and a young Jewish neighbor, also a widowed mother of a little girl. As they waited their turn to enter the gates, the Germans lined them up sending some Jews to the right, others to the left. M.'s group stayed together and found shelter in a one-and-one-half-room apartment that ended up housing eighteen people. Only later did they learn that they had been assigned to the part of the ghetto that would be condemned for early liquidation.[20]

M. continued to work for the Germans. Every morning at 5 A.M., guards came to the gate of the ghetto and marched two thousand women seven kilometers to the site of the new airfield. Even though M.'s neighbor accused her of being a "cruel stepmother" for abandoning her daughter, M. kept going, leaving her child behind in the care of her mother-in-law. She knew that only those who worked received rations. Those who remained in the ghetto were starving to death.

During her trips between the airport and ghetto, M. slipped away to trade with peasants. Wearing layers of clothing as she left in the morning, she could exchange a sweater or dress for a potato or two. When she had the opportunity, M. also stole from the fields she passed on the way. However, as the weeks went by, it became increasingly difficult to get food back into the ghetto. Once, near the end, she lost the potatoes, but did manage to sneak by with a small amount of butter that she had hidden in some cloth worn like a sanitary napkin.

As M. described the horrors of the ghetto and her eventual escape, two themes came up over and over again. One had to do with her ability to pass as a Pole and the other with the strength she gained from being a mother. Hiding her condition of "otherness" as a Jew, she found the courage necessary to survive by assuming her situation as a traditional woman.

On Yom Kippur, as the Jews were returning from their long day of work, M. heard from some bystanders that there had been a roundup in the ghetto. Starting to run, pushing her way through the crowds, she heard people say, "Look at that Polish woman running towards the ghetto. Why is she in such a rush?" On that terrible day, Jews who had attended synagogue to atone for their sins said their final prayers at Ponari, a favorite woods for outings that the Germans had transformed into a mass cemetery. Among those who perished were M.'s in-laws.

Now M. did not even have G.'s mother to take care of her child. Still she continued to work, and as she left in the mornings, she had to endure her daughter's cries, pleading with her not to go. Those piercing screams tore M. apart, but she felt that she had no other choice if she wanted to save her little girl from starving. It was a risk, as her neighbor warned, for when parents went to work, children often disappeared in surprise roundups.

Among the guards who watched over the forced laborers, there was a German with dark hair whom everybody called the "Jew." One day this guard stopped to chat with M. and told her that she did not look Jewish. She should escape. According to him, M. did not carry herself like a Jew, have the coloring of a Jew, or talk like a Jew. Why did she not simply take her child out of the ghetto and leave? The German soldier planted the idea and Polish peasants cultivated it.

One day M. stopped at the home of some peasants with whom she regularly exchanged clothing for food. The wife was alone and had just suffered a miscarriage. She needed M.'s help and convinced her to remain for the day. Nobody would miss her. When the woman's husband returned, he invited M. to spend the night, to enjoy the warm fire in their home and a good meal.

Throughout the evening, the husband repeated that M. could not be Jewish. She was too well-built, too blond, too honest and good. If he were not married already, he would take her for his wife. But when M. asked if he would be willing to hide her and her daughter, the Pole said no. It was too dangerous. So M. returned to the ghetto and waited a little longer before making her escape.

During the first months the roundups of Jews had a predictable rhythm and the complete cooperation of the Jewish police. The Germans told them that they wanted one thousand Jews on a certain day, and the police delivered, sincerely believing that by sacrificing some they would be able to save the majority. But the call for one thousand rose to two thousand and came with greater frequency.

Jews with work certificates had protection in the early days as did their spouses and children under sixteen. However, if there were a surprise roundup and the worker were not present, the dependents were left undefended. To make matters worse, periodically the Germans issued new certificates, and each time they did so, they gave them to fewer and fewer Jews.

M.'s fierce determination to remain a worker was not enough. She needed to keep her health as well in order to qualify for a certificate, a nearly impossible task given the hard labor, long hours, and inadequate food. Every night she returned to the ghetto worn out, with infected blisters that would not heal.

As the end drew near, nobody was protected. You could be captured on the street during the day or dragged out of your home at night. Almost every evening Germans rounded up Jews. No longer safe in their lodgings, M. devised a primitive hideout for those living with her by closing off the small alcove with a large chest of drawers. Families crowded into other apartments in the same building often came down to M.'s little "maline" to wait out the night.

M. lived at the end of a street on the edge of the ghetto. On the final night of the roundups, the Germans got to them very late. M. could hear soldiers tearing down locked doors with axes and filing the Jews out of their homes. Even though they entered the big room of M.'s apartment as well, they somehow did not bother to look behind the commode, leaving M.'s little group to meet the morning in a virtually empty ghetto.

The guards responsible for the work crews generally did not know what went on in the Jewish quarter during the nights. Thus, on that following day, they arrived as usual to escort their laborers to the airfield. Understanding that it was now or never, M. told her group to leave with the guards and try to escape once outside the walls of the ghetto. Wrapping her baby up as best she could, M. ran out the door to meet the Germans and blend into the ranks of the Jews coming from the adjoining ghetto.

On the landing M. heard the cries of an infant from another apartment. Its mother had been arrested the night before and must have hidden the baby, hoping . . . hoping for what? M. knew the mother and child; they often came downstairs to hide in the maline. But M. had her own baby to carry in her arms. She could not manage two. Beseeching the others to take pity on the child, she could convince nobody in the group to take it.

The cries of that infant still haunt M. today. Remembering the scene was so painful that she could not go on with her story. All I know is that M. managed to escape the ghetto with her little girl, whom she gave to some peasants for the duration of the war, and hide out by herself in a small peasant village, successfully passing as a Pole.

An important part of M.'s story has nothing to do with her ability to speak Polish or perform any other cultural trick to hide her Jewish origins. Even though Sartre correctly states that there is no Jewish race, almost every European country has its Jewish type. In Wilno, M. did not fit the local caricature and thus had the option to pass as a Pole. Not everyone could have made that choice.

M. had the further good fortune of being a woman. If born a man, no matter how blond, her status of "other" would have been carved into her flesh. Since God only required Jewish males to make a carnal covenant with Him, Jewish women—devalued within the group—had a better chance than men to pass in the gentile world. The care traditional Judaism took to mark the bodies of the favored sex also expressed itself in nonmaterial ways through the emphasis it placed on the religious training of young males. Free, then, of physical signs, M. also had little to unlearn as she emancipated herself from traditional Judaism.

Given her fair genes, unscarred flesh, and minimal involvement in things Jewish, M. was free to dissociate herself from the Jews and prove true the democratic principle that everybody was really the same. The way she did this, however, was most curious. Faced with a life and death situation, M. passed as a gentile by stating the absurd: Jewish women were anatomically different. Perhaps M. borrowed this crude ethnic joke, commonly used to slur the Chinese and Japanese; perhaps she came up with an independent invention. Whatever the origin, the joke had shock value because it evoked the most important of Jewish ritual symbols: circumcision.

As Victor Turner says, The essential quality of ritual symbols is the "juxtaposition of the grossly physical and the structurally normative, of the organic and the social."[21] Taking a swipe at traditional Judaism, which leaves women out of "the social," and at anti-Semitism which despises the religion, M. naturalized the central ritual symbol of the Jews by replacing male circumcision, a culturally induced mutilation, by a biologically inherited deformity. Just like their men, the genitals of Jewish women were different; but whereas boys became Jews through circumcision, girls, M. claimed, were born that way.

M. exploited the racial horror Poles had for Jews by elaborating upon the physical differences that existed between the two groups, a strategy that further established her firm place among the gentiles. If Jews, both women and men, were dark, short, and poorly built, with protruding noses, large ears, and funny-looking genitals, how could anybody take M. for a Jew? Defending herself by looking and acting the same, M. then switched gears and sought additional protection by playing up a difference.

In a male world, M. used femaleness to her advantage. She did so, however, not as one committed to her condition as "other," but as one determined to confirm that her sexual identity was not specifically Jewish. An attractive young woman and a mother, M. transcended her situation as a Jew and joined universal womanhood. When, for example, she helped the Polish peasant in the agonies of a miscarriage, M. did so as one woman would for another. Most importantly, M. pushed herself to survive for the sake of her daughter, and this fact too brought her closer to all mothers. Her interest in children was not ethnic, but individual; thus M. could sacrifice somebody else's Jewish child—admittedly at great psychological costs—in order to ensure the safety of her own.

The symbolic system of virtually every culture builds upon the biological differences that exist between the sexes, ages, and, where relevant, races. Western democratic traditions, however, try to minimize them. Expressing an ideological commitment to the equality of all peoples, progressives have proposed only one path to freedom for Jews, women, blacks, and the proletariat: assimilation; or, at best, duplication in slightly varied tones of the dominant ideal of a national culture. Still, a residual nostalgia for difference remains, and occasionally it cries out against the democrat's intolerance for diversity. Thus, when somebody like M. makes the understandable, if "inauthentic," choice to pass, I, for one, find myself wishing that she had chosen to survive as a Jew, not just as a person. Yet, I (we), like Sartre and Beauvoir, continue to participate in a system which teaches that, to be free and authentic, the "object" must become the "subject" and that requires taking on the national traditions of those who have defined the terms of this subjectivity. M. stayed alive under fascism, a regime which fiercely cultivated differences and attempted to wipe some of them out, by following the lessons she had learned about universality and the value of national assimilation. Even under democracy she had seen how those who did not blend, or who were not allowed to do so, remained the disadvantaged "other," the very same people who were told they had no history.

Notes

1. Barbara Myerhoff, *Number Our Days* (New York: Simon and Schuster, 1978), 27–28.

2. Jean-Paul Sartre, *Being and Nothingness*, translated and introduced by H. Barnes (New York: Washington Square Press, 1966).

3. Throughout this essay, I will purposefully use the noun *man* and the pronouns *he, him, his*, when talking about humanity in general. I do so, not because I believe that *mankind* includes *womankind*, but to remind the reader, even at the level of grammar, of how inadequately the concept of difference has been treated both by proponents and critics of our democratic, universalistic traditions.

4. Jean-Paul Sartre, "The Last Words of Jean-Paul Sartre," translated by A. Foulke, *Dissent* (Fall 1980): 419.

5. Jean-Paul Sartre, *Anti-Semite and Jew*, translated by G. Becker (New York: Schocken Books, 1948), 90.

6. Ibid.

7. Ibid., 91.

8. Sartre uses history in the Hegelian sense. People have a history if and only if they become a nation-state; a sovereign political entity with a territory and relations with other states just like themselves (see: Jean-Paul Sartre, "Last Words," 419). For Hegel, minorities living within nation-states are peoples "without history" (for a discussion of Hegel's views, see Georges Haupt et al., *Les marxistes et la question nationale, 1848–1915* (Paris: François Maspéro, 1974), 22).

9. Jean-Paul Sartre, *Anti-Semite and Jew*, 67.

10. Ibid., 13.

11. Simone de Beauvoir, *The Second Sex*, translated by H. M. Parshley (New York: Bantam Books, 1961), xvi.

12. Ibid., xvii.

13. Ibid., 682.

14. Ibid., 128.

15. Michèle Le Doueff, "Simone de Beauvoir and Existentialism," *Feminist Studies*, 6: 2 (1980): 288.

16. Jean-Paul Sartre, *Anti-Semite and Jew*, 55.

17. Ibid., 117.

18. At the end of his life, Sartre believed that "the history Hegel established in our intellectual landscape sought to have done with the Jews and it is the Jew who will make it possible to emerge from the view of history Hegel

wanted to impose on us" (Benny Levy as cited in Jean-Paul Sartre, "Last Words," 419). However, before the Jews can lead us out of this kind of history they will have to stop using Hegelian categories themselves. The commitment of some to the creation and preservation of national secular Jewish cultures or the desire of others to assimilate directly into the nations where they presently live only confirms Hegelian ideas of history.

19. Constantly changing the rules, the Nazis later required that Jews wear these stars on their arms.

20. For a complete description of life in the two parts of the Wilno Ghetto, see A. Soukever, *Ghetto de Vilna,* translated into French by C. Benasin (Paris: Editeur Cooped, 1950) and Y. Arad, *Ghetto in Flames* (New York: Holocaust Library, 1982).

21. Victor Turner, *The Forest of Symbols* (Ithaca: Cornell University Press, 1967), 29.

BETWEEN RAPE AND PROSTITUTION

SURVIVAL STRATEGIES AND CHANCES OF EMANCIPATION FOR BERLIN WOMEN AFTER WORLD WAR II

Annemarie Tröger

Translated by Joan Reutershan

In this article I analyze the relations between the sexes in postwar Berlin, in a period when the German people lived under extreme economic, social, and political conditions. As the Hitler regime collapsed and Germany fell into the hands of the Allied armed forces, many suffered from hunger, cold, compulsory emigration, and flight. The time covered begins in the spring of 1945 and continues for two years.

The article considers postwar Berlin largely through the autobiographical reflections of two women who lived there. These women tell how rape and prostitution became "normal" sexual relations for them and how they thought and felt about what they did.

Rape and prostitution have always been regarded as quasi-"natural" occurrences during times of want, war, and social unrest. Yet, by isolating them as characteristic of difficult social periods and of fringe groups, we cover up their affinity with "normal" sexual relations. The following stories have the virtue of revealing the connection which exists between rape and prostitution on the one hand and socially legitimate kinds of sexual relations on the other, a connection which is usually hidden during stable periods by morality and state sanctions. It is no longer necessary to prove empirically that there is a relationship between marriage and rape and prostitution, for others have done so already, but it is important to examine concrete examples which let us see this relationship clearly.

The "case of Berlin in 1945" is significant for two reasons: (1) rape and prostitution were very widespread; (2) women from the petite bourgeoisie, as well as the educated middle class, were equally affected and participated in these forms of sexual relations. Given the extreme circumstances, this "historical experiment" raises a number of questions. What happens, for example, to the concepts of bourgeois morality and marriage when great numbers of "decent" women realize from their own experience that prostitution and marriage are not worlds apart, but rather resemble each other closely in their social and economic structure? How does the concept of love and marriage change for women when they come to see the sex "act," supposedly the highest expression of love, eros, and sentimentality, as the gravest form of humiliation and national submission? Does this expose the cultural horror which is inherent in the double function of the "act"? How do women from educated classes understand this, those who belong to a tradition, centuries old, which has trained them to believe that masculine drives have been domesticated and heterosexuality sublimated to love?

Both women and men remember the first years after the Second World War as a period in which the German woman experienced a certain sexual and social emancipation. While nobody has yet done a serious social-historical investigation of the phenomenon, there are tangible indications of this emancipation in many autobiographical recollections, like the two stories which follow. We also have supporting evidence in literary descriptions, in polls conducted by social scientists during the occupation, and finally in the endless complaints of German men in the newspapers of the late 1940s. Thus it is even more astonishing, and from a feminist point of view more disheartening, that in the 1950s women returned quickly and without noteworthy resistance to very traditional sexual and family relations.

Most explanations for this rapid return suggest that the sexual liberation after the war did not reflect the choices of women, that it was dictated to a great extent by economic necessity, by having to support a family. According to this line of argument, the women themselves fled back into the security of traditional sexual relations as soon as possible. Economic conditions after the war even played a significant part in encouraging women to accept traditional roles, for in the redistribution of jobs and incomes, men were shamefully favored after the Second World War in Germany, more than they were after the First. But then why did women fail to resist this "redistribution"? Did the women remain silent because they wanted their men to support the family? This can hardly be so, for the turn toward a new German conservatism did not only occur among women whose husbands came back from the war, or who had the good fortune to hook one of the few single men eligible for marriage. It is significant that the trend also included those women who could never hope to be "provided for" or "protected" by a man: the millions of war widows, divorcées, and unmarrieds. The social and psychological conditions of their lives in the conservative society of the "economic miracle" were brutal. Defined solely by what they lacked, by not having a man, they were treated—even by other women—as second-class citizens and felt themselves to be such. Although by the mid-fifties most of these women no longer lived in bitter economic circumstances, they never gained such a sense of a positive social identity as did the widows of the First World War in their mothers' generation. And although having a profession was taken for granted by the generation of young women after the Second World War, they never achieved the self-confidence of unmarried working women of the Weimar Republic. Was the phase of women's emancipation in the forties, therefore, only a blossom of chaos, a short, insignificant episode between two patriarchal orders: fascism and bourgeois democracy? Or can we see signs and indications in the process of emancipation itself, which *in nuce* reveal the trend toward a return to old values? How far could the process of becoming conscious of self-emancipation go at all, even in the most favorable cases, given the contemporary conditions of want, hunger, and danger to life and limb? Where did the historical situation itself impose limits?

To examine these issues I have chosen two personal testimonies which are to a certain extent extraordinary. They *cannot* be considered "typical" of the way Berlin women speak about that period *today:* Both A. in her journal from 1945 and B. in her recollections from 1981 wrote and spoke in a more open manner and in more detail about the rape and prostitution which they themselves experienced than did their contemporaries. They reported more honestly and at the same time in a more self-critical manner about what they thought and did. It is especially noteworthy that both conceived of themselves as actively functioning, decisive, and thinking persons, and not merely as victims of the contemporary situation. But while their testimonies are extraordinary, the experiences of these two women are in no way unusual: Thousands of Berlin women were raped at the end of the war (the numbers given by serious sources vary between twenty thousand and half a million), and thousands prostituted themselves for shorter or longer periods, in order to survive.

A.'s Journal

The fate of the book *Eine Frau in Berlin*[1] *(A Woman in Berlin)* embodies a piece of postwar history in itself. The author, who has remained anonymous until today, and who will be designated below as "A.," released her journal for publication in the early fifties. It first appeared abroad in 1954. In the United States alone some 300,000 copies were sold, since its content, if not its intention, was well suited to the atmosphere of the McCarthy Era. Not until 1959 did the book appear in a German edition.

> We know little about the author. She characterizes herself thus:
>
> A pale blond, always dressed in the same winter coat rescued by chance, employed by a publisher, until he closed his store last week and released the employees "til further notice."[2]

Since she was thirty years old in 1945, she must have been born in 1915. Unmarried, A. had a "fiancé" at the front, for whom she wrote the journal. She probably came from an educated middle-class family. We can deduce this from her linguistic style and her manner of observation. She is a woman from the army of female white-collar employees, of which there were thousands in Berlin, whose degree of education varied somewhat and who came from a more or less "good" home. She corresponded to the type of New Woman of the twenties: independent but economically insecure, curious and critical, without party affiliation and without an established philosophy, but with a mind of her own. She was ironic to the point of self-irony. Her type was representative of the women who participated in Berlin's cultural life, the ferment, "the heady feeling" of the city during the "golden twenties." Although they were repressed and condemned by a male mass culture during the Nazi period, these women, as we will see in the case of A., were not destroyed by it.

A. lived in a middle-class quarter. The social composition of the apartment house consisted of mid- to high-level white-collar employees and civil servants, and independent petit bourgeois. There were also some "proletarian implants," a Belgian forced laborer, the doorman's wife with two daughters, and the baker's two women assistants. The proportion of women to men and young (under forty) to old might be considered "typical" for the Berlin population of those days: twelve older women, twelve younger women, five older and three younger men (including the Belgian), three children. An unknown man, who later turned out to be a high-ranking Nazi, and his girlfriend, as well as a German deserter, joined this group. In this community A. lived out the end of the war; it was here that she recorded in her journal the disintegration of bourgeois morality, scenes of plunder, the proximity of the petit bourgeois rituals and threats to life and limb, the risk of one's own life for another.

The "cellar community" became the most important social group for Berliners in the last two years of the war. People spent almost every other night, in the last months every night, and in the last weeks day and night in this community. During the days of the battle of Berlin it became the most important conveyor of news, as well as a cell where opinion was formed.

After her attic apartment became uninhabitable because of a bomb attack, A. moved in with a druggist's widow on the second floor. The latter became A.'s closest confidant in the days of rape. Even the last barrier fell between these two women, who had known each other for only three months in the cellar community: namely the food barrier. Any food that one managed to plunder, or otherwise get hold of—including that which she gained through sex—belonged to the other. In short, they formed one of the many "war families."

On April 27 the Russian troops entered A.'s neighborhood and discovered the cellar on the very first day. (Some cellars in Berlin remained undiscovered in the labyrinth of underground passageways beneath Berlin apartment houses.) In the course of the next ten days A. was "defiled" five times. On every occasion she was subjected to brutal physical abuse. A. did not count the many times she had more or less compulsory relations with her Russian "protectors" and "providers." On May 8—ten days later—she wrote in her journal that she had just spent the first night without a strange man in her bed. That was not, however, the average "score" for a Berlin woman in those days. Several things made A. a preferred victim. She was young, blond, not pregnant, and had no small children (such women were generally taboo for the Russians). Furthermore, on the basis of her minimal knowledge of Russian, she became an interpretor for her neighbors, and through this she attracted attention to herself.

After the second rape on the first evening, A. noted in her journal:

> What does defilement mean? When I said this word out loud for the first time in the cellar on Friday evening, an icy shudder ran down my spine. Now I can already think it, already write it down with a calm hand. I say it aloud in order to accustom myself to its sound. It sounds like the absolute worst, like the end of the world, but it isn't.[3]

The author of the journal used the old-fashioned, biblical word *defilement* throughout, although *rape* was the more common word in the 1940s. Whatever her reason may have been, by repeating "defilement" over and over again, the idea lost its threatening religious overtones and began to seem ridiculous.

On the second day during the third rape—A. had one of her worst experiences:

When I got up I felt dizzy and wanted to vomit. My ruined under-clothes fell round my feet. I staggered along the passage, past the sobbing widow, to the bathroom. There I vomited. In the mirror I saw my green face, in the basin what I had vomited. I didn't dare rinse it as I kept on retching and we had so little water left in the bucket.

Then I said aloud to myself: Damn it!—And made a decision.

It suddenly came to me: I must get hold of a wolf—to protect me from the wolves. An officer. As high a one as possible, Commandant, General—whatever I can get. What's my brain for—and my little knowledge of the enemy's language?

I felt much better now that I was once more planning and wanting something, instead of being nothing but a silent victim.[4]

Only an hour later, still green in the face, she made a date with a First Lieutenant, Anatole, who visited her that very same evening. She spent this night and the following with him. On the third "Russian day," April 29, she wrote:

By now the situation is clear: In the daytime open house for the friends of the family (if that's what one can call them) and for any member of Anatole's gang. At night, however, only for the chieftain, Anatole. At the moment I really seem to be taboo to anyone but him—at least for today. What will happen tomorrow? No one knows.[5]

Although relatively protected now against brutal attacks, her body reacted to the "voluntary" rapes:

I felt wretched and sore and crept around like a lame duck. . . .

What makes me so wretched at this moment is not the too-much, it's the abused body taken against its will, which reacts with pain. . . .

I remember a married school friend confessing to me once at the beginning of the war that since her husband had been drafted she felt physically better, because sexual relations with him had always been painful and unpleasant for her—a fact she had done her best to conceal from him. This is probably what's known as frigidity, her body had not been aroused. And frigid is what I have remained during all these copulations. It cannot, it must not be different: I want to remain dead and without feeling, as long as I am prey.[6]

Meanwhile, A.'s "war family" gained a new member: Mr. Pauli, approximately fifty years old, the tenant of the druggist's widow, who returned from the *Volkssturm* on the second day after the arrival of the Russians. This unit was the last defense force of the "Third Reich," which consisted of old men and children without weapons or am-munition. Mr. Pauli's detachment had dissolved itself. The widow's hope of finding a protector in him was, of course, in vain. From the day he returned, he put himself to bed with a "neuralgia," allowing himself to be cared for, fed, and protected by the two women. Only after the Russians withdrew did he get out of bed, healthy and fully recovered.

The "official" struggle went on. While A.'s neighborhood no longer suffered from bombardments by the Allies after April 27, it now had to withstand German artillery attack. And over and over women were raped. Bruised and defiled, they returned to the female community to be consoled. Reminiscent of a ritual, these victims were received into the circle of "normal" women.

By the sixth day there was female resistance in the quarter against the hordes of armed soldiers.

> Yes, the girls are becoming scarce. The hours at which the Russians go on their hunt for women are now common knowledge; the girls are locked up, hidden in lofts or herded together in the "safe" apartments. In the water queue word went around that a woman doctor had established in the air-raid shelter a hospital for contagious diseases, with huge signs in German and Russian announcing that the place was devoted exclusively to cases of typhoid. The patients, however, consisted only of very young girls from the neighborhood, whose virginity the doctor had rescued with her typhoid trick.[7]
>
> We have opportunity enough to practice it. This morning, for instance the woman with the eczema on her cheek had, contrary to all my prophecies, to succumb. . . . A short while afterward she came staggering into our apartment where some time elapsed before she was able to speak. We comforted her with a cupfull of Burgundy. She finally recovered herself and grinned: "And for this I waited for seven years!" (This is how long she has been separated from her husband.
>
> All in all, we are slowly beginning to look upon the whole business of defilement with a certain humor, albeit of the grimmer kind.[8]

First Lieutenant Anatole, A.'s "protector," was suddenly transferred, and, without her knowledge, A. was "handed on" to a major. The major was a career officer who came from a middle-class family. His manners, developed to perfection, made his all too obvious "interest" in her embarrassing, even to him. A. was perplexed:

> This is a new state of affairs. I can in no way claim that the major rapes me. I'm pretty sure that one word from me would be enough for him to leave and never come back. Thus I'm voluntarily at his service. Can I be doing this out of sympathy, out of need for love? God forbid! At the moment I'm sick to death of all men and all their male desires. I cannot even imagine that I could ever long for such things again. Am I then doing it for bacon, butter, sugar, canned meat? To some extent, yes. It has worried me that I have been living off the widow's stores and am

pleased that now, with the major's help, I can repay her. I feel freer this
way, eat with a better conscience. On the other hand, I do like the
major, like him all the more as a human being the fewer claims he
makes on me as a man. And he will never make great claims, I feel that.
His face is pale and he's bothered by the wound in his knee. I'm sure
he's looking for more human, feminine sympathy than for mere sexual
satisfaction. And this I'm willing to offer him, even with pleasure. . . .
All of which fails to answer the question whether I should now consider myself a whore, living as I do off my body, acquiring by its
surrender the food we need.[9]

The major remained A.'s protector/provider till May 8, when the
Russian troops pulled out of the quarter. When he left, she felt
"somewhat pained, somewhat empty"; and "I have to tell the widow of
his departure carefully." Since the major's supply of food came to an
end, her situation in the "war family" became more difficult. A. tried
one more time—and this time without caring about her relationship
to prostitution—to make a date with a Russian officer, but nothing
came of it. She continued to tend to almost all the necessities of daily
life (fetching water, combustibles, etc.) together with the widow. That
meant that the relationship among the women "held up" despite the
difficult food situation. However, her relationship to Mr. Pauli became
more and more tense: "I felt that he had simply had it with me. Before
the widow was there for him alone, took care of him day and night. I
get in the way." She also sensed how important a masculine "protector" was to the widow at her age—no matter how little one could
expect of him. So A. moved back to her attic apartment, but the
friendly relationship with the widow remained:

This collective form of mass rape will also be collectively overcome.
Each woman helps the other by speaking about it, by airing her experience and giving the other the opportunity to air her experience, to rid
herself of her sufferings.[10]

With this A.'s story of rape comes to a close. One might want to add
something, however, about the social relationship between German
men and women, as it is reflected in A.'s journal. German men could
be excluded from the episodes just depicted because they were marginal; that is, they had marginalized themselves. The most positive
thing one could say about them was that they didn't add to the
problem. The story about the tenant Mr. Pauli was no exception,
rather the rule; and this is confirmed by other sources.

The myth of masculinity had already been dismantled to such an
extent that neither collective protection nor individual heroic deeds
were expected from men. Nonetheless most women, like A. herself,

hoped that in a specific situation the individual human being (man) would act in an "honorable way": take care of himself without becoming a wolf for others; share in the care of the sick, the elderly, and the children in the difficult living conditions amid the ruins without food, water, gas, or electricity, and protect himself without adding to the danger of the women. And perhaps these women hoped for a little solidarity. With few exceptions, nothing of the sort happened. On the contrary, the men had their "excuses to hide":

> The bookseller has Party membership, the deserter his desertion, and several others their Nazi pasts for which they fear punishment by deportation, and behind which they barricade themselves when it comes to water-fetching or other activities. The women themselves do their best to hide their husbands and protect them from the enemy. For what, after all, can the Russians do to us women now? They've already done their worst.
> So we women put our shoulders to the wheel, which is logical. Nevertheless, a strange feeling remains.[11]

Men had lost the means of their power: weapons, privileges, hierarchies, and masculine alliances, all of which had gained them collectively and individually their dominance over women and children. With this loss of power, they revealed themselves as parasites and let themselves be cared for and protected by those they formerly oppressed.

Many women understood—at least at the time—that they fell victim not only to the "armed, blinded primordial swine from Caucasia," against whom any defense would have been hopeless and suicidal. They also suspected that they were doing time in Berlin for the crimes committed by German men in Russia. They began to ask the guilty question, and as one response A. translated a Russian soldier's story for a group of younger women: how German military men had stabbed children to death in his hometown, grabbed the children by their feet, and shattered their skulls on the wall.

But what did the German men feel? Did they learn from the war? Did their self-image change their concept of masculinity? It appears that the overwhelming majority refused as individuals to give any thought to it at all.

A. noted in her journal on May 8, the day the Russians pulled out:

> This is the first time in weeks that I've heard German men talking in loud voices, seen them move with any sign of energy. They were acting in a practically masculine way—or in the way that used to be called masculine. Now we're going to be on the lookout for a better word, one that can still be used even in bad conditions.[12]

B.'s Story[13]

B. was born in 1926. Her father was a musical entertainer. In order to build up his own group, he taught his wife and daughter how to play musical instruments. In 1942, B. participated with her father and mother in the "Hawaii-Trio" and entertained groups at the German front. In the Fall of 1944 all tours were stopped. Her father was drafted, even though he was fifty-two years of age. Her mother and brother were evacuated from Berlin. She herself was required that winter to work in a munitions factory in the Sudetenland. Pregnant by then, she collapsed on the job and returned to Berlin a few weeks before the Russian army arrived. In the meantime, her mother, brother, and an aunt returned to Berlin and gathered in their old apartment, which was still intact. For three weeks they lived day and night with other occupants of the house in the cellar. On April 20, the "Führer's Birthday," Russian troops entered their quarter. She herself was not raped, protected as she was by her pregnancy.

> What feelings did I have when the Russians arrived?—I don't know—I wasn't even really frightened, I only knew in that moment the war was over, thank God. But that stinks, I thought, that the Russians are here now. Why couldn't the Americans have gotten to Berlin sooner? I had actually prayed: "Dear God, let the Americans arrive in Berlin first, not the Russians." Because everybody knew already, everyone had already heard, that the Russians raped a lot of women, etc. and that the Americans, they would hand out chocolate.

With her fervent prayer, B. expressed quite precisely the somewhat simplistic ideas and hopes of Berlin's petite bourgeoisie in those days. Her dreams too were representative:

> I always have the same dream . . . I arrive in America. I've had that dream over and over again, every year a few times, always the same dream, I get on a big ship and sail to America.

Similar fantasies of escape, wanting to leave all the German misery behind, are found in many of the stories by women in B.'s generation. At the end of June 1945, "the Americans actually do arrive." B. gave birth to her daughter in a clinic around then. In October she went for the first time with two young women from her street to the fashionable *Kurfürstendamm* section of Berlin to see what they could "roundup." They took along their fathers' war medals and other things they thought the Americans might be interested in. It was not only hunger that drove these young women. During such excursions they could forget the gray misery of their daily lives for a few hours.

Her first boyfriend was a cook in the army. After their first date he prepared a large package in the barracks with milk powder, chocolate powder, and coffee—royal morning gifts for that time—and went home with her. To the remark that these gifts couldn't have been for free, B. answered:

> Oh, well, of course, what can you get in life for free—um—that he of course—let's just be blunt about it—wanted to go to bed with me, well, of course. And so I was with him for a while, and he even rented me a room (near his barracks) in the house of a very nice old couple. And well, he practically saved my daughter's life. We did have milk rations and such things, but we didn't get anything with our ration cards. It really was that bad. So I just said to my family: "Listen, I'm young, it doesn't bother me," and just did it. Why not?

The cook left her, but soon afterwards she met the next boyfriend and fell "head over heels" in love with him. She stayed on in the same room. One day before Christmas 1945 this boyfriend suddenly had to return to America. She tried to commit suicide, but failed. At first she never wanted to meet another man and returned to her family.

> But I couldn't stand it there for very long. Now I wanted to meet an American, somehow, I was determined: I wanted to go to America.

In the Spring of 1946 B. already had another room near the McNair Barracks in Zehlendorf, a good middle-class district. It was a "wonderful room decorated in Rococo style, with a balcony." The room cost two packs of cigarettes a month, which an American gave her so she would take care of his dog.

> And for that he practically supported me, well, not exactly supported, but he brought me lots of things, milk powder and whatever there was; he smuggled the ration tins out of the barracks. And now since I had everything again and a very nice room, I took my baby back.

B. tried to maintain her brief, constantly disrupted friendships with American soldiers through letters, in the hope she would still somehow get married. (According to a decree of the military government, American soldiers could only marry German women after they had returned to the United States.) But she landed in military prison, rather than at the marriage bureau, because she had tried to send her letters through the military mail. Much to her regret she was released two days later: "There was such good food there, oh, did I have a feast."

She very quickly understood that in 1945 it was practically impossible to marry an American. In the meantime another girl friend had joined her and her two friends, so that they were now a group of four. Having already learned a lot, the four women became somewhat more "professional." In the summer of 1946 they rented two rooms in a pension near the *Kurfürstendamm*—two to a room—"in order to be more on top of things." At this same time their work became more dangerous. They tried to protect themselves by never going out alone, but rather always in a group of two, three, or even all four. B. witnessed rape attempts by American soldiers twice: one ended with the death of an unknown woman; in the other, a friend of hers was attacked, but saved by the clique. Both cases were covered up by the American military government.

Early in 1947 B.'s father got work in a band playing at an American club. The pay, however, was poor: "They practically worked for a sandwich." She was hired as a singer; that is, occasionally she sang a song, and the rest of the time she made new acquaintances—under her father's nose—and collected cigarette butts. B. thinks her parents were always very generous with regard to her work; they let her do what she wanted. (After all she supported the family to a large extent.) However, she must have perceived a certain double standard on the part of her parents, even then.

Later on, when B. was no longer in Berlin, a former German boyfriend came to her parents' place to ask about her. He was an officer whom she had met during her entertainment tours at the front, the one German she cared about at all.

> And my mother said to him that there was absolutely no use, I had become a G.I. whore. . . . But she never said that to me. If she had honestly said that to me, then maybe I would have been different. . . . Those very words she said [to the German man], I was only a G.I. whore.

The "terms of the trade" in B.'s relationship to the Americans were always clear:

> I mean, I can't simply ask for something without giving something myself, and what did I have to give? I only had myself to give. And when they were so nice: They took me out to the club, gave me food, gave me cigarettes and chocolate—then I couldn't say: "Watch out, you've given me everything—but from me—excuse me, I'm a lady, get it!" [Berlin dialect].

Still, she never entirely gave up the hope of getting married, for she didn't understand the criteria used for choosing a bride until much later.

I thought, somehow I will find one who's going to take me back to America, who will marry me. I was very naive at the time to believe that a woman who had had contacts with so many Americans would still be married. They usually want someone quite "untouched".

In the summer of 1947 B. got pregnant for the second time, and her social decline began. Because she didn't want her parents to find out about it, she decided to leave Berlin. A girl friend from her group came along. For a while they lived as the girl friends of British pilots in Celle, a small town in North Germany. The pilots were transferred. Then her girl friend returned to Berlin. "She left me in the lurch all of a sudden, and there I was." Without "relationships," without the group, and visibly pregnant, she had no other choice but to seek refuge as a "pregnant resident"[14] in a hospital. During this time B. met her next American boyfriend. "Another great love of mine. I've remembered all my great loves by name."

Released from the clinic with an infant and no means of support, she found shelter with a woman where she contracted childbed fever. Then, one day on a streetcar she met a German man who wanted to adopt her child. On Christmas Day in 1947 she dropped the infant off at this man's house. "Well, so I was practically free again." Then she went to live with her new American boyfriend, who soon left to return to America, and she went to Munich, also a zone occupied by Americans.

> So somehow I always managed to muddle through . . . of course it was very hard . . . always this uncertainty: what's going to happen tomorrow, where will you sleep tomorrow? It was really cruel somehow. But I was young. I thought: Oh God, if you manage to get through the day tomorrow, you'll also manage to get through the day after. I was in a situation in which nothing made much difference. Despite that I have pleasant memories. . . . When I think back today, the Americans were always so sweet and nice to me. . . . The only thing is that I never got to marry a G.I. [laughs], although I always wanted to go over there.

Only "One Summer of Freedom"?

In 1945 the ideological fetters of traditional femininity were undone. Or so it appears after reading autobiographical accounts from this period. According to these texts, the young women of the postwar era began their sexual emancipation in several significant areas, including the demystification of both heterosexuality and the (German) man. Moreover, they practiced "new" forms of life and work beyond traditional women's roles: "Women's households," families headed by women, and a women's public sphere emerged. Some twenty-five years later we, the generation of their daughters, had to reclaim precisely these elements of consciousness in order to commence with our own liberation. In contrast to our experience, however, not only the conscious perceptions of the postwar women, but also their real lives and their concrete actions, departed entirely from traditional women's roles. Nevertheless, they did not arrive at a consciousness which was articulated politically, not to mention one which was shared by all women—that is, they did not achieve consciousness as a "historical subject."

Many different reasons can be given to explain the repression of their progressive social tendencies and emancipatory impulses, for example, the traditional sexual politics of the occupying powers and the extraordinarily heavy burdens placed on women then. But none of these reasons explain why the majority of women themselves did not resist the return to old values. To find an answer to this question we must look to the issue of the collective identity of women during this period.

Referring to the two texts quoted at length above, I will address the issue of whether the postwar situation itself—especially the sexual enlightenment brought about for these women through their experience with prostitution and rape—contributed to, or blocked, the creation of a collective identity. As I proceed, a bizarre dialectic of sexual enlightenment will emerge. This dialectic arises when sexual enlightenment is not accompanied by concrete changes in the economic and social situation of women. The problem, it seems to me, is not only of historical interest, but of concern to the women's movement today.

"And for this I waited for seven years!"

This statement, made by A.'s neighbor after she had been raped, expresses succinctly the disillusionment Berlin women felt with regard to sexual "love." In A.'s journal we can clearly observe two phases of what I would call the "demystification of sexuality": First she overcame her "virginity complex"; second, she consciously decided to become a prostitute. The second step was unthinkable without the first. "It [the rape] sounds like the absolute worst, like the end of the world, but it isn't." While this observation may appear to reveal an icy coolness which came from growing accustomed to rape, it is not the case. A. continued to suffer when she was abused. What this statement signals is the consciously effected separation between her woman's body as an object of masculine dominance and her sense of self. Expressed in another way, "I am not what is inflicted upon my body, but rather I am what I *want* and what I *do*." This division of the person is a step toward emancipation, because it allows the preservation, or the development, of an identity as a human being, even though an identity as a woman is negated by the circumstances. Though A. still suffered when she was subjected to rape, the suffering stemmed less from the "stain" inflicted upon her body and the "shame" which stigmatized her as a woman; rather, she was full of anger that her body was taken against her *will*. Her will and her anger were the foundation from which she could both struggle for her right to determine what happened to her own body and begin to formulate her own understanding of a uniquely female sexuality.

"May I offer you a little abuse?"

The conscious separation between the female body and the sense of self is also necessary if women want to try to deal with the reality of rape in a collective manner. Only if a woman no longer views herself as "soiled" and "dishonored" will she be in a position to speak about rape with others. Such central and intimate "spheres" as sexuality are included in the "women's public sphere," the emergence of which was vividly described by A. This space was the practical prerequisite for the development of these women into a historical subject. In addition to facilitating practical functions like mutual psychological and material aid, barter, and exchange of information, it was a social space, in which—at least in their rudimentary form—women's own standards and norms, a morality independent of men, in brief their own "language" was able to develop. Women created this space which they referred to as the "women's public sphere," but they never understood it politically. They never defined it. And that which is not conceptualized cannot be defended.

The women's public sphere existed for only a short period—more briefly than the "war families." As soon as German men crawled out of their beds and hiding places, or returned from prisoner-of-war camps, as soon as they again dared to speak loudly and to move energetically "like men," they attacked and destroyed the space women had created with the instinct of the formerly powerful fighting for their last bit of power. Women were "without language." The basis of their community was still too fragile and the old bourgeois ideology still too powerful in their minds. In A.'s journal there is a

brief scene, which described this process precisely: Her fiancé Gerd
had "returned from the war" several weeks after the Battle of Berlin.
A few days later their first fight occurred:

> "You've turned into shameless bitches—everyone of you in this house!"
> And he grimaced. "I can't bear to listen to these stories. You've lost all
> your standards, the whole lot of you!" What could I say? I crept into a
> corner and sulked. I couldn't cry. All this seemed so silly, so hopeless.[15]

After a male public sphere had been reestablished, a much more
dangerous phenomenon emerged. German men wanted to enjoy the
so-called "loose morals" of German women. Taking advantage of a
situation that had come about for very specific reasons, German men
claimed their share of the booty and further destroyed the taboo,
which traditionally protected the woman's body, with such vulgar
invitations as "May I offer you a little abuse?"—a compliment "meant
in fun" and heard frequently at the time. Such a joke was characteristic of the boorish, sexist tone of the language of the late forties. By
holding fast to the coattails of Russian and American uniforms, German men demanded access for themselves to the bodies of German
women, which, thanks to the Allied forces, were supposedly free now
from moral sanctions. The more German men succeeded in regaining
control of the economic resources by, among other things, monopoliz-
ing the job market, the more concrete and threatening became their
demands for sex. Considered from this point of view, we can understand the conservative turn at the beginning of the fifties. Women flew
into the arms of the Christian-bourgeois block which promised them
security and protection within traditional norms.

But the renewed Christian-bourgeois taboo surrounding the
female body existed primarily in the minds of the women themselves
and changed little in the attitudes of men or in the social power
relations. It led women to fear their own sexuality. Many of them
today are our mothers, and many of them support most aspects of the
contemporary women's movement. But when it comes to the sexually
libertine ideas of feminism, they react with panic ("You're the ones
pulling women into the dirt"). Not only does their response reveal a
fear of their own sexuality, it also expresses a sense of guilt which still
has not worked itself out. Finally, it contains as well a serious allega-
tion against us, namely that we are partially responsible for the new
wave of brutal pornography that has gained popularity in the last few
years.

The Step into Prostitution

The second step of the demystification of heterosexuality can be seen in A's decision to use her body as an instrument (object) in order to secure her survival, that is, in her conscious entry into prostitution. What then is the emancipatory element in this? The affront to bourgeois morality? A. observed with some amusement that bourgeois morals were dropped by her bourgeois surroundings like an old hat: Already on the fifth "Russian" day, all the women who could not otherwise protect and provide for themselves were in "secure hands." A. and her neighbors were no exception.

The speed and relative scrupulousness with which many Berlin women could "surrender" themselves to total strangers, who were moreover men described to them for years as "subhuman," animalistic monsters, shows that at least the older women were little influenced by fascist race hysteria. Instead, the effects of the "sexual reform" movement of the twenties appear to have continued into the postwar period among those women who were between twenty and thirty years old. To the "daughters of Vandervelde," the "act," the result of a series of sexual techniques, was no longer a mystery, nor an expression of a transcendental communion between the sexes. If sexuality was technically producible for marriage and love, then it was reproducible *without* marriage and love. The original goal of the sex reformists, to "free" female sexuality for love, had already transformed itself during the Weimar Republic to sexuality freed *from* love. This "dialectic of enlightenment," which Horkheimer and Adorno warned us about, made it easier for many women to enter into prostitution in order to survive because the prostitution of one's own body demanded—in pain of psychic destruction—the separation of (hetero) sexuality from one's own sexual and "higher" sensibilities. For these women, this would—theoretically—signify their complete disjunction from heterosexuality. In reality their path to another, self-determined sexuality was blocked by just as many obstacles as before.

The Negation of Identity

The conditions under which prostitution becomes necessary at all dictate a dangerous contradiction: to avoid being the *unwilling* prey of many men, or in order to survive, I offer my body *"of my own free will"* to one man as a sexual *object*. In doing so I recognize his claim to possess my body because only then does the man function as protector and provider. Toward the outside world, in the social sphere, I sup-

port and strengthen the old power relationships: the man possesses
and holds power of disposition over my female body. Because I
"freely" agree to this, he also possesses and disposes of me, the woman
as *person*, because "I" and that which I *want* and which I *do*. As a result
of this process, I reverse the positive step I had taken toward an
identity as a woman. I lose what I had won when I overcame the
virginity complex and could say: I am not what is done to my body, but
rather what I want and do. Now I have become precisely what I do *not*
want and what I do *not* do. Now I am something totally different. I am
what I think, feel, and wish. My identity as person is pushed into the
imiginary and is no longer recognized by the outside world; it is no
longer socially manifest. Toward the inside realm, on the subjective
level, I must—in order to hold up my identity, at least for myself—
declare my seemingly free action as a conscious maneuver of decep-
tion vis-à-vis "dumb men."

The case histories of A. and B. both show how difficult it is to
balance deceit and a true sense of self, to separate the sexual act from
one's feelings. Deceit, we see becomes self-deception. Even A., an
enlightened and self-critical woman, who could find her identity in
her intellectual profession and for whom the phase of prostitution
was very short, had to assure herself: "It cannot, it must not be
different; I want to remain dead and without feeling, as long as I am
prey." Despite that she feels a "bit of pain, a bit empty inside" after the
major's departure. In the case of the much younger B, who was not
able to construct an identity beyond the traditional feminine role,
recidivism was unavoidable. She fell in love over and over again, and
so made herself more than just economically dependent upon the
American soliders. She became vulnerable to the point of attempting
suicide. She surrendered again and again to the illusions of a marriage, and this prevented her from realistically evaluating her situation.

The Myth of Marriage

The myth of bourgeois marriage survived intact despite everything
the Berlin women had undergone in 1945. In fact, it was elevated to
an even higher status. This happened even though the myth of the
German man was totally destroyed and the number of divorces in the
initial postwar years skyrocketed, that is, even though reality made a
mockery of myth. Individual women activists sought changes in the
bourgeois/fascist marriage and family law, as well as in the abortion

regulations. They also sought official recognition for "women's families", especially in conjunction with the tax law, etc. But these initiatives had no support among the masses of German women. On the contrary, as the theoretical considerations about identity presented suggest, women's experiences with prostitution in no way threatened the myth of bourgeois marriage. The myth could not be destroyed: Marriage was the necessary "other," the imaginary identity which women needed in order to hold up under prostitution and not be shattered by it. This is especially clear in B.'s case: For her, "marriage" merged with the dream of the other country, with another life, with another self. The actual man was secondary to this; he was only the vehicle.

This was not very different for the majority of women, who were spared prostitution. Sustaining the myth of marriage as the warm and secure refuge in difficult and unsafe times, the women themselves reconstructed the image of the German man. Ironically, this was easiest for the war widows and the single women. The idealized figure of a man who has died almost always appears in their interviews and life stories: the fallen husband, fiancé, or brother. They tried then—and still do now—to justify to themselves their marriageless state, for which they suffered much discrimination. They have done this by placing the institution of marriage on such an ideal plane that finding an adequate partner was out of the question. During the years of the economic miracle, the woman "with a man" harnessed herself to the cart she supposedly shared. She pulled, pushed, and worked herself to the bone for his economic rise, so that "he" became "something" again and "stood for something." And all of this so that in her sixties she could be "let go" and exchanged for a younger woman, more appropriate to his new social status. Under such conditions the German woman did not consider her own economic or social interests.

German men—with the physical and spiritual aid of their "reconstruction companions"—succeeded in forcing single women into economic marginality. As people returned to old values during the postwar period, the numerous "women's families" were pushed more and more into ideological and social backwaters. The were increasingly tagged as communities of the "needy," the last resort for economic and social losers. The following generation of young women and girls saw a communal life-style among women more as a vision of horror than as concrete utopia. They would never make it a realistic alternative the way women did during the Weimar Republic. Instead, in the 1950s and early 1960s, the postwar generation of women tended to marry early.

The Limits of Sexual Enlightenment

This "historical experiment" in Berlin shows us the limits of sexual enlightenment as an instrument for social change, and it is instructive for the contemporary women's movement, which prides itself on having successfully demystified heterosexuality. We have achieved this goal easily because the seemingly impenetrable wall of bourgeois morals, which we initially struggled to break down, has proved to be nothing more than a paper wall of "repressive tolerance." With the world economic crisis the "dialectic of enlightenment" confronts us once again, as we can see most clearly in the United States. Until now the women's movement has only been able to respond with further sexual enlightnment because it has not developed goals for the trans- formation of society in the economic sphere. There are hardly any concrete utopias, "designs for living" to replace the institutions of marriage and the family. The lesbian movement has, it is true, made women's communities possible again on the ideological level, but the question of whether they can become a realistic alternative for the masses of women is an economic as well as a sexual problem.

There are very few strategic plans in the contemporary women's movement which connect sexual enlightenment with the economic question. Some of them are dangerously simple, like those which would free women from their economic, social, and psychological dependence on men through universal prostitution, or by carrying elements of prostitution into marriage and the family (remuneration for sex, love, and housework). They ignore the fact that collective and individual identities are not created by prostitution but, rather, de- stroyed by it. Here the women dreamers of the turn of the century were more realistic—that small, international group of great women, who designed the image of the New Woman. They wanted to release female eros from the fetters of marriage by directing it to broad goals of transformation in art, science, and society. For them sexual love was a revolutionary power and not a commodity for trade, a commodity with which one could buy the emancipation of women. According to them, only when the individual woman had her own identity and women had become a "subject of history"—only then could women enjoy sexuality "like a glass of water," without suffering. The Berlin "historical experiment" proves they were right.

Notes

1. *Eine Frau in Berlin, Tagebuchaufzeichnungen* (Geneva and Frankfurt: Verlag Kossodo, 1959).

2. Anonymous, *A Woman in Berlin,* with an Introduction by C. W. Ceram, translated from the German by James Stern (New York: Harcourt Brace & Co., 1954), The original English version by James Stern is the basis for the translations here. On the whole, Stern's language is much more literary than A.'s journal form would indicate, so that A. loses some of her spontaneity in translation. I have made changes in sections where A.'s meaning was distorted by upgrading her style. [J. R.]

3. *Ibid.,* 85.

4. *Ibid.,* 87–88.

5. *Ibid.,* 110.

6. *Ibid.,* 120–21.

7. *Ibid.,* 125.

8. *Ibid.,* 157–58.

9. *Ibid.,* 150–51.

10. *Ibid.,* 189.

11. *Ibid.,* 191.

12. *Ibid.,* 197–98.

13. B.'s story, together with two others, was recorded for a broadcast by North German Radio in 1981. The transcription was made by the author.

14. "A pregnant resident" *(Hausschwangere)* is a participant in a social program for poor pregnant women at German university clinics. The women are permitted to deliver their babies for free in the clinic in exchange for their work there as cleaning women and kitchen aids.

15. Anonymous, *A Woman in Berlin,* 316.

Women and Culture

This section reflects recent international thinking about women and culture and raises questions that will be significant far into the future.

In Marie-Jo Bonnet's provocative essay, "Farewell to History," she asks what questions still need to be asked to change how we know what we know, how we can know more, and how we imagine that we do know—"as if women revealed everything they did and did everything they dreamed of doing!" Marie-Jo Bonnet argues that the barriers to real knowledge are great. Even in her own research on lesbian relations from the sixteenth to the twentieth century, for example, she succeeded "in piecing together the fragments of a history," but was "forced to see them through the distorting eyes of men, . . . and to hear them speak a male language." What became of this "ardent passion of lovers played out on the margins of society?"

Love between women, politics between women; women generally were relegated to the margins of history—where they disappeared into mandated roles of wife and mother or were trivialized and distorted. According to Gudrun Schwarz's essay, by the middle of the nineteenth century women who sought independence and personal satisfaction outside or beyond the male-dominant order of heterosexual marriage and motherhood were branded medically sick. Several generations of medical men, beginning with Westphal (1869) and Krafft-Ebing (1877), violently intruded their masculinist fantasies into their interpretations of women's capacity to love women. By denying the possibility that women may love women because they are women, they erected the myth of the "mannish lesbian," the diseased and dangerous "virago"—sinful and sick.

Despite all the dire predictions of madness and physical collapse, of social ruination and ultimate damnation, the New Women developed their own languages, their own styles, and succeeded in widening the acceptable areas of women's work and culture. The ongoing struggle for equality and acceptance, despite the brutal barriers to change, was accompanied by notable victories and an ever-growing awareness of the full dimension of the problem.

Marcelle Marini's essay explores the meaning and legacy of an entirely male-dominated culture. Now, with a culture in dispute and rapidly changing, Marini argues that as a literary critic it is clear that women are challenging male traditions at every level of custom and creativity. The nature and balance of persuasion and power are being reordered. Feminist culture, the feminist effort to understand and expand what we see and what we know, is a "profoundly democratic program." With real freedom to explore the full range of human possibilities a real plurality and universality will be allowed to emerge, strengthening culture and society as mean-spirited reliance on in-equality—on dominance and subservience—diminishes and disappears.

Catharine R. Stimpson, Carole B. Tarantelli, and Marie-Claire Pasquier analyze the traditions of male dominance and women's enforced subservience in literature and theatre, and celebrate the challenges and the changes over time.

Catharine Stimpson emphasizes the work of the "cultural rebels," the women writers who made a difference, giving us all new strength and vision.

Carole Tarantelli focuses on the distortions and the destruction which occurs when women have no "normal" way to express "male" power. The monster and the mad woman in literature reflect the full tragedy of our misogynist traditions.

Celebrating the power of the theatre, Marie-Claire Pasquier analyzes this "area of freedom, where *play* is permitted." Using examples from both traditionally misogynist and recent feminist theatre, Pasquier introduces those many spaces in fantasy and fact where "through ritual, our fears are exorcised" and everything becomes possible.

FAREWELL TO HISTORY

Marie-Jo Bonnet
Translated by Debra Irving

Many who have observed the huge strides taken by women's history in the past decade wonder if it has challenged traditional history and renewed its methods. For the moment we must, like Michelle Perrot, acknowledge that the only way we have to approach history differently is to ask new questions.[1]

Yet it seemed that feminism would enable us to do more. We were going to break with traditional theories of knowledge as feminists had done in the other human "sciences," like sociology. It was with this in mind that in 1971 three American historians outlined the foundations of a new approach to history in an article entitled "The Problem of Women's History":

> We are learning that the writing of women into history necessarily involves redefining and enlarging traditional notions of historical significance, to encompass personal, subjective experience as well as public and political activities. It is not too much to suggest that, however hesitant the actual beginnings, such a methodology implies not only a new history of women but also a new history.[2]

So what happened? Why haven't we succeeded in revolutionizing this ancient discipline from within, in finally leading to differentiate between the sexes in ways other than simply rediscovering gender roles and functions historically defined by male societies?

Are we condemned to produce only a "parallel history," even though it may have the advantage of uncovering whole vistas of our past, like feminist struggles, the existence of women-loving women, the role of women in work and—why not?—in the family?

I believe that our problems with these questions arise in part from our not having meditated enough on the specific features of our subject. In the first place, as we study our past, we are applying intellectual categories which are not part of our own history, but of history per se.

Furthermore, history has become such a catch-all nowadays—proponents of the "new history" speak of its "splitting"[3]—that the very meaning of history, and, all the more so, of women's history, has been lost. Thus, side by side with studies of the environment or cuisine, we see the proliferation of biographies of famous women and historical novels (*La Chambre des Dames* by Jeanne Bourin, exemplifies the current confusion by its amazing success). In demographic history, we even find scholars who believe they can analyze the attitude of a population toward contraception, for example, by looking at birthrates, the number of children born out of wedlock, and statistics on marriage, as if there were a correlation between the institutional behavior of women (marriage) and their love and sex relations, as if women revealed everything they did and did everything they dreamed of doing!

Instead of allowing ourselves to be infected by the passion of current historical research for "new objects,"[4] a passion which barely masks the theoretical void left by the materialistic view of history which has influenced much of this century's research, we must determine why writing the history of women is not quite the same thing as writing the history of the worker's movement, for example, or even the history of the body and of sexuality.

Why? Because the worker's movement has already, and by definition, gained a very definite place in social dynamics and has consequently become an unavoidable participant in economic and social history, whereas women have no specific historical role other than that of "working, obeying, and keeping quiet," as Mme. B. so bitterly put it in her *Journal of Grievances* written for *the Etats Généraux of 1789*.[5]

Why? Because one of the first facts we encounter in writing the history of women is their silence, their having left very few marks of their own on the historical materials we use. And this raises a number of questions of historical method as well as content. What is history for women, how do they participate, or fail to participate, in historical processes? What is the substance of the material we work with? We analyze facts, events, political systems, institutions, social and intellectual structures, ideologies—in short, a whole set of data whose importance for women has never been investigated.

It is one thing to say that women have no real grasp of historical events; it is quite another to ask what an event is in the life of a woman. The same is true for awareness of historical time. Do women, who are responsible for perpetuating and preserving life almost indefinitely, see time exactly as do men, who have the choice, the option, of changing the social system, leaving a heritage behind them, defending or extending their familial or national territories, and, as has so far been the case, making war one of the main motives of historical change and fundamental means of domination?

This is why I believe that women, be they worn down by their oppression or be they politically active, do not live, and have no part in, a history identical to men's. This is why the idea of women's history is so difficult to develop.

When half of humanity has been persuaded that it has no voice in its own future but must merely live out its destiny, how is it to acquire what is termed historical consciousness? When thousands of sleeping beauties spend their lives waiting for something to happen to them and identify that something with a Prince Charming, how are they to feel that their country's affairs affect them and to communicate to other women a desire to experience anything but the dulling repetition of work and days and the prospect of an uninspiring future?

Is this women's history? This time, which slowly wears them out, from mother to daughter, marriage to childbirth; this long suffering of lives which have failed to win the lottery and are so oppressed by material relations that they no longer know whether light comes from heaven or from hell? Or must we acknowledge that women's history begins when one of us halts the infernal cycle and begins to live in the present, as the source and substance of social dynamism: in other words, when we break with the history of men and their laws?

Isn't this, after all, what we meant when we proclaimed 1970 "the year zero of women's liberation"? The clean slate of memory told us that it was the "year zero," and it was not exclusively out of ignorance of our history that we called it that. No, we had to reject history to find our own. Without a radical departure from the past, no women's revolt could transcend the barrier of its own beginnings.

We must not forget, however, that the interest in women's history was revealed only after, and not before, this break: when, faced with the challenge of defining our feminine identity, we had to look to the past to find the roots of our oppression and our rebellion.

But this still does not explain our relationship to tradition and historical memory, and above all the role they play in the reawakening and liberation of women.

Whence came this impetus? Where are the roots of the feminist movement? Are they really in the memory of our past? I think this question deserves to be brought up because, although we often get the impression that women have been afflicted with amnesia and that history is repeating itself, this might be due to the inability of the collective memory to determine what women did to break free of their bonds.

It is as if each of us began to tell the same story all over again, underwent the same experiences, and reproduced the gestures and words of our elders, because the message that we sought to convey through our repeated attempts at emancipation was not incorporated into a single culture, tradition, or consciousness.

And it is here, in my opinion, that we see the primary contradiction of the discipline that calls itself women's history. Once we define it, our "object" escapes us; either it melts back into the patriarchal unconscious, or it adds to historical memory only what memory wishes to know, in other words, what is part of the masculine standard and integrated into masculine history.

So although we know that the history of feminism is confined neither to the struggle for equal status nor to the "war of the sexes," we have difficulty reconstructing it in all its richness and diversity, not only because history has retained only what beckoned to it, like the rights to vote, work, and education, but also because the feminists themselves forgot, concealed, or did not divulge their true nature, no doubt fearing to damage their cause by revealing the enormous disparity between their lives and their desires.

I found the same to be true with my historical research on love relations between women from the sixteenth to the twentieth century.[6]

In the beginning, I wanted to expose that conspiracy of silence which had shrouded women who loved one another in order to restore to them a real place in history. I must admit, however, that although I succeeded in piecing together the fragments of a history, it is not the history of lesbians per se.

Why? Because I was forced to see them through the distorting eyes of men, to be introduced to them by men and to hear them speak a male language.

Behind the moralizing, repressive, or libertine speech of the sources, I was, fortunately, able to spot the acts of revolt and liberated behavior of women whose times had gagged them and who had been denied an identity. But what has become of this female world, this ardent passion of lovers played out on the margins of society?

Did it fade off into eternity, to remain unscathed by the wounds of time, or has it been transformed into creative energy, even into a feminine consciousness?

Who can tell, since this experience has not become historical fact, since the secret was so well guarded that it emerges from history without having marked it?

One can certainly compare differences between periods, trace developments, highlight the special moments when something was possible, primarily as a result of the crises in masculine civilization, in short, invoke the relativity of things and people, time and space—but ultimately, does this concern us, does it help us to understand what it is in patriarchal history that resists change?

This is really the question I am asking myself today, having searched in vain for my roots in the past and hunted for an origin which loses itself in the mists of time.

"Men-History, must I block my ears to what you say?" asks Charlotte Calmis in one of her poems.[7]

Perhaps . . . perhaps . . . since that history reconstructs for us the shreds of dead memories from the past.

Especially, perhaps, since it threatens to engulf us once again in these horrible convulsions that it takes for revolution.

When a civilization can strike no balance other than that of terror, how can we continue to tie our fate to its destiny?

Feminism is, perhaps, the last utopia of our time; and it could hardly be otherwise since women's liberation is related not to event, but to advent.

> "We ourselves were surprised by the energy we unleashed among women," said Sofia Sokolova from her enforced exile. "Sooner or later, this energy will break through again. An irreversible moment, that of the awakening, has been reached."[8]

And who was not astonished by the explosion of the 1970s? Who could have foretold its scope, its radicalism? What historical theory can explain this phenomenon? Who, moreover, would have believed that women—those poorly loved creatures—would have the audacity to break with men to form their own movement?

It's a small world, isn't it?

Because history always leaves out an essential element—the unpredictable.

When suddenly, and I would even say spontaneously, women gain a new sense of themselves, even though nothing in the past prepared them for this.

When times change so substantially that events in themselves can no longer contain or weaken the feminine explosion.

When the wind blows so hard over history that we lose all sense of chronology and forget "historical" dates. Need I recall that at the start of the movement, we invariably neglected to date our writings, newspapers, and posters, and that even today, barely ten years later, we have great difficulty in reconstructing the chronology of the events we ourselves precipitated?

We created the event, but in order that it should be recognized, we had to blow it up out of all proportion; today, however, no one can assess its importance or its impact on what was to come.

So although history has a feminist consciousness, it has thus far failed to uncover the potential of that awareness.

This is not surprising. History crushes utopia and perpetuates power. Even when it treads ever so carefully in order to promote our social integration, it does so only as a means of refusing to question its own moving principles and patriarchal roots.

March 8, 1982, was the first Women's Day in French history. We were officially recognized by a leftist government as a social movement. This can be interpreted as historical progress or as the fruit of our struggles. Far from uniting women in communal joy, however, this historical footnote merely intensified the prevailing confusion about feminism while exacerbating women's dispersion to the various political camps. It cruelly demonstrated that any form of feminism that linked and limited its efforts to social action fell very quickly into the beaten political path once it lost the energy of a collective explosion. Thus, on March 8, 1982, we witnessed the extinction of the first breath of a social movement which has lost its taste for utopia and habits of subversion. For what is losing ground and endurance is not feminism, but a certain type of politicization which clings to the oppression of women as if it were its only justification and source of energy. The past will stay with us until we stop seeing things in terms of oppressor and oppressed, until we discover alternatives other than the rejection of patriarchal society, until we can establish ties of solidarity other than those among victims.

In the nineteenth century, Suzanne Voilquin, a follower of Saint-Simon, thought, "The equality of the sexes will, by feminizing society, uncover its mysteries."[9]

Today, this principle has come upon us, but the mysteries are still beyond our reach, at the threshold of the visible and the invisible where a new concept of feminism is being tested.

And it is there, in my opinion, that we will find out second wind—in this ageless, boundless groundswell which goes back so far that we no longer know whether matriarchy is the myth which gave rise to patriarchal history or the lost paradise of women.

This is why I believe that we have an unprecedented opportunity to show that there are problems which go beyond evolution—that there is a feminine coming-to-be which challenges the very concepts of social change, historical determinism, and progress.

"To become is anti-memory," said Michele Cause, for to become is to begin to be what one was not; it is to bring out this vast feminine potential which has been stifled by history. There is no future for women in patriarchal history precisely because, in contrast to the concept of becoming, that of the future relates to a reality cemented in linear time, the evolution of things which already exist, whereas the strength of feminism is that it develops in women that which does not exist. But beware! To quote Marguerite Duras: "Women must not fall prey to the theoretical error of thinking that what is not seen is less real than what is seen."[10] This is precisely the problem feminism currently faces: our becoming emerges from the shadows and gravitates between the two poles of an explosive dynamic: the feminine experience, which is governed by historical conditions, and the feminine reality, which transcends them.

Men-History, must I block my ears to what you say?
I am the present memory of a future language.[11]

Notes

1. Statement made by Michelle Perrot on February 18, 1982, at a meeting of the Groupe d'Etudes Feministes at Paris VII on "What's Happening with Women's History?"

2. Ann D. Gordon, Mari Jo Buhle, and Nancy Schrom Dye, "The Problem of Women's History," in Bernice Carroll, ed., *Liberating Women's History*, (Urbana, Ill.: University of Illinois Press, 1976), 89.

3. *Faire de L'Histoire—Nouveaux problèmes* (Gallimard, 1974).

4. Ibid.

5. Quoted by Paul-Marie Duhet, *Les Femmes et la Revolution. 1789–1794*, Col. Archive, Julliard.

6. Marie-Jo Bonnet, *Un Choix sans équivoque: Recherches historiques sur les relations amoureuses entre les femmes du XVIᵉ au XXᵉ siecle*, (Paris: Denoël-Gauthier, 1981) (Thèse d'histoire, 3ᵉᵐᵉ cycle, Paris VII).

7. Charlotte Calmis, "Gaia" (psalms of incarnation), *Le Nouveau Commerce* Nos. 36–37 (Spring 1977).

8. "Les femmes russes ont brisé le tabou," interview in *Libération* (February 7, 1981).

9. Suzanne Voilquin, *Souvenirs d'une fille du peuple ou La Saint-Simonienne en Égypte*, introduction by Lydia Elhadad (Maspéro, 1978 [1865]).

10. In *La création étouffée* by Jeanne Socquet and Suzanne Horay (1973).

11. Charlotte Calmis, "Gaia."

"VIRAGOS" IN MALE THEORY IN NINETEENTH-CENTURY GERMANY

Gudrun Schwarz

Translated by Joan Reutershan

In 1869 C. Westphal, psychiatrist and coeditor of the *Archive for Psychiatry and Nervous Diseases,* published an article in his journal which caused a stir among colleagues in the profession. He reported on a kind of "pathological case," the "main manifestation [of which was] a symptom," that until then "had seldom, or never been described." Westphal called the symptom *inverted sexual temperament** and diagnosed it as a "neuropathic" (psychopathic) condition."[1]

Westphal based his research on a patient in the psychiatric ward of Charité Hospital in Berlin, where he was "Professor and Head Physi-

---

[Translator's note] The German term *Mann-Weib* (literally "man-woman") is usually translated in contemporary texts as "mannish lesbian" or "masculine woman." The word *Weib* during the latter part of the nineteenth century had a particularly pejorative connotation, and when hyphenated with *Mann,* it described an outrageous, strong woman, who had defiantly taken on a "masculine style." After looking for a translation which accurately reflected the vocabulary of the period under study in the article, I settled on "virago," the term used in Magnus Hirschfeld's *Sexual Anomalies* (New York, Emerson Books, 1948), 190.

*[Translator's note] The German term *conträre Sexualempfindung* has been translated as "contrary sexual mentality," "antipathic sexual instinct," "contrary sexual feeling," and "inverted sexuality." The contemporary literature usually calls it "sexual inversion" or "homosexuality." This, however, oversimplifies the meaning of the term used by sexologists of the period. In their attempts to classify sexual behaviors, they constructed a scale of physiological and pscyhological characteristics with the "traditionally" masculine and feminine heterosexual types at either end. The scale then included a series of "intermediate sexual types" (transvestites, hermaphrodites, androgynes, etc.). The term *inverted sexual temperament* refers to those on this scale who have the physiology of one sex, but (supposedly) the sexual psychology of the other, and who feel, therefore, as the opposite sex does toward their own sex. (See the literature listed in the author's notes.)

cian." Miss N. entered the hospital on April 30, 1864, and her medical record stated the following reason for having committed her:

> Miss N. has allegedly suffered since she was *8 years old* from a mania of loving women and, furthermore, of playing, kissing, and masturbating with them.[2]

With Miss N.'s story, the psychiatrist Westphal wrote up the first case study of a lesbian in German medical history.[3] Although he had only one example, he established categorically what woman-love was and the distinguishing characteristics of women-loving women:

> There is no question that in the case of this 35 year-old girl, the phenomenon of an inverted sexual temperament, the feeling she has of being masculine, has been with her since childhood. It is independent of any intentional or misleading self-deception.[4]

And further:

> As our case teaches us, perhaps for the first time, we may take it for granted that in men . . . as well as in women, an inverted sexual temperament is *congenital.* A man feels like a woman; a woman like a man.[5]

With this summary of his work on Miss N., Westphal established the foundation for his theory of the inverted sexual temperament. Despite the obvious limitations of his research, the description and interpretation of the case of this one woman served as the point of departure for all further analyses of such sexual behavior for the next fifty years.

"Acting Assistant Physician" H. Gock of the Psychiatric Clinic in Würzburg was inspired by Westphal's study. In 1875 he published— also in the *Archive for Psychiatry*—his own contribution to help clarify the "peculiar condition of the congenital inversion of the sexual temperament."[6]

> On May 24 of this year, a Jewish servant girl, *Jette B.*, 28 years old, came of her own free will to the psychiatric ward in Julius Hospital. She stated that she felt sick and unhappy, that she was totally miserable and wanted most of all to die. (The patient had attempted to drown herself a few days earlier.) Asked why she felt so miserable, she indicated, without hesitation, and in a lucid manner, that she was in love with her girl friend; she had had this passion for a long time, and had already struggled against it, because *she recognized it was morbid.* However, she could not control her feelings. She only thought about her girl friend. If she could embrace and kiss her just once—but she did

not dare admit her wish to her girl friend—then perhaps she would feel better. On many occasions she got angry for she could not embrace her girl friend when she felt driven to do so. Afterwards, she would become indifferent to everything going on around her; she could not work and *stared blankly ahead,* still always thinking about her girl friend. Now she desperately wished to be helped in the Hospital. But, she added immediately, she could not really be helped anymore. She was so immersed in her thoughts of love, "that she had forgotten her own ego."

For Gock, Jette B.'s life history suggested "obvious analogies to Professor Westphal's serious case," and he described his patient in terms of Westphal's theory of women-loving women. However, both his description of the "interesting pathological structure" of Jette B. and Westphal's original essay on Miss N.'s life contradicted the proposed theory. The two women served, supposedly, as proof for the thesis that the "inversion of the sexual temperament" existed in the "female" when she "has the feeling she is a masculine being." Yet Westphal and Gock provided case histories of women who had no such "feeling."

If we summarize the "truly compelling similarity"[7] between the two women, the following emerges: Both women reported that they had no interest in men at all. Jette B. "says she has never had any contact with men, because she is not interested in them in the least. Yes, at times she has even felt a real repulsion towards men, excepting those who have something womanish in their appearance and behavior."[8] Westphal reported, "According to [Miss N.'s] own statements, the patient never had even the slightest interest in men, and talking about the subject left her completely cold; she declared with great confidence that she could live and sleep among men without any excitement."[9] Both loved women in their childhood days. Miss N. experienced her first love at the age of eight: "from her *eighth year* on she felt an attraction to young girls, not to *all,* but to very *particular* ones, who captivated her from the *first encounter*"[10] At the age of twelve and a half, Jette B. felt herself attracted to girls for the first time, that is, to "very particular" ones.[11] Both Jette B. and Miss N. told their doctors that they had been attracted by a special "expression in the eyes." Miss N. explained: "It is strange, it is in the eye—it is a kind of magnetism which attracts me."[12]

At the time they entered the hospitals, the two women were in love with women who did not love them in return, and this led, in both cases, to enormous distress. The doctors indicated that, due to this unrequited love, the women felt that their love for women was "morbid." Both Westphal and Gock observed disapprovingly that although the women had indeed recognized their "morbid condition," Jette B. "did not in the least realize its full significance,"[13] and "a more complex, true understanding of the occurrences and relationships connected with her condition eluded Miss N."[14] Undoubtedly the doctors made these judgmental comments, because each of the women had her own idea about her "recovery." Jette B. thought "she would only become healthy, if she could just once really embrace and kiss her girl friend."[15] Miss N. considered her commitment and treatment senseless because her excited state had been "a more than understandable result of her girl friend's behavior."[16] The beloved girl had indeed created a violent scene when Miss N. made advances and expressed her love. This led to Miss N.'s "intense excitation," and in turn to her hospitalization at Charité.

Miss N. and Jette B. worked in domestic service. Jette B. took care of children; Miss N. directed the "household" of an older sister, "who had founded a boarding school for young girls." Both wished they could change jobs. Miss N. told her doctor, "Feminine occupations were always abhorrent to me; I want to have a masculine occupation. For example, I have always been interested in machine building."[17] Gock wrote about Jette B.: "She was not acquainted with any of the better feminine handicrafts, and during instruction she showed herself to be most incapable of learning such skills."[18]

It was the fate of Miss N. and Jette B. to serve as "proof" for Krafft-Ebing's theory about "female-loving females." R. von Krafft-Ebing, psychiatrist in Graz (later Vienna) and one of the best-known representatives of his profession, dealt with "inverted sexuality" for the first time in 1877. In his essay, "Concerning Certain Anomalies of Sexual Instinct and the Medical Forensic Evaluation of the Same as a Probable Functional Degeneration of the Central Nervous System," which also appeared in the *Archive for Psychiatry,* he summarized the previously collected information about this "enigmatic phenomenon."[19] Applauding the "empirical method" used by psychiatrists and the knowledge gained therefrom, he went on to discuss only nine cases of male inverted sexuality and two lesbian women. Krafft-Ebing considered this to be a thoroughly reliable sample on which to base his theory and went on to proclaim that his conclusions were universally valid.[20] Miss N.'s story, described by Westphal, and Jette B.'s life, interpreted by Gock, now came to serve as proof for Krafft-Ebing's theory.

In 1886 Krafft-Ebing published his famous book *Pyschopathia Sexualis,* which was printed fourteen times in German and in several foreign translations. It became known the world over. In this book, "inverted sexuality" received special consideration and Krafft-Ebing described the sexual inclinations of "female-loving females." No longer depending solely on Westphal and Gock, he based his findings on two of his "own observations," and recorded what was, in his estimation, typical of women-loving women.

> The female-loving female feels sexually like a man; she takes plea-sure in proclamations of courage, of masculine bravado, because these qualities make the man desirable to the female. The woman homosex-ual, therefore, loves to wear her hair in a masculine manner and it is her greatest joy to appear occasionally in masculine attire. She is only interested in masculine occupations, games and pleasures. Her ideals are those female personalities known for their intellect and admirable deeds. In the theater and in the circus, it is only female artists who command her attention, just as in art exhibits only female statues and pictures awaken her aesthetic sensibility and her sensuality.[21]

This pronouncement in the guise of scholarship should be more closely examined. Krafft-Ebing formulated a theory here which is contradictory in and of itself. Moreover, this contradiction has the distinctive function of declaring woman-love to be nonexistent. On the one hand he argued that the love women have for members of their own sex arises from a deeply rooted, "innate," "congenital" masculine identity, which leads to masculine behavioral traits. Yet on the other hand, he said, such women are forced by circumstances to behave like men because only then will they be desirable to the "fems," whose "innate" sexual interest is directed toward men. So, while Krafft-Ebing posited a same-sex identity with the man as the reason for the love for one's own sex, he also maintained that "masculine" behavior appears as a mere reaction to the "desire" for "fems," that is, a necessary adjustment to external conditions. In both arguments, men play the leading roles. That women might love women because they are women did not even occur to Krafft-Ebing. He could not see this as an expression of relationships within the feminine sex. In-stead—by authority of masculine fantasy—he described it in terms of the predominance of the masculine sex.

The claim made by Westphal and Krafft-Ebing that women-loving women strive for sexual and emotional identity with men lays the foundation for subsequent psychiatric and popular publications on the theme. From the countless number of works, I want to mention a few typical examples.

Between 1900 and 1914, W. Hammer, physician in Berlin, published a series of essays about women-loving women, some of which were printed in popular-science magazines and became quite well known.[22] He added "major symptoms" to Krafft-Ebing's catalog. The uranian, as he called the woman-loving woman, "is not inhibited in male society; a vigorously robust, self-confident style distinguishes her from her sisters"; "her gait is usually firm," her "stride is long." "She meets men's gaze with self-confidence"; "her manner of expression is usually clear." "Blushing in the company of men" is unknown to her; "a flush of anger [is] more likely." She is conspicuous because of her "gift of precise judgment" and "rhetorical capabilities." She shows "clarity of thought and relentless consistency in the formation of her judgments and conclusions, such as are otherwise seldom developed to this extent among the fair sex." All of these traits were supposedly masculine and thus—according to Hammer—permitted the "practiced observer to distinguish the uranian from the average girl with some certainty, even on the basis of external appearance." Of course he also mentioned the "short cut of the hair" and the "preference for men's clothes" as distinguishing characteristics.

A. Forel, psychiatrist in Zurich, published his book entitled *The Sexual Question* in 1907. It appeared in a "scholarly" and a "popular" edition in several printings. He wrote in terms almost identical to those of Hammer about women-loving women.

> The uranian woman, however, feels like a man. The idea of sexual contact with men is abhorrent to her. She loves mostly to wear men's clothes and she assumes masculine habits.[23]

I. Bloch, who considered himself the "father of sexology," created a similar image of the woman-loving woman in his famous book *Sexual Life in Our Times* (1906). But he went one step beyond the previous theorists, describing the anomalies, which were supposedly observable in women-loving women, as physical anomalies:

> The same-sex instinct appears often long before puberty, where even in external appearance the girl differs from her heterosexual girl comrades. Sometimes there are suggestions of a masculine body structure (weak development of breasts, narrow pelvis, development of a mustache, deep voice, etc.), but these may also be absent.[24]

In 1925 B. Bauer, a specialist in gynecology, published a sequel to his book *How Are You Female?* (1924) with the revealing title *The Female and Love.* Devoting an entire chapter to women-loving women ("Errant and Deviant Paths to Love"), Bauer summarized earlier themes on the subject and emphasized in particular the aggressiveness of women-loving women, which he attributed to their masculine psyche.

> We also find here the active, initiating, masculine type, who in outer behavior and gesture lets herself be known as a "virago." Even in her

style of lovemaking she assumes the role of the man, in the sense that she mimes the passionate lover by means of the circuitous route of masturbation and other love games. She torments the beloved female not infrequently with the most insane jealousy; not over men, but exclusively over women.[25]

M. Hirschfeld, physician for nervous and psychic disorders in Berlin, Head of the Scientific Humanitarian Committee[26] and publisher of *The Yearbook for Intermediate Sexual Types*,[27] also accepted the positions established in psychiatry at the time, but went farther on one point. In contrast to his colleagues in the profession, he designated even the "female-identified female individuals" as "innately" homosexual. Despite this theoretical refinement, he still characterized masculine-female and feminine-female homosexuals according to the already familiar conventions. In his book *Homosexuality of Man and Woman*, published in 1914, he wrote:

> Here also a type of women can be found who exhibits something decidedly virile in costume, hairstyle, stance and gesture, and in her manner of speaking, drinking and smoking. Many also have a rough, deep voice, strong masculine facial features, small hips, as well as a bone structure in general reminiscent of the "stronger" sex. Among themselves they frequently give their names a virile form. In addition, however, there exists a group of homosexual women, *not fewer in number*, who on the surface can hardly be distinguished from other women of their social sphere. They wear make-up and hairstyles according to the same fashion as other women, disdain neither corsets, nor high heels, and appear in their expression of feeling, taste and thought so thoroughly feminine, that no one would consider them to be homosexual. And yet they are this in exactly as fixated a manner as their virile companions in misfortune.[28]

Although Hirschfeld conceded that these—as he expressed it— feminine-style female homosexuals were homosexual in "just as fixated a manner" as their "virile companions in misfortune," he described them nevertheless as a distinct group and attributed competitive behavior to them:

> While feminine-style homosexual women want to know nothing of the "viragos," masculine-style homosexuals, for their part, make fun of homosexual "fems."[29]

Still, he maintained, only the "masculine-style virago" and the "feminine-style fem" can enter into a love relationships with one another.

The more femininity is in her and the less she deviates from the norm, the more she loves women who have masculine characteristics— powerful, intellectually strong females, artists, writers; and the more virile she herself is, the more she feels attracted to young, genuinely feminine girls.[30]

In sum, according to the logic of the psychiatrists discussed here, a "virago" must desire a "fem" or be desired by a "fem." The love of one "virago" for another, or one "fem" for another, was entirely out of the question. Once the category "fem" emerged as a complementary counterpart of the "virago," a system to describe her behavior also had to be formulated. The system of norms used for the "virago" and the "fem" was based on the heterosexual, standardized couple rela- tionship. Thus, the "virago" was supposed to attempt to subjugate the "fem," turn her into a housewife; and the "fem", accordingly, was supposed to want to be subjugated. While the psychiatrists all agreed that the "virago" was innately homosexual, most of them, with the exception of Hirschfeld, classified the "fem" as an innately heterosex- ual women who was seduced into woman loving.

From his first essay on inverted sexuality (1877), Krafft-Ebing had already differentiated between two groups of inverted temperaments:

In the attempt to fathom the essence and significance of this enig- matic phenomenon, it becomes necessary to divide the available mate- rial into two groups: a) cases in which the inverted sexual temperament is a congenital phenomenon, habitual for the individual, and at the same time the only possibility for sexual functioning; b) cases in which the inverted sexual temperament is in no way congenital, but reveals itself to be a temporary anomaly in an individual capable of other (and normal) forms of sexual intercourse.[31]

Krafft-Ebing classified women who had an innate sexual inversion in the category of "perversion." Those belonging to the group of the noninnate, he classified in the category of "perversity." Perversion, for him, was a "disease", perversity a "vice."[32]

The innate homosexual woman was the "male-identified female individual," the noninnate was the "female-identified female individ- ual," a heterosexual woman who was seduced into homosexuality. In 1906 Bloch made up the terms *pseudo-homosexual* and *pseudo-homosex- uality* for the group of so-called noninnate homosexuals, in order, so he explained, "to express correctly the fundamental distinction be- tween them and the genuine homosexuals." In his further discussions he said that pseudo-homosexuality was primarily a "female" phenom- enon.

> If compared with male homosexuals, the number of real female homosexuals, the "viragos," "sapphists" or "tribades" is relatively small, while the number of so-called pseudo-homosexuals is far greater than among men. . . . If one attends, for example, a male-urning's ball, one can be sure that 99% of the male homosexuals gathered there are genuine homosexuals, but at a female-urnings's ball—even these can be found in Berlin—certainly a much smaller percentage is "genuine"; the majority is composed of female pseudo-homosexuals.[33]

Other authors also differentiated between the high incidence of innate homosexuality among men and the predominance of pseudo-homosexuality among women. They attributed this difference—as they called it—to women's friendships, to their exchanges of tenderness and caresses, the likes of which would be unthinkable between men. So, wrote Bloch:

> For the heterosexual man it is usually impossible to empathize with a homosexual way of feeling, or to acquire a taste for homosexual acts. This comes much more easily to the heterosexual woman. Even between normal heterosexual women tenderness and caresses play a role. This helps us understand the easy appearance of pseudo-homosexual tendencies.[34]

According to Forel, for example, such women's friendships facilitated the "virago's" seduction of a "fem."

> When a homosexual female wants to seduce a normal girl, she usually succeeds easily by rousing the same enthusiastic love, which is not very unusual for the feminine disposition, even with regard to other women. Kisses, embraces, lying together in bed, caresses etc., are much less peculiar among girls than among boys, and do not usually elicit disgust even in the normal female, who becomes the object of such affections.[35]

What the authors called a "lack of repulsion towards intimate physical contact with a member of the same sex"[36] became, therefore, the main cause for so-called pseudo-homosexuality among women. Such an explanation is both a monstrous and helpless reinterpretation of why women love women and it forces us to suspect that the scholarly formulation serves to hide, rather than reveal, the cause: "Lack of repulsion" toward women should read "lack of attraction toward men."

Those writing about female homosexuality complained regularly that women felt an "enthusiastic, spiritual inclination toward, and a "physical intimacy"[37] with their girl friends. In 1907 Dr. Philos discussed this phenomenon at some length:

from youth onwards we are accustomed to see intimate love relations between females. We perceive kissing, embracing, the exchange of caresses and flattery of females with each other to be natural, perhaps at times somewhat laughable, but never offensive to our sense of purity and modesty, to our sense of decency. . . . The everyday sight of effusive feminine affections permitted clever female homosexuals to demonstrate completely openly their inclination toward the beloved of the same sex, without those around them becoming aware of anything other than a somewhat exaggerated, passionate friendship.[38]

Doctors cited still other causes which were supposed to explain why it was easy for women to seduce women. Krafft-Ebing, for example, mentioned *"faute de mieux* homosexual intercourse" among inmates in prison and among daughters of the upper class; the latter were protected from seduction by men and/or were afraid of pregnancy. He called such cases "cultivated inverted sexuality." Seduction, of course, was the necessary prerequisite to initiate women into *"faute de mieux* intercourse": "Frequently female servants are the seducers; sometimes it is sexually inverted girl friends, and even teachers in boarding schools."[39]

By introducing the categories "virago" and "pseudo-homosexual," those writing on the subject attempted to confine homosexual women within standardized norms. As soon as one subgroup of women was classified as "viragos," all others became potential "pseudo-homosexuals," that is, innately heterosexual, but at any time vulnerable to homosexuality, potential victims of the "viragos." Women identified as "virago" became the seducers, a danger to all other women. The way these authors diagnosed "virago" seduction followed the logic of masculine thinking about male sexuality. From the authors' point of view, it was clearly the masculine psyche (which male authors of course knew very well, or believed they did) which compelled the "virago" to seduce women again and again. The same masculine psyche prevented the love of one "virago" for another, just as the feminine psyche would make the love of two non-"viragos" for one another impossible. Some authors went so far as to maintain that "viragos" could only be each other's enemies.[40]

While the psychiatric texts described the "virago" as a seducer, pornographic writings of the period portrayed her as a rapist of women.[41] In doing so, the pornographic literature corresponded to masculine logic just as much as the scientific works did. The "viragos" seduced/raped non-"viragos" and made them "pseudo-homosexuals." "Viragos" were branded nonwomen, deprived of membership to the female sex, and assigned to a category of monsters. Moreover, women-loving women were divided from one another into the genuine, the "virago," and the false, the "pseudo-homosexual."

We see the creation of the figure of the "virago" and the invention of the special category of the "pseudo-homosexual" as an attempt to divide women from one another. Within the limits circumscribed around women loving, women had precious little space to move beyond heterosexuality. Moreover, this scientific approach defined all love friendships among women according to the standardized power relationships (masculine/feminine, active/passive, aggressive/submissive, seducer/seduced) which had been established since the eighteenth century.

It is important to question the historical significance of the theories of human sexuality which arose during the second half of the nineteenth century and remained very popular until the 1920s. Unfortunately women's scholarship in Germany is not advanced enough to do so adequately. If space permitted, we might begin to approach the subject here, however, by considering historical developments between the eighteenth and twentieth centuries. In particular, it would be valuable to examine the new research on the "polarization" of women's and men's spheres,[42] the emerging definitions of gender in the literature of the biological sciences in the nineteenth century, and the transformations of the social significance of "sexuality" in general.[43] It would also be worthwhile to look for connections between the theories of sexologists and the reality of women as home workers,[44] as well as for the connections between home workers and those in the first feminist movement. Representatives of the women's movement were frequently defamed for being "masculine" or "lesbian"; and, in fact, some of these early feminists did enter into "masculine" spheres and/or were "lesbian."[45]

How do we serve women today, and what do we contribute to historical research about women and lesbians, when we study texts like the ones here and expose their contradictions and male-identified classifications? What happens to women's history in the process? I think that by analyzing these very influential texts, many of which inspired contemporary theories about women and lesbians, we begin to dissolve some of the ossified concepts about lesbians and women. The texts I have examined reveal ideas, opinions, and clichés which still receive serious attention today, even among lesbians and heterosexual women themselves.

In Europe we have just begun to do historical research on women-loving women, on women who considered themselves to be lesbians or whom we, for many reasons, have decided to call "lesbian" even if they themselves did not use the term.[46] What we have learned in the last few years is that friendship and love between women have historically changeable forms. As we try to place the nineteenth- and early twentieth-century male theories about women into proper historical context, we have come to understand that we must do more than simply show that lesbians "in reality" were totally different from the way male scholars diagnosed them. For if we talk about these women only in relation to the male categories, we make women's history entirely dependent upon men's history.

In the last third of the nineteenth century, men created the "virago" and made her the main category of lesbian. Since it could not describe lesbian reality, they subsequently invented the "pseudo-homosexual." The work of these male theorists occurred during the very same time period which produced both a transformation in the relations between the two sexes and an organized women's resistance to the new forms of gender relations that were emerging, i.e., the women's movement. When women refused to accept the new norms, people, especially men, frequently understood this resistance as "masculine" behavior and attacked it as such. In 1904 Johanna Elberskirchen, author and women's rights advocate, published a fiery protest against theories and theoreticians which attempted to lock women-loving women into this framework:

> It is said that the love a woman has for another woman shows a propensity for the masculine—just as emancipation does. The woman is striving, grasping for "specifically masculine" character traits and "specifically masculine" professions. . . . What is the essence of homosexuality, of love of one's own sex? Of course, the exclusion of the opposite sex, the masculine, or the feminine, respectively. How can the love of one woman for another woman show a propensity for the masculine? It is the masculine which is being excluded. One could almost maintain just the opposite and say that when a woman loves a woman, the propensity for the feminine is manifested! And in fact this is the case. The male or female homosexual loves his or her own sex. It is always both, not only one member of the union who loves his or her own sex in the other, and has more or less turned away from the opposite sex. So when two women love one another, this interesting fact is by no means explained by saying that the one represents the man, she feels masculine; and the other represents the woman, she feels feminine, therefore normal! If the one felt feminine in a normal way, her instinct would necessarily drive her to a man, to the normal man! *Both* feel abnormal, both feel feminine.
>
> *Both* are driven by *instinct to the woman, to their own sex.* Both love in the other the same sex—the feminine. Not the masculine. Otherwise a

homosexual relationship would simply not be possible. Therefore, we are dealing here with a propensity for the feminine—on the part of the feminine for the feminine.

In conclusion, she continues,

And furthermore, if we women in the movement for emancipation are homosexual, then let us be so! Then it is our own good right to be so. Whom does it concern? Really only those who are homosexual. Those who have to reconcile themselves to their abnormality, as others do to their normality.[47]

Notes

1. C. Westphal, "Die conträre Sexualempfindung. Symptom eines neuropatischen (psychopatischen) Zustandes," in *Archiv für Psychiatrie und Nervenkrankheiten* 2 (1869): 73–108. Westphal's article was the first psychiatric treatment of homosexuality in women. Compare *Der unterdrückte Sexus. Historische Texte und Kommentare zur Homosexualität*, ed. by J. S. Hohamm (Lollar/Lahn, 1977).

2. Westphal, "Die conträre Sexualempfindung," 73.

3. The "established" term for women who love women today is again *Sapphist,* after the poet Sappho, who lived around 600 B.C. on the island of Lesbos and loved women. From Sappho's times to the middle of the nineteenth century women who loved women were called Sapphists. They "embraced lesbian, or Sapphist love," as the *Brockhaus* [a standard German encyclopedia, J. R.] expressed it. Another—though in German less used—term for women-loving women was the concept which arose from Latin: *tribadism, tribades.* The psychiatrists who were working on the new image of women-loving women after the middle of the fifteenth century gave designations *Sapphist* and *tribade* another content. From then on the term *Sapphist* or *tribade* no longer applied to *all* women-loving women. For some authors the concept *Sapphist* was only supposed to be applicable to bisexual women; others wanted to apply the term only to the so-called pseudo-homosexuals; still others thought that only the innately homosexual woman should be called a Sapphist. The concept *tribade* and the name constructed by K. H. Ulrichs in 1868, namely *Uranian,* were used only for the so-called "virago." Lesbian women themselves weren't much concerned with this struggle about terminology. They adopted—at least in their publications—none of these names. They called themselves simply girlfriends and women who love women. The recently organized lesbian movement, which originated in Berlin around 1970, distanced itself both from the concept "homosexual woman" and from the designation "Sapphist." They called themselves lesbians, and still do today.

4. Westphal, "Die conträre Sexualempfindung," 91.

5. *Ibid.,* 94.

6. H. Gock, "Beitrag zur Kenntnis der conträren Sexualempfindung," in *Archiv für Psychiatrie und Nervenkrankheiten* 5 (1875): 564–75; quote 564, following quotes 565.

7. *Ibid.*, 571.
8. *Ibid.*, 566.
9. Westphal, "Die conträre Sexualempfindung," 76.
10. *Ibid.*, 75.
11. Gock, "Beitrag zur Kenntnis," 566.
12. Westphal, "Die conträre Sexualempfindung," 75.
13. Gock, "Beitrag zur Kenntnis," 572.
14. Westphal, "Die conträre Sexualempfindung," 80.
15. Gock, "Beitrag zur Kenntnis," 572.
16. Westphal, "Die conträre Sexualempfindung," 81.
17. *Ibid.*, 74, 80.
18. Gock, "Beitrag zur Kenntnis," 572.
19. Compare R. v. Krafft-Ebing, *Psychopathia Sexualis*, 7th edition, (Stuttgart, 1903), 42.
20. "Sexual inclination towards the same sexs [is present when]: 1. Man to man (3.4.5.6.7.8.9.10.11.), and specifically in the sexual role of the female (3.11, Zastrow felt like a female at least in his erotic dreams), or without a specific sexual role (3.7.9.10.). 2. Female to female (1.5), whereby the individual feels like a man." [The numbers in the quote refer to the individual "cases"; 1. represents Miss N., 5. represents Jette B.] R. v. Krafft-Ebing, "Uber gewisse Anomalien des Geschlechtstriebes und die klinisch-forensische Verwertung derselben als eines wahrscheinlich functionellen Degenerationszeichens des centralen Nervensystems," in *Archiv für Psychiatrie und Nervenkrankheiten* 7 (1877): 305–312, quote 307.
21. R. v. Krafft-Ebing. *Psychopathia Sexualis. Eine klinisch-forensische Studie*, 2nd edition (Stuttgart, 1887). 65 f. *Uranism, Urning, Uranien, Urninde:* Catalog of concepts developed by K. H. Ulrichs in 1868. *Uranian, urninde* are used as designations for the so-called innately (or congenitally) woman-loving woman.
22. Among other places, he published his articles in the popular science studies called "Metropolis Documents," which were published by Hans Oswald around the turn of the century. They were primarily concerned with "sexual problems." See W. Hammer, "Die Tribade Berlins. Zehn Fälle weib-weiblicher Geschlechtsliebe aktenmässig dargestellt nebst zehn Abhandlungen über die gleichgeschlechtliche Frauenliebe," in *Grosstadt-Dokumente* (Berlin and Leipzig, no year [1902]); quotes according to the 3rd edition (1906), 30 f.
23. A. Forel, *Die sexuelle Frage. Eine naturwissenschaftliche, psychologische, hygienische und soziologische Studie für Gebildete* (Munich, 1907), 268. The abbreviated popular edition appeared in 1913.
24. I. Block, *Das Sexualleben in unserer Zeit in seinen Beziehungen zur modernen Kultur* (1908), 12th edition (Berlin, 1919), 555.
25. B. Bauer, *Weib und Liebe. Studie über das Liebesleben des Weibes.* (Vienna, Leipzig, 1925), 458.
26. The Scientific-Humanitarian Committee was founded by M. Hirschfeld in 1897. It was the first organization of homosexuals in Germany and existed until 1933. Its main goals were the removal of Paragraph 175, which punished homosexual acts between men, from the Penal Code and the enlightenment of the public about homosexuality.
27. The yearbooks were a publication of the Scientific-Humanitarian Committee from 1899 to 1923.

28. M. Hirschfeld, *Die Homosexualität des Mannes und des Weibes* (1914); 2nd edition (Berlin, 1920), 271.

29. *Ibid.*, 272.

30. *Ibid.*, 276. M. Hirschfeld is still known today as a "fighter for the rights of homosexuals." He can just as well enter history as a "despiser of women" since he maintained, among other things, no woman could be raped if she didn't want this herself. Hirschfeld wrote expert opinions in rape trials! Compare M. Hirschfeld *Geschlechtskunde. Aufgrund dreissigjähriger Forschung und Erfahrung*, 2 vols., *Folgen und Folgerungen* (Stuttgart, 1928).

31. Krafft-Ebing, *Uber gewisse Anomalien*, 306.

32. Compare C. Laker, "Uber eine besondere Form von verkehrter Richtung ('Perversion') des weiblichen Geschlechtstriebes," in *Archiv für Gynaekologie* 34 (1889): 293–3–0, 293.

33. Block, *Das Sexualleben in unserer zeit*, 555. Tribadism, tribades (gr.), Expression for women-loving women, known since the Roman Empire. Is used from about 1870 for so-called innately homosexual women.

34. *Ibid.*, 554.

35. Forel, *Die sexuelle Frage*, 268.

36. I. F. W. Eberhard, *Die Frauenemanzipation und ihre erotische Grundlage* (Vienna, Leipzig, 1924), 510.

37. *Ibid.*

38. Dr. Philos, "Die lesbische Liebe. Ein Beitrag zur Sittengeschichte unserer Zeit," in *Zur Psychologie unserer Zeit* (Berlin, Leipzig, 1907), Book 9, p. 8.

39. R. v. Krafft-Ebing, "Neue Studien auf dem Gebiet der Homosexualität," in *Jahrbuch für sexuelle Zwischenstufen* 3 (1901), 24 f.

40. Eberhard, *Die Frauenemanzipation*, 511.

41. Of the many pornographic texts, which always contain a passage in which a "Sapphist" rapes a woman, we mention the following here: H. H. Ewers, *Vampyre* (Berlin, 1903); F. Rodenstein, *Lingramfeste* (Berlin, 1908); A. Pithon, *Das Quartier der Sappho* (Leipzig, ca. 1890). As opposed to the books which appeared after 1890, the novel *Anandria, Bekenntnisse der mademoiselle Sappho* (Paris 1770, German edition in a translation by H. Conrad, Berlin 1907) contains no relationships that follow the rules of heterosexual couples nor any rape scenes.

42. Compare K. Hausen, "Die Polarisierung der 'Geschlechtscharaktere'," in *Sozialgeschichte der Familie in der Neuzeit Europas*, ed. by W. Conze (Stuttgart, 1976), 363–93 and B. Duden, "Das schöne Eigentum. Zur Herausbildung des bürgerlichen Frauenbildes an der Wende vom 18. zum 19. Jahrhundert," in *Kursbuch* 47 (Berlin, 1977): 125–42.

43. Compare M. Foucault, *Sexualität und Wahrheit* (Frankfurt/M., 1979).

44. Compare G. Bock and B. Duden, "Arbeit aus Liebe—Liebe aus Arbeit. Zur Entstehung der Hausarbeit im Kapitalismus," in *Frauen und Wissenschaft* (Berlin, 1977), 118–99.

45. Compare here L. Fadermann, *Surpassing the Love of Men. Romantic Friendship and Love between Women from the Renaissance to the Present* (New York, 1981); C. Smith-Rosenberg, "The Female World of Love and Ritual. Relations between Women in the 19th Century of America," in *Signs* 1 (1975): 1–29 (German in *Listen der Ohnmacht. Zur Sozialgeschichte weiblicher Widerstandsformen*, ed. by C. Honnegger, B. Heintz, (Frankfurt, 1981), 365–92. See also the autobiographical works of Ch. Wolff, *On the Way to Myself* (London, 1969); *An Older Love* (London, 1976); *Hindsight* (London, 1980); and her

investigations: *Love between Women* (London, 1971) and *Bisexuality* (London, 1977).

46. Women-loving women called themselves in the nineteenth century girl friends, or women who love women. See also B. W. Cook, "Women and Support Networks" (New York, 1979); B. W. Cook, "Women Alone Stir My Imagination. Lesbianism and the Cultural Tradition," in *Signs* 5 (1979): 718–39; L. J. Rupp, "Imagine my Surprise. Women's Relationships in Historical Perspective," in *Frontiers, A Journal of Women Studies* 5:3 (1980): 61–70; *Weibliche Homosexualität um 1900 in zeitgenössischen Texten,* ed. by I. Kokula (Munich, 1981) (anthology).

47. J. Elberskirchen, *Was hat der Mann aus Weib, Kind und sich gemacht? Revolution und Erlösung des Weibes. Eine Abrechnung mit dem Mann. Ein Wegweiser in die Zukunft* (Leipzig, 1904), 3, 9.

FEMINISM AND LITERARY CRITICISM
REFLECTIONS ON THE DISCIPLINARY APPROACH

Marcelle Marini
Translated by Carol Barko

I am called a "feminist literary critic": a label given me by my friends and enemies (male and female), which, then, certainly must have a meaning; but does it mean anything other than being socially, politically, indeed polemically oriented? I consider it first as equivalent to an identity card: sex? female; occupation? university professor and literary critic; political affiliation? Women's Liberation Movement.[1] Now, just as happens to other women in other areas of society, the third characteristic emerges here out of the difficulty—or from the present impossibility—of clearly expressing the first two; that is, of being recognized, as women, for our ability and our right to create— and not only to procreate—to maintain and transmit—various forms of language, of sociocultural organization, and, in a broader way, a picture of society which unites a community around shared symbolic values.

In literature and literary criticism, the areas that concern us, once we stop tackling only the most glaring effects of sexual inequality to try to compensate for them, and tackle the very roots of the system, by inquiring in what name one of the two sociosexual groups would hold the power, in its own hands, to symbolize the whole of human experience for both groups, we cause a fundamental shift: no longer are we limiting our criticism solely to *terms used* which, linked in complex ways to existing social *practices*, pretend to define, to determine, to picture and theorize about the difference of the sexes; we are questioning *how the terms work*, which is linked to social *practice* itself. What is at stake thus goes beyond our place within the establishment. It involves denouncing the insult made to women when they are denied the possibility, individually or collectively, of being creators of culture in the same way as men.

Any woman, in whatever circumstance, who speaks up in public to tell, along with her history, her experience and, in her words, how she sees the world, what she refuses, what she desires, what inventive solutions for the future she suggests, is disturbing the principle which is supposed to govern the socialization process. For she is demonstrating, be it for a brief moment of daring, that *homo faber-socius-loquens-sapiens-*etc. means, well! . . . woman as well as man. She reveals, even fleetingly, what is deliberately hidden: the monopolization (constant monopolization) in every instance *here and now,* by one sex, of abilities nevertheless attributed to human beings in general and, through this same occasion, the wealth and power that derive from them. Through this fact, popular and scholarly theories that present the inequality between the sexes as the basic act of all socialization show themselves for what they are: as attempts to legitimize actual violence, by ascribing sexual inequality to an initial cause—natural, transcendental, or historical, depending on the circumstance—but always protected from being truly called into question.

With even more reason, women who reflect on their condition in order to end it are led to withdraw their support for the belief that serves as a pact with the society in which they live: the belief that makes the male sex the indisputable model of the defined human subject, according to Levi-Strauss's expression, through man's aptitude for "taking apart and putting together nature and society."[2] So these women are intervening in every area to exercise their power of thinking, of innovation, of initiative, and of decision: within the family, in the professions, in trade unions, culture, religion, law, politics, etc. One can understand that their primary concern will not be to honor either the compartmentalization or the hierarchies conventionally set up among the various types of power, knowledge, and social roles. From their point of view, what pertains to culture is no more at odds with what pertains to economics or politics than the private is opposed to the public sphere and the individual to the societal, even if there is good reason to distinguish them from each other. It is, therefore, a culture—in the anthropological sense of the term—in dispute: customs, creations, and institutions which, through their interdependence as with their conflicts, make up a society to give it its particular character. And the dispute touches both their two aspects, impossible to separate in the reality of experience—I would say their double aspect: material and symbolic.

We are asking questions which, though trite, are nonetheless basic. For example: in literature and in literary criticism, who is writing what, for whom, and in what contexts? In the framework of what inherited or adopted kinds of speech? From what position in the society? At what moment in a remarkable history enmeshed in the intersecting links of a domestic history which itself is enmeshed in the history of a community made up of different kinds of continuity, of breaking apart, of dissimilar events? And further, who is entitled to speak the language in these places? Who receives social recognition, meaning entrée into the culture referred to as typical, when it isn't universal? By virtue of what criteria? But also; in schools, in universities, in publishing, the various media, what is read and what are people made to read; therefore, what is actualized? Why? And how does one read and teach others to read? What models of literary writing, of reading, of critical writing are favored as valid for everyone, even if, or because, they are in the possession of an elite that calls itself enlightened? In our Western society, what modes of speech are enshrined, while others are rejected for being naive, inconsequential, inadequate, too specific, indeed peculiar, to the point of being doomed to oblivion or to the garbage of the official culture? What processes of knowledge and what types of knowledge are ranked at the top of a given hierarchy as taken for granted? And how are individuals and social groups divided up with respect to this hierarchy? Who, in the end, is credited—and by whom?—with originality, with definite inventiveness, with radically new ideas and ways of seeing things? What, moreover, is the validity of those notions that continue—even among the most vociferous detractors of the author's name—nevertheless to appoint the founders-creators-masters? Symbolic kinship, problems of birthright, of inheritance, and of usurpation, are serious matters in our cultural history.

I could go on, but the essential of what I am saying stands in this observation which comes out of our long experience: if, when we ask these questions on behalf of underprivileged classes, of popular, regional, black, non-Western cultures, of religious minorities, etc., they tend to provoke violent controversies, they nonetheless remain admissible, as if we were respecting an unwritten rule demanding that the male always be the legitimate representative of his group (ethnic, social, cultural, and even biological). In contrast, should we ask these questions from our concrete experience as women who live, read, write, think in the society that is ours, we are immediately recalled to order: our intelligence is wanting. Or are we just being stubbornly persistent? In that case, bluntly, we are endangering The Culture. It seems unthinkable that we are exercising the quite ordinary right to contribute to changing certain ways in which our culture operates that do not suit us.

The problem (and the outrage) of "selecting a special group of speaking subjects,"[3] which Michel Foucault has clearly analyzed as being a pretense to the universality of the language(s) of the dominant with respect to the language(s) of the dominated, therefore make up part of our cultural horizon: on the express condition that these languages not be approached in terms of sexual difference.

It is this (implicit) law of silence upon which we are already infringing, when, following the lead of Louise Labé, Virginia Woolf, Alba de Céspedes, and so many others, we denounce the monopolization by men, to the detriment of women, of the material and symbolic possibilities of creativity. But we infringe upon it even more when we ask why certain remarkable texts by women are absent from literary studies or treated as insignificant addenda; when we angrily discover so many works of which we have been deprived, when we note, along with Annette Kolodny,[4] a strange and yet so banal a phenomenon as men's unconscious neglect—almost sincere—of texts by women (she cites Henri Peyre who, in his book *French Novelists of Today,* asserts that half the talents are women's only in order finally to devote one chapter out of twelve to them). We dare to examine what, precisely, the commentators say about the works of women whom they deign to read. We give our point of view on male masterpieces, like Simone de Beauvoir in *The Second Sex,* Kate Millett in *Sexual Politics,* Luce Irigaray in *Speculum de l'autre sexe,* and Anne-Marie Dardigna in *Les Châteaux d'Eros:*[5], the relative point of view (and assumed as such) of a woman relativizes the man's, which is offered and accepted as general. And now that we're becoming bolder, we consider that there is nothing which allows one objectively to measure the extent of a work's definite innovativeness; that the way in which they are ranked is variable and often irrelevant; that Virginia Woolf, Marguerite Duras, Nathalie Sarraute, and Anna Akhmatova have profoundly changed narrative and poetic modes of discourse—neither more nor less (how can one judge?) than James Joyce, Alain Robbe-Grillet, and Boris Pasternak. In our eyes, the love poetry of Ronsard is not more obviously universal than the love poetry of Louise Labé is obviously particular. And why shouldn't Doris Lessing's *Children of Violence* and Elsa Morante's *La Storia*[6] be great social, historical, and political novels in which men, as much as women, would discover the problems of our contemporary world in order to ponder them? Let's change levels: why, in actual fact, would men succumb to the most degrading cultural alienation by writing, and especially reading, "little" romantic novels while women would begin to move up the ladder of the culture by reading, and especially writing, "little" pornographic novels? In a general sense, there would be a lot to say about the hierarchy of genres and themes in terms of society's image of the respective value of the sexes: in magazines, in literature, in film, in the arts and the crafts.

As literary critics, we don't bloody the world or set it on fire; we don't submit men's books to inquisition and book burning; instead, we devote some time and attention (hence a part of our lives) to them, which contrasts with the expeditious manner in whch men treat the works of women when they happen to speak of them. We are still proving our knowledge of the modes of analysis and the theories in use in our time—almost exclusively male. Thus, how is one to understand the massive indifference, the uneasiness, the irony, the foolish, stereotyped, and so often venomous statements that we get as a response? One would think we were disrupting the workings of the establishment by breaking down the implicit consensus that sustains it.

We are bringing to light from the past, and the present, those works by women that are unnoticed or that are glimpsed, far off, on the periphery of real Literature; works read by a shadowy people—women, and sometimes men, who are vulnerable to the bizarre in their pursuit of exoticism, or simply society types—moving to the edges of the real Society; works of instant consumption, intended for newspaper review ever since the nineteenth century (it is most important to keep the public in mind) or, in unusual circumstances, meant for sociological review, but unworthy of the attention of the experts, who have the power and the duty to define real values, for, quite obviously, these works, in their eyes, *cannot* ever make an impact, meaning a break from the whole of artistic and intellectual production; they *cannot* be inventive; and hence, judged in principle to be ephemeral and particular, they *cannot* have a lasting effect on the collective memory which gives a culture its vital substance. And we who read these texts with the attention and the respect they deserve are revealing the existence of a marginalized culture within a dominant culture which is losing in this way its claim to being the only culture. We are showing that in a relation of inequality and of domination between the sexes, variable according to time and place, women have participated de facto in the image-rooted, language-rooted, and intellectual creativity of their community. Exceptional cases, they often retort. But where it involves what is human, the exception does not confirm the rule: it obliges us to revise the theories.

In "Women and Fiction," Virginia Woolf was already emphasizing, in regard to English women writers of the nineteenth century, that not only was "the author's presence"—but "a woman's presence"—detected in their writings, and that this disturbed the reading "as if the point toward which the attention of the reader is directed, was suddenly double instead of being single."[7] This wavering can become a more conscious practice meant to produce "an incurable double vision" as Luce Irigaray aptly puts it.[8] And this practice attains even more complexity as soon as one decides—and agrees—to have texts by women and texts by men interact as *relative to one another*, without a hierarchy. This kind of process leads one to question another hierarchy which intersects the sexual hierarchy without getting confused with it: the one that decrees what texts are literary, critical, and theoretical. Automatically, the very notion of *universality* as being indispensable to the reigning dominant ideology is found to be weakened at its base.

In a remarkable article—"Imprisoned Women: Toward a Socio-Literary Feminist Analysis"[9]—Elissa Gelfand denounces the fact that the unexamined adoption of universalizing viewpoints by theoreticians leads them to give greater importance to works which, in their eyes, have general value, and therefore to underestimate, indeed totally to ignore, texts by women which are guilty of not fitting their categories. In order to reexamine the give and take between society and literature, she suggests taking into account precisely those works that are excluded: concretely, in this case, those of women in prison as against the writings of male prisoners upon whom socioliterary studies are based. And right away, certain concepts that are accepted as universally valid turn out to be improper generalizations based on a biased sampling which has eliminated from the outset, for the sake of theoretical requirements, any conflicting texts.

In reading Elissa Gelfand, I had a sense of recognition since, with another critical process, also empirically based but in another field—reading literature from a psychoanalytic point of view—I had arrived at analogous reflections. I noted how inadequate, and even ineffective, certain orthodox concepts of analytic theory were to an understanding of how, in certain texts by Marguerite Duras, connections between body and language were symbolized; between individual fantasy and socialized fantasy; between experience, desire, and what is written; between self and the world, self and the others—stated in terms of paternity and maternity, of feminity and masculinity, etc. Reading these works in connection with my own psychoanalytic experience taught me more about it and in a different way: they were finally providing the right forms and words for what the theory left out or distorted. This must be said: when psychoanalytic theory pretends to set up absolute truths whose frame of reference is binding for all (that is, male, and hence female), it becomes deaf and blind to all the image-based, language-based, and reflective creations that do not fit its speculative framework, becoming dogmatic and precisely missing the truth in this way. Now, at the same time, I found that the narrative structures commended by formalist theories were scarcely helpful to me in delimiting the complex organization of certain works by Duras. What to do? Mutilate these texts in favor of the abstract truth of diagrams. Judge them or reject them as nonconforming? We know all about the myth of poorly constructed female writings. . . . Or question the validity of the models? Indeed, question the very notion of a model? These texts pin down the difference of the sexes at the heart of the speaking performance, of the spoken words and the subtle links between what is said and the words that are used. Often, a double set of voices, a double mythical version, a double family saga, a double view of the society, a double symbolic rendering make impossible any reduction to a single major form or meaning, to any hierarchical order or simple opposition, as the connecting links are so complex, variable, and changing. Far from having what is more than one refer back to singleness, doubleness opens up on an indefinite plurality that nothing can close off.[10]

To view the theoretical process as a pursuit of universality would then demand that women's writings be dismissed, relegating them to a specificity that excludes them from the so-called typical culture, except to appear as the negative, complementary other side, or decorative extra; or again, their identification with Sameness makes them the (nearly useless) other face of representative masterpieces of men, permitting the theoreticians, other men, to construct models whose concrete literary examples in turn do no more than reflect the theories. These mirroring games do not take place without sometimes violent conflicts among men. But this doesn't interfere with their collective agreement when it comes to presenting the literary work as "universally singular" or "singularly universal," in accordance with the two Sartrian expressions.[11] They accept diversity and multiplicity provided they are simple variations reflecting a *similarity* which is reassuring to them, for it would permit writers, readers, and theoreticians to recognize one another as the subjects—by nature and by right—of symbolic literary practices. Now this pursuit of similarity can be based only upon the denial of any real difference—and of the most basic one, the sexual difference, which threatens in a very direct way the narcissistic dream of all-powerfulness: the wish to portray-create-define the general human type by the self alone. Men don't mind being relative to one another, relative to the Same, above all not to the other sociosexual group, for this would mean confronting a painful truth: their basic unfulfillment as human beings who are subject, in the same way women are, to that irreducible limitation constituted by

sexual difference. Their literary, critical, and theoretical works end-
lessly develop and redevelop the difference of the sexes in such a way
that they can protect themselves against this intolerable truth which,
however, crops up here and there, in the rambling phrase, at the
curious juncture of several arguments, in the revelation of an image,
in the feverish course of a speech, by the sudden, seemingly inexplic-
able presence of violence or pain. Their cultural monuments are the
fruit of a specific imagination which clearly has the advantage of being
more supported, flaunted, and actualized than ours to the point of
being able to pass itself off as the imagination of the whole community.

This is why an emphasis on women reading texts written by women,
in the midst of an almost uniformly male culture, *can* change the
whole range of questions and responses. Our concrete situation of
being female, relative to being male, should mobilize our energies to
resist being alienated by a universal type; also to keep us from wanting
in turn to appropriate for ourselves the creation and the definition of
a general human type, for we cannot afford the luxury of denying or
scorning male activities and creations. It should also move us further
to invent other modes of living-imagining-reading-thinking-writing—
on the side of what is uncertain, partial, unpredictable, unfinished,
and unfinishable, in a continual give and take where differences
would be richer in potential for the future than would reductive
sameness. Indeed, I will come back to this; for us, it involves a
potential for change that the fact of being a woman cannot alone
realize; we must constantly struggle against this ideology of the universal so profoundly imprinted in us and which informs the everyday
world about our perceptions. And yet we find how disturbing is this
potential as already exercised by this or that woman. That is how, for
example, I understand this phrase of Lacan which is intended to pay
"homage" to Marguerite Duras: "She turns out to know, without me,
what I teach."[12] So, for a man, is this the highest degree of creativity
awarded a woman? It is therefore unthinkable—intolerable—that a
woman is able to say, to discover, to invent things he does not know.
There is nothing new to receive-learn from women: at best, a man
would only be able to read in the other the reflection-echo (created
almost unconsciously) of his own language of Truth. He identifies the
other with himself—the highest compliment: thus José Cabanis
praises Marguerite Yourcenar because she "writes like a man"[13] and
Sartre does the same for Simone de Beauvoir by acknowledging in her
"the intelligence of a man."[14] As for women, their place in the inter-
subjective system is narrowly construed: elsewhere I've said that, in
my view, this pigeonholing that traps us is part of the "sex snare":

> To be mute, to secrete the (devalued) language of daily life, of mother-
> ing, of the emotions, which only men (poets and theoreticians) would
> be capable of transmuting into cultural values; to repeat the words
> used by men, saying "I" where they say "they,"* to plagiarize men,
> culling their language about everything, even to saying "I" and "they"
> like them.[15]

But now we have women getting together, reading each other,
commenting on each other to produce a culture they share, while also
responding to the mass of men's writings in order to adopt or to reject
their viewpoints, as the case may be. This is all happening as if a
chorus of usually unheard voices were rising from every corner of the
establishment in the accepted culture—literature, philosophy, the humanities, etc. Indifferent to the favor they've been granted by being
allowed into the harem, these women are not bothering to prove they
deserve it through efforts on their part to replicate-confirm the language of the master-men. One might say that they grant each other,
almost from birth, the right to a socialized, socializable speech, which
can move with ease in every field of exchange. Male anxiety is taking
on serious proportions, for these women are encroaching upon the
authority of what men say. So, men are going to try to disqualify
women just where they are most threatening, precisely in the area of
what is said, by carefully avoiding any discussion of the words they use
(in which they would risk getting ensnared anyway), and that revolv-
ing around a single issue—femininity—which reveals the real stakes
of power: mastery over the other. Cannot they proceed to acknowledge the difference of the sexes, then, except by reasserting a relation
of inequality and domination?

A recent statement by a well-known psychiatrist, Jean-Bertrand
Pontalis, seems to me to illustrate perfectly this type of profound
violence, despite its softened outward appearance. Interviewed in *Le
Monde* on the possible effects of the new kinds of language of women,
he first answers: "There is no assurance that feminine language concerning femininity is *by circumstance* closer to the truth than masculine
language."[16] This I grant him willingly, though I already doubt that
he would have dared to declare from the outset something like
"There is no assurance that Jewish (black, working-class . . .) language
concerning Jewishness (blackness, the working-class condition . . .) is
by circumstance closer to the truth than Catholic (white, middle-
class . . .) language." I therefore grant him this willingly, on the condition that he agrees in turn to run through the various possibilities of
this brilliant formula. We could begin with "There is no assurance that

---

*[Translator's note] "they," feminine pronoun in French, clearly refers to the "others."

masculine language concerning femininity is by circumstance closer to the truth than feminine language." This is a considerable improvement, since it would weaken the present system in which all our education of women consists of learning who we are (and should be) from the texts of men. To go on: "There is no assurance that masculine language concerning masculinity is by circumstance closer to the truth than feminine language." Here we are verging on pure outrage. And, nevertheless, we have to tell them other things about themselves besides what they tell each other—and this isn't necessarily bad news.

Beyond the never-ending question of castration (symbolic or not) from which they never seem to recover and with which they beat us down in order to rid themselves of it; beyond their countless stories of war exploits, finance, love, and politics which seem to increase their standing solely on the side of aggressiveness and conquest; beyond their verbal and intellectual sparring where so often the most minor concrete truth is sacrificed to the wish to impose upon everyone a system that would at last tell All about Everything; beyond our refusal to accept both their domination and the society they are building; we can tell them the simple pleasure of being different. Thus, to read Proust is not a way of discovering Childhood or Memory, any more than Homosexuality; no—following the drift of our readings, nourished by our own experiences, it is a way to find what is irreducible in the experiences of a little boy, of a man, and of a writer and what may be irreducible in our own, even amid sociohistorical idiosyncracies and distinctions. We are sharing, we are identifying with each other, we are astonishing each other, we are not confusing each other—we are communicating. In our reading-investigation of many poetic, narrative, and theoretical works, there are these moments of surprise: is this, then, the way a man lives, imagines, feels, thinks, acts—and most especially when he momentarily sheds his armor of obligatory virility? How is it, then, that so few men are capable of seeking this pleasure of difference, this phenomenal source of enrichment, by reading and, above all, by commenting on, outside of conventional patterns, the numerous texts by women? This pleasure of a world vision, of a narrative or polemical construction, of a poetic rhythm, to some extent slightly, but unquestionably, divergent: all close, always a bit off, never completely unfamiliar, neither opposed, according to a binary principle, nor reduced to a dreary sameness.

The statement by Pontalis aims to cut off this open possibility of a dialogue between men and women in which intersecting views and words would be exchanged: the truth about either sex would not be the exclusive possession of any group but would emerge from in between the two, always uncertain, tentative, limited. And similarly, step by step, the truth about the natural world, the family, society, art, the imagination, language, etc. Besides, in this case, there would be no question of *one* feminine language and *one* masculine language; rather, in the end, of a plurality of languages, without definite ownership, in which flexible identities would be in a constant state of becoming, amid agreement, disagreement, conflict, encounters, understandings, and misunderstandings. Between women, between men, between women and men. This project always comes up somewhere between the real and the utopic, without ever managing to take shape to the point of becoming society's image for an entire community. It is this profoundly democratic project that frightens Pontalis as it does many of his peers: men who are certified masters of the nature of Knowledge. By imposing his presupposition, he is defending the monopoly on the Truth which serves as his basis. In this respect, his attitude does not fundamentally differ from that of the doctors of law who wanted to silence Christine de Pisan for the sake of their academic dignity (exclusively male) and for her "woman's ignorance," even though she was a great poet. We don't know anymore if it is knowledge that creates power or power knowledge; the two reinforce each other in a closed system; we do know, on the other hand, that the licensed owners of this knowledge-power will not let it get into an honest debate—there are too many risks: at the moment of danger, they show themselves for what they really are by resorting to the argument of authority. Plainly, today the combat has been broadened and has shifted: it is taking place within institutions built by men, which women are gradually starting to occupy. The enemy is within.

Whether it concerns economic or symbolic interchanges, this saying of Marx is still of value both as an observation and as a wish: "Every man looks at himself and first recognizes himself in another man." It is against the mothers and through the subordination-devaluation of women that men continue today mutually to attribute to one another the virtue of being men. What they want, despite all opposition, is to converse among themselves, to converse all by themselves. Such is the way of narcissistic harmony—the only truce in the middle of their wars between fathers, sons, brothers—which we disturb by our intrusions. Our actions and our writings they judge to be radical; we know, however, the degree to which they include precautions, compromise, unconscious respect for the dominant values; they appear to be radical because they are, in fact, getting in touch with a radical operation of society. Here, I'm happy to quote Georges Ballandier since he is one of the rare contemporary French anthropologists not to feed, in the name of universality, the solipsistic dream of a male power than has ruled, almost devoid of conflicts, since the dawn of time; on the contrary, alert to the real self-actualizing movement of so-called ahistorical or historical societies, he is restoring to struggles between the sex-based classes, as much as to struggles between the age-based and socio-economic classes, their true dynamic character. In *Anthropologiques*, he states:

> The man/woman relationship is the most profound basis of all unequal relationships; which explains that challenges (real or symbolic) to it contest it at the same time as other rapports, once the challenges become widespread. And when the man/woman relationship is attacked, society appears to be even more threatened than by the dissidence of the impoverished "classes," because it is damaged in its "foundations."[17]

We find ourselves up against something unfathomable that is not really explored by any biological, economic, socio-domestic, or psychological explanation: what is so terrifying about the prospect of women taking social action rather than being passive objects or troublemakers sowing disorder? Ti-Grace Atkinson is correct in affirming that the ideological boundaries that confine women to the class of the oppressed have not yet been touched.[18] This, however, is the project shared by women in their struggles, despite their social, geographic, and cultural dispersion. We are working on this with difficulty, torn among ourselves and within ourselves; caught, in general, in a sterile and rather despairing alternative. For, on one hand, we are preoccupied by the desire to go beyond assimilation, driven as we are by the necessity of making ourselves accepted, thanks to repeated evidence that we can do-and-say as well as men the same things they do-say: whether we like it or not, we are therefore confusing equal status with conformity to a model of prestige, in a monolithic view of humanity. It is in this sense that Simone de Beauvoir maintains:

> I think that the liberated woman would be as creative as man. But that she would not bring new values. To believe the opposite is to believe that there is a feminine nature, which I have always denied.[19]

On the other hand, directly opposed to this view, we might, for example, consider this manifesto by Hélène Cixous:

> It is essential for woman to write herself; for woman to write about woman and to make women come around to the writing from which they have been separated as violently as they have been from their bodies.[20]

This time, there is the desire to claim the specificity which, in our culture, seems the only imaginable means of recognition for women, and to support it in case of equal competition. I cannot analyze here the complexity of these two viewpoints, placing them within their numerous contexts. I would merely like to emphasize that these two antagonistic positions in fact make reference to the same universal (ultimately essentialist) categories—"woman" and "man": one by suggesting a peculiar equivalence between "the liberated woman" and just "man" (if I may be permitted to point out) in a figure of the Same where the idea of a type of human nature presently more evolved in man than in woman sneaks back into the picture; the other, by transforming a devalued, less-than-universal "woman" into a fully realized universal type which all women—except if they are no longer *real* women?—would be called upon to achieve. Can we not look for other ways than these two routes leading to a similar dead end?

If we do not allow ourselves to be intimidated by the demand made upon us to present *one* theory that is at last clear, definitive, and all-encompassing, if we pursue our patient critique of all those universals that feed upon us like parasites (Man, Masculine, Feminine, Language, Art, Writing, Socialization, History, etc.), if we learn to practice a joyful pessimism, we have perhaps some chance of inventing new modes of living-imagining-acting-thinking with men, who themselves are suspect, too, because they are willing to take into account their subjectivity and their relativity as sex-differentiated beings. Real women. Real men. Concrete approaches and works in concrete contexts, which are always different. Multiple strategies. Against a consistent uniformity, against the systematized struggle of two uniform groups, that is directed, pictured, and interpreted as if there were never a place for two—where the other kind, of sex, of race, or of class, functions as the inhuman—to go on creating a vital cohesiveness out of a plurality of differences: this is the picture I share with others, of societies that are truly in the process of becoming. This is the sense in which I understand, for example, what Ballandier says of African women: "Progress, for them, has the meaning of progress which is accomplished by different categories of the oppressed"[21]—ours as well, keeping in mind the cultural differences between ourselves and them.

This declaration of principles has perhaps tried the patience of my readers, unless, their sense of humor getting the upper hand, they have noticed the various examples of conformism in my language which narrowly places it in time and space: that theoretical style of language which I tried out this time is not the least. . . . Nevertheless, this detour was necessary in order for me to justify my title, which shows the connections between feminism and literary criticism to be problematic.

This title may sound like a provocation, indeed like a dangerous regression, at a time when an important body of publications, notably in the United States, accepts the de facto existence of a "feminist literary criticism." Now, if I have been struck by the dilemma of American feminists in defining this expression, it is because I have been living this dilemma since I began my research. Of course, this heading is useful to bring together the many ways of thinking and texts whose kinship we affirm in this way. Even more, it indicates an immense field of reading, of reflection, of explorations that enable us to discover a continent with no boundaries: that of women's inventiveness. Looking at it this way, I share the position held by Annette Kolodny[22] and Domna Stanton,[23] when they emphasize that it is fortunately impossible to reduce so many voices and different texts to a single body of language. Nevertheless, a wish that lies dormant in each of us takes hold of some: from now on, to go beyond what is thought to be an outworn stage of an (overly) empirical, partial, and scattered literary practice in order to crown it at last with *one* theory and *one* method valid for us all. You will notice that what is involved here are two characteristics required by our present Western society for anyone who wants to receive full and complete recognition from the scientifically oriented establishment. What price will we pay for this (dubious) certification as licensed experts? Facing this danger, I will clearly say that the expression "feminist literary criticism" does not in itself have any epistemological or even heuristic value for my research. That in itself it tells me nothing about what is essential, as I see it: what is really at stake for us in those vital activities which are to read, to dream, to think, to write such and such a book—*with* such and such a book.[24] That to ally oneself with a theory and a method laid down for all women is to have this label lock us into what I would call, in the double sense of the term, a disciplinary approach. Subjecting the very impulses that have urged us on—Hope, Pleasure—to the risk of dying in a cage.

I will explain myself by asking a question which appears to be stupid, but which, in practice, is not unimportant: are we concerned with establishing a feminist *literary criticism* or a *feminist criticism* of literature? In the first instance, our task would be to convert literary criticism, by accepting from the outset the current presupposition which would give it the unchallenged status of an organized discipline, clearly defined and autonomous in the area of knowledge. We would, in this case, finally be making it truly universal by the addition of objectives and concepts. In the second instance, feminism would take on the appearance and the role of basic theory and method: on the insufficiently criticized model of marxism, but, again, of existentialism or psychoanalysis, that is, of any system with an all-encompassing design whose principal terms apply (or adapt) to every domain. The nostalgia for the universal nourishes the dream of a "feminist science"[25] paradoxically like that of a philosophy of "feminine writing"[26] (*écriture féminine*) which ends up by being the key to every kind of liberation for women. We might almost be talking about a super-discipline. And then, between the two viewpoints, a compromise solution sums up the ambiguity of our ordinary literary approaches. Nancy Miller puts it this way:

> formal analysis of narrative structures does provide a coherent demonstration of the strategies of fiction. And from the findings of this heuristic process . . . feminist critics can proceed to elaborate the superstructure, the ideological framework, within which are played out the politics of what we have called the feminist text.[27]

Here, we have rid ourselves of the categories and oppositions that make up our schizophrenic existence: form/content; universal/particular; eternal/historical; essential/contingent; neuter (general)/feminine.

But let us examine more closely this notion of discipline which is so fascinating to us that we are tempted to see our intellectual salvation in it. I will group together here certain analyses by Michel Foucault that specifically oppose "discipline" to the "principle of commentary" and to "that of the author" in order to define it thusly:

> ". . . an area of objectives, a set of methods, a body of postulates considered to be true, a game of rules and of definitions, techniques, and tools (. . .), a sort of impersonal system at the disposal of anyone who wants it or who can make use of it." Where "what is presumed at the outset," is the possibility "of indefinitely formulating new postulates from procedures already set up—and all of that tied, obviously, to an institutional whole. This indeed involves "the control of different kinds of language" (and hence of the applications of knowledge), not only in accord with the dividing up of what is true and what is false by virtue of an internal consistency, but in accord with conformity to "a certain type of theoretical horizon" without which any postulate becomes a figment of the imagination or a preoccupation with "the monsters of knowledge."[28]

We, who in raising the issue of the difference of the sexes at the heart of humanistic studies in regard to objectives as much as to subjects of knowledge, have been so easily placed on the side of error, delusion, and a preoccupation with the monsters of knowledge, are we in turn going to push back into the margins of institutionalized knowledge which we are restoring or which we are making it our business to systematize, the wealth of applications, of imaginative works and theoretical approaches that have come from women who admittedly did not go along with the establishment? To reestablish the hierarchy between writers (male)/(ordinary) readers (female)/critics (male)/theoreticians (female)? To censor ourselves in the name of our own knowledge which, reconstructed once again as a wild hope for absolute knowledge, would turn against us to rule us?

Feminist approaches—none excluded—ought to allow both the idea of knowledge and the boundaries that today determine the fields of knowledge to shift. As literary critics, we can do some reexamining of literary criticism itself: recall its historical origins which link it to a new division of power throughout the nineteenth century; challenge the ties of authority it would establish with literature, language which it transforms into a mere object of its metalanguage; demonstrate the extent to which it remains a collection of heterogeneous texts, of personalized texts, of unrelated terminologies, of theories without a future, of techniques rarely capable of being imitated except to become fruitless, of ideas borrowed from various fields, including, without always admitting it, from the literary text itself; and say that it is precisely because of this that it is worthwhile in our eyes, for it can make it clear—if it accepts its mixed and changing character—that literary writing is a totally separate *mode of knowledge* while theoretical thought is also an area of the imagination, as in the splendid expression of Maud Mannoni, *Theory as Fiction:*[29] she, too, is largely unaware of its tendencies and directions.

Against certain theoretically based militant beliefs, we can equally recall that language is not opposed to action, that it accompanies it, is transformed by it, and transforms it; that the imaginary is not mere *illusion* in face of a *reality* that only socio-economic conditions and struggles would directly represent, and in face of a *truth* in possession of the humanities, systems, even political doctrines; that language is a process of *experimentation,* of *mediation,* and of *invention.* The world of fiction is one of the areas in which one can shape various possibilities opening up the future amid the burdensome past and the priorities of the present. It is neither passive reflection nor a near-mechanical transformation of material and social phenomena into art, no more than it is pure shadow play. Therefore, when I say "I am a feminist," or quite simply: "I am a woman," I certainly don't ask myself: "How

must that be implemented and made into theory?," not even merely:
"How is that implemented and made into theory?" but inseparably:
"How do we live this, or not manage to live it, desire it, refuse it, suffer
it, imagine it, say it, not manage to say it, invent it, etc.?"

The Words to Say It is Marie Cardinale's title.[30] For each woman,
there are *some* words to say it which help her to find *her* words to say it
and to offer them, in turn, to others through tentative, infinite, and
indefinite interchanges. This is the very movement of life. For if we
were suddenly to confound ourselves by playing it safe with the
required words to describe ourselves, to describe the world and our
relations with others, we would be as much like the living dead as we
are under the reigning dominant ideologies of today. Even worse, for
we would be the ones to have constructed our own tomb: the empty
mausoleum to the glory of The Unknown Woman. How can we save
ourselves if not by mutually recognizing creative abilities within, but
also outside of, the forms imposed by convention. Recognize them,
without sharing them, starting with the misunderstood women of the
past or those of so many different countries, viewed as peculiar social
milieus by virture of being doomed to silence—to the little girls who
bear our hopes? I ask you to think about this phrase of Rosa Luxem-
bourg's: "Freedom is the freedom to think in a different way."

Women can be at the crossroads of present-day thinking, which is
moving toward a new elaboration of sexual differences, finally recognized as the inexhaustible wealth of what we call the human race. For,
no matter what the class of culture to which women belong, they are
showing that sexual difference in the form of economic, social, and
cultural differentiation is the hidden basis (and therefore particularly
effective) of all notions of difference which, when confused with the
idea of specificity, is the source of discrimination, of inequality, domination, revolt, and revolution—too often taken to be a wish for mere
role reversal or assimilation. What is considered far too easily to be a
sign of inadequacy in feminism (among certain feminists included)—
the lack of a comprehensive doctrine, the uncertainties, theoretical
hesitations, vagueness, etc.—in fact reveals not only the wish but the
necessity of redefining difference. From this perspective, I would like
to quote Annick Jaulin, a philosopher, who seems to me to formulate
difference outside the usual ambiguities and in a manner akin to my
partial research: "The difference of the sexes requires that there be
neither a first nor a second of the species, for this difference generates
the species; it is generic, not specific."[31] Yet at the same time, women
are becoming aware in a concrete way that they are simultaneously the
products and the reproducers of other types of specificity that place

them—assigning them collectively and representing them individually—in very different ways, within the networks of privilege, prestige, and power in a given society and across societies. Our nascent thinking on the complex relationships between women is leading us, in my view, to ponder—beyond questions of discipline, science, and politics—ethical problems. It is time, I think, that together we grant these ethical problems enough importance so that we do not treat them as a separate domain. If feminism cannot be a comprehensive doctrine, it must repudiate this impossibility in order to find a free zone between denouncing intolerable kinds of violence and making pronouncements about utopic values to come. In order to return a livable world to us women, it seems to me necessary to invent (daily) a new picture of difference. How would this world be livable if it were not for whomever is excluded or dominated in the name of a specificity that is synonymous with inferiority, whatever it may be? A plurality of feminisms is a guarantee that differences will win a plurality of respect.

Notes

1. In France you must indicate that you mean the "non-copyrighted M.L.F." (Women's Liberation Movement), because a group called Psychoanalysis and Politics officially appropriated the initials.

2. C. Lévi-Strauss, *The Savage Mind* (University of Chicago Press, 1966).

3. M. Foucault, especially *L'Ordre du discours* (Gallimard, 1971). See also *L'Archéologie du savior* (Gallimard, 1969) and *La Volonté du savoir* (Gallimard, 1976). In English see *Archeology of Knowledge*, A. M. Sheridan-Smith, translator (Irvington, 1972) it includes *Discourse on Language* and *Power-Knowledge* (Pantheon, 1981).

4. A. Kolodny, "Some Notes on Defining a Feminist Literary Criticism," *Critical Inquiry* 2:1 (Fall, 1975).

5. S. de Beauvoir, *The Second Sex* (Random House, 1974), K. Millett, *Sexual Politics* (Ballantine, 1978): L. Irigaray, *Speculum de l'autre femme* (Minuit, 1974): A. M. Dardigna, *Les Châteaux d'Eros* (Maspéro, 1981).

6. D. Lessing, *Her Children of Violence* (London, 1964): E. Morante, *La Storia* (Gallimard, 1977).

7. V. Woolf, "Women and Fiction," in *Women and Writing*, collected and edited by M. Barrett (New York: Harcourt, Brace, Jovanovich, 1979). In Virginia Woolf's essay on women and the novel she sees this "female presence" as a shortcoming in certain texts by women as she sees the comparable presence in the works of blacks and working-class people as a shortcoming. Woolf poses the problem in order to contrast it with the search for a purely

feminine way of writing. But this very complex article supports the idea of a double view of the world, through the novel.

8. L. Irigaray, *Speculum.*

9. E. Gelfand, "Imprisoned Women: Toward a Socio-Literary Feminist Analysis," *Yale University French Studies* No. 62, (1981): 185–203.

10. M. Marini, *Territoires du féminin avec Marguerite Duras* (Minuit, 1977). In addition to the questions discussed here, I raise the problem of a "reading-writing" criticism which would be neither a "writing about" nor a "writing as" but a "writing with." See also "L'Offrande d'Aurélia Steiner au dormeur millénaire," *Diadascalies,* Cahiers de l'Ensemble théâtral mobile de Bruxelles no. 3 (April 1982).

11. J.-P. Sartre, especially "Plaidoyer pour les intellectuels," in *Situations* VIII (Gallimard, 1972).

12. J. Lacan, "Hommage fait à Marguerite Duras du Ravissement de Lol V. Stein," in *Cahiers Renaud-Barrault,* no. 52, (Gallimard, Dec. 1962).

13. The complete sentence: "One can like women very much, delight in meeting one who writes like a man, or rather like most of them do not write" is quoted by Jacqueline Piatier (who is very pleased with Lacan's remarks) in *Le Monde's* literary supplement on March 8, 1980, on the occasion of the election of the first woman (Marguerite Yourcenar) to the Académie Française.

14. Interview with Sartre by Madeleine Gubril in the American edition of *Vogue Magazine* (July 1965). Sartre adds, of course, "and her woman's sensibility."

15. M. Marini, "Les Femmes et les pratiques d'écriture," *Pénélope* no. 3, (Autumn 1980).

16. Interview of J. B. Pontalis with R. Jaccard in *Le Monde* (November 4, 1977). I quote it in reference to a discussion about the writings of L. Irigaray, in "Scandaleusement autre," *Critique,* Minuit no. 373–74 (June–July 1978).

17. G. Ballandier, *Anthropologiques,* Presses Universitaires de France (1974).

18. Ti-Grace Atkinson, *Amazon Odyssey* (New York: Links Books 1974).

19. Interview in 1972 in C. Francis and F. Gontier, *Les Ecrits de Simone de Beauvoir* (Gallimard, 1979).

20. H. Cixous, "Le Rire de Méduse," in *L'Arc,* no. 61, *Simone de Beauvoir,* 2ᵉ trimestre, 1975. "The Laugh of Medusa," *Signs* 1:4 (Summer 1976).

21. G. Ballandier, quoted in *Femmes Africaines en devenir,* by F. A. Diacre (Paris 1971).

22. Kolodny, *Some Notes.*

23. D. Stanton, "Language and Revolution: The Franco-American Disconnection," in *The Future of Difference,* ed. by H. Eisenstein and A. Jardine (Barnard Women's Center, 1980).

24. Marini, *Territoires.*

25. *Questions féministes* no. 1 (November 1977).

26. In France this expression is not used in feminist circles or even among women. The way it is presented varies according to the discourses. In the case of texts on women two analyses have been attempted in France: B. Didier, *L'Ecriture-femme* (Presses Universitaires de France, 1981), and B. Slama, "De la littérature féminine à l'écrire-femme," in *Littérature,* Larousse no. 44 (December 1981).

27. Nancy Miller, "Female Sexuality and Narrative Structure in *La Nouvelle Héloise* and *Les Liaisons dangereuses,*" in *Signs* 1:3 (Spring 1976):638.

28. M. Foucault, *L'Ordre du discours.*

29. M. Mannoni, *La Théorie comme fiction. Freud, Groddeck, Winnicott, Lacan* (Sevil, 1979).

30. M. Cardinale, *Les Mots pour le duc* (Grasset, 1975).

31. A. Jaulin, "La sainte famille et la différence des sexes," in *Annales* (Université de Toulouse-Le Mirail).

FEMALE INSUBORDINATION AND THE TEXT

Catharine R. Stimpson

The words *domination* and *subordination* have the complex weightiness that *sin* and *salvation* carried in more thoroughly religious periods in the West. Being dominant or subordinate is a state of being—social, political, psychological—that is as much an element of identity as bones of the body. However, modern ideologies demand that we break up ossified hierarchal structures and knit up new ones that incarnate the values of liberty, autonomy, and equality. The position of women dramatizes the tension between hierarchal practice and more individualistic, egalitarian theory. Scholars quarrel about the universality of male dominance and female subordination, but not about its presence—in past and present.[1] Yet, both men and women call out for women's freedom and independence and for gender equality. A question that inevitably emerges is how and why some women accept traditional, submissive roles while others resist them and proclaim modernity.

To answer such a query entails the ransacking of a multiplicity of materials. The ones I wish to shake out are largely literary. So doing, I feel afloat in a frail craft in a methodological swamp. Among the dank waters and hidden beasts that I fear are ahistoricity, overgeneralization, and a naive attitude toward literature that reduces it to a mirror image of reality, to mere mimesis, or to a source of role models, a set of inspirational ego ideals. I feel a dangerous closeness to that Samuel Beckett figure who murmurs, "I'll never know." Yet that same figure says, ". . . .you must go on, I can't go on, I'll go on."[2] One goes on because literature can matter for the study of female subordination, that participation in an inferior class or group, that dependence upon the rank, power, and authority of others. Moreover, literature can represent the conditions of negation and revolt and the fear, at once tremulous and arrogant, of negation and revolt. In particular, modern Western texts articulate motivation, perception, desire, scenes of interpretation—the fields of feeling and consciousness.

To serve as my compass, I will borrow from an anthropologist, Peggy Sanday, and her theory about the conditions in which women escape subordination. Because of its realism about power, the theory may be less anthropology than anthropolitics. Obviously, anthropology most often concerns preliterate rather than literate cultures. For some, like Lévi-Strauss, literacy is even a tragic intrusion into, an irreparable rupture of, a preliterate society's cohesion. Nevertheless, anthropology can provoke the literary critic through suggesting relationships between symbolic structures and material realities. Sanday explores the sexual "scripts" that various societies use to rationalize and regulate gender systems and those systems themselves. So doing, she concludes that women achieve economic and political power or authority when they have economic autonomy and when men are dependent upon their activities.[3] If Sanday is right, women are lesser when they lack economic strength and a way of making men rely upon them—if only through that strength. She also pessimistically wonders if

> women as a group have not willingly faced death in violent conflict. This fact, perhaps more than any other, explains why men have sometimes become the dominating sex. (p. 211)

She offers a tragic irony: women submit to men because they are less responsive to the howling claims of Mars.

To explore texts is to study both literature and its production. Because the West has so masculinized the creation of public culture, for a woman to write at all seriously has been, in some degree, an act of defiance.[4] Though less painfully now than before, the writing woman must oppose ideological dictates and social, familial, and material pressures that would silence her. The history of modern women writers is a collective biography of subversive self-assertion. Demonstrating Sanday's thesis, Western women could become writers, especially after the sixteenth century, because they had some access to education and to literacy. A literary education can, luckily, be partly private and autodidactic, self-imbibed outside of formal institutions of learning. Women could then speak to an audience affluent enough to help support a publishing industry that men ran. Their circumstances granted them the possibility of some economic autonomy and some male dependence. As a critic says of Charlotte Brontë:

> For Brontë, writing was also a way of acquiring property (even if only one's own words) and thus status where most Victorian women had none.[5]

However, writing is also an unsatisfactory test of Sanday's thesis. For all modern writers tend to achieve, not economic and political power, but moral and cultural and psychological influence. Because of this, the resistance to women as writers is less than that to women as financiers or premiers. Nor is writing itself, despite such militant metaphors as "the war of ideas," violent. One might have asked of Charlotte Brontë what Stalin so crudely asked of a pope: how many divisions do you command?

In wildly disparate ways, the women who write, these limited cultural rebels, combine several characteristics. Psychologically, they are able to express, not to repress, alienation. They can articulate difference: between themselves and others, between the perceived present and the imagined future. For still enigmatic reasons, they have a compulsive attraction to language. It has an overriding, even obsessive power, like divine spirits for the mystic. A recent biographer of Aphra Behn, the first professional woman writer in English, says, though in terms too redolent of the natural and instinctual:

> Aphra seems to have been one of those naturally prolific writers for whom setting the pen to paper was instinctive; a fundamental element of temperament.[6]

Socially, the woman writer seems to have the support of at least one other person—even though it may be erratic or rough. In her poignant, lyrical novel about a tormented working-class family, Tillie Olsen has a child, Maizie, ask her mother what the word *edication* means. As Anna answers, she, too, mispronounces *education,* but differently. That lack of a common sound signifies their mutual distance from what the word represents and the distance between them that education might breed:

> "an edjication?" Mrs. Holbrook arose from amidst the shifting vapors of the washtub and, with the suds dripping from her red hands, walked over and stood impressively over Maizie. "A edjication is what you kids are going to get. It means your hands stay white and you read books and work in an office. Now, get the kids and scat. But dont go too far, or I'll knock your block off."[7]

Economically, women writers are often needy. They write because they must live and because others, like the Alcott family on Louisa, depend on the daughter-author, sister-author, or mother-author for their living. They generally have greater opportunities for money, and for acceptance, if they are shrewd and self-effacing enough to enter an "empty field," a form that codifying critics may not applaud but that a consuming audience appreciates.[8]

No matter how subversive writing might be, the woman writer's life is rarely a simple history of subversion. She may have a moment of consciousness in which she overwhelmingly *sees* her place in structures of domination and submission. However, her collective history warns us against thinking of people—except in extreme moments of insight or choice—as either totally subordinate or totally insubordinate. Instead, consciously and unconsciously, out of cunning and cowardice, many women writers have devised a series of strategies that simultaneously reveal and conceal their self-assertions through language. As a whole, they have been neither rich nor confident enough to be vastly nonconformist. Some have written—but gurgling in support of the status quo. Others have adopted male names or masculinized their creative energies. Still others, as if to show that their revolt were singular rather than collective, have presented characters lesser than themselves. As Carolyn Heilbrun says:

> one *can* act, sometimes shocking oneself at one's courage, or audacity. One lives with the terror, the knowledge of mixed motives and fundamental conflicts, the guilt—but one acts. Yet women writers (and women politicians, academics, psychoanalysts) have been unable to imagine for other women, fictional or real, the self they have in fact achieved.[9]

The play between subordination and insubordination exists inevitably in women's texts as well as in their lives. Conflict structures their linguistic worlds. In English, at least four patterns of conflict have emerged. In the first, the woman writer sublimates her anger over women's condition into a protest on behalf of others. She projects a wish to change women's role by amassing evidence as to why others ought to alter theirs.[10] In the second, a reversal of the first, attacks on women's subordination accompany an inability to imagine other liberations as well. Like a great rocket that resistance inadequately fuels, the text goes up—to explode and then fall back. In *Shirley,* her historical novel published in 1849 but set in the Napoleonic Wars of 1811–1812, Charlotte Brontë deconstructs patriarchal religion a phallic dominance of politics and the economy, constrictions on female autonomy and work, a sexual double standard, the sufferings of a displaced working class. Yet, even her hatred of deprivation,[11] even her analysis of the interlocking systems of class and gender, cannot generate a revolutionary narrative. Her leaders of class rebellion are primitive, nineteenth-century, Yorkshire Jimmy Hoffas, the contentious and corrupt leader of the Teamsters Union in the United States in the midtwentieth century. Her narrative closes in a double marriage and a brooding elegy for the nature, mystery, and magic that industrialism has erased.

A third pattern is the construction of a self-contradictory text that rejects and affirms femininity as usual. So, in the nineteenth-century sentimental novel, women both

> wrote of their domestic dream and revealed a deep discontent . . . the positive, forceful message rode and was partly generated by an undercurrent of dissatisfaction and despair.[12]

The annotators of 3,407 books about women in the United States written between 1891 and 1920 by 1,723 authors have also isolated a "hybrid" heroine. She

> may act heroically but be punished, resigned or remorseful in the final pages. Many of the novels (we studied) include love stories, the inclusion of which may represent a compromise with convention or a recognition of social reality.[13]

Finally, a woman writer may pile up reasons for women's rebellion, but store them in a deterministic worldview that instructs us all to submit to large, impersonal forces. Even if Lilly Bart, in Edith Wharton's *House of Mirth,* were to become a reentry student and a suffragette, Wharton's Darwinistic theories of the power of heredity and environment would undercut such an unlikely personal transformation.

Fortunately, a reader of these texts—of sublimated or terminated insubordination, self-contradiction, and fatalism—need not passively submit to their imperatives. Nor need they provide spongy escapes that absorb the restless imagination and libido. Both more and less than a collapse of self and book, reading can be an active process.

In 1932, writing to his wife from prison, Gramsci made a "just and necessary" distinction between

> aesthetic enjoyment and a positive value judgment of artistic beauty, i.e. between enthusiasm for a work of and in itself and moral enthusiasm, by which I mean a willing participation in the artist's ideological world.[14]

Readers can do even more than choose between palatable art and impalatable ideology. They can select certain ideological features and abandon others. Shirley's critique of Milton in *Shirley,* but not her marriage, may be material for an enabling myth of women's power. So may Radclyffe Hall's protest against homophobia in *The Well of Loneliness,* but not her prayers to a patriarchal God that smoke up from her last pages. Readers, like Doris Lessing's Martha Quest, may willfully assemble from literature what they need for their reconstruction of the world. If gender marks some readings, women may pick up signals about resistance that men might miss. Reading women will secretly school themselves in the tactics of disobedience.[15]

Such processes enhance, no matter how internally, a person's sense of power and freedom. Reinforcing this is the probability that reading is an indeterminant act. Because of its very nature, a text can invite us to help create its meaning. As we decide what it is all about, we are cognitively alert, responsible, fecund, capable. We gain a sense of strength. Simultaneously, we enter into what we have left of the world of the text. We vicariously experience events and personalities we might not meet in ordinary life—including dramas of insubordination. We gain, then, a sense of possibility. If we empathize with a character, we may also mitigate some crippling loneliness, a self-perception of weird singularity. We gain, finally, a sense of community.[16]

However, women have written still another kind of text. Here they want their readers to agree with them, to be fellow partisans of change. Their narrative lines can show conflict between the forward momentum of those who desire difference and the inertia of persons and institutions that cling to stability, but the narratives rarely contradict themselves. Resolutely, cleanly, they support those going forward. Some of these texts more fiercely and unabashedly call for change than others: certain novels about the New Woman;[17] feminist Utopias;[18] and "feminist polemic," a genre that Christine de Pisan helped to originate and that proudly, defiantly asserts the rights and dignity of women against often viciously misogynistic attacks against them.[19]

Other texts, even though they confront subordination, submerge ideology more carefully. Using Western narrative conventions, they show the transactions of a central character with the self, others, society, and history. As they embed their politics in humanized passions, they are more apt to be psychological dramas than overt feminist programs. These texts are also realistic. When subordinate groups in modern Western culture are able to speak, but when they believe that their stories have not yet been adequately told, they will tend to turn to realism, the form that promises the appearance of accuracy. Because such texts can be persuasive and instructive, I wish to mention three of them, all from the United States: *Work* (1873) by Louisa May Alcott (1832–1888), the prolific and popular writer, the author of *Little Women; Burning Questions* (1978) by Alix Kates Shulman (1932–), the contemporary novelist, radical feminist, and editor of Emma Goldman; and, finally, "Sweat" (1925), by Zora Neale Hurston (1903–1960), the black writer and anthropologist, who died in poverty and obscurity.[20]

As many people know, *Work* adapts *Pilgrim's Progress* to a nineteenth-century woman's life. Christie, Alcott's Christian, is an orphan girl. Her father was the heir of urbane culture, her mother of rural strength. Christie integrates, then, the best of various American bloodlines. She leaves the provincial farm where she has been raised in order to create, for herself, a more independent and gratifying life. Having neither legacy nor husband, she must work. Systematically, Christie takes on the jobs open to women in the nineteenth-century: domestic service; the stage; being a governess, in a home with a flighty, rich mistress who has a seductive brother; companion, wife; secretary; seamstress. She also befriends a black cook, an ex-prostitute, and a laundress. Each of these jobs is demeaning, marginal, depressing. Women accept them because they have no choice, and if they survive them, it is because of their character, not because of the job. Christie's marriage is happy, but brief. Her husband dies, heroically, in the Civil War. Despite such a bleak, trying vision of the world of work and of the home, Alcott gives us a species of a happy ending. Christie, at forty, has three consolations: a daughter, whom she loves; work, with women, which satisfies her; and religious faith, which sustains her.

Burning Questions adapts, not a religious, but a political quest. A late modern secularist, Shulman rewrites the autobiographies of radical women—Emma Goldman, Louise Michel—to fit the conditions of a twentieth-century American woman's life. Zane IndiAnna is the daughter of a bourgeois, nuclear family in the Midwest. Her mother is supportive; her father supportive but strong-minded. After graduating from a junior college, at the age of eighteen, she comes to New York in 1958. She falls in among Beats and Bohemians, who exploit her sexually and mock her psychically. To earn her living, she takes on a number of secretarial jobs. Partly in order to escape from the Midwest, she marries a lawyer and has three children. She never fully represses her rebellious self. She violates some norms. She marches for civil rights; she gets arrested at an antidraft demonstration; she has an affair. Nevertheless, she largely becomes a wife and mother, who subordinates herself to the needs of others. However, she discovers the new feminism, in the late 1960s. Psychologically, she emerges. Politically, she transforms herself. Shulman, too, gives us a species of a happy ending. For Zane, nearly forty, has her consolations: her children, whom she loves; her work, with women, which satisfies her and which has made her economically self-sufficient; and her political faith, which sustains her. Her life has also personalized the Hegelian pattern of thesis, her youth; antithesis, her marriage; and synthesis, her radical feminism, which has reanimated the best parts of her youth.

Obviously, *Work* and *Burning Questions* have their differences, which, in part, reveal profound cultural shifts within America itself. If Alcott explores religious desire, Shulman explores sexual desire. If Alcott praises submission and self-sacrifice, those "stern, sad, angels," Shulman praises self-autonomy. Yet, remarkably, both sustain Sanday's analysis of the sources of female power. Both assert women's need to achieve economic and political muscle. Like Charlotte Brontë, they represent that need through showing how hard and precarious women's lives are without such strength. Both Alcott and Shulman also believe that women are better off when men are dependent upon them. Yet, their men are most dependent for love, tenderness, sex, and children. Sadly, in industrial society, these activities take place within the same home that keeps women from achieving that economic and political muscle that they ought to have. Except for little boys, men depend less upon women than upon other men with public power. Alcott's men probably need women more than Shulman's. For Shulman's take advantage of the twentieth-century loosening of sexual restraints and marital bonds. As they seek love, tenderness, sex, and paternity, they easily go from one woman to another, substitute one woman for another. They also use the supermarket and the laundromat for services the home once gave.

Neither Alcott nor Shulman wholly sustains Sanday's provocative suggestion about the relationship between male dominance and war. Nor do they refute it. Rather, they present complex, ambiguous attitudes toward war. To be sure, war is a man's game. To be sure, war exacts a terrible price—for Christie the loss of her husband and the maiming of male bodies. Yet, Alcott finds the Civil War a moral necessity that provokes its own excitement and offers its own rewards. For Christie, they include a large measure of power and esteem. As a nurse, a role in which men are dependent upon her for their comfort and their life, she finds both. Moreover, in an awful exchange, her husband's grievous death brings her the chance to do the work she ultimately finds so enabling. Shulman finds the Vietnamese War contemptible, antiwar politics chauvinistic. Yet, Zane's protest against the war is part of her process of liberation; and her feminist politics, though tactically they prefer shock to terror, are militant and often warlike.

Both Alcott and Shulman add some oddly congruent prescriptions to Sanday's analysis for the repudiation of subordination. They dramatize the features of the rebellious psyche. Both Christie and Zane have reasons to rebel: Christie a callous Uncle who makes her dependence upon him psychically intolerable; Zane a more positive radical aunt who tactfully schools her about the diseases of the world. In both cases, the rebellious personality has an element of mystery, of inexplicability. Discontent is simply there, like a gift, or talent. Christie simply says that she has more "yeast" in her composition. Zane describes herself as a "born fanatic." An element of mystery exists, too, in the conditions of their life that ultimately permit their rebellion to flourish. Chance, coincidence, helps to keep Christie from suicide during a moment of profound depression. Luck helps Zane. She broods: "Skill, will, circumstance, history in some complex mysterious balance had all combined with luck to land us here" (p. 354).

Yet, neither Alcott nor Shulman mystifies rebellion. Surrounding Christie and Zane is a culture that offers some encouragement. Christie had read the Declaration of Independence, fairy tales, and *Jane Eyre*. She knows the discourse of political equality, of fantasy, and of women's rights to dislike subordination. Zane has the example of St. Joan; *Middletown,* a sociological text that critically analyzes her environment; and the autobiographies of women rebels. Through culture, they have a supportive context in which to place the rebellious self only half-conscious of how rebellious it might be. Finally, both become a part of a strong women's world. For Zane, that women's world, erotically charged, included a long, gratifying lesbian love affair. Each narrative closes with an image of a politicized female community that seeks to cross the barriers of race and class, a female community that transfigures domesticity into resistance. In brief, in *Work* and *Burning Questions,* women who reject subordination do so in the company of other women. Together, they have a sustaining ideology and toughness. In female interdependence is female independence.

Consistently, the writing and speaking of black women in the United States has strongly affirmed the importance of a female community to the strong black woman. However, my third text, by a black woman writer, studies a rebellion executed in isolation, without the buoyant consolation of a group, culture, or education. "Sweat" tells of Delia, a black washerwoman in Florida. She has been married for fifteen years to Sykes, who has beaten her, physically and psychologically, since the beginning of their union. Audaciously unfaithful, he expresses no need for her. Nevertheless, she has stayed with him. Though the men in the local black community disapprove of Sykes, they offer Delia little support. Two other forces help her: her church, which offers the compensations and consolations of faith, and the knowledge that she owns her home, real estate she has bought with her earnings as a laundress.

Delia finally rebels—when Sykes goes too far. He touches a nerve, which no one could have seen until it responds. It tells Delia that her survival, her sense of life itself, is now threatened. The first upswelling of female insubordination is neither ideological nor predictable. Rather, it is an abrupt reaction to a suddenly intolerable pressure, to an intolerable dissonance between what is happening and what must happen if a woman is to go on. Sykes has been openly consorting with a woman to whom he promises Delia's house and land. Coming home one Sunday, he drapes a bullwhip over her shoulders as she kneels to sort out piles of laundry. He then installs a caged rattlesnake in the yard, knowing sadistically how snakes terrify her.

Delia's first rebellion is verbal. Appropriating one of his tactics, she talks back to the blustering, astonished Sykes. Then, escalating brutality to attempted murder, he secretly puts the snake in the laundry basket he thinks she will open. Though a "gibbering wreck," she escapes, to hide in the barn. There, in one evening, she passes through a psychological process of revolt. She goes from coherent thought to "cold, bloody rage," to introspection, to retrospection, to an "awful calm." At dawn, Sykes returns drunk. In the bedroom, the snake strikes, to kill him. Though sickened, Delia lets him die horribly, realizing that he has seen her see him.

With the power of deciding whether Sykes will live or die, she makes him dependent upon her—although his dependence is more a fatal vulnerability that he has created through vain presumptions of invulnerability.

Having gone to war with Sykes, turning his weapons against him, she is now free. She has not lusted for violence. Indeed, she has passively, miserably accepted it for years. When she fights, she uses more chaotic cunning than physical aggression. A snake, not a fist, is her tool. Her war is private, personal; not public, social. If Delia is an Amazon, she lacks company. Yet, only her terrified willingness to kill breaks her bruising, mutilating alliance with Sykes.

Perhaps I have derived from my texts—my anthropology and fiction—little more than common sense might have uttered if I had had the modesty, simplicity, and common sense to summon it. Certainly I have blatantly evaded the sophisticated interrogations of the labyrinthian nexus of literature, writing, and "life" that poststructural and semiotic critics have so intelligently constructed. Despite these demurrers, I do suggest that if women are to resist subordination, as women writers partially did, they must command resources and men's recognition of women's necessity. Women must, as well, be willing to risk loss. Such a statement is not meant to glorify pugnacity, to romanticize death, or to endorse heedlessly women's performance in armed forces or police departments. Even if Sanday wonders if a historical cause of male dominance has been men's willingness to fight as a group and a

historical cause of female subordination has been women's unwillingness to do so, she is not prescribing that women now give up their
cabbages and become captains and kings. When I speak of risking
loss, I am realistically judging the capacity of authority to punish those
who doubt its legitimacy, supporting the worth of self-defense, and
reclaiming rituals that emblemize a passage from momentary loss to
new gain, death to rebirth.

My texts also tend to assert—as a philistine common sense and a
quantity-obsessed social science will not—the vitality of the relationship between cultural artifacts and the rebellious woman's consciousness. Those artifacts harrow and nurture that consciousness.
Neither epiphanies nor conversions are the result of some version of
the immaculate conception. They flare up after years of preparation.
So a dancer splits space in a millisecond after arduous toil. The
woman who resists female subordination—no matter how erratic she
may be, no matter how instantaneous she believes her consciousness
of the wrong of subordination to be—may have had a long engage-
ment with some signals from her culture. In a self-praising gesture
that is no less valid for being that, texts and textualizers warn us of
their patience and their own sly, peculiar power.

Notes

1. A recent endorsement of the universality of male dominance is
Michelle Zimbalist Rosaldo, "The Use and Abuse of Anthropology," *Signs:
Journal of Women in Culture and Society* 5:3 (Spring 1980): 389–417. For coun-
terarguments, see Eleanor Leacock, *Myths of Male Dominance: Collected Articles
on Women Cross-Culturally* (New York: Monthly Review Press, 1981), and Carol
MacCormick and Marilyn Strathern, eds., *Nature, Culture and Gender* (New
York: Cambridge University Press, 1980).

2. Samuel Beckett, "The Unnamable,". *Three Novels* (New York: Grove
Press, Evergreen 1965), 414.

3. Peggy Reeves Sanday, *Female Power and Male Dominance: On the Origins of
Sexual Inequality* (Cambridge and New York: Cambridge University Press,
1981), 114.

4. For more detail, see my article "Sex, Gender, and American Culture,"
Women and Men: Changing Roles, Relationships, and Perceptions, ed. Libby A.
Cater and Anne Firor Scott, with Wendy Martyna (New York: Aspen Institute
for Humanistic Studies, 1976), 201–44; my article "Ad/d Feminam: Women,
Literature, and Society," *Literature and Society: Selected Papers from the English
Institute, 1978*, ed. Edward Said (Baltimore: Johns Hopkins Press, 1980), 174–
92; Sandra M. Gilbert and Susan Gubar, *The Madwoman in the Attic* (New
Haven: Yale University Press, 1979); Tillie Olsen, *Silences* (New York: Dela-
corte Press, Seymour Lawrence, 1978), 306.

5. Helen Taylor, "Class and Gender in Charlotte Brontë's *Shirley,*" *Feminist Review* 1 (1979): 90.

6. Angeline Goreau, *Reconstructing Aphra* (New York: Dial Press, 1980), 117.

7. Tillie Olsen, *Yonnondio: From the Thirties* (New York: Delacorte Press, Seymour Lawrence, 1974), 4.

8. For a study of women novelists in Victorian England who exemplify the empty-field phenomenon, see Gaye Tuchman and Nina Fortin, "Edging Women Out: Some Suggestions About the Structure of Opportunities and the Victorian Novel," *Signs: A Journal of Women in Culture and Society* 6:2 (Winter 1980): 308–25. Obvious examples include mysteries, children's literature, popular-advice manuals, contemporary Gothic romances, early "soap operas."

9. Carolyn Heilbrun, *Reinventing Womanhood* (New York: W. W. Norton and Co., 1979), 72.

10. Ellen Moers, *Literary Women: The Great Writers* (Garden City, New York: Doubleday and Co., 1976), esp. 13–41.

11. For a fine analysis of this, see Carol Ohmann, "Historical Reality and 'Divine Appointment' in Charlotte Brontë's Fiction," *Signs* 2:4 (Summer 1977): 757–78.

12. Mary Kelley, "The Sentimentalists: Promise and Betrayal in the Home," *Signs: Journal of Women in Culture and Society* 4:3 (Spring 1979): 436–37.

13. Diva Daims, "Toward a Feminist Tradition," with Janet Grimes, Computer Print-Out, State University of New York/Albany (April 6, 1982), lines 119–23.

14. Antonio Gramsci, *Letters from Prison,* selected, translated from the Italian, and introduced by Lynne Lawner (New York: Harper and Row, Harper Colophon Book, 1975, copyright 1973), 245.

15. For an exploration of female and male ways of reading, see Annette Kolodny, "A Map for Rereading: Or, Gender and the Interpretation of Literary Texts," *New Literary History* 11:3 (Spring 1980): 451–67.

16. I am, I hope with reasonable justice, taking this argument from Wolfgang Iser, "Indeterminacy and the Reader's Response in Prose Fiction," *Aspects of Narrative: Selected Papers from the English Institute,* ed. J. Hillis Miller (New York: Columbia University Press, 1971), 1–45. For a synthesis of feminist and reader response criticism, see Judith Fetterly, *The Resisting Reader* (Bloomington: Indiana University Press, 1978).

17. For helpful comments about the New Woman and recent studies of the literature about her, see Nina Auerbach, "Feminist Criticism Reviewed," *Gender and Literary Voice,* ed. Janet Todd (New York: Holmes and Meier Publishers, Inc., 1980), 258–68. See, too, Elaine Showalter, *A Literature of Their Own* (Princeton: Princeton University Press, 1977), 182–87.

18. The best-known feminist Utopia is Charlotte Perkins Gilman, *Herland,* first published in 1915 and reissued in 1979 (New York: Pantheon Press), with an introduction by Ann J. Lane.

19. The phrase *feminist polemic* is from Moira Ferguson, Department of English, University of Nebraska/Lincoln, whose important anthology and definition of the genre is forthcoming from the Feminist Press. See, too, Joan Kelly, *Women, History and Theory* (Chicago: University of Chicago Press, 1984), 65–109.

20. Hurston is almost the coeval of Richard Wright (1908–1960), an obser-

vation that I am grateful to W. W. Cook for making. I will be quoting from the following texts: Louisa May Alcott, *Work,* introduction by Sarah Elbert (New York: Schocken Books, 1977), 125. Jean Fagan Yellin, "From *Success* to *Experience:* Louisa May Alcott's *Work,*" *Massachusetts Review* 21:3 (Fall 1980): 527–39 (a good exegesis); Alix Kates Shulman, *Burning Questions* (New York: Alfred A. Knopf, 1978), 14; "Sweat," *I Love Myself When I'm Laughing . . . And Then Again When I Am Looking Mean and Impressive: A Zora Neale Hurston Reader,* ed. Alice Walker (Old Westbury, N.Y.: Feminist Press, 1979), 197–207.

AND THE LAST WALLS DISSOLVED

ON IMAGINING A STORY OF THE SURVIVAL OF DIFFERENCE

Carole B. Tarantelli

Contemporary molecular physics has the concept of "holes" that are not at all equal to the simple absence of matter. These "holes" display an absence of matter in a structural position that implies its presence. In these conditions a "hole" behaves so that it is possible to measure its weight, in negative quantities of course. Physicists regularly speak of "heavy" and "light" holes.

Yuri Lotman, *Analysis of the Poetic Text*

I dissolve, go away, am left with nothing, nothing, nothing—unless I am the wind that blows through the immense spaces that lie between electron and electron, proton and its attendants, spaces that cannot be filled with *nothing*, since nothing is *nothing*.

Doris Lessing, *The Making of the Representative for Planet 8*[1]

I

Much feminist scholarship can be seen as an attempt to create a story for women different from the traditional one, as part of the larger

I would like to thank Myra Jehlen, whose suggestions were essential to the final form this essay took.

process which claims for women the fundamental right to interpret the meaning of our acts. These efforts have, among other things, attempted to understand individual women (literary women, historical figures) or groups of women (suffragists, women wage earners) as cultural actors, the originators and interpreters of the meaning of their acts, projected into what Hannah Arendt calls the space of appearance, the space "where I appear to others as others appear to me, where [persons] exist not merely like other living or inanimate things but make their appearance explicitly."[2]

Although feminist scholarship has shown that women are so emphatically capable of being rival intelligences, it has not shown that we have gained the all-important control over the outcome of our stories. It is one thing to be able to speak, to articulate an alternative vision, as opposed to being constrained in silence. It is another thing to be able to ensure the survival or, better, even the realization of the dissenting vision; and it is this, surely, which we are aiming for and have not reached.

The representation of the female figure in literature is a case in point. For example, great nineteenth-century English women novelists were wonderfully capable of revealing the rich interiority of their heroines, and their difference from that culture's story of women. Yet, this subjectivity was doomed to defeat when, at the end of the novel, the text allied itself with the world: the first Catherine Earnshaw in *Wuthering Heights,* for example, the antagonistic woman who cannot reduce her excessiveness to the social norm, inevitably dies, while her daughter, whose story coincides with the traditioinal female story, survives to be awarded the traditional literary prize, the triumph of the perfectly adequate marriage. Indeed, as Myra Jehlen has convincingly argued,[3] insofar as it is tied to "reality," the already existent, the novel, it would seem, *must* represent the defeat or assimilation of the rebellious heroine, for if her story coincided with the traditional story of femininity, she would have an uninteresting tale to recount; and if it differed, the imposition of that meaning on the world, the realization of her vision, would automatically necessitate a radical (unrealistic) revision of the world. So the "realistic" paradigmatic story will logically be, as in fact it is, that of the disappointment of the character's great expectations, the loss of her illusions (as with Dorothea Brooke in George Eliot's *Middlemarch,* to name only one example, a heroine whose life is "dispersed among hindrances, instead of centring in some long-recognisable deed"[4]). The novel will tell the story of the reduction of the different to the same. Or if her story is the story of her refusal to succumb to circumstance, her unwillingness or inability to stop what Sandra M. Gilbert and Susan Gubar have called her mad dance of rebellion, it will be the story of her expulsion from the "sane" world, that part of the whole human experience which can be narrated. As in *Wuthering Heights,* it will, instead, portray her death.[5]

The defeat or assimilation of the different; the inability to accord value, and hence full survival, to anything except the already existent—this is certainly an old tale. Is it, in spite of feminist scholarship's recovery of female dissent, still the necessary end for the tale of difference? Or, in social terms, can the different woman exist only by negative differentiation, that is, insofar as she affirms that she does not correspond to the story of female experience projected by her culture?

Lothman's metaphor, borrowed from molecular physics, reflects an evolution in thought which indicates that, beyond pious hopes and facile enthusiasms, another tale might have become thinkable. Looked at closely, this metaphor portrays the transformation of the traditional inability to grant reality to anything but the already visible. At the end of the evolution in thought implicit in the metaphor, value (in Lothman's terms, weight) is accorded to the different.

The metaphor sends us back beyond the conceptual transformation it portrays to the time when the "holes," which are its object, had not yet been discovered—although, of course, they (presumably), then as now, existed. Indeed, we must suppose that until their discovery, the electrons, positive presences arranged in regular structures, had seemed to compose matter, to *be* the existent; and that thought about matter, systematic as all thought, had forged its theories, made its calculations, disseminated its truths, without taking into account its own future evolution, the discovery of the holes, the as-yet unseen.

But the examination of the molecular structure revealed that the electrons did not, as had been thought, occupy all the spaces structurally at their disposition; they were related, not only and exclusively to each other, but to something else, albeit an emptiness—logically an emptiness, for if the electrons *are* the existent, where they are absent there must be nothing, a "hole," a *lack* of the only possible presence.

Then (and there the metaphor reaches its third and final turn), by some undisclosed process, the holes gave indications that they were not "a simple absence of matter" but rather an absence "in a structural position which implies its presence," with measurable ("in negative terms") weight. In other words, here the different is conceptualized in its structural and necessary relationship to "matter," the already known;[6] and more important, not as empty, but full. But of what? Lotman cannot describe this apparent emptiness (except as the negative of the electrons' positivity). Or perhaps, if we may restore futurity to the metaphor, it may not yet be describable, for future thought may possibly create a language capable of describing it *in its own terms.*[7]

The recodification of difference has been a tendency implicit in much of the thought of our century (the psychoanalytic destruction of the nuclear subject by bestowing official recognition on the unconscious is one example of this tendency;[8] and the progressive attribution of more and more human behavior to the cultural and historical rather than natural or biological causes, thus making them modifiable, is another). By establishing beyond question the historical relativity of our gender definitions, feminist thought has certainly helped to establish this relativity of cultural discourse in general. Our cultural discourse is a totality which does not contain everything—did not, for example, contain women, who were decisively not *only* the relative creatures the culture had imagined them to be. For feminist thought has demonstrated that women also existed elsewhere, an elsewhere from which, among other things, came the impulse and the courage to write or to act in their own interest.

These developments in thought were reinforced by a historical fact which provided the basis for the further evolution in the status of the Other indicated in Lotman's metaphor. For the terrible possibility of total nuclear destruction has had, among other things, the paradoxical effect of rendering objectively necessary the creation of a story of social life which would include the survival of the Other. The great Victorian women narrators referred to earlier wrote in a culture forced to contemplate the traumatic fact that the free play of its most profound productive impulses had produced the spectacle of unprecedented mass suffering (the industrial system produced by the exemplary technological and economic progress brought about by the activities of the bourgeois *homo economicus* was constructed upon the mutilated bodies of the cheap child laborers who passed sixteen hours of their day in front of the machines of Manchester). The terrible question which was posed by that spectacle of extremity—the question as to the cost of culture, as to whether the principal product of productivity might not be death—was carried to its logical conclusion in our time by the contemplation of the possibility of the total obliteration of life by nuclear destruction. The trauma for thought of nuclear destruction consisted in the fact that it was the ultimate and total expression of what was already a common, perhaps even a fundamental, practice of our culture: the application of the rhetoric of obliteration to the devalued Other. That is, death (total devalorization) had been the treatment traditionally deserved for those persons judged impure, heretical, insane, unproductive, revolutionary, reactionary, in a word Other. The bomb extended to indiscriminate physical obliteration, this meaning death. The fact that in Germany this rhetoric had so recently been applied to the Jewish Other left no room for the illusion that Western ethics would necessarily be a sufficient restraint against its urge to obliterate the Other, or the different.

The difference of total nuclear warfare from past forms of obliteration was its indiscriminate application—to the mother country as to the enemy—of the obliteration that in the past had been applied only to those persons judged Other. Thus, at a theoretical level, *it obliterated the difference from the Other.* Since it is possible to argue that the separation of the other from the plenum of human life and its devaluation (of which obliteration is the extreme version) is fundamental to our cultural system,[9] nuclearism can be said to have decisively placed in question the imperial claims of culture. The bomb rendered it imperative to imagine others.

Against the background of these developments in thought we can more accurately see the question with which we began. The survival of the different as itself, the modification of the old story of the reduction of the different to the same, in its extreme form the extermination of the Other—can we see signs of this much-to-be-augured development extended beyond our wishes or our hopes and embodied in our cultural forms? In what follows, I wish to examine some contemporary texts of the women's literary tradition of the decades in which nuclear destruction became a social, historical possibility. These texts of the 1960s and 1970s in my view indicate, however partially, a change in the fate of the different, according it, as in Lotman's metaphor, a space for its survival.

II

> . . . the edges of terrestrial reality
>
> Joanne Greenberg,
> *I Never Promised You
> a Rosegarden.*[10]

Madness, a feminist criticism has repeatedly pointed out,[11] is a central metaphor in the women's literary tradition. By existing outside of the norms and limits which structure ordinary exprience, in a dark elsewhere whose laws are not those of the diurnal world of sane discourse, the madwoman poses the problem of female indifference in a paradigmatic form.

As Sandra M. Gilbert and Susan Gubar have so brilliantly demonstrated, the madwoman, at least in the nineteenth-century English texts, represents the story of women's rebellion as the proud queen's suicidal dance in the red-hot shoes merited by her mad anger. For self-destructive rage is the traditionally available emotional alternative to the Snow White passivity of the acceptance of cultural subordination. The alternative is between the mad exit from confining social form and the "sane" acceptance of limitation. The question behind this choice and implicitly asked by the protagonists of the nineteenth-century women's novels for whose stories these were the possible outcomes was this: Given history, given structure, how can I be? And the answer, of course, was, as we have seen, I, as I, cannot.

Through Charlotte Perkins Gilman and Virginia Woolf (to name only two), texts of madness continue to pose the problem of the protagonist's difference. Our period sees a reflowering of the tradition. Several texts of the 1960s, such as Sylvia Plath's *The Bell Jar* and Joanne Greenberg's *I Never Promised You a Rosegarden,* can be used to illustrate how the status of the heroine, whose difference takes the extreme form of madness, is rendered less precarious. In the 1960s novels, the question as to the possibility for the survival of her difference implicit in the ninteenth-century texts is fundamentally modified. It becomes, as I hope to show, not "Given history, given structure, how can I be?" but "Given that *I am*, why history, why structure?"

The protagonist's madness in these two novels renders explicit her radical refusal of a world which will not allow her to constitute herself as a subject, that is, to be present to herself and others on her own terms. In Joanne Greenberg's *I Never Promised You a Rosegarden,* the heroine Deborah is part of the mad world of the "atomized armies of persons who had severed their claims to membership in all the world's other groups and orders" and exists on "the edges of terrestrial reality" (pp. 64–65). In *The Bell Jar,* Esther Greenwood makes clear her disgust at the social reality which surrounds her, taking, for example, a long look at the artifacts of modernity, the "colossal junkyard, the swamps and back lots of Connecticut . . . one broken-down fragment bearing no relation to another" and decides that "it looked one hell of a mess."

This refusal comports the risk of psychic annihilation for the un-conformed self, which is reduced to self-genesis, to mere subjectivity. No genealogy exists which will enable her to understand herself. For example, Esther in *The Bell Jar* has an impossible choice among the parade of "queer old ladies," like Jay Cee, the editor, or Philomena Guinea, the author of popular pulp novels, who exercised derivative and second-rate power in the leftover positions the culture allowed to women, or Mrs. Willard, in her sensible suits and shoses using her strong-minded self to perpetuate the priority of male meaning; or

Dodo Conway, who eternally breeds her innumerable offspring. There are no other lives which can point to and thus confirm hers, no one who can see her. Thus, although Esther identifies with her creative self, she is able to express that identification only in the trivial and ultimately self-destructive image of her self as "the colored arrows from a Fourth of July rocket"; "I wanted," she says, "change and excitement and to shoot off in all directions myself" (p. 68).

In *I Never Promised You a Rosegarden*, too, the madwoman is shown to be mad partly because the unsponsored self is unable to recognize and use its powers, which are then turned against her self. The image in which the heroine imagines her sickness is that of a volcano. That is, she *is* powerful and, having, like a bottled-up volcano, no normal way to express that "male" power, she lives her self as an immense menace to itself and others. The madwomen of this novel, in fact, are "free" to express their "masculine" powers, their physical strength, their violence, their exhibitionistic sexuality, at the price of enormous pain, like the tiny old lady, the white-haired Miss Coral who lifts an iron hospital bed off the floor and hurls it acorss the room.

As Mary Shelley had intuited in *Frankenstein*, one of the tragically logical responses of the "monstrous" subject who cannot find that confirmation in the eyes of an other, which is the necessary condition for (social) existence, is to annul the self. A self without a story cannot be "seen," and thus it does not apparently exist. A story can never presuppose only a teller, it also presupposes a hearer who confirms it. Esther Greenwood, of course, also tries to annul her unacceptable self; but though her suicide attempt is evidently an act of self-hatred, its meaning goes beyond this. For it is *also* a refusal to reconcile the self which found no space in the "junkyard" with the world. Her suicide thus implicitly asks, Why history?

Another logical response to the inability to exist within the forms of social existence is to attempt to exit from them. This exit can be expressed at all levels of psychic and social life—from the fact that the person needs to exist inside the walls and barriers of the insane asylum, which place her outside "normal" life, to the schizophrenic's adherence to the knowable laws of the "unreal" kingdom in her head, over the unpredictable and chaotic "real" world where the self-representations of persons and their real meanings never coincide, to the awesome experience of madness as the wrenching of the self from *all* levels of meaning.

> A black wind came up. The walls dissolved and the world became a combination of shadows . . . all direction became a lie. The laws of physics and solid matter were repealed . . . . She did not know whether

she was standing or sitting down, which way was upright . . . . She lost
track of the parts of her body . . . . As sight went spinning erratically
away and back, she tried to clutch at thoughts only to find that she had
lost all memory of the English language . . . . Memory went entirely,
and then mind, and then there was only the faster and faster succes-
sion of sensations . . . . These suggested something secret and horrible,
but she could not catch what it was because there was at last no longer a
responding self.[12]

In this description, madness is shown to be the self's attempt to do
totally without the psychic structure destroying her. The desire to get
out of a structure which is hostile to female life is here the desire for
an apocalypse. The mad self, like the souls of the redeemed, aban-
dons all human meaning and, thus, like the suicide, ceases to exist as a
self, at least while it is undergoing the experience of madness. But in
these novels, the identification of the story with the figures of the mad
protagonist totally involves the text's meaning with her fate.[13] In
other words, unlike nineteenth-century novels such as *Frankenstein* and
Wuthering Heights, there is no "objective" world outside her story to
survive her death and console the reader for her defeat. Her "I"
precedes the story, precedes history, as it were, and thus, since the
story exists, is by definition indestructible. The world may seem to
disappear, but the "I" cannot. However singular, this female self
exists—like the mad Sylvia, in *Rosegarden,* who breaks the two-year
silence which had made her seem "a useless piece of ward furniture,"
to assert that she is "sick, but not dead" (p. 134).

But if the exit from psychic structure involves the loss of meaning
for the mad character without the disappearance of her self, this
meaning is then clearly seen to be a social construct, the self's power
to attribute relevance to what it perceives (it is a "gift," as Deborah
says, if the self's meaning and social meaning can coincide). So when
meaning returns to the heroine, first to the physical world in the
ability to see its forms and colors, and then to the personal and social
world, it returns because the self which had "left" the culture is able to
reenter at another level, where meaning is not the imposition of the
vision of others on the self (traditional feminine meaning). The newly
sane self is able to recount its story, has become a full subject.

Other early 1960s accounts of madness, though, hardly point toward a positive solution of the problem of the female subject. At the
end of *The Bell Jar,* Esther is "reborn," but this rebirth is a return to
the place in the world she had occupied before the descent of the bell
jar—she is "patched, retreaded and approved for the road" (p. 199).

And, to take another example, at the end of *Wide Sargasso Sea,* Jean

Rhys's revisionary account of the genesis of Bertha Mason,[14] the heroine goes mad because the world is totally other than her self, and all of its expressions monolithically combine to negate her: the political world—as symbolized by the burning of her home by rebellious ex-slaves; the social world—as a child she is despised by Europeans because she is a Creole and hated by blacks because she is white; the legal world—her money, which could provide the means to escape from Rochester's desire to annul her existence, is legally his after their marriage. And on the most intimate level, where we engage in acts of self-presentation and are seen by others as we see ourselves, she finds no confirmation of that subjectivity. At the end of the novel, the mad self of the heroine is identified with the physical sensations and warm colors of her West Indian childhood, the only things which have not been appropriated by her husband Rochester, and she imposes them as fire on his cold English world, burning Thornfield, but, as we know from *Jane Eyre*, destroying herself as well.[15]

I Never Promised You a Rosegarden indicates the way out of the bewildering solitude of the unsponsored female subject who lives a mad existence in a precarious and lonely present and whose future is preempted. This is enabled by the woman doctor, who confirms her own and her patient's powers: Dr. Fried is a "lightning rod . . . the grounding path for such power" (p. 99). This power enables Deborah to recover for her own use the powers which had been repressed in the construction of the precarious ego which the social world of parents, teachers, and peers had demanded. But this ending, too, like the nineteenth-century narratives, portrays the reduction of the subject. For Deborah must abandon her gods, must choose between her "real" world and her "imaginary" world (a cure for which the readers of this autobiographical novel can only be grateful, but which should not prevent us from observing its logical implications). The end of the novel, then, implicitly affirms that the world—*this* world, *this* structure, *this* history—is logically as well as temporally prior to the subject. Thus, even though the character determines to "use" her mad experience, as the doctor had assured her she could, she has in some way closed the doors between her self and another, possible world, which, thrown back into darkness, has become precisely that, Other.[16]

Madness and suicide in these novels, then, represent the refusal to live within the narrative structure of the culture without being able to generate an adequate account of the self. These texts do not certainly imagine a totally successful outcome for the story of difference, its survival as itself. But unlike the nineteenth-century texts, the traditional forms for the female story cannot claim the absolute preeminence over the different self which would render unthinkable its existence.

III

> . . . and they all followed quickly on after
> the others as the last walls dissolved.[17]
>
> DORIS LESSING, *Memoirs of a Survivor*

There is a decisive difference between these 1960s narratives and the two novels of the 1970s which we will examine here. In Margaret Atwood's *Surfacing* and Doris Lessing's *Memoirs of a Survivor,* the protagonist is projected out of *this* world: she voluntarily exits from the sane world with its laws and limits. These two texts transform the earlier texts' vision of madness as pathology—madness becomes the self's journey beyond structure to explore that part of the whole human nature which must be driven into darkness in the interest of social order. Thus they affirm the logical priority of the female subject to the already existent.

The nameless protagonist of Margaret Atwood's *Surfacing* is not driven out of her mind but voluntarily leaves that part of it which is "sane," which is confined inside the (linguistic, social) system—or which, needing "someone to speak to and words that can be understood" is coterminous with that part of her whole nature reflected in the eyes of the male.[18] Frozen by the traumatic recognition of her own powerlessness—symbolized by an abortion, by her inability to establish continuity with the future, to bear *her* child—the narrator of *Surfacing* has repressed the memory of her past and lives in a numbed present empty of feeling. Unable to face her part in the death of "that part of myself, or separate creature" (p. 168), she wrongly remembers it as a real child she has abandoned to her ex-husband; she imagines it as a child, conceived in a body, her body, which was simply a vehicle for the masculine productive powers of her husband, intended as his claim to immortality, born in an event orchestrated by the doctor gods of male technology. Thus the child, the child self, is wholly the product of male intention, not hers. But as long as she is unable to remember the etiology and real causes of her present self, she is of necessity without power to claim hegemony over her own story and to project an alternative future. She is without power to do anything but submit in silent disdain to being a "sane" woman, perpetrating the false vision by which the culture sells itself to the child-consumers of the illustrations which earn her her living.

Only through the "abolishing" of the "wrong form that encases" her (p. 205), through a voluntary psychic journey undertaken in the Canadian wilderness into the visionary space "after the failure of logic" ("like stepping through a usual door and finding yourself in a different galaxy, purple trees and red moons and a green sun," p. 171), can she hear the "other language" (p. 220) in which her dead mother and father communicate the "vision" of the absolute impersonality of all that fills the "spaces" "between the borders" (p. 211), constitutive of social life.

> Now I understand the rule. They can't be anywhere that's marked out, enclosed: even if I opened the doors and fences they could not pass in, to houses and cages, they can move only in the spaces between them, they are against borders. To talk with them I must approach the condition they themselves have entered; in spite of my hunger I must resist the fence. (p. 211)

This journey enables the remembering of her past lives, of the etiology and causes of her situation (and among them, the truth about the abortion). She can then reenter her own time, whose authority, being limited to the space inside the borders, is no longer seen as the only time and thus cannot obligate her to accept the reduction of her self to the world's story of it. No longer dependent for her existence on the confirmation in the eyes of the male, she can project a future, have *her* child. This future is not necessarily obligated to the fatal choices of the past, "to immerse oneself, join in the war, or to be destroyed" (p. 220). Things may still be as they have been, but may also be something else. ("The word games, the winning and losing games are finished; at the moment there are no others but they will have to be invented, withdrawing is no longer possible and the alternative is death," p. 223).

Unlike the endings of the classic nineteenth-century novels, which ally the novel with the past and present world and either project the protagonist into a future that sees her happy in the reduction of her powers to their possible use in the space inside the borders or witness her death, the close of *Surfacing* is open to a future in which endings are not final but provisional. Thus it attenuates the univocal structure of earlier novels, introducing the possibility that this present may produce a new future, not a repetition of the past, one genuinely new.

Doris Lessing's *The Memoirs of a Survivor* is set in an indeterminate future after the catastrophe, where Western capitalist production is grinding to a halt—where "all forms of social organization" are "breaking up" and the world is regressing to a primitive state of autarchic production in a barter economy. Migrating nomadic bands are the new form of social organization. Lessing imagines an *exit* into a space where the different can survive as itself.

The crisis imagined in *Memoirs* leads the world back through less and less "civilized" forms of social organization (from postindustrial pseudo-democracy to "packs and tribes" which had a structure "like those of primitive man or of animals," p. 174), until it produces gangs of parentless children born and bred in the no man's land of the abandoned underground, gangs with *no* structure, whose random violence casts terror into the hearts of all those whose subservience to a social structure, however rudimentary, makes their behavior intelligible to their peers. Lessing's image of the ultimate horrible human product of social disintegration—gangs of three- and four-year-old children, feeding on offal (garbage and cooked rats), inhabiting dark caves and tunnels, who murder on whim, each other as well as outsiders—is a resonant reimagining of the age-old horror of the Other; but here, an Other who is not, as is usual, imagined at the limits of the social system, but entirely outside it. In traditional terms, the underground children of *Memoirs* are worse than the damned, for the damned exist inside the universal meaning projected and controlled by the divine Orderer, whereas these children, the narrator makes clear, exist entirely outside any structure whatever; they have, as she says, no "norms."

Lessing's children represent a terrifying paradox. They are inhuman humans. On the one hand, they are physically human. But they acknowledge no values whatsoever, including the value of human life, their own or others'. They thus are culturally inhuman. On a theoretical level, they represent the absolute priority of being to meaning, existence to value.

Their existence is an implicit threat to the bits and pieces of human community remaining in the novel: there is no imaginable community, however primitive, which could include beings like them. Thus they evoke the classic dilemma posed by the Other: the stark alternative betwen the elimination of the threat they represent to the human world or (as occurs in Lessing's novel, where there is no central authority capable of mounting a campaign to control them) their continued survival with the possibility of their overrunning what remains of the social world.

The crisis of the social life of the Western world is mirrored in the novel by the middle-aged narrator's inner crisis, which takes her "through the wall" of her sitting room ("Solid. Ordinary. A wall without a door or a window in it," p. 11) into a "somewhere else" which is an endless procession of rooms which re-present her own, the race's buried or forgotten lives, rooms, ruined by some unknown hand, full of dirt and disorder, "furnished this way or that and spanning the tastes and customs of millennia" (p. 346). "The rooms were empty. To make them inhabitable, what work needed to be done!" (p. 14).

But this visit to the larger world, beyond the walls and borders of everyday (conscious) life, is not only a visit to an anarchic, potentially destructive or unbearably constrictive realm, whose chaos the walls of the "real" city and "real" life are constructed to exclude. Unlike the imagining of the children, this trip into the unknown territory beyond "normal" structure gives access, first to a vision of hope created by a fleeting glance of the "rightful inhabitant" of that different space, and then to a vision of the potential fertility and productivity of that realm, a garden "filled with industry, usefulness, hope," under which there is another garden, occupying "the same area," and yet another.

> I looked at the food the earth was making, which would keep the next winter safe for us, for the world's people. Gardens beneath gardens, gardens above gardens; the food-giving surfaces of the earth doubled, trebled, endless—the plenty of it, the richness, the generosity. (p. 161)

When, at the "end," the "hidden pattern" in the wallpaper is "brought to life," the narrator and her ward Emily go through the wall for the last time. There in that place which "might present us with anything," they find a "giant black egg of pockmarked iron but polished and glossy" which, "by the force of their being there, fell apart." And out of this egg came rushing fragments of the scenes of the world beneath the wall, scenes of the characters' personal and racial past, scenes which, insufficient for the future, folded up "vanishing, dwindling and going." But in this "dissolving" of the structures of the old world, inadequate to the newly transformed characters, who remain themselves but "transmuted and in another key," they are not left abandoned to their own inadequacies of reaction and comprehension, but are helped by One "who went ahead showing them the way out of this collapsed little world into another order of world altogether," while the old world "fold[ed] up" and the "last walls dissolved" (p. 217).

In traditional apocalyptic literature, the entry into the other order can abolish the narrative voice of the visionary, who is taken into the ideal order, and the work is then narrated by the surviving heir and custodian of the meaning and power it generates. The visionary can also in other texts return to mundane reality, full of the significance of

that more "real," more "meaningful" space acceded to in her vision. In
Memoirs of a Survivor, though, the narrator is one of the "they" who
follow the One leading through the dissolving walls of this world, and
presumably narrates in the other world, remembering along with the
other survivors ("We all remember that time . . . the protracted period
of unease and tension before the end," p. 3). This imagination of an
other world, then, is not dependent, as in traditional apocalyptic
literature, on the death of the subject of the vision, whose reward is
her translation out of history (into Paradise) in an exchange of organic
for symbolic life, or her return to the world, a reacquisition of organic
at the expense of symbolic life. In other words, Lessing does not
project as the desired consummation of the novel the end of *all*
history, but the end of *this* history, which, no longer capable of maintaining life, has given way to another history, where the survivors are
living. The rebirth imagined in the novel is drawn, not from the
traditional ritual rebirths, which pass through ritual death (life rising
from the grave); it recovers the archaic and much more hopeful
feminine mystery of birth and generation, of life issuing from life.[19]
This new birth is not narratable: it is an un-image-inable state—for it
is without the walls which, with their separation of the subject from
the object, and one object from another, permit the perception of
images. It is a state in which the life of the person is finally absolutely
prior to structure, and in which meaning is finally subservient to
being, not the other way around. For the new world of *Memoirs of a
Survivor* is one in which the value of the subject is not predicated on
the existence of a devalued other, and the "human" world has finally
become coterminous with the number of living persons, including the
frightening children: "at the very last moment they came, his children
came running . . . and they all followed quickly on after the others as
the last walls dissolved."

IV

Feminist literary scholarship has rightly emphasized the fact that
one of the principal triumphs of the women's literary tradition has
been the recovery for visibility of the world from the female point of
view and of the hidden and unexpressed female part of the world.
But the significance of the novels examined here goes beyond this. For
their modification of traditional literary form through the modification of the moment of closure breaks the alliance between the text and
the "real" world, an alliance which, as we have seen, had witnessed
either the tragic defeat or the comic reduction of the difference of

their heroines, an alliance which had cast the prestige of the text on the side of the equation of the possible with the actual and the prediction of the future from the past. They break with the tradition of literary texts which hegemonize the whole of the narratable, from origin to end, texts where, in Jacques Ehrmann's words, "it is the past that, once interpreted, makes up the future (however ephemeral) of the present."[20] In these novels, rather, the vision of the reality of an elsewhere creates the possibility of an alliance between the text and a future which may possibly be new. The close of *Memoirs of a Survivor* prospects a future which has "transmuted" the past, and the new culture is radically different from the old, for it is allied with hope for the existence of all persons, and among them women.

Notes

1. *The Analysis of the Poetic Text* (Ann Arbor, 1976), 29. *The Making of the Representative for Planet 8* (New York, 1982), 84.

2. *The Human Condition* (Chicago, 1958), 198–99.

3. Myra Jehlen, "Archimedes and the Paradox of Feminist Criticism," *Signs* (Autumn 1981).

4. "Prelude" (New York, 1963), 2.

5. *The Madwoman in the Attic* (New Haven, 1979), especially Ch. 1. Jehlen, "Archimedes," has also made this point. Luce Irigaray, in *Ce Sexe qui n'en est pas un* (Paris, 1977), has made it on another level, affirming that women must conceive of their subjectivity (their desire) in a language whose metaphoric structure is based on the perceptions of the male body, leaving female experience no metaphors in which to conceive of itself.

6. Jehlen, "Archimedes," has suggested the need for a more conceptually adequate metaphor for thinking about women's relation to the literary tradition than the insular metaphor which underlies much feminist criticism of our literary tradition and much work in history as well. Drawn from the marxian vision of the class and the idea of the subculture which the ghettoized and relatively self-contained class develops, this metaphor allows us to concentrate our attention on the relationships among women writers in the literary tradition and the difficulties in the articulation of women's experience. But it is only partially relevant to women's experience and structural relationship to our society. Lotman's metaphor is also useful in that it offers another way of conceiving of female cultural presence.

7. Lotman's metaphor presupposes the existence of a detached scientific observer whose gaze penetrates the secrets of the molecular world. This, of course, is a common metaphor for intellectual activity and it has several problems which are relevant to our understanding of the problem of the "holes." For one thing, it arrogates activity exclusively to the encompassing eye and de facto excludes the possibility of intentionality on the part of the

phenomenon under observation. In our case, for example, it would be absurd to suggest that perhaps the holes imposed themselves on the attention of the observer. Another problem is that the metaphor of the extraneous glance inevitably totalizes its vision of the object under discussion; able to see it whole, it is not partial. Thus it effectively denies that conception of the object its proper future evolution. Stephen Toulmin asserts that this dethronement of Laplace's Omniscient Calculator has occurred in postmodern science. He observes that "the classical posture of pure spectator is no longer available even on the level of pure theory" ("The Construal of Reality: Criticism in Modern and Post Modern Science," *Critical Inquiry* 9:1 [September 1962]: 97).

8. The subject is no longer identical with the perception of himself. The other is also "inside."

9. Allen Grossman has argued this at length in a generative essay, "Why is Death in Arcadia? Poetic Process, Literary Humanism and the Example of the Pastoral," ms.

10. *I Never Promised You a Rosegarden* (New York, 1964), 65. Page numbers will follow the quotations in the text.

11. Elaine Showalter first noted this in "Killing the Angel in the House," *Antioch Review* 32:3. It is also, of course, a central thesis of *The Madwoman in the Attic.*

12. *The Bell Jar* (New York, 1972), 92. Page numbers will follow the quotations in the text.

13. *The Bell Jar* is a first-person narrative, while Greenberg's text is formally narrated in the third person. But the identification with the point of view of the protagonist is not less complete than it would be if the text were narrated in the first person.

14. New York, 1966.

15. Elizabeth R. Baer makes a similar point about the end of *Wide Sargasso Sea* in "The Sisterhood of Jane Eyre and Antoinette Cosway," in *The Voyage In; Fictions of Female Development,* edited by Elizabeth Abel, Marianne Hirsch, and Elizabeth Langland (Hanover and London, 1983), 142. I wrote this article before reading Baer's excellent essay.

16. I would not like to seem to advocate madness. In texts, both the author and the critic are permitted to play with the positive implications of the existence of the elsewhere implied by the mad experience without at the same time becoming advocates of the terrible suffering involved in the loss of a functioning ego, a loss which is inevitably part of real unwilled dissociation states.

17. Doris Lessing, *Memoirs of a Survivor* (New York, 1975). Page numbers will follow the quotations in the text.

18. *Surfacing* (New York, 1972), 222. Page numbers will follow the quotations in the text. The possibility of confirmation by female eyes is not present to the narrator before her visionary experience.

19. Cf. this statement of E. O. James in *The Cult of the Mother Goddess* (London, 1959): "The mystery cult of a goddess differed from that of a god in that the one was the mystery of birth and regeneration, of life issuing from life; the other was the mystery of death and rebirth, of life rising from the grave" (p. 179). Other scholars of ancient religions affirm the lethal nature of blood rites associated with the worship of the Great Mother. But James's representation of the mystery cult of the goddess is useful because it gives us a

paradigm of the process of transformation—be it psychic or social—which reflects real biological possibilities and is an alternative to the dominant one which passes through death.

20. "The Tragic/Utopian Meaning of History," *Yale French Studies* no. 58 (1979):28.

WOMEN IN THE THEATRE OF MEN
WHAT PRICE FREEDOM?

Marie-Claire Pasquier

Women have always had an ambiguous relation to the theatre, as writers or producers of plays, as actresses or directors, as spectators or critics, as creations in the fantasy world within drama itself (comedies, tragedies, the opera even). Let us examine this relation with the following two postulates. Although they seem incompatible at first, neither one can easily be dismissed:

1. Women *love* the theatre.
2. The theatre *excludes* women.

The two statements should stand in opposition to each other, separated by *but, even so,* or *yet*. But then which should come first? What women are we talking about? What kind, or kinds, of theatre? In response, I should be tempted to be even more dogmatic than I have been already and propose a variation on the opening postulates:

1. *All* kinds of women love *all* kinds of theatre.
2. *All* kinds of theatre exclude *all* kinds of women.

Even though I claim that women love the theatre, I do not believe that this is so because the theatre rejects them, that they are drawn to it in defiance or out of masochism. But before we can explore their attraction in more detail, we must first confront the ambivalence of the terms *theatre* and *women*.

Theatre can mean the solemn institution invented by those in power to provide people with a corpus of myths that sustain the social system. It turns disorderly carnival into "delightful measures," war into ceremony, conflict into acts of allegiance. In traditional Western culture, *women* fit into the system as society has shaped them and as they wish to remain. They have no alternative, or rather they seem unaware of any. From this perspective, nothing is more understandable than the fact that women love to go to the theatre. For them it means dressing up in gowns and jewels, getting out into a legitimate public place, parading, glittering, doing credit to a male escort dressed up in his uniform, or dinner jacket, with his decorations, his cane, his mustache (cf. Virginia Woolf's descriptions in *Three Guineas*). Women of the aristocracy, and wives of the bourgeoisie, have always had the privilege, as well as the obligation, of being the cultural alibi of their class, the illuminated face. Women are the sign and symbol of social distinction, of the subtle, but important, differences that make up the hierarchic system to which they are connected through men. They themselves are playing a role; they are celebrating. Having no power of their own, they are nothing but this celebrating posture, monuments to respectability and success. This role gives women a close affinity to that hall of mirrors that the theatre has come to be, to whatever is displayed on a stage. From the time they are little girls, women have been taught to be the "erotic snares" which men both ask them to be and blame them for being. (Few women ever escape this double bind.)

Take the theatre, take women: the same enticement, the same seduction is at play. The female spectator identifies with the actress who is nothing but an image of feminine perfection. Adorned, glittering, to be viewed by all, coveted by all, yet ultimately out of reach, forever elusive. To be an actress, or to identify with one in your fantasies, is to be Woman: heavenly, divine, out of this world. The Barefoot Contessa, Esmeralda, Cleopatra, the Femme Fatale, Undoer of Empires.

The notion of woman as a trap, as a creature who is nothing but a reflection in a mirror, with no substance, goes back to Greek mythology, to the myth about Pandora's birth, the forging of the first woman.

Appearing in Hesiod's *Theogony*, this myth answers the need to oppose men (anthropoi) with a "race of women" (*genos gynaikon*). Pandora is not born of woman since she is the first woman (men were there already). Hephaistos molds her into the shape of woman. She is an *agalma*, an image. Here I am following the analysis of Nicole Loraux, whose close reading of Hesiod's text leads her to conclude:

> the creature of *The Theogony* is not a deceptive disguise; her veil is not meant to conceal the fact that she might be something different from a

woman—a god, for instance, or a demon or a man; it hides nothing
because a woman has no substance, no inner self to mask. To put it
bluntly, in *The Theogony* the first woman is nothing but her attire, she
has no body. At least the text we read seems loath to give her one.[1]

If we follow this myth, the first woman *is* theatre, she is the picture
of femininity, just as costumes, setting, and characters are merely the
elements that combine to make up a whole system of *signs*. According
to the myth, Pandora is both seduction itself *and* humanity's curse
(before she arrived on the scene, men—*anthropoi*— constituted "humanity" all by themselves: *man*kind), an indispensible curse since
there is no way around sexual reproduction, but still a curse. In this
we encounter the misogyny that was, for the Greeks, the cornerstone
of Athenian democracy. Women did not enjoy the status of citizenship: the term *citizen* itself had no feminine form. The same
misogyny is the cornerstone of Greek theatre, to which we are heirs
today. From the time of the Greeks, to Claudel, passing through
Marlowe and Goethe, what takes place on stage is an acting out
between the gods and men, or between man and God, while the
woman is cast out as a third party. Here too I refer to Loraux: "As an
instrument of separation, woman cuts off men from the gods. She
cuts them off from themselves by intruding with sexuality, that asym-
metrical balance between sameness and otherness."[2]

But even granting this misogyny, things are far from unequivocal.
For the exclusion of women is both necessary *and* impossible. What
men do is to oppose the *value* of what is male to the *fact* of what is
female. Yet, in the Renaissance, we have an example of men appropriating the *value* of what is female, making it one prerogative, among
others, of what is male. We are also heirs to the Elizabethan theatre in
which, women being excluded from the stage though not from the
repertoire, male actors played male and female roles just as inge-
niously and as ingenuously. In a sense, men can do without women to
produce the values of femininity; they can build up, all by themselves,
a whole system of differences. The theatre is where one can exchange
identities, play, more or less mischieviously, with deceptions; multiply
delusions, indulge in fantasy games, until there is no way of telling
who is who. In our time, Jean Genet, who wanted *The Maids* to be
played by two men, was of the opinion that femininity was only borne
by women in a passive, degraded form and that it took a young man to
act it truthfully. Sartre has analyzed this with great subtlety in *Saint
Genet comédien et martyr*.[3]

Yet it is precisely because the theatre represents an area of freedom,
where *play* is permissible, that there is something in it for all marginal,
oppressed individuals, including women. The world of fantasies is not

unaware of social roles, but it deals them out differently, it exploits equivocations, late disclosures, sudden reversals: the Prince and the Pauper. Athens means the defeat of women, but also the triumph of the female principle in the person of Athena, the Virgin Goddess. If the opera, as Catherine Clément analyzes it (*L'Opéra ou la défaite des femmes*),[4] also spells the defeat of women, it is because Clément confines herself to the plots, the myths, to all those stories of women victimized, of mothers sacrificed to the overriding domination of spear, ring, sword, helmet. But the opera is not only a story; it is also music, the magic of *bel canto*. Here, even though the character may lie dying, the diva's voice holds its own to the last breath.

Thus, women have understood that an alternative to society-as-it-is can be displayed and experienced through the fantasy world of the theatre. As just compensation, the female *value* confronts the male *fact*. In opposition to a society that imposes its oppressive, inequitable, selfish values as a fait accompli, a certain kind of theatre can put forth its own values in the form of a utopia, or by acting out the overthrow of power. But even this is no easy matter. Because the theatre is *drama*, hence conflict, on the model of war. We expect the triumph of the male principle even if, in the plot resolution, women characters seem to be the winners. It leads to a dead end of which some women today are fully aware. These women try to create a theatre that soars above the battlefield, a fluid, narrative, reminiscent theatre, rich in dream-like images. In France, for example, we can mention the theatre of Marguerite Duras, of Simone Benmussa. But there is no escape from the danger that even this insistence on freedom will help spread more freely men's fantasies about femininity: what woman can pretend to be free of them?

That is why, in so critical a period as today, those women who work in the theatre try, as a transitory step, to reduce the participation of men in their work. They prefer to work on texts *written* by women, or write or adapt texts themselves. Marguerite Duras wrote *Savannah Bay* expressly for Madeleine Renaud and Bulle Ogier. Simone Benmussa adapted Nathalie Sarraute's *Enfance* for the theatre; and the actress present on stage, Martine Pascal, shared the soliloquies with the recorded voice of Nathalie Sarraute herself.[5] These women even prefer to create their own settings, so that the male imagination cannot sneak back in with flamboyantly erected stage images that silently glorify the phallus. When the very talented male director Claude Régy directs Duras or Sarraute[6], he becomes a mere vehicle for the play, with an extreme, almost asceticlike discipline which is a form of self-obliteration. But one suspects that this very asceticism, in its sparseness, is a subtle way of making Régy's mark, of signing his work, of controlling what he is serving. Surely this tension between the male and female elements in the director (his overt misogyny, his "Elizabethan" femininity) and the male and female elements of the woman writer make for excellent theatre, the best, precisely because identities are so shuffled and confused that we lose our bearings.

Yet, in the end, we should not be too confident that this is to the advantage of women or of the feminine principle.

We come to another complicated situation: that of female directors, producers, historians of the theatre even, who want to promote various forms of political theatre that could be called radical theatre, theatre of protest, or the theatre of the oppressed. In recent years, there has been the interesting development in the United States of the Chicano theatre and of the Black American (also called the Afro-American theatre),[7] and in France of a theatrical movement representing the aspirations of West Indians. Throughout Europe as well as in the United States many Latin Americans in exile have also chosen to spread the word about their people's struggles through the theatre. There is Augusto Boal, to give an example, who comes from Brazil and has worked in Stockholm, Sicily, Paris, and Portugal. But in his book *Théâtre de l'opprimé* (*Theatre of the Oppressed*) he leaves little room for women when he explains that his theatre is meant for "the man in the street." As we dreamily wonder where we might find the comparable women in the street," only the "streetwalker" comes to mind and she, theoretically, has little leisure to stop and watch "le théâtre de l'opprimé."

As for Afro-American theatre, more often than not it has been misogynist, particularly in the early years. The black men who have created and produced these plays thought they would make their stories more poignant, more immediately effective, by casting the conflict that black people have with their white oppressors in *sexual terms*. Who then assumes the whole burden of sin? The white woman, the *She-Devil*, as she is currently called, or the Devil Lady, or the Fuckingbitch. In *Madheart*, by LeRoi Jones (Imamu Baraka), an allegorical play from 1967, the hero, Black Man, drives a huge wooden stake into the heart of Devil Lady "with a loud thud as it penetrates the body, and crashes deep in the floor." At the same time Black Man says: "You will always and forever be dead, and be dead, and always you will be the spirit of deadness, or the cold stones of its promise. Beautiful. Beautiful."[8]

As an interesting example of black women confronting this form of misogyny, we should mention the very successful production in 1976 of the choreographic poetic drama *For Colored Girls Who Have Considered Suicide/When the Rainbow Is Enuf,* by Ntozake Shange.[9] To quote

Ntozake Shange herself: "bein alive and bein a woman and bein colored is a metaphysical dilemma I have not conquered yet." We should also mention the work of Adrienne Kennedy, Sonia Sanchez, Alice Childree. We may soon see in Afro-American theatre the equivalent of what has recently happened in Afro-American literature: women making their mark. The success of one is encouragement to others. We see women building up enough self-confidence to begin to assert *their* vision, in *their* style.

Still, when *black* takes on positive symbolic value, it often falls quite naturally on the side of virility. The term *white,* used with scorn or repulsion, is identified with everything that is not virile; *faggot* is the generic term. A white boy is "soft and sweet as a pimple." But soft and sweet, as we well know, is the woman's body, the woman's breast, the woman's voice. Broadway, traditionally "The Great White Way," becomes "a contented fat white cow."[10] White and female. What about the black woman? In *Madheart,* if she wants to belong to the new revolutionary black nation, she'd better submit first to Black Man. Black Woman says: "I am the black woman. The one you need. You know this. Now you must get me. Or you'll never . . . iord . . . be a man." Black Man, after laughing swiftly, *"wheels and suddenly slaps her crosswise, back and forth across the face,* saying: "I want you, woman, as a woman. Go down. *He slaps again.)* Go down, submit submit . . . to love . . . and to man, now, forever."[11] His next move will be to slap her again, to drag her to him, and to kiss her deeply on the mouth. Till he hears what he wants to hear: "I am your woman, and you are the strongest of God. Fill me with your seed. *(They embrace.)*[12] LeRoi Jones is no doubt fully aware of the outrageous, provocative virtue of a scene like this, for black and white audiences alike. As we take the scene in, we, on the other hand, must be fully aware of the "alienating effect," in the Brechtian sense, of dramatic irony. If Black Man is so violent, it is because he himself has been the victim of worse violence. Having been treated like an animal, he will treat his woman as his thing, and a white man, to him, will be a woman (again, a faggot). Black Man—like White Anglo-Saxon Man before him—thinks that the bearer-of-the-seed, and only he, has the power to transform and the power to dominate.

This, then, is one paradox that women confront when promoting or writing about this kind of theatre. But there is another. These women cannot easily identify with the women, black or white, who are present as characters in the plays. As apologists, as critics, they are outside the system, beyond insult, free to bestow their benevolent appraisal on a work of art. But it remains true that, whatever detachment you protect yourself with, any theatre relying on invective insults women first and foremost. It can be argued that by bringing into play, for everyone to see, the mechanisms of oppression, the escalation of violence, you challenge oppression and violence. Another argument can be, from the critic's point of view, that, by being scholarly, objective, about these productions, you cease to be female, or black, or Jewish, you refrain from blaming Shakespeare for Katharina the shrew, for Othello, or for Shylock.

Yet the most aggressive, the most radical forms of theatre try hard to shake this liberal, pious humanism. We have a good example of this in one of Peter Handke's early pieces, *Publikumsbeschimpfung* (1966). There the playwright creates a situation in which the actors confront the spectators, addressing them in such a way that they are shaken loose from their comfortable "voyeur's" position: "You don't have to judge us from down upward, like a bunch of frogs watching birds. You won't have to act as referees"[13] or further: "You are no longer onlookers. You are the subject of our performance. You are the focus of our vision. You are the point of our dialogue." And, toward the end of the play: "We insult you because insult is a means to enforce communication. By insulting we become neutral. We have a hold over you. We knock down the barrier that separates you from us. We knock down the wall. We come toward you."[14] Of course, in doing this, the actors destroy the fragile symbolic edifice of drama. The theatre no longer is an arena for play, an arena which allows us to see ourselves in postures and situations we would not even dare dream of. Jean Genet, a male homosexual dramatist, was the one who said this, but it is true that women too are looking for a space in which nothing is forbidden, in which one can dare to be man and woman at the same time, desiring and desired, watching and watched, protecting and protected. A space in which, through ritual, our fears are exorcised. As the Italian director Giorgio Strehler recently put it: "Theatre is the most beautiful temptation offered to the soul's mobility."[15]

For a long time it was said (let's not disturb the anonymity of that "it"): "Women have no soul." Later, it was said, "Women have no unconscious." Tagging along in the collective unconscious, I seem to hear a faint echo today of these earlier dictates in the assumption that women have no creative imagination. Thus, for women to love the threatre may be a way of asserting, not "I have a creative imagination" or "I have an unconscious" (who would ever leap to an assertion like that?) but: "we have an unconscious," "*we* have a creative imagination." If women love theatre, maybe it is because theatre has a communal and collective character. In the theatre, struggle and thought have an exemplary power, and what holds for me also holds for others.

If such is the case, why does the theatre exclude women? Because it is a social institution and, as such, the same obstacles exist there as exist elsewhere. In France, for example, the few women who have "made it" in the theatre have done so relatively late and with considerable difficulty. We can say with absolute certainty that, with equal talent, a man would have been successful ten, twenty years earlier. That in a lifetime is no trifle. Ariane Mnouchkine began with the Groupe de théâtre antique de la Sorbonne, and it took her a long time to get out of the university ghetto. She had to wait for the political wave of events in 1968 to find a marginal spot in the Cartoucherie de Vincennes, a former arsenal which nobody else wanted, and there she created *1789*. Hers is a militant, charismatic vision of the theatre which manages to ease hierarchic relationships and conflicts of authority. Viviane Théophilidès and Anne-Marie Lazarini, two other prominent directors, who act, incidentally, in their own productions, also found it hard to achieve their independence and build their reputations. They both made their debuts in a small, political group called *Les Athévains*, which only managed to receive skimpy subsidies. Then there is the case of Simone Benmussa, the successful director of *Portrait of Dora, Albert Nobbs, Virginia, Freshwater,* among others. She worked her way up from being a literary adviser for the Renaud-Barrault Company. For a long time—almost twenty years—she was stifled at least as much as protected by the institution which supported her.

Why so few women? Because the director is the *boss*. It is a position that requires authority, legitimacy. Actors blindly put everything in *his* hands, while technicians—mostly men until very recently, carry out *his* instructions. Surprisingly (or not so surprisingly), it is often women (an experienced actress, for instance, working with a less experienced woman director) who, as a result of their ingrained misogyny, have the most trouble accepting the authority of a woman. For them, also, a man is the natural-born leader.

In the United States, things have happened that have given women opportunities they have not had elsewhere. The avant-garde is one, feminism another. The Living Theatre is a superb example: thanks to Julian Beck's willingness to act under the direction of his wife Judith Malina and to the community they created which sustained their theatre for so many years. Feminism has helped women become more assertive, more autonomous. Certain types of organizations, like the Women's Experimental Theatre, have familiar advantages, but also the dangerous limits of working apart from men. Finally, such diverse talents as those of Meredith Monk, Elizabeth Swados, Carolyn Carson, and Lucinda Childs seem to show that music, or choreography, by their technical nature and the overshadowing of ideological concerns, are domains in which it is easier for a woman to assert herself than in drama proper.

To write for the theatre, to stage a play, is to bring into existence a world that competes with our existing reality. The playwright is a legislator; he (and one assumes it will be he) postulates a world which operates with its network of relationships, its conflicts, its social structure: a consistent, ordered world. This requires an authority, a legitimacy, a representativeness. A woman—as others see her, but also as she sees herself—more often than not lacks this legitimacy. She represents only herself and private concerns; she does not carry on the body of social institutions (including that of the theatre). Given the tradition, how could a woman possibly talk about war, justice and injustice, power and the abuse of power? How could she talk about anything, in fact, except homemaking, which is precisely what is excluded from the stage? The drawing-room comedy enters the home, but rarely goes as far as the nursery or the kitchen. Even the warring of couples, the love battle "whose foundation is the deadly hatred between the sexes," as Kleist says in *Penthesilea*,[16] falls outside the scope of women. It takes a man to take a detached view, to be forceful and objective, whereas a woman, trapped in her role as victim or betrayer (she-who-won't-give-herself or who-makes-him-wait or who-gives-herself-to-someone-else) is only familiar with the most urgent, compulsive side of the matter. A man can tell Phaedra's story, a woman cannot tell that of Hippolytus. A man can speak for Penthesilea, a woman cannot do the same for Achilles. That is, she cannot do it with the *legitimacy*, the *objectivity* that the theatre calls for. She cannot relate a young man's sexuality. She cannot relate a man's love for a woman if it includes his desire for conquest (what could she possibly know about conquering a woman?) and his ulterior scorn for the conquered object (what could she possibly know about the satiated male's scorn for the sexual object he no longer lusts for?). A man knows all about a man's love, because he is a man, and all about a woman, because he loves women.

The converse, however, is not true—not acknowledged at any rate. Flaubert says he is Madame Bovary, but it is always transgressive for a woman to speak for a man, as it was when Hélène Cixous did so recently, in *Le Prénom de Dieu*.

While a novelist's narrative fantasies are more easily accepted, especially today, whatever happens on stage has the appearance of objective reality, there is no getting away from that, Brecht or no Brecht. It is there for everyone to see, therefore it *is*. The author is not present in person, he is the hidden God. His absence paradoxically imparts a greater solidity, a greater authority to his creation, his built-up world. The characters are like statues which, as if by a miracle, have come to life. This is the kind of seed transmitting that only man can achieve. It is difficult to imagine a woman creating Don Juan, Macbeth, Oedipus, Hernani, the Prince of Homburg. It is *very* difficult to imagine a woman who would dare to say with a straight face: "I am Faustus."

So what is left for women? It seems that certain areas are not as closely guarded as others and that women, these days, tend to take advantage of this, trying to occupy these territories. At one extreme it is not surprising—considering the way our society shapes women—that they should make excellent writers of light comedy or detective comedy since here it is so much a matter of reproducing stereotypes without ever questioning them and of coming up with stock solutions for everything. What counts is the skill, the neatness, the patience, the flair, the finishing touch. At the other extreme, women commit themselves to the activist theatre of protest, to theatre as a political weapon. When they do this, we sometimes see that they do it with greater daring than men ("women have no super-ego"). Men remain calm, cool, and collected; they hate anything that hinges on the hysterical. Women will scream when the occasion seems to require it. It takes a woman or a child to call out in the street: "The Emperor has no clothes!" For, clothes or no clothes, the Emperor still is the Emperor just as, just or unjust war is war. To men, and to the women indoctrinated by the men, war is the chance for adventure, for heroic behavior, for sacrifice. In 1963, Joan Littlewood shocked England with her relentless parody of the First World War in the musical *Oh What a Lovely War!*[17] Three years later, in 1966, in the United States, came another shocker written by a fearless woman, Barbara Garson, *Mac Bird*. President Lyndon Johnson was the butt of this relentless parody. The same year, another woman, Rochelle Owens, wrote *Beclch*, a kind of fantasy jungle inhabited by birds, tomtoms, occult forces, and unnatural sexual practices. How related or unrelated was *Beclch* to the political reality of the time? In 1966, *everything* was related, directly or indirectly, to the Vietnam War. This was clear enough to the officials who sacked André Gregory, the director who produced the play.

Yet *Beclch* had nothing strictly realistic about it. Maybe women can move a little more freely in the realm of fantasy. To make a political statement, they resort to ritual and myth. This had been the case in England, eight years earlier (1958), when Ann Jellico had written *The Sport of My Mad Mother*. The title referred to Kali, the Hindu goddess: "All creation is the sport of my mad mother, Kali."[18] This is a good example of how a woman may use the archaic media that ritual and myth used to be in order to comment upon our modern society. This is how Ann Jellicoe herself saw the problem:

> *The Sport of My Mad Mother* is concerned with fear and rage at being rejected from the womb or tribe. It uses a very old myth in which a man, rejected by his mother, castrates himself with a stone knife.

Ann Jellicoe went on to say:

> We create rituals when we want to strengthen, celebrate or define our common life and common values, or when we want to give ourselves confidence to undertake a common course of action. A ritual generally takes the form of repeating a pattern of words and gestures which tend to excite us above a normal state of mind; at the climax of the rite the essential nature of something is changed (e.g., the mass, a marriage service, the bestowal of diplomas, etc.). This play proceeds by rituals because the insecure and inarticulate group of people who figure in the play depend on them so much.[19]

Building up confidence to undertake a common course of action; reacting collectively to uncertainties concerning one's identity or one's role in society: what holds for the Cockney kids in this play also holds for women, which may explain the appeal of ritualized theatre for women writers (just as it may explain it in the case of the outcast Jean Genet). This was very true of *Beclch*. Its political strength stemmed from the fact that the text alone, working outside any realistic context, produced a theatrical reality: dreams, memories, haunted places, drowning, suffocations, cataclysms, without anything actually occurring outside the world of fantasy.

Finally, a word should be said about a realm that women have been able to move into without too much of a fight. We could call this realm "the voices of women." In an issue of *The Drama Review* devoted to "Women and Performance," Roberta Sklar wrote an article entitled "Toward Creating a Women's Theatre."[20] By virtue of repeating: "It's women's turn to have the floor," they have taken it, a little. They have first occupied the grounds that were most clearly within their dominion; those of mother and daughter relationships, for instance. Let us mention the *Daughter's* cycle at the Women's Interart Center, by Clare Coss, Roberta Sklar, and Sondra Segal. Also, as I mentioned earlier, they have by preference adapted for the stage texts written by women, not necessarily meant for the stage in the first place: *Parole de femme,* by Annie Leclerc, directed by Isabella Ehni; *Virginia,* by Edna O'Brien making use of texts by Virginia Woolf, directed by Simone Benmussa; or, directed also by Simone Benmusa, *Enfance* by Nathalie Sarraute. But the function of directing itself remains problematic, even if women refrain from exercising it with the same dictatorial or charismatic power as men. This is why one last refuge is performance art, in which one woman alone is on stage and directs, having also conceived, her own show. Laurie Anderson, in the United States, is a wonderful multi-talented artist, who has boldly explored this new dimension. In France, the names that come to mind are those of Marianne Sergent, Sylvie Joly, Denise Péron, Stéphanie Loik, Anne Pruchal. Then there are Zouc from Switzerland and Antoinine Maillet from Canada. They have the toughness of immemorial peasant women, they have guts and daring, they are not afraid of appearing strong, of being hilariously funny or deeply touching. Turning away from the fleeting, vaporous images of femininity, they clomp along in their heavy clogs.

Notes

1. Nicole Loraux, *Les Enfants d'Athéna* (Paris: Maspéro, 1981), 86 (translation mine).

2. Ibid., 81.

3. Jean-Paul Sartre, *Saint Genet: comédien et martyr*, (Paris: Gallimard, 1952); American edition *Saint Genet: Actor and Martyr*, trans. B. Frechtman (New York: G. Braziller, 1963).

4. Catherine Clément, *L'Opéra ou la défaite des femmes* (Paris: Grasset, 1979).

5. The play, called *Childhood* in English, was performed in New York City during the month of June 1985 (Harold Clurman Theater). Simone Benmussa directed the United States version as well. Glenn Close played the one-woman role and shared her Soliloquies with the recorded voice of Nathalie Sarraute speaking English.

6. *L'Eden-Cinéma* and *L'Amante Anglaise* by Marguerite Duras and *Isma, C'est beaux, Elle est là* by Nathalie Sarraute.

7. For Chicano theatre see Philip D. Ortega, *We Are Chicanos* (New York: Washington Square Press, 1973). For the black theatre see Geneviève Fabre, *Drumbeats, Masks and Metaphor* (Cambridge: Harvard University Press, 1983).

8. LeRoi Jones, *Madheart*, in *Four Black Revolutionary Plays* (New York: Bobbs-Merrill, 1969), 71.

9. Ntozake Shange, *For Colored Girls Who Have Considered Suicide/When the Rainbow Is Enuf: A Choreopoem* (New York: Bantam Books, 1980).

10. Woodie King and Ron Milner, "Evolution of a People's Theater," in *Black Drama Anthology*, Woodie King and Ron Milner, eds. (New York: New American Library, 1972), X.

11. Jones, *Madheart*, 81 (emphasis mine).

12. Ibid., 83 (emphasis mine).

13. Peter Handke, *Publikumsbeschimpfung* (Frankfurt: Suhrkamp Verlag, 1966).

14. Ibid.

15. George Strehler, reported in *Le Monde* ("Monde des Spectacles") November 8, 1984, pp. 16–17.

16. Heinrich von Kleist, *Penthesilea,* 1808.

17. *Oh What A Lovely War,* A Theatre Workshop Group Production, under the direction of Joan Littlewood, first presented at the Theatre Royal, Straford, East London, on March 19, 1963. First published by Methuen, London, 1965.

18. Ann Jellicoe, *The Sport of My Mad Mother* (London: Faber & Faber, 1958), Title page.

19. Ibid., p. 6.

20. *The Drama Review,* "Women and Performance Issue," T 86 (June 1980), New York University.

Women and Politics

During the twentieth century, women entered the public sphere in significant numbers, both in Europe and the United States. Leaving the home and domesticity, many women began to carve out for themselves a new public identity and take their place in what had been exclusively a male domain.

The papers in this section describe how women's emergence into the public arena was fraught with conflict, even violence. Martha Vicinus's essay examines the ways radical British "suffragettes" used the female body to transform the male body politic. Led by the Pankhursts, the British Women's Social and Political Union (WSPU) forced the woman's question into the male political sphere. Hundreds of young women, recruited primarily from England's "respectable" classes, marched through the cities, lectured on street corners, chained themselves to the gates of Parliament. Their bodies became instruments of public disorder. Parliament could not operate, traffic stopped, the bourgeois home seemed in danger. American feminists too insisted on their right to public space; they used the public parade, elaborate banners, and dramatic costumes and withstood the violence of forced feeding in their efforts to transform the male body politic.

Support for suffrage in the United States did not come from the privileged classes alone. Elinor Lerner analyzes the attitudes and voting patterns in New York City of different classes and ethnic groups: Anglo-Saxons, Jews, Italians, and Irish; men and women who had been born in this country and immigrants who had come recently from Europe. Challenging commonly held assumptions, Lerner describes the complexity of family, class, ethnicity, and work patterns in determining how people responded to the idea of women's suffrage.

Feminism did not offer women their only access to the public sphere. Ironically religion, especially conservative Catholicism, provided an alternative route to the public world in France and the Netherlands. Anne-Marie Sohn and Mieke Aerts explore in detail the charitable and "social work" activites of women beyond the home. Like England's WSPU, the Patriotic League of French Women recruited its members from among the most privileged classes. Although the League was created to defend traditional values, Sohn shows how this group of conservative Catholic women changed the relations of women to the political world by encouraging members of their own sex to involve themselves in the public sphere and by molding them into a political force that frequently differed from its male advisers.

So did the varied Catholic women's movements in the Netherlands. Ideologically few groups could have differed more fundamentally than the British suffragists and these Catholic groups. Yet their insistence on women's right to public space, their flamboyance, their sense of costume and the dramatic are strikingly parallel.

As Claudia Koonz points out, scholars have often been blinded to the possibility that some women receive solid advantages from reactionary political organizations and regimes. That this is so is dramatically clear in her analysis of women and politics in Weimar and Nazi Germany. "Apolitical" Protestant and Catholic women's groups, committed to traditional feminine values and male dominance, became Nazi activists. Through the ideals and goals of National Socialism, they found ways to gain greater autonomy, a female *lebensraum*.

In the twentieth century, sexuality has increasingly become a political issue. Women's groups, on the left and right, have launched campaigns and these articles touch on some of them: the Pankhursts' war against male sexual license; the French, Dutch, and German women's fight for purity; the contemporary Italian feminist crusade to make abortion legal. Governments too in all Western countries, no matter what their political persuasion, have used sexuality to control women and expand the power of the state: the outlawing of contraception and abortion, the regulation of prostitution, compulsory sterilization and ancillary means of controlling the female body. Gisela Bock takes the extreme example—the sterilization policies in Nazi Germany—and explores the connections and full implications of racism, sexism, and genocide.

Today feminists continue to defend themselves against sexist and racist offensives. They keep fighting for their public and political rights, their rights to have abortions and to define their sexual preference. What is more, they need to protect themselves now from the more benign, but still destructive, policies of progressive, male-dominated governments. Yasmine Ergas's essay compares the conflicting goals of the contemporary Italian women's movement with those of the state, suggesting that the Italian government continues to seek ways of controlling women's bodies. Having given in on the abortion issue, this democratic state has managed to homogenize the interests of women, among other minority groups, and assimilate the administration of women's reproductive rights into the patriarchal policy of "family planning."

MALE SPACE AND WOMEN'S BODIES

THE ENGLISH SUFFRAGETTE MOVEMENT

Martha Vicinus

On October 13, 1905 Christabel Pankhurst and Annie Kenney attended a Liberal Party rally in Manchester to ask Sir Edward Gray if his party would support a bill enfranchising women. He refused to answer their question, and they refused to leave until he did so. They were arrested and briefly imprisoned. The ensuing publicity, largely unfavorable, brought new recruits and an enthusiasm for women's suffrage that had never been seen before. Virtually overnight thousands of women converted to suffrage and pledged their time, money, and energy to its enactment. Militancy was born. Christabel's policy was twofold: She repudiated the traditional method of introducing private members' bills into Parliament and insisted upon attacking the government directly, demanding suffrage as a party policy. She also exploited to the full the free publicity created by committing acts that would lead to imprisonment and temporary martyrdom.[1] For nearly ten years before World War I women created and sustained their first and most militant mass movement.

In early 1906 the Pankhursts decided to move their Women's Social and Political Union to London in order to be closer to Parliament and the centers of power. They were soon joined by Emmeline and Frederick Pethick-Lawrence, a well-to-do couple long associated with social

Research for this essay was made possible by a fellowship from the John Simon Guggenheim Foundation. I am grateful for their assistance. A version of this essay appears in *Independent Women: Work and Community for Single Women, 1850–1920* (Chicago: The University of Chicago Press, 1985).

reform. The WSPU was ruled autocratically by Christabel, her mother, and the Pethick-Lawrences; the leaders feared that their rapidly growing organization would lose its momentum if they became embroiled in the slow process of democratic decision making. The WSPU attracted women of all ages and political knowledge, but its most active members were largely young, unmarried, and inexperienced. They sought immediate change and were impatient of traditional methods of gradual reform for women. As the wealthy and sheltered Margaret Thomas Mackworth explained, militancy had let "a draught of fresh air into our padded, stifled lives," bringing "adventure and excitement."[2] The suffrage movement "meant to women the discovery of their own identity, that source within of purpose, power and will . . . . Gone was the age-old sense of inferiority, gone the intolerable weight of helplessness in face of material oppression, gone the necessity of conforming to conventional standards of behaviour, gone all fear of Mrs. Grundy."[3] In less than three years the WSPU jumped from one paid organizer to seventy-five, and an income of 18,000 pounds from subscriptions alone.[4]

The WSPU organized thousands of meetings, soapbox rallies, colorful parades, and street-corner sales of their weekly, *Votes for Women,* throughout England. Until mid-1909 militancy was restricted to heckling Liberal Party speakers at by-elections, demanding party support for a women's suffrage bill. But in June 1909, after Mrs. Pankhurst and eight well-known women were turned away from Parliament, government office windows were broken and 108 women were arrested. Most were later released, but one woman began the first hunger strike, protesting the continued refusal of the Home Office to grant women political-prisoner status. She was soon released, but at another prison women were forcibly fed. In July 1910 the so-called Conciliation Bill, supporting modified women's suffrage, passed by 139 votes in the House of Commons, but differences between the Lords and Commons led to the dissolving of Parliament. Rank and file WSPU members were growing impatient; the brutal breaking up of a suffragette rally on November 18, 1910, "Black Friday," further exacerbated a growing disillusionment with Parliament, compromise, and men.

A campaign of systematic window smashing began in late 1911. Following a second attack in the West End, the police raided the WSPU headquarters on March 5, 1912. Christabel fled to Paris, where she single-handedly led the WSPU until the outbreak of World War I, after breaking her close alliance with the Pethick-Lawrences. Henceforward the WSPU was a semilegal organization with a perpetually changing headquarters and deputy leadership. For two years a policy of arson and window smashing was pursued in the face of increasingly negative publicity. In April 1913 the Home Secretary pushed through Parliament a bill giving the government power to release any hunger striker until she had recovered her health sufficiently to be rearrested. The "Cat and Mouse Act" fed into the WSPU's insatiable need for publicity, as the "mice" proved to be remarkably successful in eluding rearrest and making dramatic appearances at meetings. The WSPU's small band of militants was caught in a spiraling pattern of arson, arrest, hunger strikes, release, and rearrest. Operating as a small guerrilla army, it had become increasingly out of touch not only with the nonmilitant suffragists, but also with public opinion, government policies, and the course of wider events. Then in August 1914 war was declared and the Pankhursts abruptly called off their campaign. Although the vote had not been won, women had gained public recognition, self-respect, and a growing knowledge of their own power.[5]

Underlying the militant suffrage campaign was an insistence upon radically changing the spiritual relationship between women and men, women and society. At a time when traditional class and sexual relations were being subverted by such movements as the new Labour Party, trade unionism, eugenics, and sexual reform advocates, the WSPU's middle-class membership and advocacy of a single sexual standard seemed to place it in a nineteenth-century backwater. But a closer examination of its activities and ideological statements reveals a conscious effort to forge a new spirituality, based upon woman's traditional self-sacrifice, but intended to transform not only the position of women in society, but also that very society itself. Women were to gain access to the male political arena by the strength of their superior morality. This naturally meant a rigorous sexual purity—strong bodily control—in order to enter safely male space. A woman's personal integrity was exalted through the decision to hunger strike, the ultimate personal control of one's body; forced feeding, with its overtones of sexual violation, simply proved the moral depravity of men. The WSPU woman sacrificed her body through numerous and varied militant actions so that her spirit might triumph in the material world. If we make the necessary mental leap into a world based upon noneconomic spiritual arguments, then the revolutionary ideology of the suffragettes becomes clear. WSPU women invaded male space, all the public areas controlled by men, in order to assert their spiritual superiority and leadership; they used their one weapon—their bodies—and were commensurately punished by men, who assaulted their physical integrity in every way possible. Until the divisions between male and female space were fundamentally altered to include women in the male public world, compromise was impossible. The suffragettes' actions over eight years were a series of increasingly risky and ferocious entries into male space, insisting upon radical change.

The repeated linking of spirituality with militant action by WSPU members came from a long tradition of women and men claiming moral leadership for women. Early twentieth-century journalists frequently debated the materialism of the age; concern was especially voiced about the corruption of public and private morals, with the decline of Victorian sexual mores and religious belief. Elaine Kidd reminded the doomsayers of "the Militant Suffragettes, whose passionate idealism and daring imagination are in striking contrast to the sluggish respectability of the 'plain man' who insists upon regarding them as criminals and lunatics."[6] The suffragettes, however, went beyond formal religion, insisting upon an innate spirituality that they alone carried into the corrupt male world. Many were theosophists, eagerly adopting a religion that appeared to offer an alternative to Victorian materialist thinking, was dominated by women, and emphasized spirituality as a mechanism for social change.[7] Pantheism, astrology, homeopathy, vegetarianism, physical culture, and other forms of individual improvement were popular among women seeking greater control of their lives. But suffrage itself was their greatest religion, offering an ideal combination of spiritual devotion and concrete action.

Joining the WSPU was akin to joining a spiritual army. The language, iconography, and behavior of the WSPU were in terms of an army at war with society. Christabel Pankhurst repeatedly spoke of battles, of war with the Liberal Party, and of the need for military discipline. The WSPU trained a drum-and-fife band to lead small marches in London, in addition to their huge summer demonstrations in Hyde Park. Members were encouraged to wear the WSPU colors (white for purity, green for hope, and purple for loyalty) on such occasions, as well as when they sold Votes for Women. A "uniform" of white dress with a broad tricolored sash worn by marchers made WSPU demonstrations colorful events, as well as important symbolic acts of taking over male space, however temporarily. Both the militants and nonmilitants were fond of portraying idealized Woman, dressed as a knight or goddess, leading civilization into a better future.[8] As illegal actions increased in frequency, participants compared themselves to soldiers in an advanced corps.[9] Mrs. Pankhurst, convinced that they would bring the government to a standstill, taunted the law to try her for sedition.

The suffragettes, however, were not able to halt the political process and ordinarily found it difficult even to gain a hearing when faced with crowds of men. Mary Richardson, for example, found that men came up to her when she sold Votes for Women, pretending to buy a paper, but then whispered obscenities in her ear. She retaliated by chasing them down the street, but she ended many days feeling depressed at the side of men she had awakened.[10] Maud Kate Smith in old age remembered the "fine yellow powder" that fell on the floor when the demonstrators returned from rushing Parliament and removed the corrugated cardboard bodices they had worn for protection.[11] All work for the Cause was spiritualized by the suffragettes, but since they breached the traditional boundaries between men and women, they were left vulnerable to sexual attack. Both police and bystanders felt that politically active women were fair game to pinch, fondle, and provoke. In order to protect their own space, men continually reminded women of their vulnerablitity and illegitimacy.

The suffragettes, nevertheless, were undaunted. Impelled "by the *wonderful* spirit of loyalty and love for the cause and for our leaders," women showed great ingenuity in drawing attention to their exclusion from male political space.[12] In October 1908 two members of the Women's Freedom League chained themselves to the grille separating the Ladies' Gallery from the Commons; they then attempted to address the men below. Since it was impossible to detach the women, the grille had to be removed and the House temporarily closed to strangers. The event was the culmination of a four-months' vigil at the door of the House during all the hours the House sat, a mute but constant reminder of the WFL's request to meet with the Prime Minister.[13] The WSPU repeatedly attended meetings forbidden to women. In Bristol on one occasion two suffragettes hid all night in the hall's organ loft in order to be ready to shout "Votes for Women" when the Liberal minister spoke.[14] Two women threw slates from a roof onto a waiting crowd before a speech by the Prime Minister.[15] In all of these cases the militants were physically apart, shouting down to a largely if not completely male audience, demanding justice. Their exclusion from the political process was exaggerated by their position—they refused to participate in meetings until they could have their full rights in Parliament. If they were powerless, they did not want a token show of influence, which their quiescent attendance at a meeting or sitting of Parliament implied. Thus the symbolic acts of disruption came to hold a greater meaning for both the participants and the onlookers.

Such actions reinforced the militants' sense of being part of a guerrilla army of dedicated fighters. The suffragettes felt that they were willing to take on tasks that others could not or would not do, in order to gain a female presence in the male world of politics, law, and government. Between 1906 and 1914, over a thousand women went to prison for suffrage; thousands more were arrested.[16] Prison represented male injustice, but it also became the militant's community, where women shared the martyrdom of hunger striking and forcible feeding. Isolated yet united with fellow prisoners, the lonely suffragette striker became "both flame and burnt offering," the self-fulfilled and the self-sacrificed.[17]

For the women who entered prison, no matter how willingly, the experience was deeply affecting. Personally they were brought face to face with their own strengths and weaknesses, under the weight of the prison's regimentation and regulations. But women, each in separate cells and under a rule of silence, managed to keep up each other's spirits. Messages were written on toilet paper and passed in hymnals during daily chapel or at exercise time. The WSPU sent a band to play every evening outside the walls of Holloway Prison, which housed most of the militants. Although the government never gave the women political prisoner status—the main reason they hunger-struck in the early days—for a brief period in 1910–1912 they were given an intermediate status that enabled the militants to speak with each other, to wear their own clothes, and to have books and pens. Every advantage was seized. At Aylesbury Prison in 1912 the suffragettes dubbed their prison "Simple Life Summer School" because so many favored a return to the land, physical culture, vegetarianism, theosophy, and, of course, social reform. Charlotte Marsh organized a sports day, complete with a potato race and "concert" on combs and paper at the end.[18] During the similar period on Winson Green Prison, Birmingham, the prisoners put together a comic magazine, dubbed the "Hammerer's Magazine," after their habit of carrying hammers in the muffs in order to break windows. They included an advice column about how to deal with the Antis, how to collect a crowd when speaking outdoors (steal a baby from a pram or have a boy drop pennies), how to lose weight (go to prison), etc. One woman, writing the "Health Notes from Hospital," described poignantly the change from her cell to a large, airy hospital room:

> In a cell you have as a companion to your pain and foes to your health, loneliness, oppression, secret fear—the silence which at home in illness is so grateful, is there full of suspicion. I remember even the rising sun thro' the small window teased me and I planned how I would keep it out—in here I chose a bed facing the dawn and many a morning I have lain and watched the golden light creep up my bed till I was bathed in it and I wondered at the difference of thought on the same subject. It has seemed to me like the dawning light of freedom in so many of us women's lives. We loved the light but in cramped surroundings or alien circumstances the light often proved a torment and a suffering. In the larger world of freedom—such as we twenty-five women made here the light grows and changes, and for my part I shall always remember these weeks as some of the happiest in a perfectly happy life.[19]

Paradoxically in prison each woman made "a larger world of freedom" for herself and other women; even as the public space of the male world was denied them, women found inspiration in creating free space within the prison. Women had always created a sphere of freedom for themselves under imprisoning conditions whether within their home or someone else's or in a hated job. Now they could look to a real prison as liberating, opening a new world of freedom.

But the fragile community of prisoners was continually threatened by their lack of recognized political status. The concessions did not grant them their political purpose and were therefore refused in late 1912. Hunger striking was again resorted to, now almost automatically. S. I. Stevenson, who struck her first time in prison, remembered the experience vividly years later:

> I blushed with shame that the cup of tea should have such power over me. I kept going to it and looking at it—the steam fascinated me—(there wasn't *much* in the steam line). "I'm not going to have any," I kept telling myself. "I'm only looking at it." . . . My mouth was so parched it stung me. Now I have to record a sad sad lapse. Without hardly knowing it I suddenly found myself again sitting over the tea, in some sort as a cat lappeth, and drew it in. It was moist and eased my roof a little; I did not swallow at all. The wonderful relief it was to me—just that moisture on my tongue. Then I remembered. I covered up the teacup and buried my face in my hands. . . . About ten minutes later the door swung open. My head was still buried in my hands in abject shame. A wardress tore off the coverings and handed the untasted (?) refreshment to a wardress outside. "That's the seventeeth that hasn't touched anything," I heard her say in gruesome tones to the other.[20]

Stevenson's apostasy was only momentary, but like all the other hunger strikers she found the mental torture excruciating.

As every prisoner knew, hunger striking was only the first step in her bodily sacrifice. Women had to face forcible feeding twice and thrice a day. A doctor would arrive with a long rubber tube and three or four wardresses. They would hold down and gag the protesting prisoner, while the doctor inserted the tube (often used repeatedly without proper cleansing) down either a nostril or if possible the mouth, and then would pour in a mixture of milk, bread, and brandy, sometimes including an antivomiting agent. Hunger strikers found the procedure utterly demoralizing, leaving them feeling nauseous, with cramps, headaches, and painful sores in their mouths, nasal passages, and stomach. Most suffered severely from indigestion and constipation. But perhaps the worst was anticipating the arrival of the doctor. The agony of hearing one's comrades screaming in pain while waiting could be unbearable. One prisoner described the ritual of offering food before beginning the artificial feeding as an ironic reversal of Eve tempting Adam:

> the food, so delicious, so tempting, is offered by man to the woman, representative of her sex, and for the sake of her sex, she must refuse even to taste it. So the woman triumphs over the man. The offering is the lesser sin, but the acceptance is the greater, in this revolution of womanhood each woman strives to remove the old stigma of the story of Adam and Eve. She refuses to accept the position of subjection so disastrous to the race, both morally and physically, so great a barrier to progress and evolution.[21]

And as she reminded those who thought they might break the suffragette's spirit, "The stronger the temptation, the more uplifting is the feeling of victory."[22]

Some women, such as Kitty Marion, found the whole experience too reiminiscent of forcible rape and struggled as long as their strength held out.[23] The sexual connection between hunger striking and the militant's desire to control her body was obvious to contemporaries; even this power was denied women when they were forcibly fed. Yet physical assault only strengthened her resolve. Although she might suffer the destruction of her body, each hunger striker knew that her spirit soared over the male physical world and would eventually triumph. If men confused the spiritual beauty of women with their physical bodies, women tended to the opposite extreme, confusing bodily sacrifice with spiritual ascension. The suffragettes believed that only by giving their bodies to the Cause would they win the necessary spiritual victory that would transform the male political world. Hunger striking was the self-transforming act that would alter not only the actor, but also the larger world. Since they continually thought in terms of moral battles and spiritual conversions, the suffragettes exaggerated the power of the symbolic act.[24]

While many were horrified at the torturing of women by forced feeding, the men in power remained unmoved. A grim fanaticism overtook those who continued to hurl themselves against an obtuse government and increasingly hostile general public.[25] During the years 1912–1914 extremism was expressed either by a desire for complete bodily sacrifice though death or by complete bodily preservation through female separatism. The outcome of the first belief was not death from hunger striking, but a dramatically public action. Emily Wilding Davison hurled herself in front of the King's horse at the 1913 Derby. The second course of action was expressed through Christabel Pankhurst's series of articles in 1913 on "the great scourge," claiming that 80 percent to 90 percent of all Englishmen suffered from venereal disease. Both extremes were a natural outcome of an organization that emphasized woman's moral superiority and the spiritual significance of bodily sacrifice. Women were never again to give their bodies to polluted men, but to give them to the Cause, in order "to possess their own souls."[26]

Every hunger striker faced and accepted death as the ultimate sacrifice she would give to save women. Mary Richardson often thought of Joan of Arc as she lay half-alive, waiting for the next round of forced feeding.[27] For over a year before her death Emily Wilding Davison considered making the ultimate sacrifice; she had already tried to end her torment once by throwing herself down a prison staircase. Sometime before her death she wrote an explanation of her decision; in highly charged language, strangely reminiscent of Christabel's "Great Scourge" articles, Davision embraced her lover, Death:

> The glorious and inscrutable Spirit of Liberty has but one further penalty within its power, the surrender of Life itself. It is the supreme consummation of sacrifice, than which none can be higher or greater.
> To lay down life for friends, that is glorious, selfless, inspiring! But to re-enact the tragedy of Calvary for generations yet unborn, that is the last consummate sacrifice of the Militant![28]

Davison's identification with Christ and His sacrifice was the most extreme statement of the WSPU's spiritual message. Her tortured consecration of herself to the Spirit of Liberty found its "consummation" not in life or love, but in death. An organization that based its political presence upon woman's publicly asserted spiritual superiority could only demand increasing sacrifice from its members when faced with male denial. Women could continue to prove their superiority only by escalating their acts of suffering, inevitably leading to death.

Davison's funeral provided a perfect occasion for women to control temporarily public space. Thousands watched as her cortège of uniformed WSPU members silently walked through the streets of London, reminding all of their superior purity, faith, and loyalty. But even here they met with obscenity, pawing, and pushing by men more interested in the fate of the King's horse than the dead woman.[29] Consistent male abuse over the years had frightened and angered women and made them ready to accept Christabel's message of "Votes for Women, Chastity for Men." They readily linked male sexual impurity, which they had experienced in a lesser form each time they went into public space as political beings, with the enforcement of woman's political, economic, and marital enslavement. Christabel, safe in Paris, could warn her *Suffragette* readers about the "infected souls" of Englishmen and the permanent loss of woman's health from marriage to a polluter. In response to the few who argued that woman's chastity was the product of her past subjection, she replied that mastery over self and sex were woman's gains that would not be given up when her subjection ended: "Warned by the evils which the tyranny of sex has produced where men are concerned, women have no intention of letting matter triumph over mind, and the body triumph over the spirit, in their case."[30] Christabel advised women to perserve their bodies intact, unsullied by men, whatever the cost, until they had won political and economic freedom.

In the heady days of the arson campaign, Christabel's advice seemed appropriate to participants in an increasingly desperate movement. Bodily preservation accompanied bodily destruction. Both the WSPU and Sylvia Pankhurst's breakaway East London Federation formed corps of bodyguards to protect their leaders after the passage of the Cat and Mouse Act. The "Bodyguard" and the "People's Army" served both to prevent the rearrest of Mrs. Pankhurst and Sylvia and also to keep opponents at a distance. On one occasion Mrs. Pankhurst successfully spoke on the balcony of a guarded house and then escaped between lines of the bodyguard rhythmically swinging Indian clubs.[31] A life spent alternating between the extremes of hunger striking in a lonely cell and recuperating in a warm and supportive suffragette nursing home left Mary Richardson prey to depression and fears for her sanity. She could barely tolerate the swings from dying to living and back again.[32] Farce and tragedy were closely aligned as the government chased after recuperating suffragette "mice". The sexual connotations of the chase and the consequent forcible feeding should they be caught underscored the militant's demand for sexual purity and personal self-control. Christabel's desperate message fit the desperate actions of her followers.

When war broke out on August 4, 1914, Christabel wrote in *The Suffragette* that the war was "God's vengeance upon the people who held women in subjection" and called upon WSPU members to stand fast for the Cause and womankind. Then abruptly on August 15 Mrs. Pankhurst sent around a memo exhorting WSPU members to place their energies at the service of their country.[33] *The Suffragette* reappeared, editorializing vigorously against the Germans and for Englishmen, their venereal state seemingly forgotten. The WSPU guerrilla army, toughened from years of discipline and sacrifice, transformed itself with remarkable ease into a fighting force for

England. One of the most active arsonists, Charlotte Marsh, became Lloyd George's chauffeur; similar changes occurred among other militants. Sylvia Pankhurst, however, continued to fight for the rights of East End women, and Emmeline Pethick-Lawrence became active in Jane Addams's international peace movement.[34] Divisions that had underlain the single-issue Cause surfaced, and the women's movement entered a new phase.

Militancy had not gained the vote nor its long-range goal of a spiritually regenerated society. Yet it did not fail its participants. They had successfully brought before the eyes of the general public a new vision of what society could be and of how women could behave. Women had sacrificed themselves in order to gain access to new spaces, public and spiritual, within themselves and the wider world. After World War I, as the militants began to enter into the widening sphere of public responsibilities made possible by the granting of a partial suffrage, they kept alive their old vision through the Suffragette Fellowship. In the mid-thirties the Fellowship sought to raise money for an Emily Wilding Davison memorial; her final sacrifice for the spiritual well-being of women seemed a central symbol for the remaining suffragettes.[35] Emmeline Pethick-Lawrence responded with passionate affection for a time when women had been willing to dare all for their vision of a better world:

> The inspiration of that movement enabled us to put into practice in our daily life some of the highest ideas expressed in philosophies and religions. It made the merging of self into the not-self easy and natural instead of almost impossible. Sacrifices were made in the spirit of joy; deeds were done which could not have been contemplated had we not been lifted above the personal self. The remembrance of many deeds of courage and complete self-forgetfulness are revived as I write. I think . . . finally [of] the culminating act of self-immolation when Emily Davison threw herself in the way of the King's racing horse and cried for the last time, for justice for all women. . . . From that day onward the bounds of women's freedom have been extended ever more widely . . .[36]

Even as we know, some fifty years later, that the "bounds of freedom" have not extended "ever more widely," the vision of the suffragettes casts its light along the path of our own generation's movement, inspiring us with what women will do in the name of freedom.

The suffragettes were wise to keep alive their own memories and to pass them on to the next generation. When most of women's history was lost, they remained known, though most often as sexually and psychically aberrant women. To this day their militancy has been difficult for historians to explain. Too often they have been labeled and dismissed. Their ideology does not fit our more economically concerned times, while their life-style, with its fierce commitment to an autocratic leadership and extreme emphasis upon bodily purity and sacrifice, seems at best dated. Nevertheless, their achievements—their courage, determination, and utterly atypical behavior have thrilled generations of women seeking a way out of the impasse of cultural stereotyping. The insights of anthropology enable us to understand better the importance of symbolic acts for the powerless, of the difficulties of breaking into alien space, of claiming a different identity. The suffragettes were clearly extremists—they gloried in such a definition—but their example and an analysis of their ideology and behavior in symbolic terms has important lessons for understanding other feminist movements. No movement understood better Simone de Beauvoir's insight that women are "the other". And no movement believed more thoroughly in the transforming power of that identity when forced into the male world. Historians are only beginning to understand the very concrete relationship of this power to historical movements.

Notes

1. The best modern survey of the militant suffrage movement is Andrew Rosen's *Rise up, Women! The Militant Campaign of the Women's Social and Political Union (1903–1914)* (London: Routledge and Kegan Paul, 1974). For his analysis of Christabel's policy, as outlined here, see p. 53. I have followed the general practice of referring to the militants who were willing to break the law as "suffragettes" and the nonmilitants as "suffragists." At the time the distinction was not clearly made until Christabel adopted the sneering epithet for her paper, *The Suffragette*, in 1912.

2. Viscountess Rhondda [Margaret Mackworth Thomas], *This Was My World* (London: Macmillan, 1933), 124.

3. Emmeline Pethick-Lawrence, *My Part in a Changing World* (London: Victor Gollancz, 1938), 215.

4. Ibid., 213–14. See also Rosen, who gives all relevant financial figures for the WSPU each year of its public reports.

5. E. Sylvia Pankhurst, in her detailed personal history of the movement *The Suffragette Movement* (London: Lovat Dickson and Thompson, 1931), 226–27 and 607–609, analyzes the reasons why women entered the suffrage movement and what they gained from their years of struggle.

6. Elaine Kidd, *Materialism and the Militants* (Hampstead: Macdonald, n.d.), 1.

7. Charlotte Despard, the leader of the democratic militant organization

the Women's Freedom League, was an important theosophist and vegetarian. See Andro Linklater, *An Unhusbanded Life: Charlotte Despard: Suffragette, Socialist and Sinn Feiner* (London: Hutchinson, 1980), 156–59.

8. For an examination of British and American suffrage posters, see Paula Hays Harper, "Votes for Women? A Graphic Episode in the Battle of the Sexes," *Art and Architecture in the Service of Politics*, eds., Henry A. Millon and Linda Nochlin (Cambridge: M.I.T. Press, 1978), 150–61.

9. See, for example, Helen Craggs's defense when she was arrested for arson: "I hold that militant Suffragettes stand in an analogous position to soldiers. You do not regard the latter as murderers because they fight in a good cause, and neither am I as a militant Suffragist a criminal" (*The Suffragette*, October 25, 1912, p. 23).

10. Mary P. Richardson, *Laugh a Defiance* (London: George Weidenfeld and Nicolson, 1953), 12.

11 Quoted by Brian Harrison, *Separate Spheres: The Opposition to Women's Suffrage in Britain* (London: Croom Helm, 1978), 187.

12. Mary Nesbitt, to Miss [May] Sinclair, unpublished letter (May 1, 1912), Suffragette Fellowship Collection, London Museum.

13. Margaret Wynne Nevison, *Life's Fitful Fever: A Volume of Memories* (London: A. & C. Black, 1926), 203–205.

14. Annie Kenney, *Memories of a Militant* (London: E. Arnold, 1924), 208–209.

15. Rosen, *Rise up, Women!* 122–123.

16. The records of the WSPU which were seized in the 1912 police raid have not survived, so it is impossible to know exactly how many women went to prison. Estimates run as high as two thousand.

17. Dr. Mary Gordon's description of Lady Constance Lytton, who gave her life to the Cause. Quoted in *The Letters of Constance Lytton*, selected and arranged by Betty Balfour (London: William Heinemann, 1925), 129.

18. Olive Walton, unpublished diary (1912), Suffragette Fellowship Collection, London Museum. See also Margaret E. Thompson and Mary D. Thompson, *They Couldn't Stop Us! Experiences of Two (Usually Law-Abiding) Women in the Years 1909–1913* (Ipswich: W. E. Harrison, n.d.), 44–51.

19. "Hammerers' Magazine," Winson Green Prison (Birmingham, 1912), Suffragette Fellowship Collection, London Museum.

20. S. I. Stevenson, unpublished autobiography, Suffragette Fellowship Collection, London Museum.

21. Helen Gordon [Liddle], *The Prison: A Sketch (An Experience of Forcible Feeding* (n.p., 1912), 63–64.

22. Ibid., 64.

23. See the prison correspondence and papers of Kitty Marion, Suffragette Fellowship Collection, London Museum.

24. See also Harrison, *Separate Spheres*, 185–86 for a discussion of the failure of the suffragettes to distinguish between their tactical violence and spontaneous mass violence, which characterized earlier reform bill agitation.

25. Rosen, *Rise up, Women!* 190, 192, 197, 201, 217, 221–22, 229, 231, 238, 242, meticulously documents the month-by-month growth of suffragette destruction by arson of famous buildings. Throughout the two-year period no animal or person was injured, despite uncoordinated and even spontaneous acts by individuals.

26. Emily Wilding Davison, "The Price of Liberty," *The Suffragette*, June 5, 1914, p. 50.

27. Mary Richardson in a note to Kitty Marion, written on toilet paper during a hunger strike, said "I have been thinking of Joan of Arc to-day— How marvellous she was so alone, with vile men night and day so tormented," Suffragette Fellowship Collection, London Museum.

28. Emily Wilding Davison, "The Price of Liberty," 50.

29. See, for example, Maud Arncliffe-Sennett's description of attending the funeral and following the body to Northumberland by train, *The Child* (London: privately printed, n.d. [1938]), 82–85.

30. Christabel Pankhurst, *The Great Scourge and How to End It* (London: E. Pankhurst, 1914), 132. The essays originally appeared in *The Suffragette* in 1913.

31. Antonia Raeburn, *The Militant Suffragettes* (London: Michael Joseph, 1973), 212–14, 223.

32. Richardson, *Laugh a Defiance*, 173–74. See also May Sinclair, *Tree of Heaven* (London: Macmillan, 1917), 225, where the heroine longs to return to her cell to escape the celebratory breakfast held by the WSPU for the released prisoners.

33. Rosen, *Rise up, Women!* 247–48.

34. See Sylvia Pankhurst, *The Suffragette Movement*, 593–94, and Emmeline Pethick-Lawrence, *My Part*, 307–317.

35. A statue in commemoration of Mrs. Pankhurst had been erected in 1930, with the names of all the women who had gone to prison around the base.

36. Emmeline Pethick-Lawrence, undated letter to Elsa Gye (1934–1935?), Suffragette Fellowship Collection.

FAMILY STRUCTURE, OCCUPATIONAL PATTERNS, AND SUPPORT FOR WOMEN'S SUFFRAGE

Elinor Lerner

In-depth studies in the United States of neighborhood organizing within the women's suffrage movement indicate that the class background of the national leaders may not be representative of the wider constituency. My work reveals that women's suffrage gained substantial support from immigrants and workers. The actual movement presents a picture quite different from the portrait traditionally drawn of a white Anglo-Saxon Protestant campaign dominated by idiosyncratic, eccentric, and politically marginal middle-class women.[1] My research also calls into question some recent feminist scholarship which has tried to legitimize the politics of women's suffrage by connecting the movement to socialism.[2] With this last perspective, women's issues have won serious recognition, not in their own right, but by association with working-class struggles.[3]

Much of the new literature still lacks empirical information about those who supported women's suffrage. In this paper, I begin to address the problem by providing concrete data on the social and economic realities of the lives of people who backed the movement and by attempting to place these findings in a feminist historical context. I base the following discussion on research conducted on the responses of residents of New York City to women's suffrage.

The suffrage movement had to convince men to share their political power. Success depended on the ability of women, who had no formal access to the vote, to persuade men to grant them that right. In order to gain support, the suffrage movement needed the strong backing of women at the local level. It also needed some channel through which women could effectively convey demands to men and a compelling argument to show men that women's suffrage was to their advantage.

In the United States ethnic politics have dominated big-city politics. Questions of social policy have largely been decided along ethnic lines. Women's suffrage, therefore, like other political issues, depended on the internal, structural characteristics of each ethnic community and the links established between a particular community and the wider suffrage movement.

Crucial factors influencing community attitudes on suffrage were the economic and social position of women within a specific ethnic group, the extent of suffrage organizing, and the interest in women's suffrage expressed by community organizations and institutions (religions, labor groups, political parties), which served as intermediaries between the suffrage movement and the community. These organizations and institutions helped interpret the issue and set the context for community sentiment in each neighborhood. Since different ethnic groups had different perceptions of what it meant to have their women vote, these various organizations and institutions played a critical role in working either with or against the suffrage movement in their local neighborhoods.

In the decade before World War I, suffragists did not consider Manhattan a likely political arena for success given its large population of immigrants, working-class people, Catholics, and Jews. In 1920, 78 percent of Manhattan's residents were foreign born or had foreign-born parents. In 1910 approximately 37 percent of Manhattan was Roman Catholic and 31 percent Jewish. At least 13 percent was first- or second-generation Irish Catholic and another 13 percent first- or second-generation Italian.[4]

New York held two elections to determine the fate of the women's suffrage amendment. After losing in 1915, women's suffrage passed in 1917, with New York City carrying the state. The Manhattan vote shows that support for suffrage crossed class lines and, except for Italians, was sharply divided along ethnic boundaries. The largest, strongest, and most consistent backing came from the Jewish community, both working- and middle-class Jews. The strongest, most consistent opposition came from working- and middle-class Irish. Italians were not unified on suffrage: most voted against, but the heart of Italian Greenwich Village was solidly and consistently prosuffrage.[5]

As a group, Manhattan's middle- and upper-class Anglo-Saxon Protestant, native-born men were neither very opposed nor very much in favor of women's suffrage. Their votes hovered around the average for Manhattan in each election. The more affluent they were, the less they voted for suffrage. Only two small neighborhoods in the city that were neither working class nor immigrant gave a large majority to the referendum: the professional area around Barnard College and Columbia University and part of Washington Heights (in upper Manhattan), inhabited in those days by members of New York's literary, artistic, and theatrical elite.

The Jewish vote for suffrage is extraordinary in several respects. Jewish election districts constituted the bulk of the top prosuffrage election districts in both elections, and no identifiable Jewish districts were consistently antisuffrage. If one considers the top fifty prosuffrage election districts in 1915 and 1917, at least 64 percent and 74 percent respectively were Jewish areas. Even more impressive is the fact that of the top one hundred prosuffrage election districts in 1917 at least 78 were Jewish neighborhoods. Votes in these districts ran from 56 percent to 72 percent for suffrage in 1915 and 76 percent to 93 percent in 1917. In the larger Assembly Districts, of the three in Manhattan that gave a majority to suffrage in 1915, two were in Jewish neighborhoods: the Lower East Side and Jewish Harlem.

Not only were the areas most strongly in favor of suffrage predominantly Jewish, but about half of the Jewish neighborhoods voiced enthusiastic support for giving the vote to women. In 1915 and 1917 at least 44 percent and 55 percent, respectively, of the Jewish election districts in Harlem and on the Lower East Side were in the top one hundred prosuffrage election districts. Striking as well is the number of Jewish votes that went for suffrage. In 1917 Jewish voters constituted at least 24 percent of the prosuffrage votes, and they increased their support by 71 percent between 1915 and 1917.

Who were these male Jewish voters; and what internal, structural characteristics of the Jewish community contributed to their support for women's suffrage? Not surprisingly, given their large backing for suffrage, these Jewish voters cut across age and class lines; the length of time they had been in America also varied, as did their place of national origin.[6]

With an average age of thirty-five, Jewish voters were as young as or younger than any other group of voters studied. They represented the lowest percentage of people born in the United States; over 75 percent came from abroad. These foreign-born voters had been in this country an average of nineteen years, a shorter time than any other immigrant voter group studied. Most of them came to the United States in the late 1890s as teenagers from all the major areas of

Eastern Europe that Jewish immigrants fled. Thus Jewish voters were, in demographic terms, the least "Americanized" of all the voters sampled.

Most of them lived with families: two-thirds were married, and many of the unmarried voters were young men living with parents, where it was common for the father also to be registered. Two-thirds of the voters lived in households with at least one working woman, and almost one-fourth had jobs in the same trade as at least one woman in the household. Most voters worked in blue-collar occupations, primarily in skilled trades. One-fourth were in the garment trades. This concentration meant that a sizable number of Jewish voters had jobs in an industry that by 1910 had 36 percent of its New York City workers unionized. Some skilled workers, such as the cutters, were as much as 80 percent unionized. In New York City, those involved in the garment trades had an unusually high union membership compared to the average rate for males in the United States, which was only 25 percent.[7]

In Manhattan, employment, marital status, and family structure were clearly related to voting patterns on the issue of women's suffrage. Important as well were the characteristics of working women in a particular community. In the Jewish areas sampled, the average age of the working woman was barely twenty-one, making this group the youngest of any studied. Furthermore, more Jewish working women were born abroad (70 percent) than any of the others. These foreign-born young women had been in the United States barely eight years, making them the most recent immigrant group of working women. They came to this country in the first decade of the twentieth century, as young teenagers.

The density of working women in Manhattan's Jewish community was relatively high. Fifty-three percent were in the garment trades, and 63 percent of them worked on the Lower East Side. These percentages should be considered together with the general statistics for Jewish workers: over 50 percent of the Jewish households sampled had at least one member employed in the garment trades. Almost 70 percent had at least one member employed in a unionized trade, most of them in the garment and building industries, two highly unionized and politicized occupations.

Over 22 percent of the Jewish working women sampled were boarders; 82 percent of these worked in the garment trades. Many of the young women had probably been the first in their immediate family to come to America, and many came in search of independence and personal autonomy. As one woman put it: "I want something more than work and more than money. I want freedom"[8] Since very few working women could afford to live alone, most Jewish single women boarded with families, creating a relatively large group of independent young women who lived outside their own families and worked in occupations where they were exposed to union and feminist ideologies. Some of them had undoubtedly been politicized before coming to the United States, for an important number of Jewish immigrant women had been active in European political and labor movements. Participating now in communal family households, these women were often eager to join contemporary political struggles.

According to the United States Immigration Commission, 44 percent of New York City's Jewish households had at least one or two boarders,[9] and in these homes political discussions flourished. Life in one family was described in this way: "After dinner the boarders . . . gathered in the front room where they gossiped, shared news of their families, and discussed the needle trades and developments in the labor movement."[10] Similarly, small shops were often neighborhood centers for informal discussions and for the exchange of community news. When there were strikes, they also became communication centers for strike activities. In these ways, Jewish women who did not work outside the home or family business were exposed to political ideas and strategies.

Unlike the Jewish community, with its uniformly strong support, the Italians were divided on the issue of women's suffrage. While most neighborhoods voted against the amendment, the center of the Italian section of Greenwich Village was strongly and consistently pro-suffrage. A comparison of Italian areas that supported women's suffrage with those that voted against it point to a series of internal structural community factors which either encouraged or blocked political backing for feminist demands.

In many ways, Italian voters resembled Jewish voters. More often than not they were born outside the United States. They were relatively young and came to this country in the 1890s as teenagers. Only about a third of them were born in the United States. Most Italian voters were in their middle thirties, and those born in Italy had been in the United States an average of twenty-two years.

Communities that voted for women's suffrage had a slightly higher degree of political participation than those that voted against. Proportionately they had more registered voters. Furthermore, a greater number of those registered actually voted in each election. Finally, in these communities, voters were more likely to vote on the suffrage referendum. While immigrants from northern Italy lived in areas that tended to vote against suffrage, large numbers of southern Italians inhabited districts that voted both for and against the amendment. Thus those areas that were most strongly in favor of suffrage were predominantly southern Italian neighborhoods, Sicilian and Neapolitan, two groups usually considered to be very conservative on feminist issues.[11] Those who supported women's suffrage among the Italians crossed class lines, concentrating at both the bottom and the middle of the occupational scale.

In contrast to communities that did not back suffrage, voters in favor of the amendment had frequent contact with women in socially structured situations, especially with working women. Thirty-six percent of the prosuffrage Italian voters had working women in their households compared to 17 percent of the voters who did not support suffrage. A higher percentage of prosuffrage voters lived in households where at least one male and one female worked in the same trade than did those who voted against suffrage. Over a third more voters in the antisuffrage areas than in prosuffrage communities were unmarried: 46 percent and 33 percent respectively. As with the Jewish voters, many of the unmarried Italian voters in the prosuffrage areas were sons living at home where often other male relatives were also registered voters. Thus, from the Italian and Jewish samples, it appears that an important factor influencing male votes on women's suffrage was the household arrangement. Men who lived in family households, especially those with working women and where the voters and women shared similar work experiences, had a greater tendency to vote for suffrage than those who did not.

More striking than differences in living situations were the characteristics of the women themselves. In areas that voted for suffrage, women were twice as likely to work, three times as likely to be working wives, and four times as likely to be mothers than in antisuffrage neighborhoods. Those women who were working also tended to be older, and fewer of them were American born.

In areas that supported the vote, over 22 percent of the working women were married and over 25 percent had children living at home. Italian working women were overwhelmingly concentrated in blue-collar, service, and unskilled jobs, with most of them employed in Manhattan's light industries. The main difference between the occupations of those living in prosuffrage and antisuffrage areas is that in the former the percentage of women in the garment trades was almost twice what it was in the latter, 65 percent and 35 percent respectively.

The importance of the role played by the garment industry cannot be overstated. Its work force by 1915 was predominantly Jewish and Italian. The Italians comprised approximately one-third of the workers in the waist and dress trade and two-thirds in men's clothing.[12] Since the work force was not segregated along ethnic lines, Jews and Italians toiled together in the same shops and shared in the same union struggles. By 1909 Italian women had begun to join garment unions, and they, together with their men, pressured for Italian locals. The first one was created in 1913.[13] Although repeated attempts were made to use ethnic and religious differences between Jews and Italians to create work-force factionalism, these were largely ineffective.

By 1915 Jews and Italians had a common union experience. Over two thousand Italian women had taken part in the 1909 shirtwaist strike. In 1911, the infamous Triangle Shirtwaist Factory fire killed many Italian as well as Jewish women and spurred on attempts to unionize Italian female garment workers. According to the union the fire caused a vociferous outcry in the Italian community: " The Little Italies of New York City were in mourning. In the flickering yellow glow of the street lights fiery labor leaders urged the girls to unite under the banner of unionism."[14] By 1913, over 10 percent of New York City's Italian working women were unionized, practically all of these in the garment trades. Seventeen percent of the shops in which Italian women worked were unionized, and in the cloak and suit industry 88 percent of them were. After the 1912–13 strike in the men's clothing industry, thousands of Italian women joined the union.[15]

Other than the garment trades, few of the small, light industries employing Italian women were unionized. And, except for the garment trades, very few Italian men worked in occupations that also employed significant numbers of Italian women. Thus, due to the relatively large numbers of both men and women employed by the garment trades in the prosuffrage areas, in these neighborhoods, twice as many women worked in unionized trades, which also hired Italian men, than they did in areas that voted against the amendment. Those women who found such jobs were also in the company of other employees who vigorously backed suffrage.

In other words, the mere fact that women worked was not enough to influence men to vote for suffrage. Women had to be in a politically active, unionized trade which employed large numbers of community men and prosuffrage workers. In such an environment women were likely to become aware of the issues, support the amendment, and take the arguments back to their communities and homes. Italian areas that supported the amendment contained large percentages of working women who were married or who lived in households with voters, indicating that positive pressure could be applied to influence the electorate. In order to test the importance of women's occupational patterns, especially at the level of workforce organization and political awareness, I compare the Italian and Jewish cases with the Irish community, which had a large female work force, but which voted heavily against suffrage.

The Irish constituted Manhattan's largest, strongest, and most consistent opposition to women's suffrage. Not even one Irish election district was among the one hundred most favorable toward suffrage in either election. On the contrary, most lower Westside Irish neighborhoods were among the one hundred districts most vehemently against women's suffrage. The degree of antisuffrage feeling was very strong: in 1915 many Irish districts voted 70 to 84 percent against women's suffrage.

Since the major period of Irish immigration to the United States occurred thirty to fifty years earlier than that of the Italians and Jews, most of the registered voters from the Irish community were born in the United States. Those born in Ireland had been in this country an average of twenty-nine years. Irish voters averaged thirty-nine years in age, slightly older than the Italians and Jews.

Irish men were concentrated in service and blue-collar jobs. They were not as heavily unionized as either Italians or Jews. When they did join unions, theirs, in contrast to the garment trades, were politically conservative. In New York City, most of the Irish union members were laborers, longshoremen, teamsters, and skilled craftsmen. And skilled craft unions where the Irish dominated, like the one for the building trades, had been characterized by conservative politics well before World War I.[16]

Given the occupations of Irish men, it follows that in the sample I studied very few Irish men or Irish voters lived in households where men and women shared the same occupation. In fact, only 4 percent of Irish households had men and women doing the same kind of work. These were all office/white-collar jobs such as bookkeeper, clerk, or typist, jobs that had few unions or even a collective identity.

Indeed, the relationship between Irish voters and Irish women, particularly working women, was quite different from that in the Jewish and prosuffrage Italian communities. Irish men and women had relatively little structural contact on the personal, social, or occupational level. Over 53 percent of the registered voters were not married, a far greater proportion than in any of the other groups studied. Most of these unmarried voters were in their late thirties or forties; and they lived with an unmarried male friend, with a male relative, or in lodging houses. That the Irish sample should have had such a low rate of marriage is not surprising, for in both Ireland and the United States Irish men tended to marry relatively late, sometimes in their forties and fifties, and Irish communities traditionally had large numbers of single, older men and women.

A number of American Irish viewed this marriage pattern as a problem. The New York newspaper *The Irish World* ran many articles about the reluctance of Irish men to marry and the lack of family cohesiveness. In "Why Bachelors Don't Marry," it was argued that men did not want to give up the benefits of bachelorhood, that is, control over their time and money, just to "marry a fool." In "Why They Don't Marry," the author explained that too many men saw "marriage ruined by girls who want a good time."[17] Articles indicated that Irish men found marriage restrictive and that they had little sense of the value of women.

In the Irish community ties between men and women were limited. Not only did the Irish marry late, if they married at all, but even after marriage they shared few activities. One study of the Manhattan Irish found that men and women rarely worked in the same occupations; rather, "They work in separate, non-competing worlds." Moreover, the study found that wives and husbands seldom spent their non-working social time together, stating: "it is not customary for husband and wife to go out in each other's company. The local organizations seem to accept this segregation of the sexes as fundamental and proceed accordingly." Women belonged to female organizations such as mothers' clubs which men were "contemptuous toward", and men belonged to lodges which did not admit female members.[18] Articles in *The Irish World* bemoaned the quality of Irish married life, noting that there appeared to be little closeness. The newspaper recommended that couples spend Sundays together or evenings playing cards, but it sadly admitted at the same time that for most Irish couples the thought of being quarantined at home "in each other's uninteresting company" was unbearable.[19]

Like Irish voters, Irish working women differed from their Jewish and Italian counterparts. The vast majority of them (88 percent) were American born. They had the least percentage of immigrants of any group studied with the exception of black working women. Those born in Ireland had been in the United States an average of twenty-four years, and they came to this country when they were infants. Furthermore, Irish working women were older than the Italian or

Jewish working women, having an average age of twenty-eight. The density of Irish working women was relatively high, and the Irish community counted a considerable number of working mothers and working women who were heads of households. Significantly, occupations of Irish working women were quite different from those of Jewish women and Italian women in the prosuffrage areas. Most Irish women worked in sales, in office jobs, or in service/cleaning positions. (50 percent were in clerical or sales jobs.) All of these were nonunionized occupations where relatively few women worked together in one place and where the job was "individualized" in the sense that most of the women did not do the same job as other workers in the same establishment. The lack of unionization, other work-place organizations, or identification with other workers, as well as the upwardly mobile aspirations of most white-collar workers, limited the introduction of liberal, radical, or feminist ideologies.

In sum, there was a great deal of structural distance between men and women in the Irish community, and they perceived their interests differently. Irish male voters and Irish women did not share the same work place, work concerns, organizations, social activities, political experiences, or even, in many cases, the same households. Most of the men worked in "male jobs," such as longshoremen, laborers, policemen, and teamsters and in the building trades, where they had little contact with women. When there were unions, they tended to be politically conservative and did not have female members. Irish women worked at jobs that were not unionized and where the work place did not lend itself readily to politicization. Finally, the majority of the male voters were not married, and relatively few men had household or family relationships with women.

The Irish case offers a dramatic contrast to the conditions found in Jewish and prosuffrage Italian communities, where women worked in unionized trades that employed neighborhood men. These Jews and Italians shared their work place, union, and home life with men; and this gave them the necessary social context to gain political awareness themselves and to press feminist demands upon male voters. Irish women did not have the same opportunities.

Let us turn now to two middle- to upper-class communities of native-born, predominantly Anglo-Saxon Protestants; an area around Barnard College and Columbia University, and an upper Manhattan neighborhood in Washington Heights. These were the only two Protestant, middle- and upper-class Manhattan areas that voted strongly and consistently for suffrage in both elections.[20] Most of these voters were married. In Washington Heights the percentage was over eighty.

One explanation for the low number of young unmarried voters is that few older unmarried sons lived with their parents.

The voters had mostly white-collar jobs, and only about 10 percent of voters had working women in their families. This low representation of working women is partly due to the absence of working unmarried daughters who still lived at home. Before they left to settle down, young women in these communities did not have to work. Many were students instead.

In several respects these voters and families differed from the stereotype of the middle class so often assumed to be the base of support for the women's suffrage movement. In the Barnard-Columbia area, for example, 38 percent of the voters were university employees, doctors, lawyers, engineers, or in the arts. Fifteen percent alone were in higher education. In Washington Heights, over 10 percent were connected to the artistic or literary world and 19 percent were professionals. Around Columbia few men worked in the same profession as the women in their households, for there were few homes headed by men that included working women. Many voters and women, however, shared the same occupations.

Although only a few voters had working women in their households, both communities contained large numbers of professional women. Compared to working women in other areas sampled, they were older (the average age was thirty-three) and more likely to be unmarried (55 percent were heads of households). These women were professionals in white-collar occupations, and they often lived alone or with another single, professional woman. They apparently earned a good enough salary to enable them to live independently in relatively affluent neighborhoods. Not surprisingly, in a neighborhood near a women's college, over 50 percent of the working women sampled in the Barnard area were associated with university life. In Washington Heights, the largest occupational grouping for working women was in the literary, artistic, and theatrical professions, with 27 percent of them so employed. Both communities had a considerable number of women engaged in business, as owners or executives.

It is interesting to compare the neighborhoods around Barnard-Columbia and in Washington Heights with other middle-class, native-born communities. These two areas differed from the other neighborhoods in that they had a large number of single, professional women and a large number of men in professional, not business, occupations. This indicates that support for women's suffrage among the native-born, upper and middle class came from a very special community—the intellectual elite. This comparison also suggests that working women in this group did not have to be members of the same household to influence votes. It was enough that they earned their living in the same occupations as men in their neighborhoods and that they gained social, economic, and political recognition within these communities.

In conclusion, my study of the voting and demographic patterns of several ethnically distinct neighborhoods in Manhattan suggests that a number of structural factors influenced the attitudes of male voters toward women's suffrage. The suffrage amendment won many votes in Jewish and some Italian neighborhoods, where women and men of the community, and often of the same household, tended to work together in the same trades, specifically in occupations that were unionized and politically liberal. It did well also in white, Anglo-Saxon, middle-class communities where working women did not necessarily live with men, but did share the same professional and artistic occupations as neighborhood men, and where they achieved a certain degree of social and economic recognition. However, the amendment did poorly among the Irish, where women worked in gender-segregrated, nonunionized occupations and the unions to which the men belonged were politically conservative. In this case, not only did women have little chance on the job to gain political awareness and influence male workers, but also they had little contact with the men in their households. Many Irish men lived apart from women, remained bachelors, or married late, and even married couples shared few community or social activities. In this situation it was difficult for Irish women to convince their men that women voting would be to the advantage of Irish men.

Political action and the formation of political opinions take place in a social context which helps to shape the way individuals see political possibilities. People tend to support social issues when they think that they will benefit from them. The social consequences of giving the vote to women filtered down to the community level through labor unions, religious and political groups, and the links established between suffrage organizations and the neighborhood. Although many have believed that race and class affiliation were crucial factors in determining the opinions of voters on women's suffrage, my research shows that the interconnections between family structure and work patterns were more important. These provided the framework in which voters assessed the concrete results of women voting. The presence of large numbers of working, self-supporting women did not, in itself, provide the necessary conditions for women to gain political influence within a community. In the absence of high economic and social status women also needed a collective base from which to press their demands and a means to have these demands heard by voting men.

Notes

1. For example, Aileen Kraditor, *The Ideas of the Woman Suffrage Movement* (New York: Anchor Books, 1971), and William O'Neill, *Everyone Was Brave* (Chicago: Quadrangle Books, 1969).

2. For studies on the base of support for suffrage see Doris Daniels, "Building a Winning Coalition: The Suffrage Fight in New York State," *New York History* (January 1979); Sharon Strom, "Leadership and Tactics in the American Woman Suffrage Movement: A New Perspective from Massachusetts," *The Journal of American History* (September 1975); and Elinor Lerner, "Immigrant and Working Class Involvement in the New York Woman Suffrage Movement" (Ph.D. dissertation, University of California at Berkeley, 1981).

3. For discussions of suffrage and socialism see Meredith Tax, *The Rising of the Women* (New York: Monthly Review, 1980), and Mari Jo Buhle, *Women and American Socialism* (Urbana: University of Illinois Press, 1981). Both of these deal in detail with the New York City suffrage movement.

4. Computed from Walter Laidlaw, ed., *Population of the City of New York, 1890–1930* (New York: City Census Committee, 1932), 51, 256, 262, 289; and Nathan Kantrowitz, *"New York City Migration, 1900–1960* (New York: New York University, March 1969), 2. 12.

5. All election results were computed from numbers published in the New York City Board of Elections *Official Canvass of Votes Cast in the City of New York, November 2, 1915* in the *City Record* Vol. XLIII, December 31, 1915, and *Official Canvass of Votes Cast in the City of New York, November 6, 1917* in the *City Record*, Vol. LXV, December 31, 1917. For New York City, the state outside of the city and the state as a whole, the percentages of prosuffrage votes were, respectively, in 1915 42.6 percent, 42.4 percent, 42.5 percent. In 1917 they were 58.6 percent, 49.9 percent, and 53.9 percent. Prosuffrage votes for Manhattan were 43 percent in 1915 and 59 percent in 1917.

6. Demographic data for this study, unless otherwise noted, were obtained from samples taken from the census manuscripts of the 1915 New York State Census. Voters were identified from lists of registered voters published in the *City Record*. Sample sizes were Jewish—271 voters, 407 working women; Irish—201 voters, 185 working women; Columbia—Washington Heights—172 voters, 103 working women; prosuffrage Italians—109 voters, 218 working women; antisuffrage Italians—103 voters, 154 working women.

7. Unionization rates from Isaac Hourwich, *Immigration and Labor* (New York: B. W. Huebsch, 1922), 326.

8. Quoted in Carolyn McCreesh, "On the Picket Line: Militant Women Campaign to Organize Garment Workers" (Ph.D. dissertation, University of Maryland, 1975), 165.

9. U. S. Congress, Senate, *Reports of the Immigration Commission,* 1911, Vol. 26, 198–200. This is the highest percentage for any ethnic group.

10. Charlotte Baum, Paula Hyman, and Sonya Michell, *The Jewish Woman in America* (New York: The New American Library, 1975), 106.

11. Robert Park and Herbert Miller, *Old World Traits Transplanted* (New York: Harper and Brothers, 1921), 147; Federal Writers' Project, *The Italians of New York* (New York: Random House, 1938), 19–21; and Lydio Tomasi, ed., *The Italian in America* (New York: Center for Migration Studies, 1972), 174.

12. Hyman Berman, "Era of the Protocol" (Ph.D. dissertation, Columbia University, 1956), 24, and Robert Foerster, *The Italian Immigration of Our Times* (Cambridge: Harvard University Press, 1919), 374. Two-thirds of Italian garment workers were women.

13. Foerster, *Italian Immigration,* 403; McCreesh, "Picket Line," 132, 166–8; Rudolf Glanz, *Jew and Italian* (New York: Shulsinger Bros, 1970), 45; Federal Writers' Project, *Italians,* 65; John Crawford, Luigi Antonini (Education Department, ILGWU, Local 89), 20.

14. *Justice* 1934 cited in Crawford, *Luigi Antonini,* 19.

15. Louise Odencrantz, *Italian Women in Industry* (New York: Russell Sage Foundation, 1919), 104–106, and *Reports of the U.S. Immigration Commission,* Vol. 2, 388.

16. Hourwich, *Immigration and Labor,* 328; Thomas Henderson, *Tammany Hall and the New Immigrants* (New York: Arno Press, 1976), 83, and Charles Leinenweber, "The Class and Ethnic Base of New York City Socialism," *Labor History,* (Winter 1981), 31–56.

17. *The Irish World* (New York City), March 3, 1917; May 5, 1917; July 7, 1917. Also see Ellen Biddle, "The American Catholic Irish Family," in Charles Mindel and Robert Haberstein, *Ethnic Families in America* (New York: Elsevier, 1976), 89–123.

18. Katherine Anthony, *Mothers Who Must Earn,* 108, 156–57, in Pauline Goldmark, *West Side Studies,* 2 (New York: Russell Sage Foundation, 1914).

19. *The Irish World,* August 18, 1917; July 7, 1917; February 21, 1917.

20. Religious data calculated from Laidlaw, *Population,* p. 292, using data from 1920.

CATHOLIC WOMEN AND POLITICAL AFFAIRS

THE CASE OF THE PATRIOTIC LEAGUE OF FRENCH WOMEN

Anne-Marie Sohn

Translated by Debra Irving

Today we know quite a lot about working-class and other militant feminists who lived in France at the turn of the century. But we still have relatively little information about Catholic women activists: the contempt of the socialists has long echoed the derision of the anticlerical republicans. In the nineteenth century, the Church relied heavily upon its parishoners both for catechism and for charity ("Lady Bountiful" is a literary convention), but after 1900, the activities of Catholic women in France broke free of ecclesiastical tutelage. Religious yet autonomous associations proliferated. Some made common cause with social Catholicism, others were firmly in the conservative camp, like the Frenchwomen's League and especially the Patriotic League of Frenchwomen (PLF) which counted half a million members in 1914[1].

This partisan League devoted itself to the defense of the "freedoms" threatened by the artificial policy of the radicals. But it was a complex movement which combined political agitation with religious proselytizing and social action. In a changing society, it sought to revive philanthropy and the Christian morality behind it. To the republican ideal of the spouse as companion it opposed another image of women which deeply affected a public opinion still dominated by the Church and its teachings. The organized, full-scale mobilization of Catholic women raised the problems of the participation of women in city life and of the interaction of the public and private domains.

A Feminine, Political Movement

A Conservative League Committed to Political Struggle

The Patriotic League of Frenchwomen was founded within the context of the conflict between the Church and radicalism. The law on freedom of association was adopted in 1901. Extremely liberal in principle, it actually penalized religious congregations, which alone were forced to seek authorization. The teaching orders seemed to be the main targets, and freedom of education was jeopardized. The Catholics struck back immediately. The legislative elections of 1902 took place in an atmosphere of feverish anticipation, with the conservatives seeking to rally against the left.

Women threw themselves spontaneously into the fray. The Frenchwomen's League, defined by the police intelligence service (Renseignements Généraux) as "an opponent of the law on religious congregations," came to life in Lyons in 1901. In 1902, its Parisian committee decided to join the electoral contest and established a new movement, the Patriotic League of Frenchwomen, which was to "defend the freedoms"—that is, the freedoms of conscience and education. Identifying with the program of Jacques Piou's Popular Liberal Alliance,[2] it resolved to support that group's candidates for deputy: in fact, it defined itself as an electoral "committee" of the Liberal Alliance. It was thus clearly entrenched in the camp of the *droite ralliée* (conservative opposition to the Third Republic). But its ideological aspirations attracted conservatives of every stripe, Catholics and nationalists, as is revealed by its name, which harks back to a lingering anti-Dreyfusism and to the League of the French Homeland (Ligue de la Patrie Française), one of whose founders, François Coppée, supported it. The police also noted the involvement of "old royalists," that is, legitimists.

As far back as 1904, the League's second president, Baroness Reille, emphasized the need for a wide range of opinion: "We are neither of the droite ralliée, nor bonapartists nor royalists, but committed Catholics who are determined to join together throughout France to defend our freedoms . . . Each of us may have her own preferences, but these cannot be expressed through the League."[3] In addition to the immediate defense of Catholic interests, League members shared with J. Piou the dream of modernizing French conservatism—an unprecedented ambition for women. The first president, Baroness de Brigode, put it this way: "We want something like the Primrose League, which became such a potent force for the Conservatives.[4]

But the League rapidly abandoned that project and confined itself to nationalist platitudes. In 1908, the Paris police reported that the movement "had begun taking its orders from the newspaper *La Croix*"[5] and the Assumptionists. As a matter of fact, the newspaper subsidized the PLF's conferences, while the latter promoted the paper's circulation. Their political symbiosis was complete. Following the example of *La Croix,* League members declared themselves to be "enemies of the Jacobin régime," of socialism, and of "Jewry." They defended the "true France, loyal to its beliefs and traditions"[6]— pre-1789 ones. From that point on, relations with the monarchists became touchy: after 1906, the League no longer ranked the royalist papers with the "moral press" that it supported. Conversely, the PLF's ideological ties to the Assumptionists supplemented rather than conflicted with its links to the Liberal Alliance.

The war of 1914 was a watershed. League members moderated their attacks on the regime and supported the government. Their exaggerated patriotism aligned them with those who wanted a fight to the finish *(jusqu'au boutistes):* they would accept only "peace through victory," and viewed negotiations with the enemy as treasonous. Having a strong tradition of charitable works, the League excelled in the organization of aid to war widows and orphans. It set up sewing circles *(ouvroirs)* for the wives of enlisted men and sent parcels to French soldiers. The election in 1919 of the Conservative Parliament *(chambre bleu horizon)* and the conservative policy of the National Bloc gave its members deep satisfaction. They identified with Poincaré and endorsed the occupation of the Ruhr. Admittedly, when the Left Bloc decided to apply the secular laws to Alsace-Lorraine in 1924, the League came out for the preservation of the concordat in the name of religious freedom, but the intellectual quarrel concerned it less and less. Relations between Church and State became easier as new perils threatened.

The Russian Revolution and the social upheaval caused by the war infected League members with fear of the masses and of civil strife. After 1916, they were apprehensive that, with the return of peace, the workers "might come to think that they had fought for the possessions of those who had plenty and had generally suffered the least from the war. Soldiers might express a desire to share the pleasures enjoyed by the rich. . . . They might then make demands which would bring us to civil war."[7]

The threat spread worldwide: "Imagine the white race virtually intermingled with the yellow."[8] In 1917, the police summarized this transformation: "Its efforts, apparently bent towards achieving spiritual goals, are now directed at promoting a favorable opinion of the re-establishment of that *social* and Christian *order* which is its justification."[9] Social insecurity replaced paternalism and religious passion from then on.

Feminine Militancy

League members swung into action. Local committees took up collections to support the candidates of the Popular Alliance. The militants garnered support for the movement, but did not meddle in the choice of future deputies, which was the party's, and not the League's, prerogative. They organized frequent denmonstrations at the height of the anticlerical struggle, from 1902 to 1910, and held meetings against "liberticide" laws[10] and during the inventories of the property of the teaching orders.[11] Emergency funds were set up to assist "persecuted" nuns and priests.

The PLF also waged an unremitting struggle against the secular, or "godless," school. It sought to convince its supporters to withdraw their children, especially their sons, from public educational institutions and worked to strengthen Catholic education. Some committees, in Bercq and Amiens, for example, set up their own schools. National congresses demanded government subsidies for "free" schools in the name of the equality of citizens in respect to taxation. Thus, League members participated actively in the intellectual war which divided Frenchmen before 1914. But, aware that the struggle betwen Tradition and the Republic would be decided by the conquest of public opinion, the PLF stressed the circulation of the "moral press" to oppose the Republican, and even the neutral, dailies—in other words, the popular press. "We are not engaged in politics—we are educating people to make good choices in the elections," declared a provincial supporter.[12] The League accordingly disseminated Catholic and conservative newspapers, primarily *La Croix,* which "clearly exemplifies the well-informed Catholic press." Acting as intermediaries, the militants began collecting subscriptions. They were aware, nevertheless, that the newspaper was too serious for anyone but the "elite," and that its political stance might alienate some readers. The secretary of the committee in the Jura noted: "We haven't dared to introduce *La Croix* in certain communities."[13] In such cases, the PLF recommended *L'Echo de Paris* or, in the provinces, the most moderate newspaper. The "moral press" encountered material difficulties, primary among which was the Hachette's monopoly on distribution, which favored the "immoral press." In order to weaken its grip, the League tried to set up newspaper depots where paid carriers could pick up copies for subscribers. Other aspects of the propaganda for "liberal" newspapers were inspired by methods developed by the left: house to house distribution, free subscription and handouts after mass and even on the beach in the summer! The results seem to have been mixed. The League claimed to have distributed many thousands of copies, but this is impossible to verify. Press secretaries were to be found in only twenty-five *départements*.

In the same spirit of struggle against Republican, atheist ideology and observing that "nowadays, everyone reads,[14] League members believed that edifying reading material should be made available. Their principal objective was to train the worker by entertaining him. The vogue of novels was to be exploited by the sale of low-priced pamphlets edited by the "moral press" or by devout Catholics like the Féron-Vraus of Lille. Catholic weeklies like *La Veillée des chaumières* were also recommended, as were compendiums of "moral songs" like those of Theodore Botrel and the historical images and military postcards which were thought to be very popular among the lower classes. To attract a clientele that did not visit libraries, the PLF intended to increase the number of reading rooms sponsored by sympathetic shopkeepers, butchers, haberdashers, etc.

League members did not hesitate to use tracts and posters to influence people's minds. Posters were costly, to be sure, but "they are very influential," the Viscountess of Velard remarked in her report on the press in 1913.[15] Some committees displayed them at the door of their headquarters. Others put up newspaper articles outlined in fluorescent paint, to attract the attention of passersby!

Publicity and mass propaganda techniques were well assimilated by Catholic women, who used the new forms of communication for their ideological purposes.

Women and Politics: From the Domestic to the Political Sphere

The political involvement of Catholic women was accompanied by a militancy which was comparable in form to that of the male parties. Its rapid growth surprised observers, who tried to find ways of explaining it.

The police thought that the movement was "indentured" to the Liberal Alliance (L'Alliance liberale) and the Assumptionists: it was thus construed as an extension of male institutions. The truth was not quite so simple, however. In contrast to the situation in Italy or the Netherlands, where the Church really controlled feminist movements, the PLF was free of ecclesiastical tutelage. The Church was asked, but did not direct. Similarly, women could not be described as mere appendages of the politicians of the Liberal Alliance. The political themes sounded by League members were admittedly unoriginal:

they echoed political statements made elsewhere, principally in *La Croix*. The wives of influential members of the Liberal Alliance were among the League's most prominent supporters. Women worked for the Alliance candidates, and the *Manual for League Members*[16] characterized politics as a masculine prerogative: in the evening, after dinner, the husband would initiate his wife into political affairs and analyze legislative texts and Parliament speeches for her. Taking this point of view, one might conclude that the PLF was created by and for men: the politicians of the right understood the importance of women in the ideological struggle and mobilized them to their own advantage. They sought first of all to involve their wives and daughters, undoubtedly feeling that while lower-class women should not enter the political arena, educated women had a social prerogative to do so. Yet J. Piou never mentions the PLF in his history of the Alliance. And the fact remains that League members broke free of masculine tutelage and acted autonomously, both in organization and in inspiration for action. They were much more firmly entrenched at the local level than was the Liberal Alliance: their image was one of pioneers rather than of followers. As a result of the internal divisions which the Alliance experienced after 1910, its involvement with the PLF declined rapidly. During the war, the League actually emerged as the principal representative of the political movement which had been fractured by the mobilization of its main militants, and it survived the Alliance's demise in 1919.

The originality of the political involvement of League members was remarked on by a number of sympathizers. In 1905, *Le Figaro* proclaimed that a new type of woman had emerged. While until then, militants—"real viragos"—had been found only "in the parties of hatred and destruction, . . . here were women who were political, but not revolutionaries."[17] Catholics had thus broken the taboo that had barred women from political affairs and had invalidated the argument that "women who dabble in politics risk looking ridiculous"— that old misogynist prejudice. The valuable support which the right discovered in women legitimized a commitment which until then had been found only on the left and had therefore been discredited.

Nevertheless, the commitment of the PLF women was prompted by particular, *private* motives. Baroness de Brigode justified their activities this way: "Next time, we will check the color of the ballots a bit more carefully, for it affects *our children's future*."[18] Similarly, the *Manual for League Members* called upon the militants to oppose divorce, "for it threatens your *conjugal happiness*," and to defend freedom of education in order to "preserve the option of *having your children educated* by someone other than an unworthy teacher." Women should join the PLF to protect their families, and it was primarily through the family that women should exercise their "political influence over their spouses, brothers and sons."[19]

The motivation of League members thus attests to an original process of politicization in private life. But is this process exclusively feminine? The Church, which saw both socialism and feminism as a threat to the family, was often tempted to make private life and the family the focus of its "politics." Catholic women were governed by those politics. But the position enjoyed by moneyed women inspired them to get involved for private reasons. These women, who had conformed to the model of wife and mother circumscribed by the home, naturally took action when their domain and responsibilities were threatened from outside: their religion was under fire, divorce jeopardized marriage, and the secular school competed with their educational functions. It was also easier, less scandalous, for "society" women to reject the sexual allocation of roles—public life for men, the domestic world for women—in the name of typically feminine, familial, interests. Finally, the PLF's success was based on a latent desire to do away with the isolation imposed by bourgeois individualism. Greater integration into a changing society and the joy of building a new network of female relationships were part of the PLF's attractions for Catholic women.

One cannot describe these new forms of behavior as feminist, however. The term was never used, and League members seemed oblivious to the existence of Christian feminism. They attacked the problem of women's suffrage, but only to refuse unequivocally to fight for political goals. "It is not a question of opposing or endorsing women's suffrage, but of pointing out that it is a utopia . . . impossible. . . . The only reason it has not yet become a reality in France . . . is that the partisans of the majority fear that they will be unseated by Catholic women, whom they well know outnumber them in France." Thus, the militants took up, but inverted, the argument of the radicals, which allowed them to fall back on the traditional position that "a man's vote is his family's as well as his own."[20]

Social Integration and Outreach

The PLF, although founded by women of the nobility and the haute bourgeoisie, wished to work for "social integration."[21] It attempted systematically to penetrate all social classes, particularly the workers, who had to be "liberated" from atheism, immorality, and socialism.

A Well-Constructed Movement

Each member had a membership card and paid a modest annual fee of about twenty-five centimes until 1914. She was active through a local, communal, or parochial committee. These committees, which were the League's backbone, met usually once a month for talks or lectures followed by discussion. The moving force in each committee was the *dizainières,* women responsible for ten League members whom they visited and whose activities they mobilzed. Their work was coordinated by a group of officers which generally included a president, who assumed the public relations duties, and a treasurer, and secretary responsible for the day-to-day work. The committees were organized at the canton, *arrondissement,* and *département* levels and could hold annual congresses.

Each year there was a national congress which played a primarily pedagogical role. Delegates analyzed their local experiences and worked out new guidelines. But the most important decisions were taken by the national council, which directed the movement. Established by the founders of the PLF, it expanded rapidly through recruitment. Elections were held every four years. The council consisted of a president and a vice-president, honorary officers, a treasurer, a secretary-general who played a key role, undersecretaries, and numerous delegates responsible for specific sectors (the press, young women, etc.).

Catholic women established young women's sections independent of the League. Their members, aged sixteen to twenty, were preparing to become good League members. Each section, headed by a secretary, was made up of a "study circle" for "young society women" and a "social circle" open to all; that is, to girls from the working class. It met once a month for talks and lectures—in other words, artistic activities.

The PLF thus built up a pyramidal structure of committees based on administrative divisions. The classical organization was intended to be strongly hierarchical: "obeying our chiefs" was the motto. However, local diversity made it hard to apply directives uniformly since room for "a certain regional autonomy" had to be left for the committees, "which often moved in different directions as a result of their insufficient grasp of doctrine and lack of discipline."[22] All-out recruitment was thus shown to have its limitations.

But the PLF rapidly became the most powerful women's organization in France. Although the figures available to us may have been inflated by propaganda, they reflect rapid growth. According to the police, three years after it was founded the League had 200,000 members divided into 250 committees. In 1909, the police noted that "the League, which has recently become extremely strong, now has over 400,000 members"[23] and 900 committees. The half-million mark was passed at the 1910 congress. The war did not inhibit its expansion: from 500,000 to 600,000 members in 1917, 730,000 to 920,000 in 1927, and to 1.5 million in 1932.[24]

The League's strength varied from region to region, however—there were a number of bastions. The north and Pas-de-Calais comprised a tenth of its forces, as did the Moselle and Meurthe-et-Moselle.

Conversely, the Ardennes, the Marne, and the Haute-Marne resisted, as did the southeastern portion of the Parisian basin, although the Parisian region itself was well represented—Paris alone had thirty-five parochial committees in 1917.

Finally, the strength in the west was solid, though uneven. Our survey shows that there was almost one committee per commune in the Finistère, the Côtes-du-Nord, L'Ille-et-Vilaine, the lower Loire, and the Sarthe, whereas league members were less evenly distributed in the Morbihan.

Recruitment seems to have met with little success in Maine and Normandy, while in southern France it was received with indifference, if not hostility. The Rhône region and the Alps were not even represented at the congresses, and the southwest and Languedoc were virtually impregnable.

At the 1909 congress, the secretary for Lot noted that its newly formed committee comprised only 1,200 women, and that even in Cahors, "there's absolutely no chance—nothing can be done there."

The recuirtment of League members corroborates France's political geography: it was most successful in the Catholic and conservative Armorican west, the industrial and patronal north and east, and the capital, which was seduced by nationalist ideas.

The Aristocracy and Local Leaders

The PLF's leaders[25] were recruited from among the aristocracy and the grande bourgeoisie. Its first president, Baroness de Brigode, was the great-granddaughter of Lafayette and linked by marriage to the La Tour Maubourg family. Her sister, Baroness de Villeneuve, was treasurer. Baroness de Reille, who succeeded Mme. de Brigode upon her death in 1906, was of the Empire nobility: she was Soult's granddaughter, but was also related to the Dreux-Brézé family. The third president, the Viscountess de Velard, came from a very ancient family of Bourgogne. Baroness de Boury, who bankrolled the "moral press," was descended from an equally venerable family of Normandy. The Countesse d'Eu, the Countess de la Rochefoucauld, and Mme. de Bernis came from the most illustrious nobility, not to mention the Marchionesses de Mac Mahon and de Villèle, who brought the support of the nineteenth-century monarchy's highest-ranking civil servants. Mme. de Montaigu, the daughter of Wendel, and the Marchioness de Juine, Schneider's daughter, were the link to the grande bourgeoisie. The list of PLF leaders reads like a "Who's Who" of French nobility. All in all, as the police noted, the "ladies of the national committee" were "very well-to-do." These women were all married, often to soldiers or deputies. They monopolized public relations, leaving to the single bourgeoises the less conspicuous administrative duties.

The same was true at the *département* level. Of a thousand officers, one-fifth was from the nobility, or claimed to be. These were château-dwelling aristocrats, well-established provincial noblewomen, and, finally, the "titled nobility." Six out of seven of these noblewomen were married, and over half were committee presidents. They predominated in Brittany, the Sarthe, and the Loire area. In the southwest, the Massif-Central, and especially the Alpes-Maritimes and the Bouches-du-Rhône, they formed the backbone of a League which had few supporters. In Paris, a survey of members of the young women's sections yields similar results: one out of five was from the nobility; in eastern France, on the other hand, very few were noblewomen.

The remainder of the League's supporters—four-fifths—was recruited from among the bourgeoisie, and nearly one in three members was single. The bourgeoises generally occupied the less prominent posts of secretary or treasurer, but predominated in executive positions in industrial France. The alliance of the patronal bourgeoisie of the north with traditionally Catholic and philanthropical families like the Féron-Vraus was typical. We have found several cases of the wives of manufacturers organizing propaganda for the PLF in their husbands' factories.

The League's constituency attests to the elitist nature of the organization. In 1908, it boasted the support of sixty-three bishops as well as of the Pope's chamberlain who, according to the police, was the "soul of the PLF"! In 1909, the Duc d'Orléans contributed 9,000 francs. Well-known journalists and writers like François Coppée collaborated for lectures.

We can thus conclude that the PLF emerged from the "better" social classes and was reinforced by a conservative ecclesiastical hierarchy. The background of the leaders sets them apart from the middle class which were the pillars of Republican France. Perhaps its leaders saw the PLF as a way of avenging themselves upon a society and régime which challenged aristocratic values. Their clientele was not equally well off, however: throughout the organization, the provincial petite and moyenne bourgeoisie, flattered by the chance to collaborate with the France of old, were dominant.

Propaganda Techniques and Local Clientele

The use of propaganda geared to the various regions and social classes shows us how support was solicited at the local level.

In the countryside, the initiative often came from fervent Catholics, as in Hérault, where a certain committee relied on the devotion of a family which was "solid in faith as unto an oak." The future president's first job was to win over the parish priest by explaining the PLF's goals and stressing the support of the bishops. Next, she had to ask his advice in choosing *dizainières* and officers from among the local "religious elite." The founders then expanded their audience through a variety of approaches, drawing on the network of families and friends, and above all on the conversion of individuals through a very subtle form of psychology: "To move souls effectively, one must advance on them slowly, gradually, sympathize with their weaknesses and woes, and patiently await the right moment."[26] Visits to the home yielded the best results, and the *dizainières* were instructed to persevere without giving in to discouragement. Religious observance, which united women, also facilitated the recruitment of new followers. The secretary in Aisne placed commitment to the cause and "intensity of devotion to the Sacred Heart"[27] in a single category. Similarly, the young women's sections recruited their members from the religious clubs for adolescents and children (patronages and *enfants de Marie*). But because priority was often given in the provinces to religious fervor at the expense of political commitment, strength of faith became a limitation. Limoges was thus considered "a very difficult area" because "nearly half the marriages are outside the church."[28]

In the towns, the same propaganda was used in bourgeois parishes. "Generally they take the most admired individual, the one with the highest standing. . . . Vanity then most often moves her fellow citizens to join."[29] The fact that the leaders were from the aristocracy explains the League's success among the status-hungry bourgeoisie.

On the other hand, it proved more difficult to make inroads into the working class. The PLF devoted much of its energy to this, and many committees had a "people's secretary." League members worked toward "the reconciliation of the classes through social contact"[30] The records of congresses always stress the special virtues of the working-class *dizainières,* like the mother of fifteen who succored the dying, or the young woman who remained in a "bad" factory "to do good." The paternalism which prevailed among the northern and eastern industrialists made contact easy. In Lille, the League organized numerous meetings in factories for workers and afterwards "they joined the ranks of League members."[31] Cooperation between factory owners and the PLF appears to have been effective, but one may be permitted to question the sincerity of followers recruited by their employers! The PLF also relied on religion to win over the lower classes. In Essonnes, for example, it exploited the creation of a new parish for paper makers to establish itself. Its success was also perhaps not unrelated to the opening of a sewing circle. It was, in fact, able to attract working women by offering services: religious clubs, charity works, and entertainments. In 1915, when League members organized a propaganda meeting in Saint-Eloi (Paris) at which films on the fighting were shown, a large crowd attended, but it melted away as soon as League recruitment began. The police, which was familiar with the lower class's resistance to religious dragooning, noted: "The working class was attracted principally by the prospect of seeing films . . . on the war."[32] Results were often disappointing. The secretary for Hirson (Aisne) pointed out that the young women's section comprised a few seamstresses but no factory workers.

At the 1910 congress, a militant wondered, "How to overturn the barriers raised by the excessive indifference of some, the anger and envy of others?" Solidarity among Catholic women seemed to stop short at the gulf which separated the classes, and which League members refused to recognize. In the provinces, however, the movement's objective of bridging the class gap was partially realized. This objective constantly inspired the social and religious activities of League members, who hoped to adapt working women to their own feminine model.

The Image of Women, Religion and Philanthropy

"Heart and Soul" of the Home

The image of women which League members promoted is traditional: it could be defined as a Christian variation on the nineteenth-century bourgeois ideal.

They all accepted the inequality of the sexes. One must leave "first place—that of master—to one's husband,"[33] and the man alone was to command: "Let him give all the orders, so that all those beneath you become accustomed to seeing him do so." Very different things were thus expected of each of the sexes: the woman was by nature "gentler . . . more religious." "Devotion is intrinsically feminine," as were "kindness" and "abnegation."

Duties were allocated on the basis of the inequality of the sexes and their aptitudes. The woman was identified with the domestic sphere, as wife, mother, and housemistress. Wife of a man who had "chosen" her as his companion, the League member sought not love, but respect and appreciation. Although marriages of convenience outnumbered marriages of choice, they were none the less stable and happy. In these marriages of convenience, reserve naturally governed the relations among spouses. Public display of affection was viewed as indecent and unacceptable. The husband respected his wife for her irreproachable conduct more than for her feelings toward him. The principal duty of the wife "who bears his name" was, after all, to "pass it on untarnished to his children." While the wife could not be "a comrade to whom one had the right to say everything," she could play an important role as "advisor and supporter," as long as she acted tactfully, respecting the man's obvious superiority. One had to "infiltrate" one's husband's mind, "inspire orders" without seeming to; this is illustrated by the model dialogue suggested by Francesca. "My dear, it seems to me that this would be the best way to handle this matter. But do as you will! After all, you know better than I."

More than anything, League members exalted the "sublime role of motherhood": willed by God, a national duty in a France that was becoming dangerously depopulated and the only area in which femininity was allowed to flower. Education was the mother's responsibility, and more in tune with the English model than with Rousseau. Girls and boys were brought up strictly in order to build character. In the affluent realm of the leaders, however, the mother delegated material responsibilities to the household help and devoted herself to the child's moral and religious education and to setting a good example. She therefore has to be "intransigent" on the subject of social contact: divorcés, for example, were never to be greeted in public. From the first communion onward, she monitored her daughters around the clock: books, outings, and friends had to pass muster. "Flirting [which] removes the main attraction of the virgin," was not to be tolerated. Although little girls were educated at home to preserve them from the "godless school," League members seemed prepared to accept school where boys were concerned, thus supporting the double standard. A mother prepared her son to "serve God and his country" and, often being the wife of a soldier, she could imagine no finer vocation that that of bearing arms. Her daughter, destined for marriage, had to learn the "domestic sciences." Religious instruction was identical for the two sexes, however: at seven or eight months, babies were already beginning to blow kisses to the crucifix and, as soon as they could talk, children lisped out their prayers.

In short, the wife reigned supreme in the home. The image of the one who "keeps the home fires burning" goes back to the Victorian "household angel." Anglomania obliges and Francesca advises each League member to beautify her home. For the sorely pressed man, "nothing is more restful than to come home to a wife attired suitably, perhaps a bit coquettishly, and a well-cooked meal."

In its practical advice, the *Manual for League Members* thus joins the ranks of the household and educational how-to books which were so popular in the nineteenth century.[34] At most it makes a few concessions to aristocratic values: the role of honor, the dream of a return to a "chivalric Nation" and, in short, a preindustrial concept of the dutiful family member.

A Good Religious Example

Daily devotions made it possible to disseminate this image of the Christian woman through example. Religion played a large role in the life of the adherents, especially in the provinces. In a movement which, according to the secretary-general, was intended to reflect "the pure Catholic spirit" but was not under the tutelage of the clergy, the "pride" of being a believer was often ostentatious. Each League member displayed the movement's special emblem: a daisy on a background of the Sacred Heart. Each committee participated in great parades under a banner: Christ on one side, the Sacred Heart on the other.

Meetings of League members were largely given over to cultural activities. Prayers and masses opened the congresses, while devotions to the Holy Sacrament closed them. There were lectures on dogma and faith. The League organized pilgrimages and retreats, while the members beautified their churches and fervently performed certain devotions. The cults of the Sacred Heart, the Holy Sacrament, and Joan of Arc were part of the entire, primarily feminine, piety movement, but were also derived from the movement's nationalist and conservative bent.

The militants offered their services to the parish priest and organized over two hundred religious instruction classes. They took charge of the religious clubs and often carried on the work of the nuns, whose teaching orders had been disbanded as from 1901.

They did not neglect the interpersonal approach, however. They strove to ensure that religious obligations, like the day of rest, were respected and set an example by giving their employees Sunday off. They encouraged regular communion, confession, and weekly mass attendance, and required that members at least observe Lent. They even undertook missionary duties: "to christianize the indifferent." These Catholic women were more interested in external shows of piety than in the problems of faith, however. In 1912, the committees of Aisne boasted of having induced four couples that had been cohabiting to marry and baptized twelve children. The president for Chateau-Thierry pointed out that "these marriages have become a regular habit in our League, for many militants have written me that, along with the baptism of a number of children, they are our most outstanding apostolic achievement."

The results were inconclusive, but still more surprising was the fact that the League experienced a number of internal setbacks. In Aisne, half of the *dizainières* failed to observe Lent in 1911. The secretary was forced to reprimand them and tried to make communion at least once a month obligatory. She also proposed to strip of their responsibilities women who did not attend mass every Sunday, but pleaded for indulgence toward the rank and file: "if we had to exclude all those who do not attend mass, alas! We should lose half of our membership." These disappointments can be explained by the weaknesses of all-out recruitment. Many League members, attracted by the prospect of social esteem and a taste for politics and sociability, were not prepared to do daily battle in defense of the faith and to rechristianize France; nor were they interested in social action.

Philanthropy and Prophylaxis

The League espoused the social ideal of traditional Catholic patronage. Its condemnation of the class struggle was inevitable, in the name of Christian unity and that cooperation between rich and poor which ensured civil peace. Equality in faith was not, however, incompatible with respect for the hierarchy. The secretary-general of the young women's sections put it crudely:"When common sense prevails, the young working-class woman understands perfectly the need for hierarchy in an organized society, and the more the young society lady treats her with affection and without affectation, the more she is inclined to recognize her as socially superior and destined to lead (Approbations)." Disregard for one's inferiors was blameworthy, but the leadership capabilities of a minority were never questioned. The League's implicit condemnation of unbridled capitalism was nevertheless exposed in its definition of the salary as "the salary of human life, not that of supply and demand," as well as in the influence of social Catholicism: some of that movement's most eminent representatives, such as Albert de Mun and Marc Sangnier, lent their support to a number of the PLF's demonstrations.

Before the war of 1914, the League organized many works of charity which were direct descendants of the ninetheeth-century tradition: clothing for the poor, nursery supplies for needy mothers. The collective "services" for mothers and children were more modern. In 1910, the League had 121 religious clubs, 24 child-care centers, and 7 vacation camps. In 1912, it created the Mothers' Alliance (Alliance Maternelle) to help find jobs for the children it had aided. Eleven mutual funds (mutualités), 16 mothers' aid groups, and the dispensaries made up a private social service to benefit the family. The League also worked to inculcate morals and "family values" in the working class.[35] Conversely, assuming that the peasant class was healthy, it paid little attention to the countryside. Through its fourteen dowry funds and sixteen trousseau charities, it prepared young women of limited means for marriage. It organized courses in household management (forty three in 1912) which were often led by nuns trained at the abbey. This teaching of home economics and religion was designed to steep the lower classes, through feminine intermediaries, in the values of order, cleanlines, economy, and decency. A certain secretary noted that "by visiting families regularly, one slowly gets them back onto the right path" and that because of this, "there will be fewer households which go wrong."[36] Suzanne de Nouaillat explains that the "moral song" courses organized by the Baume-les-Dames study circle (Doubs) have "an uplifting effect on ten workers."[37]

After the war, the League stressed preventive health measures such as establishing clinics and checkups for infants. It espoused a bolder, legally sanctioned family policy: thus, it endorsed the construction of low-cost housing and tax breaks for large families to increase the birth rate. It was no longer merely a question of alleviating the most abject poverty, but of developing a family "policy." Faced with a growing and multifaceted demand for social assistance, and aware that private charity could not satisfy it, the PLF envisaged a growing reliance on the State. It followed the latest analysis of the social question but, having renounced the classical, moralizing form of philanthropy, saw its role diminishing with successful competition from a burgeoning social service.

We have deliberately left until last the involvement in female labor which most clearly reveals the PLF's contradictions. League members found remuneration for women's work to be incompatible with their familial ideals: "Married women should remain at home in order to attend to the housekeeping and care for their children." Unfortunately, "the struggle for existence has led a great many women and young girls to seek honorable subsistence through work."[38] Confronted with a phenomenon which it could not dismiss, the PLF sought to mitigate its primary drawbacks. It orchestrated the placement of workers in order to keep them away from the union-sponsored placement services—those dens of political perdition. It established women's trade unions linked to the needleworkers' union (Aiguille) as well as "mixed" unions uniting female employers with employees, so that the trade union should not be "synonomous with revolution." These unions, which took their members chiefly from the sewing trade, organized housekeeping courses and choirs; they secured discounts from stores for their members. As a militant from Arles pointed out during the 1913 congress, "the advantages they derive from it, such as discounts on coal and basic necessities, could . . . count for something in their having joined." The Joan of Arc project, which provided housing for single women, was devised to protect young women from unfortunate contacts. Finally, the League became an employer: it opened sewing circles and "aid through work organizations," especially for seamstresses, which reconciled work to home and family. The League preferred these efforts to simple economic assistance, for they forced the beneficiary to contribute to her own well-being. But these projects also made it possible to preserve the worker from the immoral atmosphere of the factory: "The material needs of the workers are not our sole emphasis: concern for their morals plays a large part."[39] The PLF's social action, as a whole, differed little from that of the social Catholic movement. The League took up the tasks which, since the nineteenth century, had fallen to "Lady Bountiful" and her sisters.

The Catholic women of the PLF broke out of the domestic sphere to which they had been relegated by the sexual distribution of duties. Deprived of the right to vote, they demonstrated that women could take an avid interest in politics or, rather, in being politicians. Although their ideology was modeled on masculine lines, their activities were their own. Their involvement in public affairs was extraordinary in being linked to private life through its familial motives, as well as in the fact that their activities were primarily religious and philanthropical, and therefore fell into the feminist tradition which had been growing since the nineteenth century. The militants did not seek to develop a new image of women, but confined themselves to introducing new forms of collective organization. Without giving up their domestic monopoly, they tried to forge a closer link between private and public life. In so doing, the Patriotic League of Frenchwomen demonstrated that affluent, conservative women could attain a certain measure of emancipation.

Notes

1. There is a wealth of information, which is lacking for other Catholic women's organizations, on the Patriotic League of Frenchwomen. As a political group which was hostile to the government, it was closely surveilled by the police until 1918. In addition to the published information on the organization and the newspapers it put out (*L'Echo de la L.P.F.* and its supplement, *Le Petit Echo*), our work has been based on the documents preserved in the F7 series at the National Archives and on the files in the Bibliothèque Marguerrite Durand.

2. On the Popular Liberal Alliance, see Jacques Piou, *Le Ralliement, son histoire,* 1928.

3. Letter written to Mme. Labourgère in May 1904 and transmitted to the press, F7 13215.

4. *Le Soleil,* November 25, 1902. Bibl. M. Durand.

5. Report dated February 22, 1908, F7 13215. On *La Croix* and the Assumptionists, see P. Sorlin, *La Croix et les Juifs,* Ed. Beauchesne, 1967.

6. *L'Echo de la L.P.F.,* November 20, 1903.

7. Paris Police Department report (Préfecture de Police), November 21, 1916, A.N. F7 13216.

8. Paris Police Department report to the Ministry of the Interior, September 1, 1917, F7 13216.

9. Letter of September 13, 1917, F7 13216.

10. That is, the law for the freedom of association (1901) which permits without control the formation of all kinds of associations except those which come under the law of the separation of church and state.

11. In the application of the law separating church from state an inventory was taken of the possessions of each religious sect before the group in question could dispose of its wealth. This caused serious problems. See J.-M. Mayeu: *La Séparation de l'Eglise et l'Etat,* coll. Archives, Julliard, 1966.

12. *Congrès de la L.P.F.,* published by the L.P.F.

13. Ibid.

14. Ibid.

15. *Congrès de la L.P.F.,* 1913.

16. It is written by an anonymous activist, Francesca, and published in Dijon in 1909.

17. August 9, 1905, M. Durand, Dossier I LIG 396.

18. "La Collaboration des femmes aux élections," *L'Echo de la L.P.F.,* 1914.

19. Ibid.

20. The appeal by Mgr. Dubillard in *L'Echo de la L.P.F.,* March 1906.

21. Undated letter, dossier of diverse correspondences, F7 13215.

22. We found two evaluations in the reports of February 22 and April 22, 1908 (F7 13215).

23. According to the figures quoted in *La Croix*, April 1, 1927, and two reports of the police, April 7 and October 14, 1927 (F7 13215).

24. We depended on the dossiers of the M. Durand Library, the biographies in Series F7, biographical dictionaries, and those of high society (*Rex Dictionnaire de la noblesse française*, etc.).

25. Undated text (texte ronéotypé), "Le calandrier de la Ligueuse," F7 13215.

26. *Congrès de l'Aisne*, 1912, published by the L.P.F.

27. *Congrès de la L.P.F.*, 1910.

28. Police Report, April 19, 1915, F7 13216.

29. *Le Figaro*, August 9, 1905.

30. *Congrès de la L.P.F.*, 1910.

31. Police Report, April 19, 1915, F7 13216.

32. All of the quotations of this part are taken from the *Manuel de la ligueuse* and from the "Calendrier de la ligueuse."

33. See Anne Martin-Fugier, *La Place des bonnes: La domesticité feminine à Paris en 1900* (Grasset, 1979); Fanny S. Fay-Sallois, *Les nourrices à Paris au XIX siècle* (Payot, 1980): P. Perrot, *Les dessus et les dessous de la bourgeoisie: Une histoire du vêtement au XIX siècle* (Fayard, 1981); and Geneviève Fraisse, *Femmes toutes mains* (Le Seuil, 1979).

34. See on this subject J. Donzelot, *La police des familles* (Editions de Minuit, 1977); L. Murard and P. Zylberman, *Le petit travailleur infatigable, Recherches*, No. 25 (1976); also the critiques of M. Méxignac, "Travail social et structure de classe." In relation to *La police des familles* by Donzelot, see *Critique d'èconomie politique*, April–June 1978; D. Rancière's "Le philanthrope et la famille," *Révoltes logiques* (1979); and A.-M. Sohn's "Histoire de la famille, histoire de la sexualité sous la IIIᵉ République," *Bulletin de la Société d'Histoire Moderne* No. 2 (1984).

35. *Congrès de l'Aisne*, 1912.

36. *Congrès de la L.P.F.*, 1910.

37. "Oeuvre du travail de Quimperlé," undated but undoubtedly of 1913, F7 13215.

38. *Congrès de la L.P.F.*, 1909.

39. *L'Echo de la L.P.F.*, August 15, 1912.

CATHOLIC CONSTRUCTIONS OF FEMININITY

THREE DUTCH WOMEN'S ORGANIZATIONS IN SEARCH OF A POLITICS OF THE PERSONAL, 1912–1940

Mieke Aerts

> "It must be rather difficult, walking through their hills, their jungles, battling the mutated shadows of their flora and fauna, haunted by their million-year-old fantasies."
> "We try," I said.
> "You're basically not equipped for it," PHAEDRA went on.
> "But suppose you have to exhaust the old mazes before you can move into the new ones. It's hard."
>
> SAMUEL R. DELANY, *The Einstein Intersection*

"The personal is political" can be considered one of the most intriguing slogans that resulted from fifteen years of modern feminism. At first sight it seems only to coin a terse expression of a fairly trivial sociological insight: even what people tend to consider matters of personal choice and preference form part of an overall pattern of social interaction. As such they are embedded in the basic power

---

For practical reasons there are no bibliographical references in the following, as they would all be to relatively obscure Dutch sources; use was made of the journals, pamphlets, and archival materials produced by the organizations, and to a lesser extent of interviews with ex-spokeswomen and/or leading ideologists. Persons interested in further detail, please contact the author.

structure of that society. On closer investigation, however, the slogan points to a series of critical and complex questions. What do we mean by *personal?* Why do we, as feminists, assert so vigorously that what our society defines as personal is, in fact, *political?* What exactly do we mean by *politics?* Why was it the feminist movement that first asserted or demanded a "politics of the personal"?

So much seems to be clear from the work of writers such as Michel Foucault and Jaques Donzelot: feminists have not been the first in modern history to try and find ways of devising collective strategies for changing the conditions of personal life. In fact, it seems not farfetched to say that modern feminism came into being as a response to older types of politics of the personal. That is, older ways in which social power relations concerning sexuality, reproduction, socialization have been combined into distinctive strategies of social control, centered on people's existence as individuals, on "personal" life, and linking that in specific ways, often by means of gender constrictions, to the "public" life of population politics, economic expansion, war, and peace. Whereas it will certainly take a long time for the effectiveness of modern feminist discourse in this area to become visible, it might be very useful to look back at some of the older strategies and especially at the contradictory ways women have moved between them.

Looking back

Generally speaking it has often been noted that many forms of the politics of the personal are rooted in the religious practices of organized Christianity, but in a more specific sense this is true for the situation in the Netherlands. Not only have Dutch party politics from 1917 on consistently been dominated by Protestant and especially Catholic parties, but also social life in general has been deeply influenced by the various churches. From the end of the First World War up to the mid-fifties, the Netherlands knew a system of so-called "verzuiling" (vertical social segregation according to denomination and—partially—political faith). In this system Catholic individuals were supposed not only to participate in normal church activities and vote for the Catholic party, but also to marry only other Catholics; go only to a Catholic school; work only for a Catholic employer; join only a Catholic trade union or only a Catholic women's organization, or a Catholic sports club, or a Catholic cattle breeding association; read only Catholic papers and journals; listen only to Catholic radio programs; and, at need, accept only Catholic health care. Protestants faced similar expectations. Only the nonreligious socialists and liberals asserted their right to exist with a "neutral," or nonreligious, world. While the religious ideal of a totally segregated society was never completely realized, important state-financed institutions, the educational systems, health care, and radio broadcasting were, and are still, effectively split up along denominational lines.

In its favor, this segregated system has protected minority rights by preventing one group from taking over entirely and imposing its ideology on the rest of the people. During its heyday, the second half of the interwar period, Social Democrats and members of the radical left were able to establish a political and social foothold. Furthermore, and perhaps more significantly, thanks to the pluralism, fascist and National Socialist movements never manage to dominate the political arena.

In evaluating Catholic women's organizations in the interwar period, we must bear in mind the extent and power of this denominational structure. Women had not created the institutional setting within which they operated. As feminist historians we must study the ways they operated within it, how it shaped their visions and goals, how they altered, at times subverted, its restrictions.

Contours

The Roman Catholic Women's League existed between 1912 and 1942. In these thirty years the objectives of the League focused on the coordination of women's charitable and social works as much as on the social emancipation of Catholic women themselves. After a few difficult years membership rose to a peak in the period just following 1919, when Dutch women got the vote. In the thirties membership fell from about 51,000 in 1921 to about 42,000. To cover up the drop in membership on lay women, the League added the figures on the collective membership of 18,000 nuns. In all, the League encompassed about 10 percent of the Catholic female population over the age twenty-five. This figure compares favorably with, for instance, the Protestant Women's League (from 6,000 to 14,000 members), the Association of Social Democratic Women (about 12,500 members), and the feminist organization (a little under 3,000 members).

The Grail was by far the best and most spectacular of the interwar Catholic youth organizations. The Grail movement was meant to organize each and every Catholic young girl in the diocese of Haarlem from about age fifteen until marriage, and to socialize her in the ways of "Catholic Womanhood." The Grail never achieved its numerical goals, though its membership did rise to the height of 10,000 in its first three years of existence (1929/30–1932). During the thirties several girl sporting clubs joined the Grail movement, bringing membership by 1940 to 20,000.

Both the Catholic Women's League and the Grail were dissolved in 1942 during the German occupation. After the Second World War the League was replaced by a new organization of the same type, called the Catholic Women's Guild. The Grail, for its part, reemerged, but instead of working with young Dutch girls, it turned to missionary and social work activities in "developing countries." Young Catholic girls in the Netherlands were encouraged to join the Catholic Girl Scout Movement which appeared after the war. Although it tried hard not to be associated with the Grail and did indeed have a different vision and program, many ex-Grail leaders went over to the Scouts, blurring the differences between the two groups.

A third women's organization developed during the interwar period. A group of unmarried, university-trained young women met in 1931 to form the small (about twenty members) and exclusive society of friends called *De Sleutelbos* (literally "bunch of keys"). Their stated aim was to work together "with and for each other." The Second World War ended its activities as well. After the war it drew out its existence before finally dissolving in 1949. At that time Sleutelbos members joined the Catholic Women's Debating Society, a far less exclusive organization for academic women that was founded in 1947.

Shapes

The Sleutelbos group did not like pictures. Its pamphlets and its journal, *The Second Tower*, featured at the most a few statistics in neat tables.

Not so the Grail: its journal, *The Silver Trumpet*, was richly illustrated with drawings and photos, its leaflets were models of effective coloring and design, and its propaganda movies especially, some of which were in color and sound, recreated the spectacular uniforms and robes, striking combinations of wine red, light yellow, dark green, gray, ocher, salmon, dark violet, light green, blue, white, and black. And the postures: groups of Grail girls in the clubhouses, on the porch, on the beach, in the woods, cycling through the countryside, marching through the streets, carrying not one but at least ten enormous, gaily colored flags, arms lifted high in the so-called "Roman salute" in front of the bishop's palace, or bodies stretched taut in dramatic gestures when participating by the thousands in one of the typical Grail mass performances.

The Catholic Women's League could only compete by presenting in its journal, *The Catholic Woman,* time and again the same picture: a solid table with a bouquet of flowers behind which stood five (or ten, or twenty) solid ladies and their male "spiritual adviser." By looking very carefully one might note the little button on every lady's breast, with a small cross on it and the words *in hoc signo vinces* (in this sign you shall conquer).

Obviously only the Grail systematically sought to transpose its vision, that of the "exemplary Catholic young woman," into the graphically concrete. Too systematically, many of its annoyed Catholic contemporaries, commented or, to use their word, too "outward." And certainly the Grail preoccupation with visible, tangible femininity contrasts sharply with the Women's League's never abating crusade against the desecration of the female body by modern designers of bathing suits and high society fashion. Yet, the Grail's obsession with the female body possessed clear limitations. The extravagant feast of colors could not conceal how utterly decent The Grail vision was; it clothed its women in long sleeves, stockings, patent leather walking shoes, and capes ("gives a touch of flamboyance, without showing the body"). Furthermore, uniforms could only be worn when wearers were participating in Grail activities, in which situation they symbolized the way in which the organization created unity and discipline without bypassing necessary hierarchy.

Places

A geographic unity tied all three organizations together: the diocese of Haarlem, which included in this period almost the whole of urbanized Holland (with the cities Amsterdam and Rotterdam). The first local branch of the Women's League was founded in Haarlem City, and in later years about one-third of the League members lived in the diocese. The Sleutelbos group also drew its most active members from the big cities. The Grail was even more exclusively a Haarlem affair: Early efforts to organize in other dioceses had come to nothing, a curious fact given the existence of thriving Grail branches in such foreign cities as London and Berlin. The urban basis of these Catholic women's organizations is highly significant. Catholicism in the Netherlands is not an urban phenomenon, but rather thrives in the predominantly rural provinces in the southern Netherlands.

Yet, at closer inspection this sharing of a geographical place reveals itself as superficial. The Sleutelbos gave a virtually meaningless address, printed on their pamphlets as if it were an afterthought. The Women's League was easier to find: more than a hundred local branches, with, among other things, activities in each parish's community house; a central office in Utrecht; annual meetings where deputies of every branch listened to the president's reading of the annual report; and of course League representatives could be found in various other Catholic organizations and institutions, especially on boards of Catholic schools of domestic science and even as regular members of the council of the Roman Catholic State Party. The Grail movement also had local branches and even its own local accommodation, the so-called Grail Houses, at least in the first years of the movement's existence. In these houses some Grail leaders lived permanently, to oversee the meetings of the various clubs. Of course, also these houses were decked out in a distinctive Grail style: contrasting colors and sober, informal furnishing with, for instance, cushions laid out on the floor instead of chairs. Even more distinctive for the Grail style were activities like marching through the streets or performing a speaking chorus inside a football stadium.

In other words, these organizations represent three different ways of defining woman's place. Both Grail and League sought to create specific places where women could gather as women. But whereas League women tended to move from one private space (their home) into another (a small meeting hall), Grail girls occupied the place in between, the street, that terrible public place decent Catholic girls normally were not allowed to stay in. Yet the Grail's statement remained ambivalent. The street was a place any other group or individual could occupy after the Grail had gone home, whereas places on school boards and party councils were more durable. The same paradoxical situation characterized the Grail Houses: Here the movement had realized a "room of its own," but one that was completely outside normal, parish-church-and-parish-community-house-centered Catholic social life. It is for this reason that Grail Houses became a symbol for the too strong autonomy of the movement. All this does not concern the Sleutelbos, who chose a third way of dealing with defining space: their words and printed opinions went their own way, their writers remaining anonymous.

Time

For the Women's League, modern times signified the decay of religious life, growing materialism, Communism, feminism—in short, a general moral crisis. The League saw as its historical mission to counter these tendencies by protecting and promoting Catholic family life. Ironically, they sought to protect the Catholic family by stimulating Catholic women to enter the modern world. Unmarried women should enter feminine occupations. Mothers who could afford them should undertake charitable works. All should support activities favoring Catholic organizations.

The Grail movement considered the idea of a historical mission to be eschatological. They saw the modern world as the field for the Last Battle between the Forces of Light and the Power of Darkness. To tip the balance in favor of God's Kingdom, woman had to step into the arena because only she could save the world. That is why the Grail saw itself simultaneously as the God-given antagonist of communism and as the embodyment of three generations of feminists—the equal rightists, the disillusioned, and now those who were to feminize society. Furthermore, both the Grail and the Women's League subscribed in the late thirties to the ideas of the Catholic Action, that lay members of the Church had a special task in fighting modern impiety, of course guided in all things by the clergy. The Sleutelbos too focused on the meaning modern times held for Catholic women. For them modern times were special because of the possibilities they offered the unmarried woman. In earlier days she had to choose between dependence on father or brother(s) and membership in a religious order. These days presented her with the chance to live on her own, as an unmarried, working lay woman. Thus the concept of laity was very important to the Sleutelbos, but had nothing to do with propagating the faith or Catholic Action. On the contrary, religion was considered a matter of private conviction, while the influence of the clergy in public life was constantly, sometimes even bitterly, opposed.

So while each organization was very time conscious, there were three different long-term historical perspectives at work, which dominated each other in specific configurations. Each perspective was the history of a struggle: laity versus clergy, women versus male domination, and God's Kingdom versus Communism. The first one was completely absent in the Women's League, the third not discernible in Sleutelbos publications, while it dominated both the League (from the beginning) and the Grail movement (more pronounced after 1935). It should be noted that, to the League, Communism meant moral depravity and state encroachment on mothers' rights to raise their children as good Catholics. The Grail emphasized Communist militancy, which was almost never connected to specific demands or practices: Communism, and especially the Communist youth movement, was simply the adversary and in the early years of the movement an admired one, too, for its craftiness and aggressive persistence, from which the militant Catholic woman learned much.

In accordance with their distinctive long-term perspectives, all three organizations structured their day-to-day activities differently. The Catholic Women's League produced an ever ongoing stream of unspectacular activities and opinions. The Sleutelbos dropped their occasional pamphlet or reacted to a particular political event: an Open Letter against a Catholic minister who threatened to introduce a bill against married women working outside the home (1938). The Grail almost never referred to affairs of the world, but instead kept up an almost breathtaking pace in running from one spiritual emergency to another. Especially during the organization's first years, its structure changed continually, campaigns and actions succeeded one another with mad abandon. The Grail structured its year according to the Ecclesiastical Year, placing Easter and Pentecost in the year's center as glorious celebrations of sacrifice and suffering. The Women's League also observed ecclesiastical festivals, however with far less emphasis and other accentuations focused on different celebrations—on Christmas, for instance, as a typical family celebration. In Sleutelbos pamphlets Church events were never mentioned.

One important absence of time consciousness should be noted: none of these organizations, not even the more worldly Sleutelbos, considered the emergence of fascism and National Socialism worthy of more than casual attention.

Women

All three organizations centered their activities around the question of defining the qualities their own "ideal Catholic woman" should display. Unlike the Sleutelbos group, the Women's League and the Grail saw themselves as educating "women's true nature," with the Grail emphasizing the exploration of formerly disregarded aspects.

The Women's League never tired of exhorting women to care for their families, the unemployed, the sick, the poor, and the lonely. This caring should not be confused with such banalities as cleaning, floor scrubbing, or nursing; in short, working. Rather the League referred to efforts such as providing a nice atmosphere, setting a good example, bringing some beauty into the drab existence of others, and giving guidance with a light hand. Caring was seen first of all as *educating,* as moral enlightenment. This idea was most succinctly expressed in the notion of "spiritual motherhood," that featured often in the League's journal, *The Catholic Woman*. Woman's influence in society must be based on her position as a mother in her own family, but should not be restricted to family matters. The Grail never questioned the assumption that every Catholic girl would eventually be a mother. But neither did it dwell upon that future, especially in the early years. Far more important were notions like militancy, heroic attitudes, willingness to "give" oneself 100 percent here and now, all based on glorious self-denial and the spirit of sacrifice. Both *self-denial* and *spiritual motherhood* were deemed totally unfit and even dangerous guiding principles by the Sleutelbos. These women denied the possibility that some general ideal of femininity could be valid for all women and in all life's situations. At least the unmarried woman should give *work* the central place in her life, and by that was meant every professional activity a person really wanted to perform. No woman should feel herself restricted to the so-called "feminine occupations."

Corresponding to different central notions, the organizations developed different strategies to make them come alive. Whereas the Women's League produced mainly didactic expositions on the many complicated modern world problems a Catholic mother should know something about, and whereas managing and organizing activities constituted typical League activities, The Grail Movement experimented with various combinations of words, symbols, and postures. One of the Grail's characteristic combinations was the chant, or speaking chorus, performed not only as part of the spectacular so-called "lay theatrical performances" (German: *Laienspiele*) like *The Royal Easter Cross* or *Pentecostal Blessings*, but also in the clubhouses or on street corners; furthermore maybe the Grail salute: "Excelsior, Alleluja, Forward!" with one arm raised in the "Roman" salute. Central Grail symbols included the Cross and the Holy Grail itself. Grail language explicitly addressed the emotions and was meant to create in readers and listeners distinctive states, like selfless rapture or unflinching militancy. Sleutelbos language seemed to belong in another universe, sharply contrasting as it did with its impeccable matter-of-fact tone and academic idiom.

One more thing can be said about these three organizations: they shared a common class background. The Sleutelbos was the only organization that stated openly its exclusive and academic interests, but even without such honesty it would be clear that for this group *work* meant the creative work of the professions, and the supposed reader of its pamphlets was a fellow intellectual, man or woman. And although the Women's League claimed to speak for all Catholic mothers, it was obvious that those who should have been the object of so much motherly care and guidance were not among the members. Indeed, one of the modern world problems that *The Catholic Woman* continuously discussed was "the servant question"—and not from a servant's point of view. Compared with the task of identifying the "unmarried aunts" and "mothers," it is a little harder to find out exactly whose "daughters" the Grail sought to organize, because here too the claim was a very general one (all girls) and the references to concrete social conditions were scarce. But given such small clues as a photography column in *The Silver Trumphet* which presupposed many members possessing their own camera, combined with the time-consuming and often expensive character of Grail activities, it seems fair to conclude that most members belonged to a reasonably well-to-do family (in the thirties!) and/or held better paid jobs.

Men

In *The Catholic Woman* two types of men appeared: ordinary men (laymen), some of whom gained women's love, care, and children; and others, charitable assistance from the parish, neighborly love, and an extra pair of shoes. Then there were the Reverend Sirs (the priests) who instructed mothers in how to treat ordinary men.

In *The Silver Trumphet* Reverend Sirs were mostly seen from far off, especially on the steps to the bishop's palace or the grandstand. Husbands were not seen at all. On the other hand, *The Silver Trumphet* discussed "masculinity" at length using it as the negative point of reference in developing a "really feminine" style. *The Silver Trumphet* saw "masculinity" as responsible for the state of disorder the world was in. Only women could save the world and they must in no way be tainted with masculine notions and practices. This, the movement added, is the message of Percival's quest for the Holy Grail. Percival could become a savior only by renouncing his masculine worship of violence, stalwartness, and arrogance.

The Sleutelbos dismissed the idea of dependency on men, but without attacking men in general or propagating an ideal femininity. As they put it: differences between men and women are less important than differences among women and among men themselves. One such difference is undoubtedly that between clergy and laity. The clergy and its views were attacked often enough by the Sleutelbos, but never because they were men or held masculine views, at least not publicly.

Both the Sleutelbos and Women's League kept practical relations with the clergy in accordance with their views, be it on opposite ends of the scale. The Women's League was harmoniously integrated in parish activities, and every local branch had its "spiritual adviser," the parish priest. The Sleutelbos from the first refused the idea of an ecclesiastical "guide," which can only be done by refusing official permission to organize by the bishop. This brought with it real freedom to think and write what they wanted, but it resulted as well in the lack of official recognition and a restricted audience.

The Grail's situation was more complicated. In the first years of its existence, it was led by an exclusive female "lay order," the Women of Nazareth, who were only accountable to the bishop himself. Both the parish clergy and the Women's League were passed over and reacted to the situation as wronged parents. From 1934 on, complicated, behind-the-scene maneuverings resulted in organizational changes of the Grail in the direction of traditional parish life, until it became rather like the Women's League. One by one the Grail houses closed down, and the local branches were divided between the parishes—each received its inevitable "spiritual adviser." When the old bishop died in 1935, all protection from above ended. The new bishop—a former parish priest—alluded to the movement in his first speech and said he was sure an organization that had put so much emphasis on self-denial would gladly adjust itself to the new circumstances. The Grail leaders managed to do this, though not always with good grace.

To understand the Grail movement fully, however, we must recognize the deep-seated hostility the regular clergy felt for the movement—and attempt to understand the sources of that hostility. The framework of both the Women of Nazareth order and the Grail Movement was originally thought out by a man, the eccentric Jesuit professor Van Ginneken. He trained—and, some say, thrilled—the first generation of Grail leaders. Van Ginneken taught the women to exercise psychological control over themselves and others; psychology was one of Van Ginneken's many hobbies. Methods of discipline and control of the "soul" at first intended for the Women of Nazareth found their way into the Grail. And so, Grail leaders meticulously kept a card index in which they recorded the spiritual development of every individual member and her participation in Grail activities. But this did not end their efforts: they noted whom she befriended and how she behaved in general. Leaders regularly conducted critical examinations of individual Grail members, their object, the inculcation of humility, and the establishment of a female version of the confessional relationship. One can hardly resist the conclusion that Van Ginneken successfully passed on some of the traditional priestly technology for "spiritual care." He encouraged Grail leaders to assume priestly roles and priestly powers over other women. He created an institution that rivaled the parish for the loyalty of its female parishioners. This was exactly what other priests objected to. Whether the spiritual technology Van Ginneken taught the women Grail leaders constructed a new feminine religious style or a female adaptation to male ways remains a question.

Constructions

Organizations like the ones dealt with here are often called "traditional," a misleading term in so far as it suggests these women did nothing more than reassess traditional views of femininity. But, then, the appellations *conservative* or *reactionary* are equally misleading—*react* these organizations indeed did. Of course there was a lot of talk about the eternal values of Catholicism. But that does not release the historian from her obligation to investigate very closely how much was really "conserved" of old "traditions."

First of all, to organize with the stated aim of propagating a certain feminine lifestyle—a general characteristic all three organizations shared—was not traditional at all, certainly not within a Catholic framework. It was the urbanized diocese of Haarlem that provided their social frame of reference, not the rural southern Netherlands with its traditional Catholic culture. The idea of *women* as a social group and the possibility of a femininity created by this group were made visible in these organizations. And if all women participants did not realize this, most of the clergy did, leading them to seek so anxiously to control the organizations.

And there is another thing: by lumping these women all together as "traditional," important differences between their "traditions" might get lost. We have seen that each organization addressed, redefined, broadened a particular aspect of the pre–First World War female experience. As a result three female figures emerged that, while drawing on traditions and norms, constituted significant variations upon traditional female roles. I refer to the caring spiritual mother, the militant daughter, and the working unmarried aunt. Each type constituted a self-consciously crafted response to "modern times." Each construction of femininity was the production and the focal point of a distinctive type of the "politics of the personal." Each featured its own central notions and its own mode of actualization. Whereas all moved in the tension that is basic to the politics of the personal, that is the opposition of two spheres, the private and the public, every one of them also related in a specific way to social definitions of femininity. In both the Women's League and the Grail, the distinctiveness and complementarity of Woman was built up, while the idea of complementarity was forcefully opposed by the Sleutelbos women. The Women's League saw itself as creating a limited public sphere for women to wield power in, albeit marked off from and subordinate to the wider sphere of male power. The Grail movement insisted on occupying the public space where girls–young women could celebrate their femininity, but totally outside the "trivial affairs" of everyday public life. The Sleutelbos demanded women's rights to participate in every aspect of existing public life. They did not address themselves to those "feminine" matters of morality and the family that were taken so seriously by the other organizations. Yet neither did they question the male structuring of the public sphere—or male dominance within it. Of course it should not be forgotten that these struggles for definitions involved not only women and that not all women were involved. Yet we have also seen that the Grail and the League—with the clergy lending a hand—rather successfully played "feminism" off against socialism/Communism. They did so not only in a superficial sense (the often overtly stated anti-Communism of both organizations), but also in the sense that these women's search for self-control was subtly transformed into one of social control over other women (and men) of the working classes. And so in the end, the terms *conservative* and *reactionary* as discriptions of their activities may not be so totally misplaced after all.

And Looking Back Again

Of course neither feminism nor Catholicism of the 'eighties is that of the 'thirties. But even so research into these three Catholic women's organizations raises significant political issues for our times. They suggest questions concerning the possibility, desirability, and limitations of a politics of the personal, of counterposing holistic visions of "femininity" on the one side and a brains-only approach in terms of catching up with men on the other. Then there is the most disturbing question of all: What relation exists between feminist "politicizing" in the 1980s and Catholic "moralizing" in the 1930s? Have we left these women's visions and concerns so very far behind?

SOME POLITICAL IMPLICATIONS OF SEPARATISM

GERMAN WOMEN BETWEEN DEMOCRACY AND NAZISM, 1928–1934

Claudia Koonz

Just over a half a century ago, the National Socialist Party began the last stage of its astonishing rise to power. A disreputable fringe movement in 1928, it moved to second place by 1931 and, in July 1932, attracted nearly 14 million votes (compared to the second place Socialists' eight million). With over a million party members, a paramilitary force of 400,000 SA men, and 37 percent of the vote, the National Socialists presented a formidable threat to Weimar democracy. Just half a year after the fateful July 1932, Hitler was named chancellor, and by early 1934, the nation had fallen into the mailed grip of Nazi rule. The Third Reich casts a backward shadow as we ask how one-third of the German electorate could have supported a regime we know to have been founded on genocide, terror, and war. Witnesses to the spectacular success of this dynamic organization, no less than its historians, still wonder how Hitler's party rose so quickly and why the Weimar Republic collapsed with so little resistance.

The answer to this question begins with an understanding of the continuity between several German traditions and Hitler's promises. Hitler launched his crusade in the name of familiar values, using revolutionary rhetoric and technologically sophisticated media—releasing, as it were, the latent poison in a broad range of conservative beliefs. Like his rivals on the right, Hitler swore to end class war and avenge the First World War; but he had the audacity to demand as well

the end to two biological "wars" that other politicians only dared hint
at: the "race war" between "Aryan" and Jew and the "war between the
sexes." Historians have thoroughly investigated the popularity of
Hitler's militarism, anti-Communism, and anti-Semitism; in this article I will investigate the appeal of the "war between the sexes" as a
contributing factor in Nazi popularity. Although antifeminism certainly attracted men to Hitler's movement, I will emphasize women's
motivations for opposing their own emancipation.

Hitler waged war against political opponents, "racially undesirable
elements," and "enemy" nations; in each case he aimed to defeat and/
or annihilate his declared targets. No one anticipated that the van-
quished would participate in the "solution." Still less did anyone
expect the defeated to cooperate within a hierarchy dominated by the
victors. The outcome of the "sex war" would be different. If men
leaders had their way, women would eagerly relinquish their newly
won political rights and rush to participate in the restoration of
patriarchal institutions. National, class, and race war would destroy
Hitler's opponents; victory in the "war between the sexes" would
separate the combatants. Hitler put it simply, "The wonderful thing
about nature and providence is that no conflict between the sexes can
occur as long as each party performs the function prescribed for it by
nature."[1]

The question arises: why—as Simone de Beauvoir noted in *The
Second Sex*—have women frequently reinforced their own oppression?
Since the Third Reich, observers and historians have commented on
the fact that women surrendered to male authority without investigat-
ing it as a problem. Journalists registered surprise as they watched
throngs of women cheering wildly during Hitler's speeches; feminists
despaired when they learned that between 1928 and 1932 women
voters supported Nazi candidates as strongly as men.[2] After women
had been granted suffrage in 1918 and guaranteed fundamental legal
equality by the Constitution of 1919, all political parties included
women candidates on their electoral lists, recruited women into party
work, and paid lip service to women's equality. Only the National
Socialists categorically prohibited women from holding any office
whatsoever and promised to undo the 1918–1919 reforms as soon as
they had the power to do so. In today's parlance, we would have to
conclude that no "gender gap" existed in the support for an overtly
antifeminist movement.

From that day until this, assumptions about the female psyche often
lead us to make assumptions about women's "innate" liberalism or
hatred of violence. During the Nazis' rise to power, journalists noted
Hitler's "fascination for the weaker sex" and left the explanation to

psychologists. A British feminist, however, took up the challenge and speculated about the reasons for Hitler's popularity among women.

> Hitler, the lonely bachelor, the non-smoker, the crusading teetotler, the glorious fighter for Germany's honor who had once gone to prison for his convictions—it is a richly emotional picture to gaze on in their day and in their nighttime dreams.[3]

Women's support for the National Socialist cause, most observers concluded, lay in women's irrational needs; and Sylvia Plath's "Daddy"[4] reverberates still.

> Not God but a swastika
> So black no sky could squeak through.
> Every woman adores a fascist.
> The boot in the face, the brute
> Brute heart of a brute like you.

Italian feminist, Maria-Antoniette Machiocchi, asked more recently how women could have been made "available" to fascist propaganda. What undercut their "natural immunity" to militarism, imperialism, and racism? The answer, she suggests, must lie in "the connection between fascism and female sexuality," in powerful psychological forces which attracted women to that blatantly male-dominated movement.[5]

I suggest that women have no "natural immunities" or ideological proclivities. Myths of either a superior "feminine" morality or an inferior "feminine" psyche have blinded many scholars to the possibility that some women receive advantages from reactionary political movements, especially in the context of economic crisis, decaying democratic institutions, and resurgent patriarchy. Women joined the Nazi movement because of short-term self-interest rather than misguided self-sacrifice. They remained willfully ignorant of Hitler's lethal goals because so much of what Hitler promised had already become deeply embedded in their "feminine" belief system. Moreover, their upbringing had conditioned them to ignore the rough masculine world which often offended their sensibilities.

The Nazi insistence on a rigid separation between "masculine" and "feminine" spheres attracted women who had been educated and socialized in traditional roles of nineteenth-century bourgeois womanhood. On the "woman question," Nazi doctrine differed from the ideals of the middle-class women's rights movement only in degree. But Hitler's promise to remove women from the public sphere avoided a logical trap into which many advocates of women's rights fell. Leaders of the middle-class women's movement generally supported the ideal of full equality for exceptional (and unmarried) women, while opposing the average woman's emancipation from the oppression of family life and patriarchal law. Women who renounced marriage, they believed, deserved rights; but for the masses of women, motherhood constituted life's major commitment and provided the mainstay of their social identity. Middle-class crusaders for women's legal equality enmeshed themselves in a contradiction because of their ambivalence about conflicts between individual liberties and the collective good. This hesitation was reflected in their strategy to expand women's rights during the 1920s.

For decades, leaders of the middle-class women's rights movement in Germany (as in other European nations) had based their claim to equality on the proposition that women, if emancipated, could offer invaluable services to the national community. Instead of threatening men in areas conventionally designated as "masculine," women promised to carve out their own public sphere. By surrendering, in other words, to the status quo in role division, they hoped to win equality without a battle within a male-dominated system. The first steps toward emancipation in 1918–1919 had come, it appeared, as a reward for services rendered in the war effort, not as the result of a victorious suffrage campaign. Hence, women politicians in the next decade followed what they believed had proved to be a winning strategy and stressed women's potential contributions to the patriarchy when they worked to improve their status. In the face of antifeminists' hysterical anxieties about "masculinized" women, proponents of emancipation relinquished their claims to equal human rights and instead vowed, "We want our special nature to be especially esteemed."[6] Women in politics scrupulously avoided the Enlightenment rhetoric of individual rights and emphasized instead Romantic notions of women's special nature. Leaders of the middle-class (as well as socialist) women's movement shunned the very term *feminism,* calling themselves instead women socialists or *Frauenrechtlerinnen*—an awkard term which translates best as "women's rights women."[7]

Beneath women's compliant tone, however, lurked a more ambitious agenda. Their discourse attests to these covert dreams of power. In the late 1920s women began to adapt a metaphor common in nationalists' arsenal of bombast: *Lebensraum.* Hitler used this term to refer to the rich agricultural lands to the east of Germany—land which he claimed Germany needed to feed its growing population. This ranks as one of Hitler's most blatant lies, for everyone realized that the German population had been declining since the late nineteenth century.[8] Nazi leaders, to be sure, did not consider women a part of their *Lebensraum* plans, except as breeders of more children to vindicate their imperialist dreams. But middle-class women writers used the term in a very different way, calling for their own women's *Lebensraum* within German society and culture. Perceiving finance and formal politics as irrevocably male, women demanded their separate sphere within public life beyond the reach of male hegemony. In times of crisis (like the First World War and the Depression), women leaders insisted that only they could bring social peace *(Burgfrieden)* to the potentially dangerous elements of the German population. Cooperating with the national state, middle-class women volunteered to act as agents of social control and to unify politically and culturally dissident elements.

Despite claims to restore national solidarity and attack all "selfish" materialistic interests, the class-linked aims of this rhetoric had never been far from the surface. Marianne Weber, Democratic delegate to the Reichstag, for example, worried about "propertyless masses," who had "sunk into a deplorable moral state"[9] Women "as the bearers of culture," she argued, could "reconstruct the general ethical level" and head off the threat of revolution. More overtly, the powerful German Housewives Association worked to undercut servants' demands for better conditions, shorter hours, and higher status. On occasion they cooperated with conservative politicians in promoting home economics courses as a method of diverting rebelliousness in both daughters and servants.[10] Protestant, Catholic, and Jewish women rescued women from prostitution rings, attacked pornography, sponsored programs to combat venereal disease, and opposed divorce reforms and abortion. By attacking men who abused their patriarchal privileges, these conservative women sought to impose their own control over the private sphere; by fighting to contain sexuality within the family, they endeavored to bind husbands, fathers, and sons more closely within the female sphere; and by setting themselves up as guardians of morality, bourgeois women transformed their private anxieties into public outrage long before they heard of the National Socialist Party.

Early advocates of suffrage had always assumed that women, once enfranchised, would rush into political party life and usher in further reforms. As it turned out, the reverse occurred. Women did "go public," but they did so by participating in the same traditionalist organizations which their mothers and grandmothers might have joined. Far from pressing for further victories, they organized against feminist demands which they believed would further erode their status as wives and mothers. By the early 1930s, over two million women had become active in various Protestant women's organizations, and Catholic associations counted just over half that number.

Membership in the Jewish Women's Federation doubled in the last years of the Republic to include over 50,000 members. Of the approximately 750,000 members of the Federation of German Women's Associations BDF, most belonged to associations which lobbied for special women's occupational or charitable goals with little concern for broad feminist issues. The Federation of German Housewives Associations, for example, counted just under 100,000 members by 1931—with the second-place white-collar women workers' union claiming over 100,000 members. Approximately 40,000 teachers belonged to the women teachers' union, and 20,000 to the Catholic Women's Teachers Union.[11] Fundamentally conservative, these women did not join political parties—not even the ladies' auxiliaries. That would have violated their notion of separate spheres. Instead, they operated in religious, civic, and cultural programs, far from the suzerainty of male politicians.

Middle-class women's organizations defined themselves as apolitical, but that was true only in the narrowest sense, for they waged a powerful covert war against democracy and feminism. Politically, they responded like disaffected middle-class men who organized single-issue, protest parties within the political system. These men typically came from endangered segments of the "old" middle class.[12] As small shopkeepers, government employees, nonunionized workers, and craftsmen, they felt the rapid modernization of the economy threatened both their livelihood and their status. Competition from powerful monopolies drove them to bankruptcy, while streamlined production processes devalued their skills and the feminization of unskilled branches of the labor market undercut blue- and white-collar men's ability to find new jobs. Even before the Great Depression, modernization closed the economic vise and drove millions to search for a "third way," in the form of a hierarchical and authoritarian state which would hamper freedom but also provide structures within which the middle class might once again enjoy autonomy and status. Historians routinely note the importance of these trends as a crucial factor in Hitler's appeal, but they have neglected to consider the housewife counterparts of the men who flocked to single-issue and fringe political movements. For most middle-class women, the home provided both a work place and a source of pride. To defend this "turf" against cultural and economic erosion, they formed powerful national associations to protect the patriarchal family upon which, they believed, women's traditional roles depended.

Although statistical records on the women who adhered to the Nazi Party before 1933 are rare, the available evidence suggests that women Nazis were the female counterparts of the insecure middle-class voters who shifted to the Nazi Party between 1928 and 1932. In the earliest official membership surveys, "woman" as a category meant "housewife."[13] Background information on a large sample of early women party members is scarce, but in Hesse-Darmstadt the applications for party membership have been preserved. In a 3 percent randomized sample of the data, it is clear that virtually every woman who applied to the party considered herself a housewife.[14] The few women who listed other occupations defined themselves as white-collar workers or sales personnel—never as factory workers, servants, or other working-class occupations. A second source of information on women who joined the party prior to 1933 and then rose in the women's bureaucracy is provided by a collection of 950 autobiographies of women chosen to attend special leadership courses between 1933 and 1938. Once again, the overwhelming majority of these women had grown up in a middle-class milieu and over half had attended lyceums. Only a few, however, had completed university-level education (and only one, a physician, worked as a professional); a handful mentioned domestic service and waitressing as their occupations prior to marriage. Interestingly, women with aristocratic backgrounds were overrepresented, with about 5 percent. Most women's fathers had been civil servants, small tradesmen, artisans, teachers, or office workers. When these women married, they sought husbands from similar backgrounds. None noted any form of industrial work in her previous experience (although one woman's father had been the foreman of a lace-making shop). Over 65 percent identified themselves as Protestants, as compared to 11 percent Catholic; and the remainder described themselves as either "believing in God" or German Christian. Other variables appear to have set Nazi women leaders apart from their middle-class counterparts. Only 48 percent were married when they attended the leadership training courses, and 36 percent had never been married. The remaining 16 percent were widowed or divorced. Ideology aside, the pragmatic demands of marriage and motherhood precluded major party responsibilities, no matter how loyal women may have been. Despite propaganda urging women to bear many children, the mothers in this group had borne an average of fewer than two children each. About a third of these women lived their adult lives near their places of birth—which suggests that the others experienced some form of disruption in their social life. Women leaders appear to have been released from the ties of traditional communal institutions and the burdens of child rearing. Autobiographical accounts and records from the pre-1933 period suggest further that Nazi women felt spurned by their social "betters." Rather than joining the more staid religious and civic ladies' organizations, they may have looked to the loosely organized, dynamic Nazi movement as a more likely outlet for their ambitions. This became especially true when economic dislocation and political chaos threatened during the Depression. Like women in traditional organizations, Nazi women felt threatened by cultural decay, downward mobility, sexual license, and Communism. But unlike their more respectable counterparts, women Nazis had lost faith in traditional male structures to solve these problems—as one early leader put it, "We are not just another tea and crumpets *(Kaffee und Kuchen)* organization!" Women, like lower-middle-class men who followed Hitler, took their special interests into the rapidly growing "catch all" movement *(Sammelpartei)*.[15] But Nazi women's activities and perceptions differed dramatically from men's because women knew they would remain the second sex in the Third Reich.

Hitler and his deputies recruited men, but ignored women. When they mentioned women at all, their pronouncements were consistent with Joseph Goebbels's call for a return to nature.

> The mission of women is to be beautiful and to bring children into the world. This is not at all as rude and unmodern as it sounds. The female bird pretties herself for her mate and hatches the eggs for him. In exchange, the mate takes care of gathering the food, and stands guard and wards off the enemy.[16]

This statement (and the style!) indeed epitomized male Nazis' attitudes. If these sentiments motivated women to vote Nazi, we might be justified in assuming they were culpably naive. But women distorted Goebbels's intent to suit their desires for power in their own sphere and elaborated their own version of what mother bird ought to be doing in the nest while father flew away. Paradoxically, Nazi men's very lack of concern with women gave Nazi women the sense that they really could operate in their own *Lebensraum*. Whereas men leaders in church and political organizations monitored "their" women's groups and worried about any display of autonomy, Nazi men saw themselves as a revolutionary masculine movement and ignored women altogether. Their arrogance provided women with the opportunity to develop their own concerns while enjoying the feeling of power associated with membership in a dynamic political organization. For women, the Nazi Party united the advantages of a national political movement and a party, combined with the emotional appeal of a religion.

Women's own explanations for their "conversion" emphasize their need for self-respect, political influence, and autonomy. Again a winged metaphor might be appropriate, but it would be taken from

Virginia Woolf's description of the eternal "Angel in the House" who followed a few simple maxims:

> The shadow of her wings fell on my page; I heard the rustling of her skirts in the room. Directly, that is to say, I took up my pen in my hand to review that novel by a famous man, she slipped behind me and whispered, "My dear, you are a young woman. You are writing about a book that has been written by a man. Be sympathetic; be tender; flatter; deceive; use all the arts and wiles of our sex. Never let anybody guess that you have a mind of your own. Above all, be pure. . . ." I turned upon her and caught her by the throat. . . . Killing the Angel in the House was part of the occupation of a woman writer.[17]

The Angel may have been lethal for writers, but traditionalists found her strategy familiar—and effective in the short term for women without genius or scruples. Whereas Woolf needed to challenge the male writer, average women have felt more secure acquiescing to male authority. In exchange, they expected to be left alone in their house (or nest), while men attended to "more important" affairs.

A brief survey of a few national women leaders in the Nazi movement attests to the wide range of options open to the women who swore allegiance to Hitler before 1933. The oldest pro-Nazi group, Guida Diehl's Newland Movement, predated the Nazi Party by at least six years. Diehl had founded this patriotic association during the worst years of World War I and continued to preach her spiritualist, quasi-Christian, and nationalist message throughout the 1920s. "Mother Guida," as her followers called her, opposed women's suffrage, called for a national women's parliament, endorsed state subsidies to mothers whose husbands could not support them, and believed women ought to work only within a household setting.[18]

In the late 1920s, other supporters of Nazism rallied to the strident tone of Elsbeth Zander's "Red Swastika" and unquestionably obeyed her dictatorial orders. She saw herself as the female equivalent of Hitler—and summoned women to motherhood in much the same terms as he recruited men to the paramilitary. Despite her scandalous personal life and her heretical proposal to run women as Nazi candidates, Zander retained her party's confidence.[19] Lydia Gottschewski, a dynamic woman in her early twenties, offered Nazi women still another alternative. This forceful organizer called on women to form their own fighting union—to close ranks and march against the enemy on the "spiritual" front. Men, she believed, would "clean up the streets" while women would undertake the more arduous task of doing missionary work among the unconvinced. Forming the Nazi personality, in her view, presented a more exciting challenge than street brawling.[20] A group of women Nazi academics even carried racial theory into social science and proposed that, while women of "lesser" races might be inferior to their men, Germanic women in prehistoric times had grown to equal size and performed equal work. Decadent Western civilization had degraded Germanic women; Nazi society alone would restore true equality between men and women, they predicted.[21]

In several districts, local leaders galvanized their followers into a wide variety of actions. Paula Siber in Duesseldorf, for example, blended Christianity and a colorful rhetorical style to win over thousands of converts from this densely populated industrial area.[22] Among her most successful activities were establishing charitable collections for impoverished Nazi families, setting up shelters for wounded storm troopers men, working with neighborhood groups, sponsoring knitting evenings at which Nazi ideology was discussed, and distributing food to the unemployed.

Nazi women remained independent—free either to sew or to wear brown shirts. In the political chaos of the Depression, male leaders cared little about women's activities; all contributions and ideals were welcomed. One rural group might gather to knit socks and sing Nazi songs of an evening; and in another village, women might run secret missions through police guards or smuggle illegal weapons to an underground SA cell. An early convert to Nazism relished the feeling of tranquility after returning from an exhausting day of conflict with anti-Nazi demonstrators. As she rested sipping a cup of tea, she heard the family next door (also devoted Nazis) playing a Mozart string quartet. This, she recalled, is what she fought for—to save culture and virtue in a world polluted by materialism.

Nazi women rarely reported any political activity before they joined the Hitler movement—although most mentioned their religious and conservative family background. Upon entering the Nazi party, they prided themselves on activating previously apathetic women—telling them that they could place their traditionally "feminine" skills, emotions, and spirit in the service of a national movement. One woman orator, Irene Seydel, who drew hundreds of women to hear her speeches, reflected on the secret of her success after a tour of Westfalia in 1932.

> From my own experience I can tell you about women who have responded to our appeal and begun to see things clearly because they discovered they could once again serve the *Vaterland*. Women have something to offer their *Volk*—the purity of their hearts and the power of their spirits! Women long to hear that politics emanates from love,

and that love means sacrifice. . . . The German woman's talents wither at the harsh sound of commands barked by northeastern (Prussian) trumpets. But she is eager to work for whoever sends a friendly ray of sunshine her way.[23]

Seydel wove slogans and homely metaphors into a unique style, inspiring simple country women and factory workers alike with lavish praise for just those womanly traits which men so often decried as "merely female." These qualities alone, she insisted, would restore unity to the badly fragmented nation. Like all women Nazis, Seydel did not describe herself as a member of a "party," but instead used the term *movement* or *freedom movement,* by which she meant a total doctrine which guided every aspect of life and values. While liberals praised the freedom of Weimar Democracy, Nazi women called it derisively "the system," by which they meant a political network of opportunism, materialism, and corruption which excluded them and devalued their status as mothers. To regain a mythical social world in which women held power and status over the private realm, women Nazis joined a fanatical, dynamic, and marginal elite. Women's participation in this male-dominated movement complimented SA men's brutality by offering "feminine" virtues and social services to members of the subculture. However, men's antifeminism prevented them from simply merging into the movement. Because male Nazis routinely ignored or insulted them, women created their own solidarity as double outcasts—scorned by non-Nazi Germans and looked down on by male Nazis.

Wearing swastika armbands, they marched in the streets of their hometowns or neighborhoods to taunts of "Hitler whore!" "brown goose!" or "Nazi pig!" Often they compared themselves to the Christians in the catacombs and spoke of their joy at being able to participate in a genuine community. "What did it matter that we were nearly always ridiculed and stoned by Communists lurking in the shadows. . . . We were so despised in our neighborhoods that we hardly dared to walk alone in the streets."[24] Scorn and ridicule forged a unity among them that in itself overcame the feelings of alienation and helplessness that they had experienced before they joined the Nazi Party. Once in the movement, however, the world began to appear both simpler and more secure; in the words of an early party member, Maria von Belli, "In those days there were only two types of people—those who followed Hitler and those who did not."[25]

Nazi women's records testify to their having created their own institutions which they believed would remain autonomous after Hitler's "revolution." Taking up the ubiquitous rhetoric, women Nazis demanded their "*Lebensraum* for the woman in the state and the culture" of the Third Reich.[26] Before Hitler became dictator, women Nazis submerged themselves in the Nazi *Gemeinschaft* and simultaneously in their own women's subsections of the movement. They surrendered to the collective drama of the crusade and discovered their own individuality in the fight. Instead of challenging male domination, they applied traditional survival skills and demanded recognition in exchange for fulfilling traditional expectations. "Female consciousness," in addition to general adulation of Nazi goals, created a separatist women's movement within Nazism.[27]

These women saw the world in terms of "us" and "them," meaning, in the first place, men and women, and, in the second, "Aryan" and Jew. They contributed to Hitler's political, national, race, and sex "wars" by strengthening female solidarity and by creating the image of a total movement. Elias Canetti recently restated a central tenet of "crowd" psychology which describes the relationship of polarities to the *Gemeinschaft* as a whole.

> The surest, and often the only way by which a crowd can preserve itself lies in the existence of a second crowd to which it is related. . . . [G]iven that they are about equal in size and intensity, the two crowds keep each other alive. The superiority on the side of the enemy must not be too great, or, at least, must not be thought to be so. In order to understand the origin of this structure we have to start from three basic antitheses. The first and most striking is that between men and women; the second that between the living and the dead; and the third that between friend and foe.[28]

Nazi women before 1933 rendered a vital service to the party by creating an alternative subculture for men, women, and children. Thanks largely to women's dedication, Nazi Party membership provided the faithful with a sense of community, complete with social services, an image of virtue, and shared values.

Nazi women dreamed of "more masculine men" and "more feminine women" but not because they longed to surrender to authority; rather, Nazi women predicted that if only men would fulfill their "proper" roles, they would leave women space in which to cultivate their own communities. Democracy homogenized people into conformist masses, wrote a Nazi woman psychologist.[29] Class and religious alliances tore Germans apart; a return to "social health" necessitated a substitution of religion and class by sex and race as the defining attributes of community. In keeping with this general view, Nazi women extolled a classless, *volkish* female community and criticized the "blue stockings" for cooperating with Jewish women and attending international conferences. "We long for the day when every German woman will call other women, 'sister'," one woman put it. For all their rhetoric about solidarity, however, women Nazis viewed poor and peasant women as clients in need of their help rather than as equals.

The Nazi Party did not allure women with promises of an "escape from freedom" or with Hitler's hypnotic powers. Rather, it attracted women who longed for freedom from male scrutiny—who sought a vent for their anxiety about women's status in the world and saw in the loosely organized Nazi movement an outlet for their ambitions. Pledging themselves to goals common to middle-class women's organizations everywhere, they utilized the autonomy afforded them by Nazi antifeminism to create their own communities and forge their own doctrines. The illusion of independence lasted only until Nazi victory.

Hitler's seizure of power changed everything. Overnight the party of disreputable outcasts became the very core of the Nazi state. Before 1933 only renegades dared risk the ostracism of joining the National Socialist movement. After that date, only the courageous dared to resist it. Ironically, the stalwarts from the old days experienced Nazi power as a greater shock than did most non-Nazi middle-class women leaders; for within months of Hitler's appointment as chancellor, his deputies purged every independent woman leader and recruited instead the civic and church leaders whom women Nazis had earlier regarded as rivals. With Hitler as dictator, "respectable" women's civic and religious organizations purged their Jewish members and integrated themselves effortlessly into the Nazi state. The ease of this transition cannot be explained by middle-class women's cowardice (since they indeed vehemently protested against specific policies of which they disapproved); nor does Nazi efficiency provide an explanation (since the women's section of the new state remained in chaos until late 1934).

The National Socialist solution to the "woman question" had been prefigured in the goals of middle-class women's organizations. With little difficulty, German women accepted a society based on biological distinctions, for they had always seen the world as bifurcated along sex lines.[30] After 1933, as before, organized middle-class women, by working within their own sphere and outside the formal political system, cultivated their ignorance of the world they defined as "masculine." They continued to bargain for women's rights on the basis of women's ability to make a unique and vital contribution to patriarchal middle-class institutions. The logic of millions of German women found its expression in the words of Gertrud Bäumer, leading women's rights advocate and founding member of the German Democratic Party. "We do not oppose National Socialism as a party, but only its position in relationship to women," she declared.[31] Bäumer, eager to ingratiate herself with the new leaders, lost no time in declaring she had supported National Socialist ideas for years and called on women to continue their fight for equality under the new political circumstances. In Bäumer's mind, one male party would follow another, and women had little choice but to carry on their struggle within every context. Women's long-standing reluctance to link their demands for inalienable rights within a broader concept of human liberty had eroded their ability to advance nonnegotiable demands of any kind and rendered them docile vis-à-vis any political system or policy. Like a single-issue lobby, they declared themselves willing to cooperate with any male state—for a price. They bargained for privileges rather than fighting for equality.

In conclusion, women working within the National Socialist state, by following traditional "feminine" dicta, epitomized the quotidien "banality of evil." Despite encounters with anti-Semitism, political terror, and injustice, women Nazis did their best to convince their fellow "Aryan" citizens and foreign observers that all was well in the familiar, domestic sphere. For decades, middle-class women had advanced claims over their own *Lebensraum* within society and outside formal politics. They prided themselves on creating a realm where purity reigned no matter what. As the Nazi state destroyed morality in the public sphere, women did their best to guard the private space and make personal life pleasant for the men who executed Hitler's murderous plans. Separatist thinking on the "woman question" contributed as much to Hitler's success as his shopworn nationalist, racist, and anti-Communist notions. While Nazi men expanded German territorial *Lebensraum* and made the nation *Judenrein* (literally "purified of Jews"), women contributed to evil by ignoring it.

Notes

1. Quoted by Susan Griffin, *Pornography and Silence* (New York, 1980), 168.

2. Hans Beyer, *Die Frau in der politische Entscheidung* (Stuttgart, 1932); Gabrielle Bremme, *Die politische Rolle der Frau in Deutschland (Gottingen, 1956);* W. Phillips Shively, "Party Identification, Party Choice and Voting Stability: The Weimar Case," *The American Political Science Review* 66 (December 1972), 1203–225.

3. "The Battlecries of Hitlerism," The New York *Times*, VIII, 3:1 (July 10,

1932). Katherine Thomas, *Women in Nazi Germany* (London: Gollancz, 1943), 32; cf. also Hilde Browning, *Women under Fascism and Communism* (London: Lawrence, 1943), 5. Hitler's promise of husbands "had an enormous effect, touching deeply as it did, the innermost feelings and desires of millions of women for whom 'equal rights' meant until then merely the right to be exploited." Clifford Kirkpatrick, *Nazi Germany: Its Women and Family Life* (Indianapolis and New York: Bobbs-Merill, 1938), 43.

   4. Sylvia Plath, *The Collected Poems*, ed. Ted Hughes (New York: Harper and Row, 1981), 223.

   5. Anna-Maria Machiocchi, *Jungfrauen, Muetter, und ein Fuehrer. Frauen im Faschismus*, tr. Eva Moldenhauer (Berlin: Wagenbach, 1976), cf. Jane Caplan, "Introduction," *Feminist Review* No. 1 (1979): 72–80.

   6. "Rede von Frl Julie Velde, gehalten auf der ersten Nationalversammlung der deutschen Volkspartei," BA Koblenz, ZSg 1 42/45. Maria Schlüter-Hermkes, "Die Frau und die geistige Kulturentwicklung" in *Die Kultur der Frau* (Berlin: Herbig, 1929), 191.

   7. The debate on women's rights in the National Assembly, *Stenographische Berichte*, 58th Session (July 16, 1919), 1597 ff. On the history of "feminism" in the American context, cf. Ellen DuBois's *Elizabeth Cady Stanton and Susan B. Anthony, Correspondence, Writings, Speeches* (New York, 1981), 193. After the American women's movement had opted for "reliance on the simple fact of gender to unite women politically, . . . no longer understood itself primarily as a part of a larger political effort to transform society and achieve true democracy, ÄandÜ . . . no longer connected itself with the radical transformation of the sexual order and the emancipation of woman from coercive sexual stereotypes," the *new* term *feminism* emerged to "distinguish the small minority who called for radical transformation of women's lives. . . ." In other words, *feminism* in its very nature *is* a radical movement. On "women's rights women," cf. Nancy Cott, "The House of Feminism," *The New York Review of Books* (March 17, 1983): 36–39.

   8. Friedrich Burgdorfer, *Der Geburtenrückgang und seine Bekämpfung. Die Lebensfrage des deutschen Volkes* (Berlin: Schotz, 1929).

   9. Marianne Weber, "Die Besonderen Kulturaufgabe der Frau," *Frauenfragen und Frauengedanken: Gesammelte Aufsätze* (Tübingen, 1919), 252.

   10. Hannover Hausfrauverein to OberstLeut. Feldmann, Hannover (Chairman of the local *Vaterland* Party), May 26, 1932, Hann/320 I/69. Hannover State Archives.

   11. Evans, *The Feminist Movement in Germany* (London: Sage, 1976), 175–201. Renate Bridenthal, "Class Struggle around the Hearth: Women and Domestic Service in the Weimar Republic," *Toward the Holocaust: The Social and Economic Collapse of the Weimar Republic*, ed. Michael Dobkowski and Isador Wallimann (Westport, Conn: Greenwood, 1983). Fritz Mybes, *Geschichte der Evangelischen Frauenhilfe in Quellen* (Gladbeck: Schriftenmissions-Verlag, 1975), 56–57. The most rapidly growing membership in the nation was Silesia. In 1928 600,000 German women belonged to the *Frauenhilfe* alone (in 5,000 local associations); By 1933 all women's branches of church organizations totaled over two million. Cf. also Frauengruppe Faschismusforschung, ed., *Mutterkreuz und Arbeitsbuch* (Frankfurt: Fischer, 1981); Tim Mason, "Women in Germany, 1925–1940: Family, Welfare and Work," *History Workshop* 1 and 2 (1976). These totals exclude other conservative women's associations, such as the elitist Queen Louisa League with 150,000 members, Buch to Krummacher, September 29, 1933, Berlin Document Center, hereafter referred to as BDCÜ. Cf.

Agnes von Zahn-Harnack, *Die Frauenbewegung: Geschichte, Probleme, Ziele* (Berlin: Deutsche, 1928), 20–28, breakdown of sixty supposedly nonpolitical women's organizations.

12. Thomas Childers, "The Social Bases of the National Socialist Vote," *Journal of Contemporary History* 11 (1976): 17–42; for a different interpretation, cf. Richard Hamilton, *Who Voted for Hitler?* (Princeton, 1982), 9–86, 309–361. Alexander Weber, *Soziale Merkmale der NSDAP Wähler. Eine Zusammenfassung bisheriger empirischer Untersuchungen und eine Analyse in den Gemeinden der Länder Baden und Hessen* (diss. Freiburg, 1969), esp. 159–64, 176–77.

13. Robert Ley, ed., *Parteistatistik* II (Berlin, 1935), 192–92. Recent discussions of male Nazis' policies toward "the woman question" include Dorothee Klinksiek, *Die Frau im NS-Staat* (Munich: DVA, Stuttgart); Jill Stephenson, *Women in Nazi Society* (New York: Barnes and Noble, 1975) and *Women in the Nazi State* (London: Croom Helm, 1982); Georg Tidl, *Die Frau im National Sozialismus* (Vienna, Zurich, Munich: Europa, 1984); Rita Thalmann, *Etre Femme sous le III Reich* (Paris: Lafont, 1982); Dörthe Winkler, *Frauenarbeit im 'Dritten Reich'* (Hamburg, Hoffmann und Campe, 1977).

14. Hessisches Hauptstaatsarchiv, Wiesbaden, Darmstadt, Rep. G 12/B, "Neuaufnahmen," 1931–33, May 6, 1932 (Bl. 483-596); May 23, 1932, July 1, 1932 (Bl 66–74); Nov. 10, 1932 (bl.1–232); and March 20, 1933 (bl.232–259), April 13, 1933; through May 15, 1933. cf. Eberhard Schoen, *Die Entstehung des Nationalsozialismus in Hessen* (Meisenheim am Glan, 1972), 100.

15. Thomas Childers,114–18, 188–89, 260.

16. Joseph Goebbels, *Michael: ein deutsches Schicksal* (Berlin, 1929).

17. "The Death of the Moth" (1931) in *Virginia Woolf, Women and Writing*, ed. Michele Barrett (New York: Harcourt, Brace and Jovanovich, 1979), 59.

18. Guida Diehl, *Die deutsche Frau und der Nationalsozialismus* (Eisenach: Neuland, 1933). "If women sink into a cultural abyss, the entire nation sinks; if the *Volk* sinks, then women bear the largest share of the guilt. And probably that American trend, emancipation would be to blame." For an outstanding collection of documents from this period, cf. Annette Kuhn and Valentine Rothe, eds., *Frauen im deutschen Faschismus*, 2 vols (Düsseldorf: Schwann, 1983).

19. *Opferdienst der deutschen Frau*, BA Koblenz/NSD 47/1–2. Cf. also Marie Baltzer, "Die Frau im NS Staat," *Nationalsozialistische Monatehefte* 3:22 (January 1932), in which the author claims to follow the "organized motherliness" espoused by Gertrud Bäumer and the women's movement, 19–25).

20. Lydia Gottschewski, *Männerbund und Frauenfrage* (Munich, 1934). Lydia Gottschewski, "Neu deutsche Frauen!" *Teutonia*, Dortmund, 262 (September 22, 1933) in DCV-A/CA VIII/a)B.13. Gottschewski, *Amtliche-Frauenkorrespondenz* I (October 25, 1933), 4.

21. Irmaggard Reichenau, *Deutsche Frauen an Adolf Hitler* (Leipzig, 1933). Pia Sophie Rogge-Borner, ed., *Die deutsche Kämpferin*, periodical at Institue für Zeitgeschichte, Munich; idem, *Die innere Gestalt der nordischen Frau* (Berlin, 1938); and idem, *Am geweihtem Brunnen. Die deutsche Frauenbewegung im Lichte des Rassengedankes*, (Weimar, 1926).

22. Paula Siber, *Die Frauenfrage und ihre Lösung durch den National-Sozialismus* (Berlin, 1933).

23. Irene Seydel, "Volk und Familie," correspondence SAM/W-N/NSF/405. Her recurrent message was that women ought to lose their *Ich* (ego) and discover the *Volk*. Cf. Seydel to Hitler's sister, December 27, 1933, ibid., folio 393.

24. Dornberg, interviewed by Frau L. Koller, 1940, SAM/W-N/NSF 128. For example, cf. the autobiography of Helene Radtke, in the Theodor Abel collection at the Hoover Institution, Stanford University, hereafter referred to as HIÜ.

25. Similar expressions occur in about half of the women's autobiographies collected by Theodor Abel. This quotation comes from 212.

26. Dr. M. Unger, "Die Frau im national-sozialistischen Deutschland," *Amtliche Frauenkorrespondenz*, No. 11 (April 1, 1934); Florentine Hamm, "Die Frau in Deutschlands Niedergang und Aufstieg," *NS Monatshefte* 3:22 (January 1932), 17; and Leonore Kuhn, "Lebensraum für die Frau," *Die Frau* 40:9 (June 1933).

27. Temma Kaplan, "Female Consciousness and Collective Action: The Case of Barcelona, 1910–1918," *Signs* (1982) 7:3, 545–61. Frances Fox Pivin, in her address to the 1984 Barnard Women's Conference, used the term *domestic moral economy*.

28. Elias Canetti, *Crowds and Power*.

29. Anna Zühlke, *Frauenaufgabe und Frauenarbeit im Dritten Reich*, special issue of *Das Dritte Reich: Bausteine zum neuen Staat und Volk* (Leipzig: Quelle und Meyer, 1934), 9–12. In democratic society, "the women loses her ego *(Ich)* by loving everyone equally. Liberal equality *(Gleichmacherei)* dissolves the individual into the mass."

30. On contemporary implications of this paradigm, cf. Zillah R. Eisenstein, "The Sexual Politics of the New Right: Understanding the 'Crisis of Liberalism'," *Signs* (1982), 7:3, 567–77, and Judith Stacey, "The New Conservative Feminism," *Feminist Studies* 9:3 (Fall 1983), 559–83.

31. Gertrud Bäumer, "Umwege und Schicksal der Frauenbewegung," *Die Hilfe* 39:9 (June 1933), 385–87, quoted by Barbara Greven-Aschoff, *Die bürgerliche Frauenbewegung in Deutschland 1894–1933* (Göttingen: Vandenhoeck Ruprecht, 1981), 186, 158–95. Even before 1933 she had written of the "narrow, asphalt democracy, the Jewish atmosphere of Weimar." Since I wrote this article, Christine Wittrock has described the links between the women's emancipation movement and Nazi policy, *Weiblichkeits Mythen Das Frauenbild im Faschismus und seine Vorläufer in der frauenbewegung der 20er Jahre* (Frankfurt a.M., 1983).

"NO CHILDREN AT ANY COST"

PERSPECTIVES ON COMPULSORY STERILIZATION, SEXISM AND RACISM IN NAZI GERMANY

Gisela Bock

Translated by Joan Reutershan

On July 14, 1933, six months after Hitler came to power, the National Socialist government enacted a law for "the prevention of congenitally diseased progeny." People identified as "inferior" *(Minderwertige)* would be sterilized. The official commentary on the law explained that sterilization was a means to "eliminate inferior genes" and articulated the following goal: "Sterilization will lead to the gradual purification of the people *(Volkskörper)* and to the eradication of pathological hereditary traits."[1] Section 12 made sterilization enforceable by the police and Section 14 forbade voluntary sterilization. Thus the law intended that all cases of sterilization would subsequently become compulsory. Available sources permit us to estimate the number of legal sterilizations in Germany between 1934 and 1945 at around 400,000. In addition, an unknown but considerable number of people were sterilized outside the law without their knowledge or against their will.

The issue of compulsory sterilization in Nazi Germany has received

Preliminary results of my research were published in *Signs* 8:3 (1983): 400–421. The paper published in this volume is expanded upon in my forthcoming book: *Zwangssterilisation im Nationalsozialismus: Untersuchungen zur Rassenpolitik und Frauenpolitik* (Köln und Opladen: Westdeutscher Verlag, 1985).

little serious attention by historians. When they do mention it, most scholars regard the policy of "eradicating inferiors," by preventing them from being born, as a prelude to the policy of "exterminating worthless life" which began in 1939. Both policies were supposed to "liberate" the *Volkskörper* from "alien bodies" *(Fremdkörper)*.[2] The crimes committed in the name of the sterilization policy, most of which occurred during the first six years of the regime, have understandably received less attention than the crimes committed by National Socialism in its last six years in power. Yet historians cannot ignore the former because they are less horrible than the latter. It was primarily the perpetrators, not the victims, who talked about gradations on a scale of injustice. According to the race hygiene movement, sterilization was "more humane" than murder, even "protective and loving." Sterilization rendered murder "superfluous" in the long run. It was considered a "milder" version of such practices as setting children out to die in Sparta; witch burnings in early modern times; the killing of the mentally ill; and—by some of the defendants in the Nurenberg Trials—the mass murder of Jews.[3]

The crimes committed under the sterilization law should not be judged by a standard only National Socialism could set. This earlier program for dealing with "inferior" people was an injustice of its own kind. Even without an explicit plan for murder connected to it, the sterilization policy was inhuman. Its significance extends beyond that of a mere prelude, and it must be studied as an integral component of the more encompassing procreation policies of National Socialism.

The sterilization law has been overlooked, in part, because much of the early research on women under National Socialism did not go beyond popular notions and images. It was believed that the National Socialist policy toward women was exclusively pronatalist and that promoting childbearing was pursued by all means—from keeping women out of the labor market to the elevation of mothers through a "cult of motherhood," to "compulsory" childbearing. Adequate research about the Nazi image of women is still lacking in Germany, but the most important contribution on the subject so far challenges these stereotypic assumptions. Leila Rupp has shown that this image was highly complex. Exclusive motherhood referred only to a small portion of women.[4] For the others, image and reality consisted of a double or triple burden. Women's employment was not taboo in either propaganda or praxis, and it increased after 1933.

Research on the sterilization law confirms further that the stereotypes are misleading and that the Nazi policy toward women must be reevaluated, especially with regard to childbearing. National Socialist propaganda and policies did not encourage "more, more, more children." It did not call for a "triumph of numbers," "Kinder, Küche, Kirche," or "children at any cost." In fact, the words *woman* and *mother* were never "synonymous terms," neither for Hitler nor for the other leading National Socialists.[5] A huge campaign for the sterilization of the "inferior" of both sexes dominated Nazi propaganda before and after their rise to power and it often addressed women specifically. In 1933 it was proclaimed that "a reasonable reduction in the birth rate would actually be a blessing for humanity, if it would primarily affect the unfit. But this is, unfortunately, not the case." The "free right to propagate" was vigorously condemned, especially for the "incurably worthless." National Socialists spoke out against the biblical phrase "Be fruitful and multiply."[6] In 1937, for example, the *Partei Archiv* contradicted the assumption that "the state wants children at any cost." Instead, the correct version read: "The state wants racially valuable, physically and spiritually unencumbered children from German families." Propaganda directives reflected this: "The slogan is not 'children at any cost,' but rather: the largest possible flock of children from the genetically healthy German family." As for the others: "Their very increase, which is almost always higher than average, represents a danger for our people." In 1944 the assumption "that virtually all women are worthy of propagation" was called "utopian" and "too optimistic."[7] Under National Socialism 10 to 30 percent of the population was considered "undesirable" for purposes of procreation; only 10 to 30 percent ranked as truly "desirable."

Previous investigations of National Socialist pronatalism have regarded the issue solely from the perspective of childbearing and thus as a woman's issue. Nobody has considered it from the point of view of begetting a child, that is, as a man's issue. Pronatalist propaganda, however, often addressed men in particular and, together with the actual policies, revealed a cult of fatherhood, not motherhood. Financial rewards, to cite a significant example, given to people who had children, were granted to fathers, not mothers. These were propaganda and policies of men for men.[8]

National Socialist pronatalism was the complement of National Socialist antinatalism. If procreation has incorrectly been seen exclusively as a woman's issue, then the prohibition of procreation has incorrectly been viewed as a man's issue. Men alone were not sterilized; women were too. The story of these female victims of antinatalism should be part of women's history, in keeping with the double goal of the field: "to restore women to history" and "to restore history to women."[9]

To summarize the significance of the Nazi sterilization policy, let us stress two points: First, compulsion, violence, terror, and murder—characteristics of National Socialism—are identifiable not in the pronatalist, but in the antinatalist policy of the regime. It was for the latter, not the former, that the Nazis established a huge and efficient state machine.[10] Second, antinatalism was the one original, consistently executed, and "successful" National Socialist policy for controlling procreation. National Socialism declared it a matter of the state, and it did so not by promoting births as much as by preventing them. It was not by chance that the official commentary and propaganda for the sterilization law proclaimed it as the enactment of "the supremacy of the state in the area of life and the family." Nor was it by chance that common parlance referred to sterilization as "the Hitler section," in contrast to the Caesarean which facilitates parturition.[11] National Socialist gender policies consisted not of pronatalism and a mother cult, but of antinatalism and a father cult.

Since women and men were sterilized in equal numbers, students of the period have concluded that the sexes were treated "equally" and that the sterilization policy was gender neutral. It was considered inappropriate to analyze the subject as part of women's history. At best, some agreed that there was a special "woman's problem" within the more general history of sterilization, a female variant of the issue. To accept this position, however, obscures important aspects of the sterilization policy, some of which will now be reviewed briefly.

There were obvious gender differences between the perpetrators and the victims of sterilization. While women comprised half the number of victims, the sterilization policy itself was invented, decided upon, and executed by men.

The hypothesis of "equal" treatment of the sexes reduces women's history to the issue of "equality" or "inequality" of numbers and assumes that by recording the statistics by sex it has adequately recognized the female half of the victims of the sterilization policy. But just as women's history differs from the history of men in important ways, the history and experiences of female sterilization victims are not the same as those of men. For example, the criteria used for selecting those to be sterilized, based largely on psychiatric evaluations, measured a woman's deviance from female gender norms and a man's deviance from male gender norms.[12] Since gender is culturally constructed and therefore a social category, the selection of individuals for sterilization was not "genetic" but social and cultural.

The notion of gender neutrality in the sterilization policy ignores the fact that childbearing and begetting a child are two clearly gender-specific social activities and that women and men are affected differently by at least three aspects of sterilization: the separation of sexuality from procreation, the imposition of childlessness, and the physical intervention necessary to sterilize the victim.

The separation of sexuality from procreation was the subject of intense discussion among important politicians between 1934 and 1936, and their debates made clear that the sterilization policy was a conscious sexual policy. Innumerable women who wanted "to have nothing to do with men" and had had no sexual intercourse were sterilized because—according to contemporary juridical notions— rape had to be taken into account as "a natural law of life" and the ensuing pregnancies had to be prevented beforehand. Thus, according to the commentaries, "a different evaluation of the danger of propagation is necessary for men and for women."[13] Many reports show that in reality involuntary and mass sterilization raised both the risk and the actual number of rapes of "inferior" women.

Childlessness means something different to women than it does to men. Since women without children are frequently identified with the positive gains of "emancipation" or "feminism," much of the research concerning with the misogyny of Nazism looked only at the policy of promoting procreation. But a woman's right to choose includes not only her right not to have children but her right to have them as well. While both male and female sterilization victims protested against their treatment, women, virtually alone, objected to being unable to bear children.

As for Nazi policies on abortion, they differed little from those that existed in Germany before 1933 and after 1945 or from those in other countries, for that matter. Indeed, contary to current views, the number of convictions for voluntary, that is illegal, abortions between 1933 and 1943 was 20 percent lower than it was between 1922 and 1932. Thus, the contemporary view that sees the National Socialist position on abortion as the distinguishing characteristic of its policy on procreation must be reevaluated. The anti-abortion law of Weimar Germany was actually suspended in 1935 in order to allow for abortions in those cases in which women were to be sterilized.[14] Under National Socialism, abortion was no longer prohibited but professionalized. Medical doctors, psychiatrists, judges, and antropologists decided on the medical, eugenic, and ethnic reasons for legalizing abortion. Pregnant "inferior" women could be not only sterilized, but also given an abortion.

The physical intervention necessary to sterilize men (vasectomy) and women (salpingectomy) is significantly different. The "unequal" operation, much more dramatic for women than for men, has not only involved an invasion of the female body, but has also threatened female life. Beginning in 1934, about 5,000 to 6,000 women (and about 600 men) were killed during the Nazi period as a result of sterilization. Most of them died because they resisted the operation and the struggle increased the risk of complications and death. For members of the female sex, the sterilization policy was therefore not merely a prelude to mass murder, but, given the numbers who died, it can be identified as the first stage. To the 5,000 to 6,000 we must also add the unknown, but considerable, number of suicides (mostly female) which occurred among sterilization victims.[15] This form of mass murder, implemented for the sake of the *Volkskörper*—the first of the Nazi mass murders—has been obscured until today because women's history within sterilization history has been overlooked.

It has been suggested that the sterilization policy is irrelevant to women's history in general because only 1 percent of the women in Germany of childbearing age (between fifteen and fifty) were actually sterilized. According to this argument, it would only have been important if all women or a majority of them had been sterilized. Such a perspective, however, disregards important characteristics of women's history. The history of the female sex differs from that of the male sex, but this does not mean that all women share an identical history. Not only those issues which affect all or most women are relevant, but also those which affect female minorities: women factory workers, prostitutes, and women historians, for example.[16] We can measure the general condition of a society, historians agree, by looking at the ways minorities are treated. By the same token, we can gain an understanding of the situation of women in general by studying the history of female minorities. Indeed, historians of National Socialism have considered it important to analyze the condition of those few women who lost their jobs in 1933 and of the 30,000 who were convicted for illegal abortions.

Yet no attempt has been made to analyze the situation of women under National Socialism by studying the 200,000 who were sterilized against their will. Similarly, nobody has drawn any conclusions about the condition of women by looking at such female minorities as the approximately 100,000 German Jewish women who were murdered; or the many millions of non-German women, Jewish and non-Jewish, who were also killed; of the over two million women among the forced laborers, mostly from the East, who lived and died in Germany during the Second World War. All of these groups had one thing in common: they were minorities not necessarily in statistical terms, but because of their "little value." National Socialism saw such minorities as a "threat" for the majority. To "solve" the majority's problems the

Nazis found a "solution," then a "final solution": eliminate these minorities.

In order to gain a fuller understanding of the Nazi policy toward women, it is essential to focus on the women of "inferior" minorities. While the procreation policy directed toward "valuable" women did not differ significantly from what was in place before 1933 and after 1945, it changed dramatically for women of "inferior" minorities. But since sterilization and other racist policies concerned "only" a minority, they encountered little resistance.[17] These policies, however, affected all women, for they gave a strong indication of the disregard National Socialism had for the female body. Furthermore, these policies demonstrated that the line between "inferior" and "valuable" women was not clear-cut. Few women could be sure they belonged to the "valuable" 30 percent or the "normal" 40 percent, to those whose children were welcome or acceptable. The sterilization law affected not only the 200,000 women who were actually sterilized, but the hundreds of thousands as well whose relatives, men and women, had been sterilized for "hereditary" defects. If your family had been touched, you too were vulnerable. Moreover, there were hundreds of thousands of others who had been scheduled for operations which were postponed during the war, but which were supposed to take place after the "final victory."

The numerical relationship between "inferior" and "valuable" groups was relative in still another sense. Himmler stated in 1943, when a continent of "inferiors" was about to be annexed: "The moment we begin to doubt our faith, our racial value itself, then Germany and the Germans are lost. Because the others are a majority in relation to us. We, however, are of greater value in relation to them."[18] By this time, the "war on childbearing" had entered a new phase and was directed especially against Jewish, Gypsy, and Slavic women, but it also continued against "inferior" women of "German blood."

Since National Socialist racism, like all other kinds of racism, was not limited to men, Nazi policies dealing with women should not be characterized as "secondary racism."[19] These policies were just as racist as were those enacted against men. Although, from the regime's point of view, Nazi racism had no specific "woman's policy" in the sense of a homogeneous gender policy, the laws enacted had the effect of determining a policy against women. The relationships between social categories and realities of gender and race, the intertwining of sexism and racism, have become an important field of research in the United States and must become equally as significant in Germany. Just as women should not merely be considered a "special problem" of "general" history, women of discriminated-against minorities should not merely be considered a "special problem" of women's history, particularly when we look at National Socialism. The fact that this regime subjected minority women to "special treatment"[20] makes it necessary to see them as central to the history of National Socialism as well as to the history of women.

As we try to understand the significance of the sterilization policy for women's history, we must pose new questions about National Socialist racism. Until now, those writing about racism in Germany have primarily focused on anti-Semitism. This has led some German scholars to argue that National Socialism "was not primarily 'racist,' but only anti-Semitic."[21] Recently, however, good work has begun to appear on Nazi racism in relation to Slavs, Gypsies, and blacks; even before the necessary connections between sterilization and euthanasia, and the assassination of the Jews have been made.[22] Comprehensive analyses of Nazi racism are rare and are usually limited to the history of ideas.[23] German scholars usually conceptualize racism as an "ideology" or "Weltanschauung." While one school of historians, therefore, sees German racism as a product of ideas, others doubt the historical validity of looking only at ideas and attempt to explain Nazi crimes by "real" social forces, such as the class struggle, economics, and politics (the right versus the left), or by political institutions which seem independent of racism.[24]

Racism is not merely an ideology, but a real and historically significant social force, a form of relations between ethnic or comparable socio-cultural groups, most often between minorities and a majority. It is a social relation, however, not in the sense that it can be reduced to class relations, professional categories, or political positions on a scale from right to left, but in the sense that it is an authentic and independent relation between human groups. (A similar perception of the "social" is necessary for a historically adequate understanding of sexism which is also a form of relations between two human groups that is reducible neither to ideology nor to traditional social and political categories.)

The sterilization policy was one of many manifestations of Nazi racism. It was directed against "deviating" or "undesirable" minorities: against "inferior" members of the ethnic majority as well as against members of such "inferior" ethnic minorities as Gypsies, Poles, blacks, and Jews. Beginning in 1933, Jews, to take the most dramatic example, were gradually excluded from the "people's community" *(Volksgemeinschaft)* and from the laws which governed that community, but they were included in the sterilization law. As "inferiors" they were subjected to the same laws as "inferior" non-Jews. Jews were only excluded from the sterilization law in 1942 when the "Final Solution," the program to bring about the complete annihilation of the Jews, made sterilization "superfluous."

Not all members of discriminated-against ethnic minorities were sterilized, nor were those sterilized among them selected exclusively because of their ethnicity. Still, Western Jews were considered more susceptible to "schizophrenia" than the average population, and Eastern Jews and Gypsies, to "feeble-mindedness." In 1941, a Jewish woman was sterilized "as a schizophrenic," not "as a Jew," and the reason given for the need to operate was that she had "depressions." Clearly she was being persecuted as a Jew. Since psychiatric explanations were given and since many Jews and Gypsies were not sterilized, apologists have concluded that the sterilization policy had nothing to do with racism.[25] Racism, however, does not necessarily affect all members of an ethnic minority in the same way, nor does it limit itself only to members of the marked group: the Nurenberg laws which prohibited sex and marriage between non-Jews and Jews is a case in point.

Racism involves not only discriminating against "alien" ethnic groups, but "improving" the quality of the racist's "own" ethnic group by means of discriminating against the "inferiors" from the ethnic majority. The "master race" (Herrenvolk) was not a given; it had to be created: "Initially, the racial doctrine of the Third Reich was concerned with the Germans: It was a tool which was supposed to model the German people."[26] Sterilization was to service that end.

According to National Socialism, in addition to the Jews and Gypsies, there was another cause for the "racial degeneration" of Germany: millions of non-Jewish and non-Gypsy "inferiors." All of these groups were considered to be "parasites" on the people. In other words, some groups threatened the German people from "within," others from "without."[27] Himmler praised the sterilization law in 1936 in this spirit with the following words: "The German people . . . have learned once again to look at the human body, to measure its worth or lack thereof, to cultivate the body given to us by God and the blood given to us by God for our race."[28] Together with the economic and political restrictions placed on the Jews, the sterilization policy would become the most important action of Nazi racism until 1939, when racism took on increasingly murderous forms.

Nazi sexism was not race neutral, and Nazi racism was not gender neutral. The cult of masculinity, characteristic of racist traditions, has frequently, if not systematically, been cited. Racism glorified a "masculine ideal type" and "the true Aryan [was] a Westerner of the male sex." National Socialism was a male movement (Goebbels) in a male state. Sexuality, blood, and violence were inseparably mixed in racist language and images. Jews perceived anti-Jewish racism as "sexual anti-Semitism."[29] Not only did the "Jew" supposedly exploit the "German" worker as "capitalist," "Marxist," or "trade-union boss," together with the "Negro," he was supposed to be a "rapist" of the "German" woman, a "pimp," one who "penetrates the body of the German people" and "slowly and persistently disseminates his seeds." German women who entered into relationships with Jewish men were considered "whores," and women's emancipation was presented as a "Jewish" product, especially of Jewish women.

The "final solution" of the "Jewish question," of the "Gypsy problem," and of the "race question" in general also contained a "solution to the woman question."[30] While traditional European wars had been battles of men among men, in the race war women also became immediate objects of male warfare. Himmler explained this change to his ss-men in 1943: "If I felt compelled to attack partisans and Jewish commissars in some village, I usually gave the command to have the wives and children killed as well. . . . Believe me, I did not give this command lightly. . . . But we must recognize more and more that we are engaged in a primitive, primordeal, natural race war."[31] Among the German Jewish victims of the Holocaust, the number of women was one-half higher than that of the men.[32] Also, more Gypsy women than Gypsy men were killed in Auschwitz.

National Socialist racism was a conscious program, formulated largely by the Ministry of the Interior, to "improve" the *Volkskörper* by regulating the relationship between the sexes. It led to the transformation of traditional patriarchal culture into a cult of masculinity which was unknown before. In 1937 Reichsminister Hans Frank spoke of the "concept of fatherhood originating in the eternal depths of the process of nature," and Hitler proclaimed in that same year: "*We* will regulate the relations between the sexes. *We* will form the child!"[33] National Socialism attempted to subjugate gender relations to male racism at the state level, and the sterilization law was one of the first measures institutionalized as part of this effort. Sexist in so far as it permitted the state to take over birth control, the sterilization policy was racist in that it distinguished between "valuable" and "worthless" births. This policy, therefore, was both a form of racism and sexism.

Notes

1. Arthur Gütt, Ernst Rüdin, Falk Ruttke, *Gesetz zur Verhütung erbkranken Nachwuchses vom 14. Juli 1933* (Munich: Lehmann, 1934 and 1936), 56–62

(further quotes: GRR). For the timing of the law see Karl Dietrich Bracher, *Stufen der Machtergreifung*, in idem, Wolfgang Sauer, Gerhard Schulz, *Die nationalsozialistische Machtergreifung* (Köln and Opladen: Westdeutscher Verlag, 2nd edition 1962), 144, 214, 284–86. For the following see, in my forementioned book, chs. 4.3 ("The quantitative Dimension") and 5 ("Zwang, Freiwilligkeit und Widerstand").

2. See especially the excellent work of Klaus Dörner, *Nationalsozialismus und Lebensvernichtung* (1967), reprinted in idem, *Diagnosen der Psychiatrie* (Frankfurt and New York: Campus, 1975).

3. See, e.g., Erwin Baur, Eugen Fischer, Fitz Lenz, *Menschliche Erblehre und Rassenhygiene*, vol. 2 (Munich: Lehmann, 3rd edition, 1931), 306; Erich Ristow, *Erbgesundheitsrecht* (Stuttgart, Berlin: Kohlhammer, 1935), 8f., 21, 38; documents in Alexander Mitscherlich and Fred Mielke, *Medizin ohne Menschlichkeit* (1948; reprinted Frankfurt: Fischer, 1978), 242f., 245; Raul Hilberg, *The Destruction of the European Jews* (Chicago: Quadrangle, 1961), 269ff., 315 Uwe Dietrich Adam, *Judenpolitik im Dritten Reich* (Düsseldorf: Athenäum/Droste, 1972), 321–23.

4. Leila J. Rupp, *Mobilizing Women for War. German and American Propaganda 1939–1945* (Princeton, N.J.: Princeton University Press, 1978), esp. chs. 1 and 4, p. 72.

5. Clifford Kirkpatrick, *Nazi Germany: Its Women and Family Life* (Indianapolis, New York: Bobbs-Merrill, 1938), 103 ("woman and mother should be synonymous terms"), 149 ("The call of National Socialism is distinct and clear . . . 'Be fruitful, multiply and replenish the earth with good Germans'"). He knew it better, though, presenting Nazi sterilization policy as "a solution of the unsolved and perhaps unsolvable woman's problem" (ch. 7). For the other quotes see Betty Friedan, *The Feminine Mystique* (New York: Dell, 1963), 32; Jill Stephenson, "Reichsbund der Kinderreichen: The League of Large Families in the Population Policy of Nazi Germany," in *European Studies Review* 9:3 (1979): 351–75, 369; Hans Peter Bleuel, *Das saubere Reich* (Bern, Munich, Vienna: Scherz, 1972), 196, cf. 197 ("Mutter können alle werden").

6. Walter Schultze, *Die Bedeutung der Rassenhygiene für Staat und Volk in Gegenwart und Zukunft*, in Ernst Rüdin, ed., *Erblehre und Rassenhygiene im völkischen Staat* (Munich: Lehmann, 1934), 8f., 14.

7. Partei-Archiv, November 1937, p. 19; Bundesarchiv Koblenz, NS 18/712; R 22/485.

8. See ch. 3 ("Pronatalismus: Frauenpolitik und Männerpolitik").

9. Joan Kelly-Gadol, "The Social Relation of the Sexes: Methodological Implications of Women's History," in *Signs* 1:4 (1976): 809; see also Gerda Lerner, *The Majority Finds Its Past: Placing Women in History* (New York, Oxford: Oxford University Press, 1979).

10. See ch. 4 ("Sterilisationsbehörden und Sterilisationsprozesse").

11. GRR 1934, p. 5; cf. chs. 2 ("Die Eroberung der Macht über das Private") and 7 ("Sterilisationspolitik als Frauenpolitik").

12. See chs. 6.1 ("Krankheit, Wert, Fortpflanzung") and 7.1 ("Geschlechter, Geschlechtlichkeit und Gewalt gegen Frauen").

13. GRR 1936, p. 121.

14. See chs. 2.2 ("Pronatalistische und antinatalistische Gesetzgebung"), 3.3 ("'Gebärzwang'? Generatives Verhalten und Abtreibung"), 7.1 ("Mutterschaft und Vaterschaft").

15. See ch. 7.1 ("Von der 'Fortpflanzungsauslese' zur 'Vernichtungsauslese'").

16. Cf. Kathryn Kish Sklar, "American Female Historians in Context, 1770–1930," in *Feminist Studies* 3:1–2 (1975): 171–84; Gisela Bock, "Prostituierte im Nazi-Staat," in Pieke Biermann, ed., *Wir sind Frauen wie andere auch* (Reinbek: Rowohlt, 1980), 70–106.

17. See ch. 5.3. ("Kritik und Widerstand von 'Nicht'-Betroffenen"); cf. Christof Dipper, "Der deutsche Widerstand und die Juden," in *Geschichte und Gesellschaft* 9 (1983); 349–80.

18. Bradley F. Smith and Agnes F. Peterson, eds., *Heinrich Himmler. Geheimreden 1933 bis 1945* (Frankfurt, Berlin, Vienna: Ullstein, 1974), 165; cf. ch. 7.2 ("Jüdische, zigeunerische, 'fremdvölkische' Frauen").

19. David Schoenbaum, *Hitler's Social Revolution* (New York: Doubleday Anchor Books, 1967), 178.

20. The nazi term *Sonderbehandlung* was both a euphemism for murder and a technical term for legalized discrimination of "special" groups; for Jewish women see Marion A. Kaplan, *The Jewish Feminist Movement in Germany* (Westport, Conn., London: Greenwood, 1979); idem, "Tradition and Transition. The Acculturation, Assimilation and Integration of Jews in Imperial Germany: A Gender Analysis," in *Year Book of the Leo Baeck Institute* 27 (1982); 3–35.

21. Hermann Arnold, *Die Zigeuner* (Olten: Walter, 1965), 66.

22. See, e.g., Dörner *Nationalsozialismus und Lebensvernichtung*, the literature on the Holocaust (n. 3); Ernst Klee, *"Euthanasie" im NS-Staat* (Frankfurt: Fischer, 1983), 367ff.; Reiner Pommerin, "The Fate of Mixed Blood Children in Germany," in *German Studies Review* 5:3 (1982): 315–23; Donald Kenrick, Grattan Puxon, *The Destiny of Europe's Gypsies* (London: Chatto-Heinemann-Sussex University Press, 1972).

23. See, e.g., George L. Mosse, *Rassismus* (Königstein: Athenäum, 1978; English ed.: New York, Howard Fertig, 1978); Léon Poliakov, *Der arische Mythos* (Vienna, Munich, Zürich: Europaverlag, 1977).

24. A classical example is Bertold Brecht's play "Die Rundköpfe und die Spitzköpfe" (working-class anti-semitism ascribed to Jews being capitalists); Andrea Brücks et al. "Sterilisation in Hamburg," in Universität Hamburg, ed., *1933 in Gesellschaft und Wissenschaft* (Hamburg: Universität Hamburg, 1984): 185, assume that "Rassenkampf = Klassenkampf"; Patrik von zur Mühlen, *Rassenideologien* (Berlin, Bonn, Bad Godesberg: Dietz, 1977), uses both procedures summarized.

25. E.g. Hans-Joachim Döring, *Die Zigeuner im nationalsozialistischen Staat* (Hamburg: Verlag für kriminalistische Fachliteratur, 1964), 178, argues that sterilization of gypsies was not racist because "a general compulsory sterilization, which was to be accomplished by a certain date, has not taken place".

26. B. W., *"Keine Rassenforschung mehr?"* in *Frankfurter Hefte* 1:17 (1946): 585.

27. "The German race question is mainly defined by the Jewish question. Less in view, but not less important, is the gypsy question. . . . Corrosive effects on people occur not only from without by alien races, but also from within by the uninhibited procreation of those of inferior heredity": Werner Feldscher (Ministry of the Interior), *Rassen- und Erbpflege im deutschen Recht* (Berlin, Leipzig, Vienna: Deutscher Rechtsverlag, 1943), 26, 118; cf. chs. 1.4 ("Anthropologischer Rassismus und eugenischer Rassismus") and 6 ("Sterilisationspolitik als Rassenpolitik").

28. Himmler, in Bradley and Smith, *Heinrich Himmler*, 54f.

29. This term was used in Comité des Délégations Juives, *Die Lage der Juden*

in Deutschland 1933 (Paris 1934; repr. Frankfurt, Berlin, Vienna: Ullstein, 1983), 468; the other quotes: Mosse, *Rassismus,* 103; Poliakov, *Der arische Mythos,* 317; Joseph Goebbels, in Walther Gehl, ed., *Der nationalsozialistische Staat,* vol. 2 (Breslau: Hirt, 1935), 155f.

30. As proposed, e.g., by the Minister of the Interior Wilhelm Frick, *Bevölkerungs- und Rassenpolitik* (Berlin: Reichsausschuss für Volksgesundheitsdienst, 1933): a famous speech announcing, among others, the sterilization law; cf. ch. 7.3 ("Die 'Lösung der Frauenfrage'").

31. Himmler, in Bradley and Smith, *Rassismus,* 201. For the Second World War as a "race war" see Andreas Hillgruber, Die "'Endlösung' und das deutsche Ostimperium als Kernstück des rassenideologischen Programms des Nationalsozialismus," in *Vierteljahreshefte für Zeitgeschichte* 20 (1972): 133–55.

32. In 1941 men constituted forty percent and women sixty percent of a total of 167, 245 Jews. Cf. Monika Richarz, *Judisches Leben im Deutschland,* Volume 3 (Stuttgart: Deutsche Verlagsanstalt, 1982), p. 61.

33. Frank, in Bundesarchiv Koblenz, R 61/130; Hitler, in Max Domarus, *Hitler. Reden und Proklamationen 1932–1945,* vol. 2 (Munich: 1965), 762; cf. ch. 2.3 ("Sterilisationsgesetz, Rassismus und nationalsozialistische Herrschaft") and 2.4 ("Männerstaatlicher Rassismus und weibliches Geschlecht").

CONVERGENCIES AND TENSIONS BETWEEN COLLECTIVE IDENTITY AND SOCIAL CITIZENSHIP RIGHTS

ITALIAN WOMEN IN THE SEVENTIES

Yasmine Ergas

Citizenship and Collective Identity: Convergence or Tension?

Examining contemporary citizenship rights, T. H. Marshall focused on the paradox of societies which maintain in operation two apparently contradictory principles of organization: equality (of status) and inequality (of social class).[1] Modern history—Marshall concluded—shows that "citizenship has itself become, in certain respects, the architect of legitimate social inequality,"[2] although he also thought conflict between the two principles increasingly likely. Twenty years after the publication of *Sociology at the Crossroads,* the monetarist renaissance and welfare cuts confirm Marshall's clairvoyant doubts regarding the persistent compatibility of market mechanisms and social rights. Even before the fiscal crisis undermined the ever-precarious equilibrium between state-guaranteed equality and economically generated differentiation, however, the "new movements" of the past two decades had raised another problem concerning the equalizing effects of citizenship: Why do societies within which common, ascriptive status is increasingly important systematically produce mobilizations predicated on specific collective identities that cut across the traditional divisions of class and yet appear to refuse assimilation into the general unifying category of the *citoyenneté?*

Discussing the emergence of those post-1968 movements which generated conflicts located outside the labor market, authors such as Touraine, Pizzorno, Habermas, and Offe—to name only a few of the most significant—have stressed the importance of themes linked to *identity*. In Claus Offe's analysis, for example, the emerging new paradigm of political action is seen as discarding parties and choosing movements while also essentially neglecting traditional issues such as those concerning distribution, security, and representation in favor of autonomy. Gays and feminists, ecologists and city dwellers thus seek "to establish a sphere of freedom, that is safely protected from the reach of both the market and political authority. In contrast to earlier social movements, the freedom that is demanded is not the freedom of individuals, but that of collectivities sharing a notion of identity."[3]

The "new movements," therefore, tend to highlight social differentiations that are independent of the market's workings. While politicizing largely ascriptive and life-style-based distinctions, the same movements have also led to an increase in institutionally secured rights, especially those pertaining to social well-being. The public policies they have fostered, throughout Europe and in the United States, have enriched the meaning of citizenship, enhancing the egalitarian connotations of the status associated to partaking in a common national identity.

Thus, the "new movements" have affirmed difference while promoting similarity; they have implicitly sought a "minimal state," whose function could be reduced to that of an external guarantor of freedom, and actually engendered a maximum expansion of public institutions. It remains to be understood how these peculiar and complex "perverse effects" of recent social movements came about. Yet, in order to do so, another problem must first be faced: To what extent have the principles of citizenship and identity functioned as mutually reinforcing; and to what extent, on the contrary, have they activated conflicting forces and trends?

This is the question which I will address in the following pages with reference to women in contemporary Italy. Two aspects of the interrelationship between citizenship and collective identity will be examined: first, the ways in which the development of citizenship has itself raised the problem of, and provided the institutional bases for, the political mobilization of women as a specific collective identity; and, second, the paths whereby once the emergence of a specific collective identity had led to an expansion and enlargement of citizenship, citizenship itself has favored or hindered the political viability of women as a specific collective identity.

Women's Proper Role in a "Democratic Republic Founded on Labor"

Like many of their Western counterparts over the past two decades, Italian feminists have focused on a wide variety of themes from women's sexuality to their position in the labor market. Notwithstanding the range of topics, one essential problem has persistently seemed to underly the questions which have captivated activists: Who/what is a woman? Feminism thus still dwells on the same problem Virginia Woolf raised in 1928 when she wrote, " 'I' is only a convenient term for someone who has no real being"[4] and Simone de Beauvoir took as the point of departure for her classic enquiry, *The Second Sex:*

> If her functioning as a female is not enough to define women, if we decline also to explain her through "the eternal feminine," and if nevertheless we admit, provisionally, that women do exist, then we must face the question: what is a woman?[5]

Although ontological queries permeate contemporary feminist thought and existential angst haunts many women, in actual fact, something very similar to a feminine identity must exist for the question to have been voiced. The problem—it seems worth stressing—is not couched in terms of the Hamletian dilemma. Rather, feminists have asked, given that one is, what is one? By phrasing its basic motive in this way, the feminism which developed in the sixties and seventies in Italy and in other western European countries, set its sights beyond the theoretical horizon delineated by the concept of discrimination which has guided traditionally emancipatory women's movements. Emancipation—the end of discrimination—implies the attainment of rights as these are already defined in a society. In contrast, the culture of liberation, as many ethnic and nationalist movements had remarked before the resurgence of feminism, seeks both a qualitative redefinition of these rights and the specific right to nonassimilation, to maintain distinct ways of being without having therefore to pay the price of subordinate social status.

For similar problems to be raised at all, a female subject must exist. I certainly cannot take it upon myself to reply to the definitional questions which several generations of feminists have left unanswered. Instead, I propose to examine cursorily the role played by postwar Italian state policies in constructing and molding the collective identity of contemporary Italian women. I will argue that, in twentieth-century Italy, the state has played a key role both in shaping a female political subject and in laying the bases for the quandries concerning women's identity which have permeated feminist debate.

State policies have reflected the biases and uncertainties of general discourses on women. The history of Western thought, as has often been remarked, is replete with disquisitions on the second sex that have crystallized femininity in a condition of otherness hardly conducive to collective action.[6] But in the modern world, as the private realm has become increasingly public and, more specifically, as sexuality has increasingly become an objective of collective speech and intervention;[7] as the family has acquired a "modern" shape; and as reproductive roles have become ever more visible, important, and specialized, the foundations have been placed for women to acquire a specific, positive relevance of their own.

The passage from devaluation to recognition has, of course, been uneven and subject to oscillations and variations dependent on the historical contexts in which it has occurred. In Italy, recognition itself has been played out in constant tension between two poles: the value of woman-as-mother and the value of woman-as-worker. The first identity has dominated political discourse and has been described as a natural, positive attribute of femininity. The second has been posited as an acquired right. Neither natural nor essential, it represents a concession which the polity has on occasion granted women rather than the recognition of an inherently positive quality pertaining to them as social beings.

The significance of this duality extends beyond the specific question of women's intrinsic or conquered claims to worthiness. As the (paradoxically) prolific madonnas dear to Catholic doctrine, the fascist regime, the Christian Democratic Party, and to deeply engrained leftwing traditions, Italian women have been extolled for their mothering capacities. This particular mode of validating womanhood has left its mark in almost a century of protective legislation that has formally granted the working mother more safeguards of her reproductive activities than is common in most of western Europe.

The political theory implicit in this mode of validation has fittingly found its empirical counterpart in women's weak position in the "official economy" and in the stronger segments of the labor market, favored by protective legislation which has been unaccompanied by affirmative action. Moreover, focusing policies toward women on motherhood has meant implicitly theoretically anchoring women's worth to their generative and caretaking abilities. Their marginal position in the labor market thus provides a metaphor of their place in a culture which sees in them those who create the conditions of, and contextualize, a setting they do not animate.

As a mode of validation, "woman-as-worker," on the contrary, places women "in the heart of the action." Italy is—the postwar Constitution emphatically states—"a democratic Republic founded on labour": a dictate which unequivocally grants the laborer a privileged position in the country's "moral economy" and a special right to citizenship. Thus the recognition which has occasionally been granted to women, in recent decades, of their right to be laborers has denoted a willingness to incorporate them fully into the *citoyenneté*.[8]

The flaw—from women's point of view—is that this mode of validation obscures the importance of ways of being (histories; cultures; in general, identities) which cannot simply be reduced to that of "the worker." In other words, although recognizing that women constitute an integral part of the society's "productive forces" may ensure that they are granted the status of actors, it postulates a process of assimilation to the dominant male model which—at least in theory—obfuscates the relevance of all that is specific to the female experience.[9]

A rapid survey of some of the major postwar policies toward women can illustrate the ways in which this bipolar process of validation, based on the alternative between specificity and marginality on one side, and integration and assimilation on the other, has been operationalized.

After two decades of authoritarian management, in the Constitutional Assembly the "woman's question" once again became a topic of political debate and negotiation, leading to the granting of suffrage, constitutionally guaranteed equality, and the protection of reproductive rights. The discussion which occurred in the Assembly emblematically expresses the paradigm within which women's rights were defined. The third article of the Constitution declares that all Italian citizens are equal and that the state must remove all impediments to the attainment of effective equality. The thirty-seventh article of the Constitution states that "the working woman has the same rights and, for equal work, the same retribution as the working man. Working conditions must allow her to fulfill her essential family functions and must guarantee mother and child special, adequate protection." This article of the Constitution—on which a great deal of the subsequent legislation concerning women has been based—expresses the compromise reached between Catholic and nonclerical forces after a long debate centered around two questions: the meaning of equal work and the "essential" quality of women's familial roles.[10] Initially, the Christian Democrats had requested that an explanatory clause be added to the phrase *equal work,* specifying that it signified "equal productivity." The Christian Democrats themselves, however, subsequently withdrew this request, arguing that "'equal productivity' is

implicitly understood in the concept of 'equal work'."[11] Since it was
also implicitly understood that women do not produce as much or as
well as men, this interpretation of the Constitution was to ensure the
survival of legally accepted salary differentials which contradicted the
principle of equal pay. As for women's "essential family functions" the
Christian Democrats refused to delete this statement of principle; but
the left accepted it, and not only as an unavoidable tribute to be paid
for the unity of the major antifascist forces. That the left had no
intention of revolutionizing relations within the family was still evident long after the new Constitution had been approved.[12] The new
Republic granted women unprecedented recognition and political
rights, but it also immediately postulated the identity between femininity and maternity which was to dominate and orient the definition
of their social rights. Coherently, the "Republic founded on labor"
approved progressive legislation protecting the reproductive rights of
working mothers in 1950, while the ILO principle establishing equal
pay—approved by the international organization the following year—
was not ratified by the Italian government until 1956 and did not
become operative until 1960.

This emphasis on women's reproductive roles has been considered
emblematic of a "compromise against women," tacitly agreed to after
the war by all the main political forces.[13] Although such a compromise may well be discernible in the public policies of the postwar
period, in actual fact protectionism had strong female support.[14] The
compromise provided the legal basis for the socioeconomic model of
the subsequent two decades, which—as has been repeatedly demonstrated—relied heavily on women's roles as homemakers to compensate for the lack of public services,[15] and it was not until the end of the
decade and the early sixties that the "woman's question" once again
became the object of political attention.

From the first law regulating work done in the home (*lavoro a
domicilio*) approved by Parliament in 1958 to that which, in 1964,
established that only "just causes" could motivate layoffs, innovative
legislation profoundly modified women's legal status. In this period,
for example, layoffs due to employees' marriages were rendered
illegal (1962); housewives secured pension rights (1963); and sexual
limitations regulating access to careers in public employment were
abolished (1963). The concession of pension rights to housewives
offered political support to mothering roles; but, in effect, the acceptance of equal pay had heralded a period in which egalitarian state
policies essentially centered on women's position in the labor market.

A second period of relative "silence" followed the reforms of the
sixties; then, in the seventies a literal onslaught of new policies and

legislation radically altered women's status in the family, in the labor force, and in the polity. Women's status and roles in the family were affected by a series of measures: laws extending and reinforcing the protection of reproductive rights (in particular, of maternity leave); the legalization of divorce and the reform of the family code (which has been considered one of the most advanced in western Europe); the organization of "family centers" which specifically tender to women's reproductive health; the legalization of abortion; and the institution of public child-care services. Over the same period, laws protecting women in the "irregular economy" (in particular, those performing piecework in their own homes), granting special incentives to employers hiring women under a scheme devised to alleviate youth unemployment, and banning sex-based discrimination in the labor force were enacted. Furthermore, a special undersecretariat for women was instituted in the Ministry of Labour and most regional governments set up women's advocacy bodies *(consulte femminili)* to ensure women's interests specific political representation.

As a consequence of these measures, women's general condition has—on the books, at least—changed very significantly over the past decade. Although no affirmative action has been implemented,[16] their formal right to equal participation in the labor force has been codified. At the same time, the state has extended the realm of collective responsibility into reproductive spheres once entirely delegated to the family and, specifically, to women. Finally, a bill recently formulated by the government (and now pending parliamentary approval) has—for the first time in Italian history—incorporated women into the nation's defense system, permitting them to enlist in special, voluntary corps of the armed forces.

A close look at many of these measures shows that, to a significant extent, they legalize and promote women's ability to control their reproductive capacities and alleviate some of their responsibilities as mothers. This is fitting with the modern welfare-state definition of mothering roles, which is far more oriented toward making women into the administrators and household managers of a complex set of resources (public and private) that must be gathered and reorganized so as to meet the specific needs of individual families,[17] rather than promoting rapid demographic growth. At the same time, this redefinition of female familial roles makes place for the integration of women into the labor force, also the objective of many policies of the seventies.

Notwithstanding the varying features which characterize the legislative measures adopted in each period considered, the decisions taken have mainly pointed in two directions. On the one hand, they have tended to reinforce and provide social support for women's domestic roles; on the other, they have purported to favor sexual equality in the labor market. Since the war, moreover, other equally important public policies have tended to promote equality while grouping women in specific arenas evocative of their domestic-maternal vocation. Throughout the fifties and sixties, the remarkable expansion of schooling was accompanied by a rapid increase in female enrollments. Although women's presence in the upper echelons still tends to be lower than that of men, their access to educational institutions has attained hitherto unprecedented dimensions. Yet, until recently, such access to traditionally male reserves was accompanied by massive channeling of women into effectively sexually segregated schools. At a secondary-school level, large numbers of girls enrolled in "women's professional institutes" which taught future seamstresses or household managers; in teacher-training schools; and, in commercial-technical institutes designed to prepare the labor force of the service sector: essentially, shopgirls and secretaries. University streaming followed similar patterns: while men still dominate the scientific, technical, and more generally, professional faculties from law to engineering, letters, and the arts have become female pastures.

The growth of the service sector and, within it, that of public administration agencies has both favored women's access to paid employment and concentrated them in particular segments of the labor force. Thanks largely to government posts, massive numbers of women today are clerical workers, teachers, nurses, and social workers. Furthermore, the expansion of the Italian welfare system has not only generated female employment; it has also transformed increasing numbers of women into state clients. Although formally public services generally address a sexually undifferentiated audience, they in fact activate a female constituency. As mothers of school-age children or as caretakers of the aged and the sick, women both enter into contact with, and meet each other in, the premises of the welfare state.

While social policies have grouped women in specific institutional contexts (education, public employment, welfare agencies), by reiterating the peculiarities of women's problems—the complexity of conciliating dual roles, the tenacity of sex-based discrimination, the persistence of male privilege in the family—and by tacitly acknowledging women's demands invoking positive state intervention, postwar legislation has implicitly stressed and legitimized the existence of specific female interests. Even though such recognition has tended to reduce women to either one or the other of two identities, that of the mother or that of the worker, the compounded effect of legislative measures and social policies has been to support and mold a specific female collective identity.

Women's Political Citizenship: Is Voting Enough?

In the postwar period, state policies furthered rights which, at particular times, provided the institutional bases supporting the political activation of a specifically female collective identity. Moreover, the existence and strength of those autonomous movements for which citizenship often helped lay the foundations frequently proved essential in securing Italian women new gains. Although women obtained the vote in 1946, their interaction with the polity has therefore been marked by discontinuities which do not simply descend only from their exercise of electoral strength.

Since the war, women's problems have entered into political discourse and generated new policies primarily in three periods: between the fall of the regime and 1950, at the beginning of the sixties, and in the seventies. Moments of political upheaval have, therefore, been beneficial to women, for their gains have been concentrated, first, when the entire political order was being redefined; then, when the crisis of *centrismo* and the first center-left governments signaled the closure of the arrangements which had dominated the fifties; and, finally, when mass mobilizations in all sectors of society both announced and imposed the disruption of preceding political agreements. These same periods also witnessed peak moments in women's postwar mobilizations. Thus, during the Resistance and in the period immediately following the fall of the fascist regime, women had mobilized in large numbers, thereby once more acquiring, after the fascist interlude, a relatively high degree of political visibility. Then, in the early fifties, their relevance declined and their associations lost much of their organizational autonomy. In particular, the UDI—the main organization of women, linked to the left-wing parties—was increasingly suffocated and essentially transformed into a device for conveying the parties' (in particular, the PCI's) strategy. After 1956, however, with the crisis of the Stalinist model of the party and the loosening of party control over its collateral associations, UDI regained some of its autonomy: much of the legislation of the early sixties came in response to the *nouvelle vague* of women's agitation. Once more, in the seventies, the emergence of a forceful feminist movement led to legislations and social policies designed to remedy some of the greatest imbalances in the relationships between the sexes.

Yet notwithstanding the fact that equality still has not been attained and that, therefore, at each point in time women could posit new objectives, the existence of autonomous women's movements has been subject to oscillations and their political presence marked by brusque interruptions. To a certain extent, the precariousness of women's movements may be explained with reference to their dependency on other actors' political mobilizations and, generally, on the conditions of the political system which allow them access both to resources and exchange. It may also, however, be the direct consequence of the way in which women's demands have been interpreted, mediated, and translated into policy decisions by the policy. The policies established in the seventies concerning three key problems—abortion, women, and family centers—will therefore be briefly examined to determine their effects on the feminist movement as a political actor.

Between 1974 and 1976, the campaign for the liberalization of abortion became the focal point of feminist initiative and brought the movement decidedly into the political market. Mobilizing around the slogan "free and assisted abortions" (aborto libero, gratuito ed assistito), the feminist movement gained unprecedented political visibility, and its capacity to affect decision making within the spheres of conventional politics increased noticeably. Thus, for example, the Italian Communist Party was forced to revise, under the pressure of mounting female protest, its first, highly restrictive proposal concerning the legalization of abortion. And, in the Socialist Party, the polemic between the supporters of completely free abortion and the party leadership created significant internal problems.

Through the campaign for abortion, the feminist movement emerged as the primary organizer and political representative of women's political demands. That this particular issue should have acquired such relevance is largely due to the plurality of meanings interwoven into the campaign itself.[18] First, the campaign constituted a crucial moment in the "construction" of the movement.

Adopting a combination of tactics based on direct action, feminist militants instituted organizational centers which both performed illegal abortions and organized group expeditions to legal abortion clinics in the United Kingdom. These initiatives gave rise to recruitment which extended into social groups previously untouched by feminism's early development. Moreover, by actually solving the problem of undesired pregnancies for large numbers of women in all social brackets, the feminist movement extended its area of support. Finally, by establishing coordinating centers in all major cities to deal with the plurality of initiatives undertaken, the movement developed a structural format based on the delegation of representation which increased its credibility as a potential negotiating partner on the political market.[19]

Abortion as an issue also expressed symbolic demands. On the surface, the request for free abortion concerned an obvious material need, easily verified by statistical data concerning the diffusion of illegal operations. On a deeper level, however, by touching on an element common to all women—their scarce control over their own reproductive powers—abortion favored women's identification as a particular, homogeneous, and discriminated category. Abortion cut across class divisions and age groups, uniting women. Moreover, by claiming the right to choose maternity freely, women implicitly called for a more general right to self-determination, in effect, challenging their subordinate status in the social and political order. The campaign for abortion can therefore be seen as synthesizing the emergence of a new female collective identity.[20]

The new law, approved in 1978, greatly liberalized the provision of abortion. While therefore responding positively to the concrete issue raised by the preceding mobilization, it nonetheless generated a series of negative consequences for the feminist movement as the bearer of new values and as an organized political actor. From the point of view of the values implicitly contained in the feminist campaign, the law expressed a substantially hostile stance. The right to abortion is limited to specific cases and subjected to medical authorization. Moreover, the approval of the "presumed father of the conceived" is solicited. At the same time, the final decision is left to the individual woman, for she is allowed to disregard negative evaluations by medical personnel (except when abortion may cause serious physical injury), to exclude her partner from decision making, and to invoke a loosely phrased clause legitimizing "social circumstances" as reasons for interrupting pregnancy. The net outcome of this paradoxical formulation of the law is that women are granted the right to self-determination in practice but denied it formally. Other symbolic meanings embedded in the campaign were also negated by the law, which disarticulates women's unity by attributing rights and constructing procedures differently according to age, length of pregnancy, and urgency of the abortion required. Thus, the new legislation conceded material benefits but withheld symbolic recognition and effectively reduced abortion to a particular problem requiring the provision of health services.

Once the approval of the new legislation had settled abortion as a matter of relevance to national politics, the problem of implementation remained a concern of the feminist movement. However, the implementation of the law severely undermined service institutions around which the movement had grown. As the initiatives based on direct action collapsed, the movement lost both centers of recruitment and organization and legitimating functions. Moreover, when the delivery of abortion services became the responsibility of public health institutions (and of specially authorized private clinics), tensions once concentrated around centers of national government were dispersed, obliging the movement to comply with a microterritorial articulation of conflict which undercut both its mobilizing capacities and its political visibility. Finally, with the start of implementation, personnel involved in professional capacities acquired new political relevance. Abortion became an issue within the medical profession, a point of demarcation between conservatives and progressives. As the loci of conflict changed, so, too, did the relevant political actors.

In 1975, Parliament approved a law instituting "family centers." The law set the guidelines within which each region was then to formulate its own policy. These family centers had been fostered by the women's centers planned (and in some cities effectively established) by the feminist movement. The redefinition of the issue at hand—from "women's" to "family" centers—was confirmed by the regions' identifications of their new policies' clientele. Women virtually disappeared as a specific category, giving way, instead, to "the individual," "the couple," "the family," and "the community." Thus, as was to be repeated by the law on abortion, the family centers, though ostensibly responding positively to a need highlighted by feminist mobilization, denied the values embedded in the latter and circumscribed the problem being dealt with to a question of services.

Because they encompassed the specific functions performed by the women's centers, the new public institutions made feminist forms of organization outdated. Again, as in the case of abortion, the extension of the services of state agencies led to the crisis of centers whose organizational and legitimating functions had played a significant part in the construction of the feminist movement.

While provoking the dismantling of movement institutions, the establishment of family centers also limited the movement's ability to affect the services delivered. As Parliament had delegated authority to the regional governments, the latter also attributed key decision-making roles to a multiplicity of actors: town governments, intermediate state agencies, governing boards of individual centers, and professionals employed within the centers themselves. Multiplying the number of negotiating partners and fragmenting implementation into separate—and fairly discrete—processes controlled by different actors, this continuous interagency delegation of authority and resources complicated the paths which the feminist movement (or other collective actors) would have to follow in order to influence the quality of the services being delivered. Thus, the state agencies' "insulation" with respect to organized feminist pressure increased as the movement's political effectiveness declined.

Beginning in 1976, regional and municipal governments established new centers for the advocacy of women's rights. By creating these ad hoc bodies within the institutional framework, local governments cast doubt upon the feminist movement's effective representativeness. Once again, feminism appeared as a particular strand of women's politics, losing the status it had previously acquired as the most visible—and most meaningful—spokesman of women's political demands.

As women's representation was reintegrated into formal political institutions, the statutes governing the new centers regulated access in ways which undermined the influence of feminism, compared to other components of the women's movement and to traditional social and political actors. Moreover, they preventively defined (albeit in very loose terms) the range of issues which could be examined and the rules through which negotiation should proceed. On the whole, the *consulte femminili* reduced the significance of feminism as a political actor while also limiting its access to, and possibilities of exchange within, the political market.

The crises which affected the feminist movement in the final years of the seventies—the dismantling of many of its primary organizational structures (consciousness-raising groups, collectives, coordinating committees); the accentuation of its orientation toward cultural and microsocial objectives, with only sporadic forays into the broader political realm—can thus be traced back both to the general effects of the transformation registered by the political system since 1976[21] and to the specific impact of the new public policies generated in response to the feminist movement on the movement itself. The latter, in short, delegitimized it as the primary spokesman of women's interests, negated the value of some of its most important symbolic requests, demobilized some of its key institutions, and introduced new "filters" hindering its access to the political market.

Destructuring of the feminist movement—followed by a significant decline in women's political presence—thus accompanied the increase of social rights attained in the seventies. The recent vicissitudes of Italian feminism might therefore seem to confirm Tocqueville's forebodings about the leveling and homogenizing consequences of democracy: equality effaces identity; citizenship and specificity inevitably collide. Yet a similar conclusion would, indeed, be shortsighted, for although women once again appear far removed from the political sphere, a myriad of feminist initiatives have, in recent years, denoted the persistence of a collective identity which may have been eroded by interaction with the state but is certainly not extinct.

Notes

1. T. H. Marshall, *Sociology at the Crossroad* (London: Heinemann, 1963).
2. Ibid.
3. C. Offe, "The emerging coexistence of two paradigms of the political," *Mimeo* (1980): 14.
4. V. Woolf, *A Room of One's Own* (Harmondsworth, 1974), 6.
5. S. de Beauvoir, *The Second Sex*, trans. and ed. by H. M. Parshley (New York: Bantam Books, 1961).
6. For an excellent, recent analysis of women in Western political thought, cf. J. Bethke Elshtain, *Public Man, Private Woman: Women in Social and Political Thought* (Princeton: Princeton University Press, 1981).
7. Cf. M. Foucault, *Histoire de la Sexualité*, vol. 1: *La Volonté de Savoir* (Paris: Gallimard, 1976).
8. Cf. T. Treu, *Lavoro femminile e uguaglianza* (Bari: De Donato, 1977), and M. V. Balestrero, *Dalla tutela alla parità* (Bologna: Il Mulino, 1979).
9. Cf. U. Prokop, *Realtà e desiderio: l'ambivalenza femminile* (Milan: Feltrinelli), and J. Bethke Elshtain, *Telos* (1981).
10. Cf. T. Treu, *Lavoro femminile*, and M. V. Balestrero, *Dalla tutela*.
11. Cf. M. V. Balestrero, *Dalla tutela*, 116.
12. For example, in 1978 the Communist deputy G. Berlinguer insisted that any new legislation concerning abortion should grant the "father of the conceived" a role in the relevant decision-making process.
13. Cf. A. de Perini, "Alcune ipotesi sul rapporto tra le donne e le organizzazioni storiche del movimento operaio," in F. Bimbi, ed., *Dentro lo specchio* (Minal: Mazzotta, 1977), 236–80.
14. Cf. M. V. Balestrero, *Dalla tutela*, 109–128.
15. Cf. L. Balbo, *Stato di famiglia* (Milan: Etas Libri, 1976).
16. The law on youth unemployment (no. 285) contained specific incentives for employers hiring women; however, the law itself has not proved very effective and the special provisions concerning women have been particularly ineffective.
17. Cf. L. Balbo, "Crazy Quilts: Rethinking the welfare state debate from a women's perspective," *Mimeo* (1981).
18. Cf. Y. Ergas, "1968–79, Feminism and the Italian Party System," *Comparative Politics* 14:2.
19. On the conditions which affect a political actor's credibility in the political market, cf. A. Pizzorno, "Scambio politico e identità collettiva," C. Crouch and A. Pizzorno, eds., *Conflitti in Europa* (Milan: Etas Libri, 1977), 407–433.
20. On the concept of *collective identity* as used in this context, cf. A. Pizzorno, *Conflitti in Europa*, and "Le due logiche dell'azione di classe" in *I soggetti del pluralismo* (Bologna: Il Mulino, 1980), 257–96.
21. Cf. Y. Ergas, "1968–79"; S. Tarrows and L. Graziano, eds., *La Crisi*

italiana (Turin: Einaudi, 1979); P. Lange and S. Tarrows, ed., *Italy in transition, West European Politics* 2:3 (1979); A. Martinelli and G. Pasquino, *La politica nell'Italia che cambia* (Milan: Feltrinelli, 1978); M. Fedele, *Classi e partiti negli anni 70* (Rome: Editori Riuniti, 1979); and C. Donolo, *Mutamento o transizione?* (Bologna: Il Mulino, 1977).

Political Theory:
Socialist Feminism, a Critique
from Within

In this section we present a series of papers rich in detail on a broad range of topics: from the shirtwaist workers' strike in New York in 1909 to the French press's coverage of Alexandra Kollontai in the 1920s; from the activities of American socialist feminists to those of French "bourgeois" feminists, to the importance of the Napoleonic Code, Natural Law, and socialism in feminist thought. Despite the variety, an important theme runs through these papers. Each author touches on the late nineteenth- and early twentieth-century debates in France, the United States, and the Soviet Union among socialist and other progressive feminists about whether women should fight for their rights in capitalist society or delay feminist programs and devote themselves first to the socialist revolutionary struggle. As Geneviève Fraisse points out, feminism and socialism emerged in Europe at pretty much the same time. Both movements sought ways to improve the conditions of social groups; both challenged a system that discriminated against women and the laboring classes. Many of the early feminists in Europe and the United States were socialists: Hélène Brions, Marguerite Martin, Madeleine Alletier, Crystal Eastman, Theresa Malkiel, Alexandra Kollontai. Many of them did not believe that one should have to make a choice between feminist and socialist causes. However, as the Socialist Party gained legitimacy in France and the Communist Party took over in the Soviet Union, the leaders marginalized women's issues and encouraged female party members to dissociate themselves from the demands of "bourgeois" feminism.

Only the problems of women at the work place continued to be seen as a party issue, and even this, Françoise Picq observes, led to conflicts of interest. In 1913, for example, the Women's Socialist Group of the French Socialist Party voted not to support Emma Couriau in the famous case of the female typographer who tried to join an all-male union in Lyons. While these socialist women were unwilling to break ranks with the party, "bourgeois" progressive feminists, who for years already had been defending working women, enthusiastically embraced Couriau's cause. Even in the United States, where the Socialist Party played a dominant role in the struggle to unionize women, Françoise Basch recalls how the socialist journalist Theresa Malkiel complained about the Socialist Party's neglect of immigrant women laborers.

The example of Alexandra Kollontai, discussed by Blanche Wiesen Cook and Christine Fauré, is a particularly disappointing chapter in the history of feminism within socialism. Blanche Wiesen Cook compares Kollontai's early contempt for "bourgeois" feminism with the attitude of the American socialist-feminist Crystal Eastman, whose primary alliance was with feminists across class lines. Despite Kollontai's party loyalty, she was isolated and eventually exiled. As a diplomat she spent most of her public life away from the Soviet society she helped to create. In her later years, her work long banned at home, Kollontai found herself surrounded and sustained by the liberal feminists she had earlier dismissed. Tying together the themes of the past with those of the present, Christine Fauré reminds us that dissident voices on the left today, within the women's movement and elsewhere, those people who are crying out against totalitarianism in all forms, are the ones who have brought back from obscurity Kollontai's revolutionary ideas about free love and reproductive rights.

The authors in this section, like the vast majority of the other contributors to this volume, identify with the contemporary feminist left. They came to the women's movement through socialism, after having struggled in the 1960s with the male-dominated left and/or peace movements in their countries, much in the way that many of the women they write about did earlier this century. Conscious of the tensions that still exist between two ideologies which they believe should be compatible, Geneviève Fraisse and Françoise Picq expose the problems and contradictions that continue to plague us today. Geneviève Fraisse looks for the philosophical foundations of feminist thought in France and locates them on all sides of the political spectrum: from Enlightenment philosophy and the French Revolution, through utopian socialism, to marxism. Françoise Picq analyzes the development of the concept of bourgeois feminism, a concept largely invented by women members of the Socialist Party who found themselves in competition with nonsocialist progressive feminists for the loyalty of working-class women. Feminism, they both argue, has borrowed ideas from the left, but it has also made use of democratic traditions to demand rights for women. Interestingly enough, it is among members of the American Socialist Party at the turn of the century that Françoise Basch and Blanche Wiesen Cook draw the most optimistic picture of the union of socialist and feminist ideals. Theresa Malkiel and Crystal Eastman understood the universal nature of real change and sought to make wide-ranging alliances in order to gain effective support for their goals.

NATURAL LAW AND THE ORIGINS OF NINETEENTH-CENTURY FEMINIST THOUGHT IN FRANCE

Geneviève Fraisse

Translated by Nancy Festinger

Charles Fourier usually receives credit for introducing the term *feminism* into the French language. Associated with his name, feminism has been linked to socialism as well. Although Fourier had very radical ideas about the emancipation of women, he never actually used the word *feminism* in any of his writings, either as a noun or adjective. The social critic and moralist Alexandre Dumas-fils, on the other hand, did employ the term in 1872 in *L'homme-femme,* a small work which dealt with the oppression of women in marriage and with their right to divorce. But his use of the neologism signals only a recognition of a conflict of ideologies, not a commitment to the issues. In 1892 *feminism* finally became official at the Feminist Societies Congress.[1]

Reviewing the history of this new word, we trace the diverse ideological, moral, and political origins of the French women's movement and see the gradual development of what was to become, by the early 1900s, not just a state of mind or an isolated action, but a doctrine independent of other ideologies of its time. We should point out that if feminism means a protest against oppression and a demand for the transformation of women's condition, every Western culture, at some point in its history, has experienced events or periods which could be called feminist. In the case of France, we learn that during the 1830s, even before the term gained fashion, feminism had emerged as an attempt by a particular social group to define women's place and identity in society.

If feminism is a doctrine or even a social ideology, what are the foundations on which it builds its theoretical assumptions? What are the philosophical bases of feminist discourse, of the demands and proposed reforms? How do feminists justify making changes against the existing social relations which are founded in the differences between the sexes?

As we look into these questions, we should study certain ideas in democratic and in socialist thought. Feminist ideology, occurring contemporaneously with the growth of socialist theories, derived inspiration both from Enlightenment philosophers and from nineteenth-century socialist utopians. It did not have a direct link to a particular philosopher; there was no founder of feminism in the sense that there were founders of the various schools of marxism and socialism, but there were certainly major figures. Furthermore, it bears noting how feminism shares ideas and experiences with socialism. While the relationship between the two is first and foremost historical, as feminism and socialism emerged at the same time (in 1830 and again in 1970), we shall see that there are also major structural connections at the level of theory. It is true that a socialist like Proudhon rejected feminism, but still the ideology of the two movements asks similar social questions.

Since feminism drew on the philosophers of the Enlightenment and French Revolution, as well as on socialist theory, in addition to identifying one political/philosophical tendency or another, it would be useful to explore questions which lie at the very root of feminist expression. For example, the fact that there is objectively a difference between the sexes challenges the assumptions of the Enlightenment concept of the universality of law. What is the relationship between the reality of woman before a civil and political law which, in theory, should not exclude anybody, but which does so in fact because it does not recognize differences? We should also examine what there is in the political order that might validate feminist claims. In other words, it is necessary to see what justifies the rights of women: is it the nature of women (the definition of which is problematical) or the state of society which invokes the historical and anthropological discourse of the period? In the discussion which follows, we will address these issues.

The Democratic Enlightenment and Utopian Socialisms

We would like to stress that it is very difficult to identify the bases of feminist thought. To attempt to do so creates two problems: (1) it

becomes necessary to define the philosophical foundations on which
the theory affirms the multiplicity and diversity of feminisms; and
(2) it becomes necessary to uncover the theoretical and political principles which permit us to think of the unity of feminism as a doctrine.
The introduction of the all-inclusive term *feminism* occurred during
the last years of the nineteenth century, at the very same time that the
women's movement developed many different factions. As it diversified between 1880 and 1914, women's clubs and publications grew by
leaps and bounds and distinct groups began to identify themselves.
There were Christian feminists, free-thinker feminists, philanthropic
feminists, and freemason feminists. There were republican feminists
and socialist feminists. Paralleling developments in the workers'
movement, these different types of feminist "tendencies" emerged
together with the splits occurring among French socialists. What is
remarkable is that the variety of feminist groups did not shake the
image or weaken the idea of feminist unity. Léontine Zanta, *agrégée*[2]
in philosophy and the first woman to earn a doctorate in the field
(1914), compared feminism to any doctrine professed by its author
(like Calvinism or "Spinozaism") and described it as "a philosophy
specifically formulated by women."[3] As suggested by the title of her
work, *The Psychology of Feminism,* she remained vague about the philosophy itself.

The adjectives associated with feminism at the end of the nineteenth century acknowledge the influence certain philosophers had
on feminist groups because they expressed views on women or on the
place of women in society in some of their writings.[4] In general,
however, authors of feminist texts referred to these philosophers to
defend ideas which otherwise lacked theoretical legitimacy. They did
not develop arguments on the basis of a particular philosophy; rather
they used texts and authors as support for a specific problem in
feminist thought.[5] As a result, it is nearly impossible to ascertain the
philosophical foundations of feminist discourse.

With respect to socialism, by 1840 it was clear that Saint Simo-
nianism could not serve as an authoritative source for feminism. Even
though it did offer a theoretical opening, in practice it proved abusive
and contradictory. There remained the writings of Charles Fourier
and the ideas of Victor Considerant expressed during the 1848 revolution, but interestingly enough it was Proudhon's misogynist socialism that feminists cited the most. This use of Proudhon underlines
the fact that if feminism has claimed socialism as part of its heritage, it
has done so with critical clarity, rather than blind faith.

After the era of the utopian socialists, Marx and the marxists fueled
the fires of debate. With them the discussion shifted, for Marx and

Engels voiced a greater interest in the analysis of the family than in the specific problems of women as outlined by the feminist movement. It was their followers, August Bebel and Paul and Laura Lafargue, who were cited in feminist literature. But since these disciples concentrated mostly on distinguishing between good (working-class) and bad (bourgeois) feminism, their thinking did not provide feminists so much with an analysis of the status of women and feminist needs as it did an authoritative source for the position that the woman's struggle should be subordinated to the class struggle.

The democratic-republican movement and eighteenth-century philosophers also inspired feminists. Yet, if Condorcet, on the one hand, became a permanent positive reference, Montesquieu, Voltaire, Diderot, and Rousseau served both as examples of precursors of feminism and of those responsible for the modern subjugation of women. Feminists praised Montesquieu for his chapter on government by women in *L'Esprit des Lois,* but rejected some of his scornful characterizations of women.[6] They found Voltaire to be indifferent to women's condition, but in his relationship with Madame de Châtelet, they said he favored the emancipation of women.[7] Condemning Diderot for the sensualism with which he viewed women as objects, they also recognized in him an unprejudiced man, convinced of woman's creativity.[8] Feminists generally despised Rousseau for the fifth book in *Emile,* devoted to Sophie, a characterization which closely resembled too many nineteenth-century women; but they applauded him for Julie in *La Nouvelle Héloise.*[9]

In Christianity, the contradiction was even more blatant, and it was difficult to judge if Christianity contributed to women's oppression or to their advancement. Some feminist texts cited the Gospels as the cause of Western women's subordination and Saint Paul as the one who bore prime responsibility. Other texts harkened back to the "woman of valor" in the Old Testament, whom they took to symbolize the way all women ought to fulfill their social obligations.[10]

At first glance, we note a simultaneous rejection and acceptance of certain philosophies. Feminists used texts for dual purposes, demonstrating thereby the apparently superficial relationship between their writings and the philosophical works they employed. Perhaps, then, we ought to look at that period when feminism as an expression of a given social group was both unified and diversified.

According to Léon Abensour, the idea of democracy explains why the feminist movement has been important since 1830. Although the feminist question could arise under other forms of government, it does so without challenging basic principles. It is only under democracy that feminism cannot be ignored or made short shrift of. But

Léon Abensour's observation is paradoxical, for by the end of the French Revolution women had already been precluded from participating in public and political life. Then, while The Declaration of the Rights of Man and the Citizen did not exclude women from social and political spheres, what it did was far worse; it established their absence.

By studying the apparent contradiction between democratic theory and practice, we can truly address the issue of the foundations of feminism. Throughout the nineteenth century, feminists themselves pointed to women's mores* which both were avant-garde and challenged the law. These women were conscious of their sexual difference and of their particularities as women. They knew that they were living in a world which proclaimed universality and democracy, and they demanded of that universality that it recognize women with their gender differences. A male feminist called this paradoxal position "integral Humanism."[11]

To reconstruct the paradox we must set aside the matter of mores to confront the problem of women's rights, or what is called here natural law. We will see that natural law was not always consistently defined and that within feminism there were divergent theoretical positions which did not necessarily follow the cultural and philosophical traditions I have outlined, but pointed to a more basic distinction. As a result, we must reassess the choices feminists made for their philosophical inspiration.

Slaves or Citizens, Helots or Enfranchised: Woman Subjects of the Law

The main reason French feminists of the nineteenth century agreed to accept the definition of human rights as embodied in the law was that they firmly believed that the laws governing human life within society had finally, after many centuries, emerged victorious over brute force. Feminists thought that, in order to demand laws which were in keeping with the mores of women, they had to be sure that they belonged to an age in which right had replaced might. It was a surprising conviction, one which flew in the face of history and social dynamics, but it was a commonly held assumption. People believed that the new laws of democracy held out the possibility for a true social contract, in ways that no other previous legal system had been able to accomplish.

---

*[Editors' note] We have translated the French *moeurs* as "mores" to capture the nineteenth-century flavor of the debate.

The rights issue was a constant in feminist discourse; civil rights as well as civic rights were the subjects of discussion. Interestingly, many historical accounts refer only to women's demands for rights as citizens—in particular, their demand for the right to vote—thereby reducing feminism to suffragism and making of feminism a bourgeois movement in the finest republican tradition. Yet such a view does not stand up to historical scrutiny. In fact, it was socialist women who, up until the turn of the century, participated in greatest numbers in dramatic actions (registering on ballots, campaigning for parliamentary candidates) designed to apply the principle of universality; republican feminists like Maria Deraismes gave voting rights secondary importance, after civil rights.

From the outset, then, the question of rights began with a paradox and a misunderstanding. It was a paradox, because those who felt that voting rights were an urgent necessity did not consider universal suffrage in a republican state to be a sufficient political act. Consequently, these feminists, together with socialists, stigmatized the struggle for the right to vote as a bourgeois issue. A misunderstanding arose because the demand for suffrage (since overemphasized by historians) was not the main goal of any feminist group. At most, as Emile Faguet points out, supporting women's suffrage after 1900 became the criterion which could be applied to distinguish between opportunistic feminists—those who joined, willy-nilly, an inevitable social movement—and "integral" feminists, those who recognized that if they did not win the right to participate in political life, women would not have achieved anything but a relative emancipation.[12]

For these reasons, it would be ill advised to start out by analyzing the various rights demanded and their complex political ramifications. A better approach would be to start back with the Napoleonic Code, to get a sense of the status of women in nineteenth-century society. It is unnecessary to list the prohibitions on women's activities and the obstacles put in their way—which were legion—but it is important to stress that, even so, one could not exactly point to a principle of exclusion in the law. Indeed, although the details of such constraints are identified, it is impossible to locate their source. On the contrary, as Léon Richer remarked, the Civil Code created a strange discrepancy: Article Seven distinguished citizens, from among the totality of persons, as those who exercised civil rights, while Article Eight provided that all the French were entitled to civil rights, Since women enjoyed only certain civil rights,[13] who were they? Should they claim their rights as French citizens or as human beings? The discrepancy could be traced to what remained unformulated in the Civil Code and in other legislative documents; and it became a weapon to be turned against the law itself. Women were not expressly forbidden from earning the baccalaureat, gaining access to higher learning, or registering on ballots . . . therefore, the pioneers proclaimed, all such activity was permissible.

As we look closer at the status of women in nineteenth-century society, matters get even more confusing. Madame de Staël wrote in 1800 that "Women's existence in society is still uncertain . . . in the present state of affairs, most are neither part of the natural order nor part of the social order."[14] Were they undefined beings, that is, hybrid beings?

Women were not citizens, that was for certain. Were they slaves, taken as a result of ancient territorial partitions? There were many of both sexes who, like John Stuart Mill, saw married women as barely better off than slaves, and it was true that marriage deprived women of various rights. Yet it would be misleading to attribute women's slavery to their married state since widows and "old maids"—while they might have had a few additional civil rights—were not considered citizens either.

Neither citizens nor slaves . . . were they enfranchised? Madame de Staël thought so, because they were hybrid beings from whom neither great ambition nor excessive disobedience was tolerated. Claire Demar thought differently; for her, women had not yet attained such a state: she called for *the enfranchisement of women*.[15] The term itself was reductivist and minimized the feminist ideal; it was replaced by *emancipation*.

One does not emancipate a slave, one emancipates a helot, declared many pre-1870 feminist texts. Ignoring the Spartan origin of the term, they used *helot* according to the definition accepted at the time, taking it to mean a person "reduced to the final state of abjection and ignorance," what we would call a person oppressed by material and moral means.

The term was thought appropriate because it was vague and expressed the confusion about the social status of women. It was not a matter of enfranchisement, of granting or returning lost rights, but of emancipation, of shaking to its very foundations the dynamic of oppressor/oppressed in order to achieve liberation. "Secular helotism," wrote Julie-Victoire Daubié, "has roots that run far deeper than the purposeful discrepancies of the Civil Code."[16]

Besides the Civil Code, the *Declaration of the Rights of Man and the Citizen* is the fundamental reference text, the expression of natural law which established the principle of equality between white and black, man and woman. It was a declaration based on applied logic, as was John Stuart Mill's book *The Subjugation of Women*, in which he denounced the contradiction between society's principles and its reality. Logic was also used by Joseph Barthélémy, a jurist: he disagreed with women who treated the vote as an expression of their natural right (for him, it was a social function, exercisable by a group just as well as by all members of a society); nevertheless, he recognized that a democracy could treat voting rights as a natural right in a situation where, if it did not grant the vote to all its citizens, it would be contradicting itself. Thanks to this logical reasoning, suffrage became universal by 1848 rather than remaining a right possessed by male electors who qualified by their property holdings.

However, feminists did not often refer to this argument, probably because the confusion over women's legal status caused certain uneasiness. They did not live within the legal sphere, and logical argument was unfamiliar territory to them in that it "forced" them, with a willful naiveté, into the legal arena. For this reason, the argument that prevailed among feminists was to invoke the evidence that social customs justified the transformation of their legal status. In 1850 they called it "mores"; in 1930 Léontine Zanta referred to "facts, acts, reforms" accomplished by women. The proof adduced was not the principle of belonging, but the reality of equality.

Proof of the factual reality, as opposed to the problem of proof by law (a problem recognized by John Stuart Mill), led women to reflect upon universality, in the sense of a primary equality between man and woman. Curiously enough, Olympe de Gouges, in her *Declaration of the Rights of Woman*, published in 1791, made the distinction between man and woman, even though her purpose was to show their kinship. She did not say that men's rights were also women's rights, but that women had such and such a right, just as men did. The nuance is important: she did not erase the differences, even while listing similarities. This was a frequent feminist strategy, to seek the application of universality while recognizing the reality of women's particularities, or to base rightful claims on women's "natural" or historical role.

Those who called for a revision of the law did not always present the condition of women in the same light. Louise Dauriat said in her petition to Parliament in 1837 that the reforms should benefit mothers and wives first of all since they had been the most deprived of their rights under the code. Olympe de Gouges contended that single mothers' rights should be recognized first. Others placed emphasis on women obtaining full civil rights, such as Léon Richer and Marie Desraimes in the early years of the Third Republic. Another position was that civil rights were inconceivable without voting rights, that the struggle should take the form of a battle on both fronts, though voting rights should be given priority because women would thus have a way to defend their own interests. This was Julie Daubié's argument, and she defined emancipation in those terms.

Social emancipation or social *and* political emancipation at the same time? Feminist demands for equal rights did not always specify. Consequently, theoretical choices which had little to do with political partisanship formed the foundation of feminism as a doctrine. We must analyze these choices and ask why they arose. Whether the political priority was believed to be civil or civic rights (and who can say which of the two was the more revolutionary or socialist demand?), nineteenth-century feminism had a perspective different from that of marxist doctrine, which held that social emancipation was merely a small step on the road to political emancipation, since social emancipation, according to Marx, was an individual, egotistical, bourgeois emancipation (cf. *On the Jewish Question*). Actually, among women, the isolated individual's concerns were centered on the private, domestic life of wives and mothers, not on women who were bourgeois property holders. Women's private lives had little to do with plenty and egotism; their lives were defined by their relationship to men, on the one hand, and children on the other. Such lives were as socially important as those ruled by professional and political concerns. For feminism, even within the divergent theoretical positions, the crucial matter remained the difference between the sexes. With that in mind, we can now look again at the philosophical texts which inspired feminist thought, texts which reflected upon the differences in human beings and the relation, with or without families, between the sexes.

From Natural Law to the Question of Origins

The women's rights issues, in other words the rights of wives, mothers, and citizens, date back to eighteenth-century thought. The nineteenth century was interested not in the origins of the principle of social relationships, but in the historical origins and evolution of society: it heralded the era of anthropology. Anthropology made an important theoretical contribution to feminism, and its impact can be measured through the life of a major figure, Clémence Royer (1830–1902). Philosopher, anthropoligist, and feminist too,[16] Clémence Royer's positions help clarify feminists' divergent views on the rights issue.

Clémence Royer had a rather idiosyncratic interpretation of feminist ideas. She was against voting rights, out of her conviction that so long as women received a mediocre education and so long as their living conditions and thought patterns, conditioned by centuries of subjugation, could not be structurally transformed, women were incapable of exercising the right to vote. Although only a minority shared her position in the nineteenth century, it is an interesting one because she based her conclusions on scientific studies. Rejecting the notion of natural law which justified the immediate correction of wrongs done to women, she stressed the length of time it would take to acquire certain rights. Clémence Royer subscribed to the theory of human evolution—an evolution which accounted for the state of society and the conditions required for historical progress.

She was not against the idea of women gaining the right to vote, but was opposed to the urgency of demanding it because women's mores did not provide them with the necessary intelligence to exercise such a right. Hence, her view was the opposite of the one alluded to earlier, which claimed that the progress made in women's mores gave them the right to demand a change in their legal status. According to the other position, the condition of these mores served as proof of women's right to vote, as an affirmation of voluntarism. But for Clémence Royer, women's mores were the product of a history of subjugation. And she believed that the newly established democracy (the final proof presented in the proof-by-mores argument) was precisely the political system most harmful to the prospects for women's freedom and emancipation. Democracy, unlike autocracy, she argued, strengthened civic life to the detriment of private life and thus reinforced male power while relegating to women an increasingly minor role.

This demand to transform mores, this mistrust in the all-powerful democratic law, underlines clearly the rejection of a logic of nature, one which implies that on principle all human beings are equal. Feminist legalism, although it implied a certain difference between the sexes, subscribed to a general idea of humanity. Clémence Royer, who thought in terms of evolution and not in terms of defining woman's nature, also took into consideration the difference between the sexes.

Turning her back on political theory, her arguments were anthropological in nature. Using Darwin's theory of evolution as a foundation, she studied the origin of man and societies, analyzing the relation between the sexes.[18] She believed that originally there reigned, or existed, equality between the sexes. Inequality did not result from woman's physical weakness or from her being a mother, as was generally believed at the time. For Clémence Royer, it was not woman's nature which caused her subjugation, it was the process whereby the family was set up and work was divided between the sexes. Such ideas are familiar to us today but were unheard of in 1870; with them, Clémence Royer explained why women were not only oppressed but also intellectually "atrophied." It was not a matter of a fundamental inequality between men and women, but that did not mean there was absolute equality among all human beings, either. Clémence Royer criticized Jean-Jacques Rousseau and affirmed that inequality was natural.

Instead of seeking to resolve the problem of inequality with a political program, she suggested that the only way to eliminate "institutionalized" inequality between men and women was by educating the women. Their intelligence had been atrophied because they had been left behind; and that, the theory of evolution confirmed, could be remedied. Clémence Royer in this respect agreed with the many feminists who were appalled by women's complacency in remaining oppressed. But she was the only one to set forth scientific reasons to support her positions.

It would be worthwhile to examine this relationship between science and political morality, between anthropology and the critique of democracy; however, my purpose is to identify the bases for feminist discourse, and—in that sense, Clémence Royer can be presented as an example of a discourse with two orientations: scientific and ideological.

The theoretical explanation for her two-tiered position was this: "Anthropology, the last rung of the physical sciences, which links it to the moral sciences, should be well-grounded, in order to provide a basis for morality, which is the principle of law and legislation. But anthropology can only be derived from an overall view of biology. The glory of Auguste Comte will consist in his having stated this methodological truth."[19] Elsewhere, Clémence Royer criticized Auguste Comte, but in the passage quoted she expressed a yearning that was common to her time.

In our search for the philosophical foundations of feminism we ought to pay our respects to the usual official references and, at the same time, ignore them, so as to discover where other theoretical, ideological, and scientific opinions enter the picture. It is precisely by thinking of the unity of feminism as a doctrine that it becomes possible to identify its underlying tensions, a sign of its multiple origins. To locate the currents of nineteenth-century feminist thought is to come to grips with two conflicting views: one, a reflection on the nature of woman (woman's nature as defined by her particular qualities or as part of human nature); and the other, an analysis of the relationships between the sexes and between women and society.

Nineteenth-century feminism was about socio-political aspirations and the value of democracy, but it was also marked by scientific debates which should be studied independently of the facile views of that era.

Notes

1. Léon Abensour, *Le Problème féministe* (Paris, 1927).
2. One who passed the qualifying exam (l'Agrégation) in a particular field and who then was assured a tenured teaching position by the state in a lycée. It has great importance within the university.
3. Léontine Zanta, *Psychologie du féminisme* (1922).
4. Jenny d'Hericourt, *La Femme affranchie* (1860).
5. For example, Marthe Louis-Lévy, *L'Emancipation politique des femmes* (1933).
6. A positive reference for L. Abensour; a negative one for E. Legouvé.
7. A positive reference for E. Faguet (*Le Féminisme*, 1910); a negative one for E. Legouvé (*Histoire morale des femmes*, 1849).
8. A positive reference for L. Abensour; a negative one for J. Oddo-Deflou (*Le sexualisme*, 1905).
9. A positive reference for J. Oddo-Deflou.
10. Cf. Abbé Bolo, *La Femme et le clergé*. Etienne Lamy, *La Femme de demain*.
11. Léopold Lacour, *L'Humanisme intégral* (1897).
12. Emile Faguet, *Le Féminisme*.
13. Léon Richer, *Le Code des femmes* (1883).
14. Madame de Staël, *De la littérature considerée dans ses rapports avec les institutions sociales* (1800).
15. Claire Demar, *Appel d'une femme au peuple sur l'affranchissement de la femme* (1833).
16. Julie-Victoire Daubié, *L'Emancipation de la femme* (1871).
17. Clémence Royer became known in Lausanne, where she taught a philosophy course exclusively for women. The introduction to the course was published. Later she did the first translation into French of Darwin's *Origin of the Species*, for which she wrote a preface, defining her own theoretical position supporting but also opposing Darwin. She went on to become a member of the first anthropological society as well as a winner, ex-aqueo together with Proudhon, of a competition on the theory of taxation. She published various scientific books and contributed to many feminist journals and congresses at the turn of the century. See Geneviève Fraisse, *Clémence Royer, philosophe et femme de sciences*, ed. La Découverte (Paris, 1985).
18. Clémence Royer published *L'Origine de l'homme et des sociétés* a year before Darwin's *Descent of Man* appeared; she claimed to have dealt first with the subject.
19. *Le Bien de la loi morale* (1881).

"BOURGEOIS FEMINISM" IN FRANCE
A THEORY DEVELOPED BY SOCIALIST WOMEN BEFORE WORLD WAR I

Françoise Picq

Translated by Irene Ilton

In the late nineteenth century, much like today, it was commonplace to hear that feminism was a bourgeois movement. Then, as now, it was taken for granted; it was hardly a matter for discussion. But those who dismissed feminists for their class background were no different from the people they disdained. It was not working-class women who insulted Maria Pognon at the 1896 Feminist Congress in France; "collectivist students" did,[1] a fact that made no impression on Charles Sowerwine, who blithely joined those who criticized with the disparaging remark: "She [Maria Pognon] earned her pocket money managing a boarding house."[2] According to Sowerwine, it went without saying that a feminist did not have to make a living. She was only earning a little pocket money on the side, even if, as in the case of the widowed Maria Pognon, she was forced to support herself and her children and would finally end up dying in poverty.

Did the class origins of feminists in the Third Republic make this women's movement particularly bourgeois? Or was it bourgeois because of the place these women occupied in the system of production? Did feminism really pursue conservative or reactionary ends by seeking to integrate women into capitalism? Or did it help capitalism "survive by ridding it of its most glaring inequalities"?[3] Did feminism represent a danger to the triumph of socialist objectives?

While it is difficult to answer all of these questions, asking them is often enough to show that the notion of bourgeois feminism does not fall within the realm of socio-political analysis but of ideology. It is not predicated on sociological fact, but political condemnation. To label feminism as bourgeois is, in a certain way, to challenge its legitimacy and to identify it with social conservatism, with the maintenance of class privilege.

This kind of name calling causes all sorts of problems. Women in the Third Republic had no legal status at all; consequently it is not surprising that feminists began by insisting that women be granted the basic rights of human dignity. Certainly many of their goals seem reformist to us today, but many of them also echo our own struggle. Feminists then were no more content than we are now to demand their place in society as it existed; they cast a vitriolic eye on what they call "sexualism" or the "masculinist organization."[4] And they came to have no more respect for socialist dogma than the dogma of church or state. Were they so different from many of ourselves, we, the intellectual petit bourgeois women who have come out of the revolutionary movement of the 1960s?

The condemnation of feminism as a bourgeois movement began in the early years of the twentieth century among socialists, particularly socialist women. Becoming part of the discourse, it gradually took on the importance of theory, unchallenged, taken for granted, familiar to all. Yet how could this have happened when Engels had given women a place in the revolutionary struggle and had clearly identified the "world historic defeat of the female sex"? How was it possible that several decades after the publication of *The Origins of the Family, Private Property and the State*, women, in the name of the same revolutionary ideal, would be kept from demanding their basic rights as a necessary step toward true equality?[5]

Bourgeois and Proletarian Women

What is a bourgeois woman? One who, devoting herself to the emancipation of working-class women is guilty of having been born into a family of comfortable means? The student putting the full force of her education at the service of the working-class woman? The woman who, while leading a productive life, does not compromise the care and tastefulness with which she dresses? By calling them "bourgeoises" you commit an injustice, creating a regrettable confusion between the designation bourgeois and the moral condition which we must fight against with all our strength: the bourgeois mentality.

Fanny Clar, *L'Equité*, 1913

All too often the marxist analysis of the modes of production and class antagonism has entered the discourse of politics in summary and

reductive forms. Lacking in subtlety and without any specific treatment of women's position in the system of production, an abbreviated
interpretation has been imposed on the world of women where it is
singularly out of place.

According to marxist analysis, bourgeois men are those who own
the means of production. Because of their sex, females of the bourgeoisie are denied the majority of their class's privileges and, when
married, are not only dispossessed of all their property but become
themselves private property and a means of reproduction. As a result,
bourgeoise is not the feminine equivalent of *bourgeois*. At best she is the
wife of a bourgeois. Feminists, therefore, who spent their lives trying
to escape the fate of the women of their class understandably felt
insulted by an analysis which defined and then condemned them not
for what they were, but for the man to whom they supposedly belonged.

"You reproach us for being 'bourgeoise,' " protested Maria Pognon.
"I don't know where you draw the line between bourgeois and working-class women, because there are no idle women among us. We are
all working women."[6]

Idle or working, for Maria Pognon that was the dividing line along
which feminists clearly placed themselves. Feminists struggled for the
right to work, de jure and de facto, for opening up to women career
opportunities, for free use of their wages, for the forming of professional organizations. They were neither working-class women selling
their labor power nor bourgeois women exploiting the labor power of
others.

In France in 1900 there was one woman lawyer and thirty women
doctors, hardly enough to constitute a female bourgeoisie. But how
many of them rushed to become secretaries, elementary school teachers, postal clerks—respectable for them, but which were difficult to
identify with the ruling class?[7]

Given their professional activities, many so-called bourgeois women
might be classified with the "petite bourgeoisie," the social class Marx
believed wavered between the bourgeoisie and the proletariat, depending on the political climate, and which had to be won over to the
revolutionary cause at all costs. Then again, one might have thought,
as did Bebel, that their sexual status would ally them with the proletariat. As women, Engels himself said, they constituted a class enslaved by monogamy; they "represented the proletariat" within the
family. Thus one might have expected French socialists, claiming
kinship with marxism, to support feminist demands and consider
women—all women—as their potential allies. This point of view
seemed at first to be winning, but rapidly the reverse thesis developed
and triumphed in socialist theory and practice.

The "theory of bourgeois feminism" drew an unbreachable class line around women. All feminists, without differentiation, were considered *bourgeoises,* while socialists put themselves forward as proletarians, whatever their class origin or way of life. Most socialist leaders did not (and do not) come from the working class. But that did not stop them from calling attention to the bourgeois social background of feminists and to reject the "objection whereby, for all intents and purposes one [could] . . . say the same thing about [members of] the socialist movement."[8] The place of socialist leaders in the workers' movement has never been questioned: "the workers did not exclude from their organized ranks people like Vaillant, Jaurès, or Guesde under the pretext that they did not come from proletarian stock."[9] Their background did not keep them from "organizing under the banner of the proletariat," as Suzon explained it, for the criterion was and remains to be "able to see in social chaos deep-seated class antagonism."[10] This requirement, this ideological perception, subordinated all other considerations (particularly those of sex).

Materialism notwithstanding, for the socialists it was not one's class which determined consciousness, but consciousness which determined class. To organize as proletarians was not to affiliate oneself on the basis of class reality, but according to a real referent. One was not born proletarian. One became proletarian by adherence to the ideals and the party of the proletariat. Marxism, a doctrine forged by the intelligentsia for the use of the working class, whose conscience they claimed to be, magically transformed its heralds into proletarians. Men (or women) who did not profess their faith in it must, conversely, be bourgeois.

When socialists looked at feminists, it was another matter. Women and the proletariat became mutually exclusive. "We will organize," said Eleanor Marx, "not as women, but as proletarians, not as the feminine competitors of our worker husbands, but as their comrades in arms."[11] A bipolar opposition emerged, explicitly identifying the proletarian as male (which corresponded to the reality of socialist organization)[12] and, implicitly, identifying the bourgeois as female. While the struggle between the sexes still resembled a class struggle, contrary to Engels's thesis, by the early twentieth century the socialist analysis had assimilated the role of women into the bourgeoisie.

Feminism in France, 1878–1914

Feminism developed in the Third Republic as a movement of opinion and social reality, affecting, albeit unequally, the different strata of society. Driven by economic necessity, women from the lower classes and from the petite bourgeoisie flooded the salaried work force. It was under these circumstances that organized feminism grew. At first, however, feminism attracted mostly intellectual women. "[T]his is a critical period for the intellectual woman," wrote Charles Turgeon, who, noting the discrepancy between the education of young girls and the prospects open to them, feared that they would be "enlisted into the revolutionary army" which, at that time, was called the "intellectual proletariat of women."[13]

Feminism is neither a single unified doctrine nor a structured organization. It is a movement made up of many different groups holding conflicting ideas. The much proclaimed solidarity of the female sex masks political opposition and prevents the formulation of any splits within the ranks, but many of those who have spoken in the name of feminism have little in common. Calling it *bourgeois* further obscures the reality of a social movement which draws its strength from the fact that it cuts across class lines. The priorities, objectives, and modes of action vary from one feminist group to another; and it is necessary to separate the various tendencies in order to understand what feminism is or has been in relation to other social movements at a particular time.

During the historical period of interest to us here, there was in France a Conservative-Catholic feminism and a "respectable" Protestant feminism. In 1900 these factions organized the Catholic Congress of Women's Institutions (Congrès catholique des Institutions féminines) and the Congress of Women's Charitable Organizations and Institutions (Congrès des Oeuvres et Institutions féminines). In addition there was a third faction, often called the feminist left, which organized the Congress on the Condition and Rights of Women (Congrès de la Condition et des droits des femmes); and this is the faction which is of particular concern to us, for it was "the largest, the most active and the most revolutionary."[14] Our interest cannot be explained by political preference alone; it reflects as well the politics of the times. It is with this feminist faction that the socialists had the most trouble. Having expressed a commitment to working-class women, the feminist left entered into direct competition and conflict with the socialists.

Within the feminist left faction, as represented by the Congress on the Condition and Rights of Women, there were several different groups: Women's Suffrage (Le Suffrage des femmes), led by Hubertine Auclert; Women's Solidarity (La Solidarité des femmes), organized by Eugénie Potonié Pierre, Caroline Kauffmann, and Madeleine Pelletier; and the League of Women's Rights (La Ligue du Droit des femmes), headed by Maria Pognon and Marie Bonnevial.

Each group published its own newspaper, but they all supported as well the feminist daily, *Le Fronde*, edited by Marguerite Durand and under whose auspices the Congress on the Condition and Rights of Women met. The feminist left came together in 1892, 1896, and 1900; and in congress after congress their platforms made such social demands as equal work, equal pay, the abolition of special laws for women, and the end to the competition of unpaid labor performed in convents and prisons. They also called for the appointment of women as labor inspectors, for equal working hours for both sexes, for the inclusion of domestic work in the same category as factory or office work, and for six-weeks' paid maternity leave.

Most observers of the period—writers or journalists—saw virtually no differences among those on the feminist left, all of whom they summarily called socialists. Within the feminist left, however, the socialist women made sharp distinctions. They drew "class lines" according to whether a feminist group had affiliations with a working-class organization or not, and according to their vision of the class struggle. There was a clear split between the proletarian feminists on the one side and the bourgeois on the other.

Consciously or not, the "theory of bourgeois feminism," which emerged from the split among feminists on the left, reversed the marxist position on the woman's question. One must explain, therefore, not merely describe, the historical and theoretical development of such an anomaly. It is far from self-evident.

Women and Socialism at the Dawn of the Third Republic

At different moments in history, especially in France, feminism and socialism have met, confronted each other, and frequently clashed. The definitive establishment of the Third Republic is one of those times when the deep-seated aspirations and contradictions of the two social movements came into conflict.

In 1879, Hubertine Auclert was invited to speak at the Congrès Socialiste in Marseilles, "not because she [was] a worker, but because she [was] a woman, i.e., exploited, a slave representing nine million other slaves."[15] In the name of socialist principles, she demanded justice and equality for women and an end to privilege based on sex and class. In the name of all women, she offered to all proletarians an alliance against their common oppressors and succeeded in having the demand for the complete equality of the sexes written into the socialist program. Socialism declared itself in favor of women's suffrage even before feminism called for it.

Thus, feminism and socialism, the two social movements which were just beginning to take shape and to organize themselves, decided to join forces: "Women and proletarians of all countries, unite," wrote *L'Egalité*.[16] No doubt ulterior motives played a small part on both sides of that alliance and the feminists soon could judge its limitations. Having given their support to women, the socialists, in return, expected women to show their confidence in socialism. Women were asked to settle for a declaration of principle and to put aside their own demands while awaiting the revolution which would put an end not only to legal inequality, but also to its cause—economic dependency. Demanding women's rights in a capitalist society was to believe such a society capable of mending its ways. It was to demand nothing more than bourgeois rights, the same as those proclaimed in the bourgeois revolution of 1789. To put it bluntly, socialists saw any attempt to improve the lot of women under capitalism as an act of defiance toward the workers' movement, the only movement capable of resolving the woman's question. In other words, it was bourgeois feminism.

The latter part of the nineteenth century saw the creation of two feminist-socialist groups, the Women's Alliance (L'Union des Femmes) and Women's Solidarity (La Solidarité des femmes). Founded in 1880, the Women's Alliance called for civil and political rights of women as well as the right to work. The group contended that these rights would only become a reality through socialism. Ten years later, in 1890, Women's Solidarity came into being, proclaiming a feminist and socialist program. Both of these socialist groups rejected the so-called conservatism of feminism and of feminist pressure groups which had been challenging socialists to live up to socialist words in socialist deeds. Assuming that they could work within socialism and despite some success, both of these groups finally ran up against the same obstacle: the refusal of socialists to give concrete support to women's demands. Neither Léonie Rouzade's candidacy in the municipal elections of 1881 nor that of Paula Minckin in the legislative elections of 1893 received the backing they sought, and these socialist women saw themselves forced to wage the struggle for women's rights in the arena of feminism alone.[17]

Yet another group, the Feminist-Socialist Group (Groupe féministe-socialiste) was formed in 1899, but it was very different from its predecessors. While they kept both terms in their name, the women here showed a decided preference for the orthodox socialist agenda. They tried to organize working-class women whose low degree of consciousness, they believed, was slowing down the struggle waged by men. The achievement of women's rights was not an end in itself, but a "means of preparing for the socialist education of women." Willingly subordinating the special concerns of women to the needs of various socialist groups, the Socialist-Feminist Group stated that there "can be no antagonism between men and women of the working class."[18] When conflicts did arise, they backed the men, deeming the interests of the Party always to be more important than any one specific problem. Despite its obvious good will, even this group could not convince the socialists of its usefulness. Unable to gain recognition within the newly unified Party in 1905, it rapidly vanished.

After a few years, during which there were no women's organizations within the party, the Socialist Women's Group (Groupe des femmes socialistes) was formed in 1913 in accordance with international directives.[19] As Madeleine Rebérioux points out, "Tainted with bourgeois overtones, the feminist reference disappeared" from the group's name.[20] However, a certain number of feminists did participate, and four of them—Marie Bonnevial, Hélène Brion, Marguerite Martin, and Maria Vérone—were elected to the first executive committee on March 6, 1913.

It was through the activities of the Feminist-Socialist Group and, later, the Women's Socialist Group that the arguments forming the framework of the theory of bourgeois feminism were articulated. In 1900 socialist feminists confronted the "bourgeois feminist" organizers of the Congress on the Condition of the Rights of Women. In 1913, the confrontation took place within the Socialist Women's Group itself. Feminists and mediators alike were subsequently excluded from positions of leadership. To protect itself from feminist deviations, the Group adopted statutes forbidding the recruitment of women from outside the Party. Ironically, these devoted supporters of socialism had backed themselves into the position whereby they could no longer bring in new members to the Party. Their fear of feminism had grown to the point where it had shut them off to all women's issues, including those of women workers.

Socialism and/or Feminism: The Terms of the Debate

For the socialist Louise Saumonneau, feminism was bourgeois in that it placed sexual solidarity in opposition to the class struggle. As an example of the conflict between the two movements, Saumonneau singled out Maria Pognon's closing speech at the Congress of 1900 in which Pognon called for friendship between bourgeois and working-class women by saying: "I know that there is a party which preaches class struggle, well I disown that party, we must demolish the barrier that you want to erect between us."[21] This was the kind of "diatribe

against socialism," observed Louise Saummoneau, "that ends all self-
respecting bourgeois assemblies.[22] In 1913, the socialist Suzon spoke
in a similar vein: "We want no part in a movement that is doing its
utmost to cast a veil over the class struggle. We reject the pathetic
compromises of Lamourette, who stirs into one melting pot of lies the
many irreconcilable interests of millionaires and wage earners, of
royal and republican princesses and the victims of the sweating system
gnawed by hunger."[23]

The confrontational rhetoric of Maria Pognon did not mean that all
feminists opposed the formation of women's groups within the Socialist Party. In the name of sexual solidarity, many feminists in 1900
rejoiced over the creation of the Feminist-Socialist Group: "Socialist
feminism, primarily economic, will make a great contribution to the
cause, by complementing, as it were, those devoted to legislative
reforms."[24] These feminists encouraged working-class women to
form unions, seeing in them women's only means of emerging from
their isolation. By fighting against their exploitation, they would gain
dignity in work. "Unity is essential, associations, cooperative systems,
trade unions; women must be admitted everywhere and they must
work everywhere with their brothers in adversity; men must learn
where their duty lies and open their ranks to their sisters."[25]

But the Feminist-Socialist Group unilaterally broke with feminism
in the name of the class struggle. When "bourgeois women," for
example, supported a strike of working-class women, far from applauding the sexual solidarity expressed through this action, Louise
Saumonneau criticized the women who accepted the support. For her,
it was the mark of a lower form of class consciousness. She was against
women forming their own unions when men refused to admit them
into theirs because it "would favor the bourgeois influence." In her
view, *feminist* was synonymous with *bourgeois* and what she feared most
was seeing "the women of the people being led astray" by feminism.[26]

Class affiliation created a sharp division between socialist women
and "bourgeois feminists," argued the Feminist-Socialist Group.
There could be no common interests between them. Having drawn
the lines in this way, working-class women became the stakes in the
rivalry between this group and other feminists on the left. Those
progressive feminists who did not belong to the Feminist-Socialist
Group and who took an interest in working-class women consequently
became the "natural adversaries" of Louise Saumonneau.

A split occurred once again in 1913, but this time within the Socialist
Women's Group. As if by contagion, those women among the socialists
who proclaimed female solidarity in spite of the class struggle were
seen as *bourgeoises*.

Were feminism and socialism really mutually exclusive? Did they have to fight against one another? Was there no way to support the same objectives? Did the class struggle rule out all solidarity among women? Points of view diverged on the subject and confronted each other on the pages of *L'Equité, La Bataille syndicaliste,* and *La Voix du peuple.*[27]

For Marguerite Martin, "true feminism is based solely on the egalitarian principle . . . it is perfectly compatible with the socialist ideal." She called for the emancipation of women and encouraged socialists to seek allies beyond the movement when it made sense: "[S]ide by side with bourgeois women every time their demands concern a specific point on the socialist agenda."[28]

The feminist faction within the Socialist Women's Group and the unions did not deny the class struggle, but they insisted that it affected women, excluded as they were from social power, in a very particular way. What is more, they claimed there existed "as a result of the male [bias in the] organization of the world, [the need for] feminist solidarity."[29] They also stressed the conflicts which divided the working class: "Like it or not, the woman wage earner owes it to herself to add to class exploitation the grievous misunderstanding between the sexes."[30] Recalling the "bourgeois law invoked at times by working men" against female labor, they denounced "the male instinct, [which] for centuries [has been] accustomed to subjugating women and which is terrified at the thought of their emancipation." They decided it was necessary to "continue the feminist struggle alongside and on the fringes of the socialist struggle."[31]

Antifeminist socialist women, on the contrary, "let everything which is not the proletarian struggle fall by the wayside." According to them, "women should not wage battle against the omnipotence of mustaches and beards," but should devote themselves generously, bring "whole reserves of enthusiasm, courage and cheerful hope," submit themselves unquestioningly to the ideals and "masculine thinking" of the party. No autonomy was tolerated; the socialist struggle dominated all others.[32]

Denying any solidarity among women, antifeminist socialists claimed allegiance instead to the alliance between men and women of the working class which, they believed, nothing could shake. Evidence to the contrary, they stated that the woman's question had been resolved and equality of the sexes achieved. Since the Party promised that "in the society of the future, women will have the same rights as men, the feminist issue does not even arise. We have resolved it by abolishing its grounds for existence, the inequality of rights."[33] This was a magical proclamation which masked the reality behind that image of the world of the future and ruled out all present and real dissent: a waking dream of a mythical class solidarity, compulsively ignoring the war between the sexes which seems so obvious to us today.[34]

Women's Right to Work

The question of women and work did become a crucial issue in the workers' movement. If many unionists were committed at that time to Proudhon's principle that women should be housewives, the socialists took a stand in favor of work for women. According to Engels, emancipation would come about "through the reintroduction of the entire female sex into public industry."[35] All the same, the socialist press, like the trade union press, showed little interest in the problems of female labor. It was in the feminist newspapers that women socialists spoke out about the conditions of working women.[36]

One might have expected that militant women socialists would have been particularly interested in developing among members of the working class the "socialist" ideal of the woman "comrade [in the] economic and political struggle for the raising of wages and the emancipation of work."[37] In June 1902, the Feminist-Socialist Group did intervene during a strike of cabinet makers who were demanding "the exclusion of women from cabinetmaking," in order to emphasize that it "would be deeply unjust to prevent women from earning a living for themselves and for their families" and that "there is only one way for workers to avoid competition: make them understand that it is in their interest to unionize and then to demand a salary [for women] equal to that of men doing the same work."[38]

But that was the only time socialist feminists took a stand. To distinguish themselves from feminists, and out of fear of a confrontation with the men, socialist women usually refused to support the right of women to work.

To fill the gaps left by unions, nonsocialist feminists promoted the creation of women's unions. Some of these organizations clashed with men's unions that were defending their male sexual monopoly.[39] Marguerite Durand, however, was not about to tolerate any insult to feminist dignity in the name of the class struggle and was not afraid to challenge those in authority.

The critical and confrontational action of the feminists proved to be more effective than the devotion of women socialists and union members who saw in that feminist action "an attempt on the part of the bourgeoisie to monopolize the wage-earning woman."[40] Thanks to the feminists, the C.G.T. (La Confédération générale du Travail")[41] finally had to respond. As Madeleine Guilbert put it, "the first attempt on a national level to promote the introduction of women into the unions of the C.G.T. arose from a clash with part of the feminist movement."[42]

At the time of the "Couriau Affair," again it was the feminists who took up the defense of Emma Couriau and supported this woman typographer who had tried to join the local union in Lyons. In order to "remain a class group" and reassure "their male comrades," the Socialist Women's Group, on the other hand, had refused to take a stand against the trade unionists who opposed the unionization of a female worker.[43]

In conclusion, despite the principles laid out in the Party's program, the "theory of bourgeois feminism" led women socialists to reject the demands of legal and political equality for women. Instead, they spent their energies criticizing the objectives of those they had turned into their political adversaries: "The principle of the feminist is . . . based upon the demand for a 'natural right' like the 'natural rights' invoked by the bourgeoisie in 1789."[44]

Was it political weakness or sexual bias? Whatever the reason, socialist women abandoned working women, dismissing their cause along with the general feminist platform which they neither trusted nor endorsed. They saw the interest feminists took in working-class women as just another indication of the nonproletarian tendencies of the movement. Perhaps it was cultural conservatism, perhaps it was the influence of the clergy, but in spite of their espoused revolutionary vision of the world, socialists did not consider women full-fledged members of the proletariat in whose name the Party spoke and with whom socialist women identified.

Notes

1. *Congrès feministe* (1896).

2. Charles Sowerine, *Les Femmes et le socialisme* (Presses de Fondation des Sciences politiques, 1978). Translated as *Sisters or Citizens? Women and Socialism in France since 1876* (Cambridge University Press, 1982).

3. Marie-Hélène Zylberberg-Horquard, *Féminisme et syndicalisme en France* (Anthropos, 1978).

4. Jeanne Deflou, *Le Sexualisme, critique de la prépondérance et de la mentalité du sexe fort* (1906); idem, *Lutte féministe, organe uniquement et rigoureusement indépendant pour le féminisme intégrale* (1919).

5. Frederick Engels, *The Origin of the Family, Private Property and the State*

(1884), Marx-Engels Reader, ed. Robert C. Tucker (Norton, 1978); "the peculiar character of man's domination over woman (in the modern family), and the necessity, as well as the manner of establishing real and social equality between the two, will be brought into full relief only when both are completely equal before the law."

6. Maria Pognon, *Congrès de la Condition et les Droits des Femmes* (1900).

7. In 1900 there were 50,000 state-employed elementary-school teachers, in 1914 there were 155,000 women civil servants; they represented 39 percent of those employed in the service sector at that time. (M. H. Zylberg-Hocquard, *Femmes et féminisme dans le mouvement ouvrier français* [Editions Ouvrières, 1982].)

8. Eleanor Marx, "La question féminine," in *Dialectiques* 8, (1887).

9. Suzon (Suzanne Lacore), *Féminisme et socialisme*. This pamphlet assembles the articles which appeared in *L'Equité* in 1913 and 1914; in are collected the arguments for "bourgeois feminism." In 1898, the Worker Party of Jules Guesde had only two workers among its deputies. (Claude Willard, in *Le Mouvement social*, October 1960.)

10. Suzon, *Féminisme et socialisme*.

11. Eleanor Marx, "La question feminine."

12. Women made up less than 3 percent of the total membership in the various socialist groups and in the Party before 1914 (Cf. Sowerwine, *Les Femmes et le socialisme*)

13. Charles Turgeon, *Le Féminisme français* (Larose, 1902).

14. Ibid.

15. *Congrès Ouvrier Socialiste de France*, session "De la Femme" (Of Woman), chaired by Hubertine Auclert, (October 22, 1879), "Egalité politique et sociale de l'homme et de femme."

16. *L'Egalité*, (March 31, 1880).

17. The refusal of Guesde's Worker Party to support Léonie Rouzade's candidacy is at the origin of the schism in French socialism which lasted until 1905: *Guesdistes* and *possibilistes* clashed over the issue of women's rights, insofar as that issue "was the concrete center of an abstract question: reform versus revolution over which the party was split." (Cf. Sowerwine, *Les Femmes et le Socialisme*.)

18. *La Femme socialiste* (1901) (from the newspaper).

19. *La Première Conférence Internationale des Femmes Socialistes* (First International Conference of Women Socialists) (Stuttgart, 1907) decided, despite the opposition of Madeleine Pelletier, that "women socialists must not ally themselves with the feminists of the bourgeoisie."

20. M. Rebérioux, Preface to C. Sowerwine, *Les Femmes et le Socialisme*.

21. Maria Pognon, *Congrès de la Condition*.

22. Louise Saummoneau, *La Petite République*, November 14, 1900.

23. Suzon, *Féminisme et socialisme*.

24. *La Fronde*, January 2, 1900.

25. Maria Pognon, *Congrès*.

26. Louise Saummoneau, *La Petite République*.

27. *L'Equité, organe éducatif du prolétariat féminin*, edited by Marianne Rauze, 1913–1919. *La Bataille syndicaliste*, Elizabeth Zemianska, "True feminism . . . is trade-unionism," August 1, 1913. *La Voix du Peuple*, journal of the C.G.T., 1914.

28. Cited in *L'Equité*.

29. Hélène Brion, *La Voix féministe* (Epone, 1917), Syros, 1978.

30. Venice Pellat Finet, *La Voix du Peuple.*

31. Hélène Brion, *La Voix Féministe.*

32. Suzon, *Féminisme et socialisme.*

33. Elisabeth Zemianska, "True feminism."

34. We can list fifty-four strikes by men for the expulsion of women between 1890 and 1908 (Madeleine Guilbert, *Les femmes et l'organisation syndicale avant 1914*, CNRS, 1964).

35. F. Engels, *The Origin of the Family.*

36. Aline Valette, who was first permanent secretary of the Worker Party, wrote the "Work Column" in *La Fronde* until her death in 1899; she was succeeded by Marie Bonnevial.

37. That is what Paul Lafargue contrasted with the idealized petit-bourgeois housewife in *La Question de la femme* (Paris, 1905).

38. *La Petite République*, "Les Grèves," June 2, 1900.

39. Unions of women typographers, typists, cashier-bookkeepers, makers of artificial flowers and feathers, midwives.

40. The C.G.T., founded in 1895, was a confederation of socialist trade unions. Today, a confederation of the same name often affiliates itself with the French Communist Party.

41. Marie Guillot, *La Vie ouvrière.*

42. M. Guilbert, *Les femmes.*

43. In 1913 Emma Couriau was refused admission to the Lyonnaise section of the Syndicat du Livre (the union concerned with all the technical aspects of newspaper and book production), which, in addition, expelled her husband for having permitted her to exercise the trade. Spurred on by the Southeast Feminist Federation (Fédération féministe du Sud-est), this case caused a great outcry in socialist and unionist circles and was the beginning of a notable shift in opinion.

44. Suzon, *Féminisme et socialisme.*

THE SOCIALIST PARTY OF AMERICA, THE WOMAN QUESTION, AND THERESA SERBER MALKIEL

Françoise Basch

Translated by Nancy Festinger

I would like to select some issues from the long and complex history of the ways socialist organizations have dealt with the woman question, in order to discuss some of the ideological and tactical controversies which stirred the Socialist Party of America (SPA) in the early 1900s. These controversies, which lie at the crossroads of socialist and feminist ideology, gave rise to, and continued to kindle, questions and confrontations. The subject is an interesting and timely one because it has to do with the identity of women as socialists and as feminists, both as individuals and as members of groups. As part of our inquiry we must examine the relationship between parties and militants and between the identities these women positively assumed and those that were imposed upon them. By studying the options these women recognized for themselves, we can see how class consciousness and sex consciousness affected their search for an identity. Since their endeavor was not merely concerned with immediate answers, but with constructing a better future, I briefly describe the socialist "utopia" dreamed of by SPA militants and then trace the outline of a new identity for women, as it was expressed in the work of Theresa Serber Malkiel.[1]

If I highlight Malkiel's writing on the subject, it is because she is, in my opinion, central to this entire discussion. Her history, the development of her identity, her experiences as a life-long militant in the SPA, all were part of a heritage that she shared with many other women of her milieu, each of whom, like her, went to great lengths to define her position with respect to the complex dilemmas she faced. Malkiel's multiple identity as a young Jewish immigrant, a working woman, then a journalist, an attorney's wife, and a committed socialist did not make her choices of priorities any easier as she tried to integrate socialism and feminism.[2]

Suffragist struggles were led by several organizations such as the National American Suffrage Association, which established its head-quarters in New York in 1901, and Carrie Chapman Catt's Women's Suffrage Party, also based in New York. Between 1907 and 1910 more suffragist groups were formed—evidence of a more widespread response to feminist campaigns and to the increasing number of young immigrant workers who became active in women's organizations. There were also groups such as The Women's Trade Union League and the settlement houses, among whose objectives was to gain suffrage for women. Although militant suffragists barely managed to get their message across in traditional political forums, they won the recognition of the New York State Democratic and Republican parties in 1916, both of which came out in support (although with certain reservations) of an amendment for women's voting rights throughout the state.

The SPA, an exception to the general indifference displayed toward women's rights, was the first political organization to welcome women into its ranks. From its inception in 1901, the SPA favored equal civil and political rights for men and women alike. In August 1907, the Second International convened in Stuttgart; it instructed the SPA and other socialist parties to endorse women's voting rights. Hence, suffragists in the SPA were officially encouraged to pursue their goals at a time when no other party had taken a stand on the issue. Around this time, a SPA militant, Josephine Conger-Kaneko, founded a monthly, *The Socialist Woman* (which was to become *The Progressive Woman*[3] and then *The Coming Nation*). In 1908 the Women's National Committee was formed, with the stated aim "to make intelligent socialists and suffragists of women and to secure their active membership in the Socialist Party."[4] From this time on, the SPA became more vigorously involved in suffragist activities, especially on the Lower East Side and in working-class neighborhoods. However, the Party was later weakened by ideological disputes, and the momentum of these activities slowed down around 1912. Hence, agitation for women's suffrage was mainly the work of women's organizations and their allied groups, men's organizations such as the SPA, and unions (for instance, the ILGWU in the garment industry) whose members were primarily Jewish and socialist women.

Integration and Separatism

In the United States, England, and France, whenever confronted by hostility or outright refusal by parties and organizations to admit them, women usually saw fit to keep their distance and organize themselves separately. Despite its pioneering role in this area, the SPA was riddled with contradictions from the beginning. On the one hand, the Party considered it desirable to maintain and encourage a relationship, even if it was an uneasy one, with autonomous women's groups; on the other, the Party wished to regain and monopolize the political initiative it had enjoyed by recruiting women members. As international pressure for women's suffrage became more pronounced and as suffragist activism increased, these two tendencies within the SPA continued to coexist, but became two distinct stages.

The separatist tendency, very strong before 1908, became less vocal after the National Women's Committee (NWC) was founded, only to come to the fore once again around 1914. During this period two types of groups were formed. As SPA regional offices were set up throughout the country, women were organized into local groups. To be sure, an increase in strength from 4,000 to 20,000 between 1901 and 1904 indicates that recruiting efforts had met with some success. At the same time, women with socialist leanings established autonomous groups of their own. While not composed of card-carrying members of the SPA these groups nonetheless enjoyed a close alliance to the Party. It was to these clubs that the early issues of *The Socialist Woman* were directed, especially the August 1907 issue. In some clubs, militants' wives, sisters, cousins, and girl friends busied themselves with the Party's good works (charity sales, Sunday schools, etc.). Such "auxiliary" activities, in keeping with the tradition of "women's missions of mercy," provided SPA militants with convenient opportunities during which to inculcate political ideas in the minds of their young apprentices. Yet, on occasion, women belonging to autonomous groups took more radical initiatives, and some discussion groups, such as the Women's Socialist League of the Women's National Socialist Union became politicized to the point of competing with the SPA on its own turf. The Women's National Socialist Union, very active on the West Coast, sought to introduce women to socialism. The SPA accused it of "bourgeois feminism" and systematically boycotted it. Its disappearance in 1904 did not mark the end of autonomous group activism, however, for the groups survived the establishment of the NWC in 1908. Even SPA militant women like Malkiel, whose political views differed from those expressed by such groups, recognized their usefulness.

The stormy relations between the SPA and similarly oriented groups illustrate one of the contradictions inherent in any political approach to feminism, for women's struggles to institute programs and form organizations did not adhere to any particular political "line" and were swinging constantly between integration and separatism.

How did front-line militants such as Lena Morrow-Lewis, J. Conger-Kaneko, and T. Malkiel define the issues, the dual dynamic of integration versus separatism, group autonomy versus SPA leadership? How did SPA feminists deal with their lack of recognition? How did they choose from among their alternatives? Two points bear keeping in mind: first, even if some women were particularly concerned with women's issues, they devoted most of their energies to SPA activities. To do political work elsewhere was out of the question. However, this did not prevent them from belonging to other groups; Malkiel, for example, dissatisfied with the Party's defense of immigrant women workers, formed a local autonomous group, Women's Progressive Society of Yonkers. Second, the SPA's functional misogyny was bound to be grist for the mill of those who opted for separatism. In 1908, in an article by John Spargo,[5] the Party's sexist attitudes were denounced by Party members, men and women alike. Similarly, in a gesture of self-criticism, Kitchi-Kaneko accused militant socialist men of lacking interest in the political education of their wives. As a result, men went to meeting halls while women settled for meetings in churches.[6] In 1909 Malkiel derided the blatant misogyny in an article by "Comrade" Cohen,[7] who defined women as living creatures and, placing them in the same category with animals, ascribed to them innate instinctual and intuitive qualities superior to those of men. Statistics confirm existence of sex discrimination with the Party: In 1904 the number of women Party members rose substantially, though the number of women in prominent positions did not increase proportionately. Exasperated by the Party's scornful attitude toward their participation in politics[8] women began demanding equality and, above all, recognition. "Women are tired of being 'included,' tired of being taken for granted. They demand definite recognition,"[9] wrote Conger-Kaneko. She heaped blame on the Party for its noticeable negligence of women, noting that the Party had not bothered to follow women into their kitchens as it followed men all the way "to their lairs—to the street corner, to the trade union hall, to the saloon."

Socialist women reacted to latent or open hostility by becoming aware of what set them apart from men. Views varied in degrees from asserting that the two sexes had no interests in common to declaring that there was indeed a "difference" which justified the establishment of a distinct and separate type of organization. A militant from Los Angeles remarked that perhaps women needed to think for themselves and express themselves in each other's company before taking up the struggle at their male comrades' sides.[10] It was a strategic separatism, based on women's need for an identity and a divergence of interests between the sexes, Kaneko and Malkiel took a maternalistic view of the matter, suggesting the need for a program directed at late beginners:

> In a separate organization the most unsophisticated of little women may soon learn to preside over a meeting, to make motions and to defend her stand with a little "speech.". . . After a year or two of this sort of practice she is ready to work with the men.[11]

The establishment of the wwc at the May 1908 National Socialist Party Congress marked an important stage in the relationship between the Party and socialist women, but did not significantly affect the existence of the autonomous groups; it merely facilitated propaganda and training efforts by providing for the production of brochures and pamphlets in a more systematic fashion. On the other hand, the new body (wwc) succeeded in being incorporated in the Party's constitution and in participating on high-level committees. Although recognition was still relative, especially as regarded financial matters, the establishment of the wwc had a positive effect both on the external activities (national propaganda, support for the "strike of the 2,000" women's suffrage) and on the inner workings of the spa.

Class Consciousness–Women's Consciousness

Suffrage

Separatism was the subject of much debate in discussions of women's suffrage and the spa's relationship to suffragist organizations. It should be remembered that the spa and the Progressive Party were the first to stand up for equal voting rights. When the Second International passed its resolution on the issue in 1907, it sent a double message: "it ordered socialist parties in all countries to support women's suffrage, but barred women from abandoning the socialist struggle for the salons of bourgeois suffragists."[12] This latter directive was construed by Josephine R. Cole as unacceptable interference in the affairs of national parties, especially in those of socialist women. In her opinion, women were free to choose their political alliances according to the prevailing circumstances. She caustically remarked that in all the years she'd worked in the SPA, she'd never heard any of its orators energetically support women's suffrage.[13] In the National Socialist Party Congresses of 1908 and 1910, pro- and anticooperation forces clashed violently. Was their disagreement tactical or strategic? The answer is not unequivocal. Malkiel, one of those who identified herself as a member of an oppressed class and whose primary concern was the class struggle, thought it was high time for the working-class party to assume responsibility for agitating and educating people about women's voting rights, the attainment of which, she believed, was surely not far off. "The right to vote is our birthright," declared a woman delegate to the 1910 Congress. Civil and political equality between the sexes was written into the SPA's convention; so what need was there to organize separate groups? And was it not absurd to divert both time and energy from the struggle for socialism in order to work politically with "bourgeois ladies"?

Those who argued for Party efficiency and ideological purity seemed to be distrustful of the ruling class and doubtful of the socialist militants' ability to "take over" the suffragist movement and infiltrate its ranks. A woman delegate to the 1910 Congress warned the young women workers that the suffragist groups were out to snatch them away from the Party.[14] Malkiel argued that, if the Party preached class struggle at the same time as "cooperation," they would lose credibility with women workers, who would be at a loss to comprehend such a contradictory stance.

Not only did they perceive the possibility of competition which might coax away adherents to socialism, but SPA militants distrusted any action that did not stem from the class struggle. Thus, during this period, Clara Zetkin quarreled vehemently with British suffragists who advocated "limited" suffrage; she accused them of ignoring the interests of the female proletariat who would not necessarily qualify to vote under the provisions of property-based law.[15] Of the same view, a woman delegate to the 1910 Congress pointed out the limitations of winning political rights in a social context that remained unchanged: she declared that it strained credulity to believe that a female boss, for example, would not continue to monitor her employees' votes. Many suggested, in different ways, that the suffrage issue did not constitute a cause common to all women and that, in a class-bound society, "sisterhood" was a hollow idea. Harboring no illusions about the balance of power, Emma Goldman predicted that, when high-society ladies acquired suffrage, they would vote in accordance with their own interests and the reign of money would continue.[16] What everyone agreed upon, in varying degrees, was that, in order of priorities, socialism came well before women's rights and that class struggle alone was the miracle cure for any inequalities: "the same blow necessary to strike the chains from the hands of the working man will strike them from the hands of the working woman."[17] Was that not tantamount to saying that there was no divergence of interests between the sexes? Was that not denying that any confrontation could arise from the struggle—separatist or otherwise—to attain the vote for women?

Those opposed to "cooperation" often made reference to Ava Belmont and Anne Morgan, whom they invoked as symbols of upperclass suffragists. Even though their organizations lent crucial financial support to the shirtwaist strikers in 1910, they were dubbed "the mink brigade" and participation by such "high class ladies" was not well received in working-class circles.[18] Indeed, these representatives of New York's high society were worlds apart from women who were exploited on the job: "the bitter cry for bread has no meaning [for them. They are] too far removed from the actual battlefield."[19] Moreover, some of their activities—interviewing striking workers in a chic nightclub, organizing a procession of cars—were considered condescending and ostentatious. Their hostility to socialist ideas was made all too apparent in a meeting on January 13, 1910, when Anne Morgan accused Morris Hillquit and Leonora O'Reilly of fanatically indoctrinating "unfortunate girls." Even if it were only foot-stamping for the press, the perfidious capitalists[20] were visibly disturbed by socialist influence on the striking women workers.

The socialists' distrust of bourgeois suffragists was not unfounded, for the last manipulative move of these women was an attempt to discredit NWC delegates and undermine socialist support of the strike by branding it as mere propaganda. Theresa Malkiel, Meta Stern, and Antoinette Kolnikow ended up having to explain themselves to the press, which they did somewhat defensively.[21] There was no mistaking it, this was no longer a time in which a sense of universal sisterhood flourished.

Those who favored working with suffragist groups supported their position by claiming that collective action was tactically desirable or by basing their opinions on an optimistic view of the influence of socialism. "Why wage separate campaigns," asked Morris Hillquit, "if the U.S. suffragist movement is for equal political rights?" One woman militant suggested that the Party make use of the voting issue in its recruitment drive. Whatever their views on the possibilities of infiltrating women's groups, those who favored cooperation were motivated by what they felt was the immediate priority that women's suffrage represented. In 1908 "Hebe" explained that the vote for women, even if limited in scope, even if it would at first accrue to the benefit of the

"parasite class," would be immensely beneficial to the workers' movement.[22] Even if women workers had private property interests to
protect, winning the right to vote could only have a favorable effect on
working conditions and the dynamics of workers' power.

Two quotations may serve to summarize the two arguments: "I'm a
socialist first, then a woman," declared Theresa Malkiel. Lena Lewis,
on the other hand, affirmed, "We must first do away with the political
gap between the sexes before making meaningful class distinctions."[23]
The first statement indicates a belief that changing society at large is
the priority; the second, that the priority is the political emancipation
of the oppressed sex.

Particular differences in opinion were overshadowed by the mini-
malist and maximalist debate that had accompanied the SPA from its
early years. Obtaining the vote (albeit limited) for women could be
treated as an immediate demand because, given a static social context,
it was considered pointless to wait for the advent of the new society
before acquiring partial political freedom. It became a question of the
short or the long term: should women get the vote immediately or in
an unspecified socialist future? Did not all political programs have to
come to grips with the now/later dilemma? Or was it implied that men
and women had a different social vision which went beyond class
solidarity? As J. Kaneko intimated, women demanded to be recognized as such because they knew that their interests had always been
different from men's or because they were still fighting for what men
had long since obtained. She quoted Bebel, "Women have as little to
hope for from men as workmen from the middle classes."[24] Malkiel
further insisted that women had to take charge of their own liberation
from oppression; what's more, that they immediately had to resolve
the contradictions they confronted so as not to "build our expectations
on the future freedom and at the same time calmly submit to the
present oppression."[25]

Work

The class consciousness–woman's consciousness dilemma surfaced
in all socialist thought of the period. The Party paid particular attention to the problems of women in the workplace. And wherever
women worked, there was intense competition between the "apolitical" suffragists and the socialists. The woman worker is exploited
just the same as her male counterpart, asserted Malkiel in a propaganda brochure,[26] and if men occupied a more enviable position it
was because they had learned to organize in a collective struggle. It
was up to women, then, to go beyond individual action; they had to

unionize and join in the socialist struggle. Women had to help build
the foundation for a new society. In the prophetic tone that often
characterized her writing, Malkiel spoke of "the beautiful universe . . .
of abundance for all" that thousands of men and women were working to build. She urged women to join those "in whom the sacred fire
burns," "those who will make the trumpet sound announcing the
advent of liberty." In her articles she clearly identified the specific
oppression women experienced. "You are not paid for your housework," she said to the worker's wife; furthermore, what the worker
knew of his own mother's life was a lesson in how marriage, far from
being liberating, ties the wife to constricting, interminable, unpaid
labor.[27] J. Kaneko went so far as to introduce the notion of a "war
between the sexes"—in her view, the degrading nature of women's
work work was attributable to their total lack of political and trade
union power.[28]

The idea of an oppression particular to women was also alluded to
in strike support activities. Response to the striking shirtwaist workers,
for example, certainly was a demonstration of solidarity with proletarian labor, but more so of solidarity with women workers who
identified themselves as such. In addition to the ILGWU, strike support
came mainly from women's organizations. And it was not a coincidence that the SPA sent a group of twelve women to aid striking
workers in New York and Chicago. The woman's proletariat worked
under particularly exploitative conditions. Ever since the turn of the
century the needle trades had been staffed by women workers who
were grossly underpaid, bullied by employers and foremen, kept
under close supervision and subject to fines and sexual humiliation.
Moreover, women usually came up against hostility from the unions,
which were far from supportive. The objective difference between
men's and women's working conditions was clear from the very beginning of the strike and was even turned to good use. Organizations
competed to make a show of enthusiasm for the moral qualities of
tenacity, generosity, and heroism the striking working women demonstrated. Playing on the heartstrings of the public, a new image of
women was created, with emphasis on the pathetic and sentimental.
The title of articles are revealing: "Two Little Heroines," "How Girls
Can Strike."[29] The poor women's heroism and generosity were contrasted to the unfeelingness and selfish egotism of the rich. In New
York and Chicago there emerged a new stereotype of women, that of
young, exploited, but heroic girls out on strike, the new heroines of
the working class. "Pale little girl, frail little girl . . . the outcast of
today but the pioneer of tomorrow."[30]

The socialists also began to point out an aspect of women's oppression that had previously gone unremarked: domestic labor, the non-remunerative, invisible tasks women had to perform, the economic value of which was not taken into account.[31] A worker's wife, as reproductive force, was indispensable to the labor force, but the importance of her role went unrecognized. Household work was considered either an anomaly or an injustice; some proposed its outright abolition, others proposed that it be remunerated as a "social necessity" with a "social" salary.[32] Against the background of the average sociological reality, there were two extreme cases of oppression: women working in nonindustrialized regions (fetching water, chopping wood, spinning, weaving)[33] and young girls, pathetic victims of male oppression, performing manual labor. Since women's work was either underpaid (workshop and factory) or unpaid (at home), be it in the countryside or in the big industrial metropolis, for the socialists this was evidence of arbitrary and unjust economic dependence.

Sexuality

Some socialist propagandists denounced the more secretive domain of sexual life as the most degrading aspect of women's dependence on men. With unaccustomed violence, Malkiel attacked the deadly egotism of man, who, in Oscar Wilde's words, "kills what he loves"—a vampire who, in the name of love, wallows in [his victim's] blood.[34] In Malkiel's articles women are portrayed as men's property, defenseless victims of a blind, unbridled appetite which denies women their desires, their integrity, and their very life. In chastising the "breeding beast" her tone borders on the Malthusian, quite unusual for socialist writing in her time.

If such was woman's expected lot, what about the prostitute who was condemned to the life of an outcast? Malkiel emphasized man's responsibility for his unrestrained appetite; she referred not to "monsters" but to the average man: "We see them enter our homes and marry some of our purest girls."[35] In an effort to demystify the stereotype of the woman who lives in sin, she declared that the prostitute's lot was neither unusual nor permanent. When all was said and done, from whichever angle the multiple manifestations of woman's servitude were viewed, it came back to woman's economic dependency "in marriage, in the shop, in the factory."[36]

A Socialist Utopia

Socialist thinkers who projected a future free from domestic, industrial, and sexual exploitation envisioned a new society where, liberated and regenerated, both sexes would flourish. Utopian dreams of happiness and regeneration were designed to stimulate militant ardor and fire, faith and imagination; in such dreams, past, present, and future were mixed. Adversaries of socialism had always charged that socialism would mean the destruction of the family unit. But articles of the period suggested that the family would be built on a new foundation, after the dusty vestiges of Victorian-era concepts of *home* were swept away. The idea of home was a fiction in a society based on oppression, tenements, unemployment, and in which woman was a servant to man. In the new family under socialism, the "free woman" would no longer be a victim as in the past. "Strong in mind and body, a capable mother, a cheerful companion,"[37] she would lay down the weapons used by the oppressed—wiliness and seduction and "childish illusions." It was predicted that once her horizons, formerly so constricted, expanded to embrace all of humanity, she would be cured of excessive emotional dependency and protected against "romantic" disappointments. Equality for men and women would abolish both her dependency and man's tyranny and would herald a new era of love relationships "on the high plane of comradeship."[38]

Women would fulfill their roles as mothers with a new dignity. From such an exalted position all problems related to motherhood and education would, for all intents and purposes, disappear. Treated as part of the "nation's wealth," children would no longer be the responsibility of one family exclusively. Women, exalted as "mother[s] of the race," would take on the laudatory mission of education. Thus the utopian vision recast the familiar notions of women's "missions of mercy" and women's power, considered not incompatible with the goal of equality. In fact, the short biographical sketches in women's socialist newspapers placed a high value on the positive qualities of mothers and wives. Edifying tales celebrated maternal love. Rather than explore new forms of social organization, women, it was believed, would devote themselves to the regeneration of the race, with their dignified spouses at their sides. What Malkiel, inspired by nineteenth-century ethnology, seemed to be wishing for was a return to an original matriarchy which would establish women's superiority and moral fortitude.

In socialist writings, attention was not drawn to the nuclear structure of the family or monogamy, both of which went unchallenged, remaining the pillars of the new family as of the old. Awareness of women's economic dependence in the home and of the tediousness of domestic labor inspired planning for collective projects, communal apartments and hotels, and the creation of a team of "professional" household workers. A home equipped with the most inviting gadgets was held out as a model: "In the summertime our housekeeper feels like having ice cream . . . one device in the refrigerator makes juice cubes, another ice cream. All these conveniences will be at your disposal in the near future." The references to gadgets (amusing in retrospect) expressed the need for pleasure and enjoyment in what was otherwise a rather austere utopian future. The projected utopia was rarely presented so prosaically, but was part and parcel of a generalized longing for "the music and the dream."

In addition to the wealth of propaganda tracts and brochures, Malkiel wrote a significant text around the time of the Shirtwaist Strike in 1909, *Diary of a Shirtwaist Striker* (1910), in which she tried to integrate an activist struggle and the view of a future life that was usually missing from run-of-the-mill propaganda. How did she express her utopian and political vision? Where did she stand amid the various alternatives referred to earlier in this essay? Her story can be read on two levels: Mary, the young heroine out on strike, struggling against dual oppression as a worker and a woman; and the vision of a socialist future. In this fictional diary, Mary, at the outset a non-politicized worker of American origin, slowly becomes aware of the class struggle by experiencing a strike, solidarity with other women workers, repression, and, of course, socialist propaganda. But Mary is also oppressed by a patriarchal family, and it is through her discovery of exploitation on the job that she begins to see the tyranny built into family relationships. A strong case is made for the link between class oppression (the proletariat) and the oppression of women. In the ardor of her struggle, Mary seems willing to sacrifice father, mother, and fiancé. At one point in the narrative, the reader may wonder if her political conversion will lead her to question the traditional basis of family life and woman's role in it. But the evolution from traditional family life to "new" family life, along with the progression from young proletarian heroine to New Woman, comes about when she reclaims the old roles of wife and mother in a new context, in which the family is perpetuated, but on a more egalitarian basis. The tyrannical lord of the manor becomes an open and flexible partner, willing to accept political guidance from a woman: Mary influences Jim to become a socialist. Thus she embodies the familiar image, so cherished in the nineteenth century, of woman as guide and inspiration. She does not lead her companion toward the divine light, but toward the light of socialism.

Even if the purpose and style of this work bear a close resemblance to propaganda, one wonders why Malkiel felt a need temporarily to forego the tone of admonishment and encouragement she used in brochures and tracts, in favor of a less didactic, more novelistic form.

Could she have felt freer working in a literary mode, freer to convey her feminist message (oppression in the family setting is challenged more energetically here than in her other writing), freer to invent a "story" and, in it, a heroine with whom the reader could identify? It is difficult to answer this question. But surely, in the history of the array of options available to women and the different stances they sometimes adopted, the transition from pure propaganda to the language of fictional propaganda marks a noteworthy stage in the development of feminist-socialist thought. However, here we leave the domain of political discourse to enter the territory of the imagination.

Notes

1. See Malkiel/Basch, *Journal d'une gréviste* (Editions Payot, 1980).

2. On the socialist-feminist dynamic at the turn of the century, see Mari-Jo Buhle's brilliant study, *Women and American Socialism 1870–1920* (University of Illinois Press, 1981).

3. Sarcastic remark by Anna Touroff, representative of Socialist Women of Greater New York during Eighth International Congress in Copenhagen, 1910: "The name *The Socialist Woman* was later 'softened' to *The Progressive Woman*, a name which is milder, and probably more 'attractive'." Report of Socialist Women of New York.

4. M. J. Buhle, "Woman and the Socialist Party," *Radical America* (February 1970), 44.

5. John Spargo, "Woman and the Socialist Movement," *International Socialist Review* 8 (February 1908).

6. "Where is Your Wife?" *The Socialist Woman* (August 1907).

7. "Where Do We Stand on the Woman Question?" *International Socialist Review* 10 (August 1909).

8. National Social Party Congress, 1910, p. 183.

9. *The SW,* May 1908.

10. Mary Garbutt, *Los Angeles Socialist,* December 21, 1901.

11. J. Conger-Kaneko, "Separate Organizations," *The SW,* April 1908.

12. "Women and the International," *The SW,* October 1907.

13. J. R. Cole, "The International and Women's Suffrage," *The SW* (November 1907).

14. National Socialist Party Congress, 1910, p. 188–89.

15. C. Zetkin, "The Limited Woman Suffrage Fight in England," *The SW* (1908).

16. *The New York World,* December 13, 1909.

17. "National Convention on the Woman Question," *The SW,* June 1908.

18. These organizations were The League for Self-Supporting Women and The Equal Rights League.

19. T. Malkiel, "The Dangers of Socialism," *The New York Call,* January 11, 1910.

20. Touroff, August–September 1909, p. 10.

21. *The New York Call,* February 8, 1910.

22. Hebe, "The Socialist Party and Women," *The SW,* July 1908.

23. National Socialist Party Congress, 1910, p. 185.

24. J. Conger-Kaneko, "Why the Socialist Woman Demands Universal Suffrage," *The SW,* March 5, 1908.

25. T. Malkiel, "Woman and the Socialist Party," *The SW,* May 1908, and "Where do we Stand on the Woman Question?" *International Socialist Review* (August 1909), 16.

26. T. Malkiel analyzes the exploitation of young girls: "Little Victims of Large Cities," *The SW,* February 1909.

27. T. Malkiel, "To the Working Woman" and "My Sisters in Toil," *The SW,* July 1908.

28. J. Conger-Kaneko, "Why the Socialist Woman demands Universal Suffrage," *The SW,* March 1908.

29. W. Mailly, "How Girls Can Strike," "Two Little Heroines," *The Progressive Woman,* February and May 1910.

30. Immortalized by Hebe (Meta Stern) in M. J. Bule, "Socialist Women and the 'Girl Strikers' Chicago, 1910," *Signs* (Summer 1976).

31. L. P. Robinson, "Work and Housework," *The SW,* August 1908.

32. W. Lanfersiek, "How Shall Mothers Be Recompensed under Socialism?" *The Progressive Woman,* March 1910.

33. May Walden, "Woman's Slavery," *The SW,* September 1907.

34. T. Malkiel, "Vampire," *The PW,* April 1910.

35. T. Malkiel, "Our Unfortunate Sisters," *The SW,* November 1908.

36. J. Conger-Kaneko, "Marriage and Divorce," *The SW,* July 1907.

37. T. Malkiel, "The Free Woman," *The SW,* October 1908.

38. J. Conger-Kaneko, "Is the American Family to Die?" *The PW,* March 1909.

FEMINISM, SOCIALISM, AND SEXUAL FREEDOM

THE WORK AND LEGACY OF CRYSTAL EASTMAN AND ALEXANDRA KOLLONTAI

Blanche Wiesen Cook

Historically, a vigorous feminist tradition united the principles of socialism with personal and sexual freedom. To reclaim the fullness of that tradition it is necessary to review why and how it was abused, neglected, and erased for so long from our consciousness.

To reexamine the work and cultural heritage of feminist theorists Crystal Eastman and Alexandra Kollontai, who considered revolution in terms of freedom, socialism, and feminism, is to challenge conventional attitudes cherished by right and left. Ultimately we have been limited to reactionary choices: Under capitalism the mythical choice is alleged to be a "free market" or uncontrolled economy on behalf of political liberty and personal freedom; under socialism it is social control on behalf of full employment and economic security. Since both Eastman and Kollontai recognized that political and social liberty were limited under capitalism to the privileged and economically dominant few, they both turned to socialism's promise of an end to economic brutality, mandated unemployment, and starvation wages as the basis of their program. But they rejected as absurd the notion that socialism involved political or personal repression. Their vision involved a transformation of humanity, social and sexual liberation, more freedom. It involved personal joy, intellectual growth, satisfying work, and fulfillment for every individual.

Eastman and Kollontai were feminists who believed that women should seek and use power to transform society and to change the

358

conditions of their private lives. I do not mean to suggest here that they agreed on all issues. On the contrary, their views reflected basic differences regarding alliances, priorities, and methods. The most fundamental difference was Eastman's primary alliance with feminists, across class lines, on behalf of women's rights, as contrasted with Kollontai's early contempt for the bourgeois feminist movement. Without a feminist support network to rely upon, Kollontai became increasingly isolated, until her years in exile when she was surrounded largely by liberal Western feminists. Eastman's centrality to the movement for equal rights feminism endured over time, despite the indifference or hostility some of her colleagues felt for her socialist views.

Eastman and Kollontai were committed to changing the role and position of women in society. They believed in the energizing power of sexual contentment. They sought harmonious and communal living arrangements. They were dedicated to individual integrity and personal independence both in and out of marriage. They deplored poverty, social repression, and war.

They were political activists whose lives were engaged in creating an environment that would nurture socialism, feminism, and sexual freedom. For Eastman and Kollontai these elements were not separate, distinct, and alienated from each other. They were connected. The history of their dissonance, of the cruel separation made between personal freedom and economic revolution, between feminism and socialism is the history of an unfulfilled and deeply flawed revolution.

Mindful of the economic, racial, and heterosexual privilege that dominates capitalist culture, Juliet Mitchell has written that while it "is true that to date the socialist countries still tend to discriminate against women—it is hardly surprising given the length and nature of their pre-history. But what is more important is that oppression of women is *intrinsic* to the capitalist system—as it is *not* to the socialist." On the other hand, Eastman and Kollontai, as well as other late nineteenth- and early twentieth-century socialists raised the issue of women's liberation, both in terms of women's oppression due to economic dependency on men and in terms of women's sexual subordination to men. Yet today these issues remain in a secondary and trivialized place within the organized male-dominated left. The extent of the continued trivialization of women and of issues of personal freedom and social transformation, remains so severe that Juliet Mitchell has called it a veritable "counterrevolution." The continuance of the personal and sexual repression of women under socialism, no less than under capitalism, and the insistence on traditional familial arrangements, on the maintenance of patriarchy, has been made possible in part by the disappearance and the ongoing denial of a tradition that promised socialism with feminism and the loss from our consciousness of the leading theorists of that tradition. The reappearance of the work and the writings of Crystal Eastman and Alexandra Kollontai has only now begun, after fifty years of obscurity as victims of a systematic historical wreckage.[1]

Both Eastman and Kollontai were widely read and respected in their own lifetime. Eastman was an attorney who specialized in labor law and civil liberties. Her investigative study *Work Accidents and the Law* (1910) was a major contribution to the workers' movement for industrial health and safety. New York's governor Charles Evans Hughes appointed her first woman commissioner of the New York Commission on Employers' Liability and Causes of Industrial Accidents, Unemployment and Lack of Farm Labor. In that capacity, she drafted New York State's first workers' compensation law, which became the model for many states and the federal government. She was also appointed to several positions within the Labor Department of the United States prior to World War I. At the same time, she campaigned for women's suffrage and birth control, as well as other issues of interest to women, including equal educational and work opportunities, equal pay for equal work, and a program for the physical "regeneration of the female sex."

With champion swimmer Annette Kellerman, who toured the United States from her native Australia, Eastman promoted the popular entrance of women into the world of sports. To promote her vision of women's power, Crystal Eastman spoke before large audiences on "women's right to physical equality with men." Journalist Freda Kirchwey, then a student at Barnard College, recalled that Eastman pictured a Utopia of athletes, with women "unhampered by preconceived ideas of what was fit or proper or possible . . . to achieve." Eastman believed that "when women were expected to be agile, they became agile; when they expected to be brave, they developed courage; when they had to endure, their endurance broke all records." According to Kirchwey, as Eastman "stood there, herself an embodiment of tall, easy strength and valor, her words took on amazing life."

Eastman began to call herself a socialist during her student years. She graduated from Vassar in 1903, received an MA in sociology from Columbia University in 1904, and graduated second in her class from New York University Law School in 1907. She worked her way through graduate school as a recreation leader and social worker at the University Settlement House. Her Greenwich Village apartment, which she shared with other suffragists and attorneys—Madeleine Doty, Inez Milholland, and Ida Rauh—became a major communications center for labor reform, suffrage, and birth control activities. Her first major expression of socialist militancy appears in a 1911 article, "Three Essentials for Accident Prevention," in which she deplored the tragedy of the Triangle Shirtwaist Company Fire, in which 140 women locked into the room that had been their "sweatshop" perished. "When healthy women and men die because of preventable disasters," she wrote, "we do not want to hear about 'relief funds'. What we want is to start a revolution." Nothing short of revolution would finally end "this unnecessary killing and injuring of workers in the cause of industry." The first step toward that revolution, Eastman believed, was collecting the information, compiling the statistics, demonstrating the reality that revolution was necessary to prevent economic disaster and human suffering.

During the war Crystal Eastman continued to champion suffrage, but her major political emphasis became the anti-interventionist movement which protested imperialism, the growing military-industrial complex, and the erection of militarist politics that stifled dissent and the celebrated Anglo-American traditions of liberty and democracy. She organized the Woman's Peace Party of New York in 1914, inspired by the antiwar suffragists whom she had met at the Budapest suffrage conference in 1913—Emmeline Pethick-Lawrence, Dr. Aletta Jacobs, and Rosika Schwimmer. She introduced Pethick-Lawrence to Jane Addams, and together they founded the Woman's Peace Party which was to affiliate with the international women's movement for peace. As executive director of the American Union Against Militarism (AUAM), Eastman orchestrated a private citizens' lobby to keep the United States neutral, to keep the United States from invading Mexico in 1916, and to oppose the growing militarism of American society. When the United States entered the war in April 1917, she and Roger Baldwin emphasized the work of the Civil Liberties Bureau (later renamed the American Civil Liberties Union) which sought to protect the rights of conscientious objectors and dissenters in wartime.

On July 2, 1917, Crystal Eastman issued a press release to introduce the Civil Liberties Bureau: "It is the tendency even of the most 'democratic' of governments embarked upon the most 'idealistic' of wars to sacrifice everything for complete military efficiency. To combat this tendency where it threatens free speech, free press, freedom of assembly and freedom of conscience—the essentials of liberty and the heritage of all past wars worth fighting—that is the first function of the AUAM today. . . . To maintain something over here that will be worth coming back to when the weary war is over."

Crystal Eastman was radicalized by her wartime experiences. She had lobbied and campaigned throughout what were, before the war, legal and generally acceptable political channels against preparedness and conscription and America's entrance into the European war. The abolition of civil liberties in wartime revealed the fragile nature of bourgeois rights even in a country that boasted fiercely of its democratic heritage. The Espionage Act and the Sedition Act of May 1918 altered the nature of American freedom. Those laws rendered all Crystal Eastman's wartime activity illegal and resulted in the removal of all radical publications from the mails, as well as the imprisonment of countless dissenters, including her brother and many of her closest friends. During the postwar Red Scare thousands of Americans were imprisoned or deported—anarchists, socialists, labor leaders, conscientious objectors.

A socialist before the war, she had maintained faith in the democratic principles generally associated with America. War, the counterrevolutionary mobilization, and the secret Allied intervention against the Soviet Union served to convince her that the only way to "restore liberty" was "to destroy the capitalist system." After the war she and her brother founded and coedited a new magazine of protest and revolution, *The Liberator.* "The world's future," *The Liberator* editorialized in February 1919, "shall not be the League of Business Politicians at Versailles, but the New International, the League of the Working Classes of the World."

In March 1919 Crystal Eastman became the first American journalist to visit Communist Hungary. Her report from Hungary is as valuable for its information as it is for her feelings regarding the contradictions such situations present to "pacifist revolutionaries." There was, she concluded, nothing simple about the dilemma of force. The activities of the invading British, American, and Japanese armies and Admiral Kolchak's "monarchist forces" helped resolve the conflict. The secret Allied intervention in Russia, reported only in *The Liberator,* intended to destroy all revolutionary movements and suspended Crystal Eastman's pacifism.

Above all, Eastman's postwar work was dominated by the crusade for equal rights feminism. After the suffrage amendment was passed, Eastman charted the next phase of the ongoing struggle for women's rights. Women wanted freedom, she explained, and "Freedom is a large word." Her December 1920 article, "Now We Can Begin," is one of the fullest statements of her postwar vision:

> Many feminists are socialists, many are communists, not a few are active leaders in these movements. But the true feminist, no matter how far to the left she may be in the revolutionary movement, sees the

woman's battle as distinct in its objects and different in its methods from the workers' battle for industrial freedom. She knows, of course, that the vast majority of women as well as men are without property, and are of necessity bread and butter slaves under a system of society which allows the very sources of life to be privately owned by a few, and she counts herself a loyal soldier in the working-class army that is marching to overthrow that system. But as a feminist she also knows that the whole of woman's slavery is not summed up in the profit system, nor her complete emancipation assured by the downfall of capitalism.

Woman's freedom, in the feminist sense, can be fought for and conceivably won before the gates open into industrial democracy. On the other hand, woman's freedom, in the feminist sense, is not inherent in the communist ideal. All feminists are familiar with the revolutionary leader who "can't see" the woman's movement. "What's the matter with the women? My wife's all right," he says. And his wife, one usually finds, is raising his children in a Bronx flat or a dreary suburb, to which he returns occasionally for food and sleep when all possible excitement and stimulus have been wrung from the fight. If we should graduate into communism tomorrow this man's attitude to his wife would not be changed. The proletarian dictatorship may or may not free women. We must begin now to enlighten the future dictators.

Eastman's enlightenment program contained four parts: To arrange the world so that women would have equal opportunity "to exercise their infinitely varied gifts in infinitely varied ways, instead of being destined by the accidents of their sex to . . . housework and child-raising." Then, should women choose housework and child raising for an occupation, it should be "recognized by the world as work, requiring a definite economic reward." To ensure access to jobs and professions, Eastman called for the elimination of all barriers to trades, trades unions, and training. She demanded equal pay for equal work and a "revolution in the early training and education of both boys and girls. It must be womanly as well as manly to earn your own living, to stand on your own feet. And it must be manly as well as womanly to know how to cook and sew and clean and take care of yourself in the ordinary exigencies of life." She was aware that "men will not give up their privilege of helplessness without a struggle" and noted the power of man's "carefully cultivated ignorance about household matters":

> Two business women can "make a home" together without either one being over-burdened or over-bored. It is because they both know how and both feel responsible. . . . Two self-supporting adults decide to make a home together: if both are women it is a pleasant partnership,

more fun than work; if one is a man, it is almost never a partnership—
the woman simply adds running the home to her regular outside job.
Unless she is very strong, it is too much for her, she gets tired and
bitter.

For Eastman the solution involved education, the rearing of "feminist
sons" in a society that honored feminist principles. First of all, economic independence depended on "voluntary motherhood." Birth
control was as essential as equal pay for equal work. Mothers, Eastman
insisted, were entitled to economic independence, and that required a
"motherhood endowment." Since "the occupation of raising children
is peculiarly and directly a service to society," the mother upon whom
"the privilege of performing this service" falls should receive "an
adequate economic reward." Voluntary motherhood, economic security, feminist education, and the removal of all barriers "in every
field of human activity" would secure the first steps of Eastman's
vision of equal-rights feminism.

She was one of four women who founded the Congressional Union
and subsequently the Woman's Party that introduced the Equal Rights
Amendment in 1923. She said at that time that this amendment was
worth fighting for, even if it took ten years. During the 1920s Eastman
lived mostly in England and was incapable of finding steady, full-time
work. From 1921 until her death, as a result of the Palmer Raids and
the "Red Scare," Eastman was unemployed, blacklisted, discontent,
and largely in exile. She and her two children traveled between
England and the United States with commuter regularity. She also
lived in the South of France with her friend Jeannette Lowe and her
children. Her essay "Marriage under Two Roofs," written largely for
money, was not written as spoof. For years, she lived largely apart
from her husband not only under two separate roofs but in two
different countries. Although she wrote for such feminist journals as
Equal Rights and Lady Rhonnda's *Time and Tide*, she thirsted for full-
time work. But the U.S. blacklist was vicious, and all efforts to find her
employment failed. She died in 1928 at the age of forty-seven of
nephritis. With her death, her writings and her vision were muted,
buried, and eventually denied, only to be reawakened with the
women's movement of the 1970s.

Like Eastman, Alexandra Kollontai was well educated, privileged,
and appointed to Party and government office. She studied political
economy in Zurich, and like Eastman, her first publications related to
women's rights and comprised learned and statistical analyses of the
dreadful conditions under which workers toiled. Her first major
work, *The Life of the Finnish Worker* (1903), was an erudite and thor-

ough marxist study of Finland's economy, and resulted in Kollontai's entrance into the ranks of radical economic theorists, which in Russia meant that a warrant was made out for her arrest. From 1903 to 1917 Kollontai was frequently in exile. But she consistently campaigned for women's rights, worked for the recognition of women's issues within Russia's social-democrat (Menshevik-Bolshevik) circles, and taught political economy to workers in a series of Communist Party schools.

In 1911 Kollontai lectured at the Russian Party school in Bologna, and for the first time talked about sexual relations in the socialist movement. In August 1917 she was elected to the Communist Party's Central Committee. After the Revolution she was the first Soviet Minister of Social Welfare (People's Commission for Social Welfare) and the only woman in the Cabinet. In 1920 she was elected to the Party's Central Executive Committee. From 1922 onward she was a leading ambassador, first to Norway, then to Mexico and Sweden. She negotiated the first successful trade agreements that ended Europe's blockade against the new Soviet state. In 1942 she was awarded the Red Banner of Labour for services to the Soviet state to mark her seventieth birthday. In 1945 she was awarded a second red banner for her services during World War II. In 1952 she died at eighty in her home of a heart attack.

To scan the surface of her career one might be impressed by her honors, her seeming power, and the simple fact of her survival through the dreadful purge trials and executions that wiped out every one of the early Bolsheviks. Of the revolutionary generation of October 1917, only Kollontai survived Stalin's terror. But she survived in exile, followed by secret police, harassed, and silenced. Kollontai's exile as ambassador began before Lenin's death. From 1922 to 1945 she was rarely in Moscow, and then only for diplomatic briefings or political recriminations. Her exile followed upon her support for the Workers' Opposition, but the full fury of the Communist Party apparatus was turned against her ideas about women, the family, sexuality, and love. Her insistence on personal freedom as well as workers' control rendered her one of the most reviled women in official Russia. Her intense popularity among workers and young intellectuals, especially both in and out of Russia, possibly saved her life; but her work was subjected to crude distortion, vicious slander, and long-term denial in the still locked files of Russia's revolutionary history.

Present at the creation, and in power, Kollontai was not, like Crystal Eastman, more or less casually lost to history. Her views were specifically rejected and discarded. Kollontai and Eastman both explored the connections between personal relationships and social change. Eastman defined a feminist as "one who believes in breaking down sex barriers so that women and men can work and play and build the world together." In an article on birth control she noted, "Feminists are not nuns. That should be established. We want to love and to be loved, and most of us want children, one or two at least. But we want our love to be joyous and free." Freedom required the political and economic equality of women and men. Until that was established, Eastman believed that women in all socialist parties, movements, and countries required separate caucuses through which to make their demands, and by which to establish their unity. Reporting on a meeting of socialist women from eighteen countries that met at Marseilles in 1925, Eastman wrote: "When the socialist parties of the world do genuinely decide to make equal rights for women a primary aim of their policy, never to be side-tracked for political expedience, then and not till then will we abolish our separate existence."

Kollontai also argued that there should be separate women's committees, indeed a Party-sponsored woman's commission, to promote the political education and interests of women. But unlike Eastman, Kollontai rejected a broad-based alliance with feminists. While they both agreed that only under socialism would women finally be economically secure enough for women's rights to be substantial, Eastman favored active alliances with women in and out of socialist circles to promote the special interests of women. Kollontai relied on the good will of her party comrades in her effort to build separate organizations for women workers and peasants.

Before the Revolution Kollontai experienced all manner of petty insult and personal abuse when she attempted to call a meeting or use party space for women's meetings. Frequently the doors were locked, and her signs reading "meeting for women only" were replaced by notices that the meeting was canceled and a "meeting for men only will be held tomorrow." Kollontai complained that the party leaders recognized the "usefulness" of her political education activities among women workers, but did nothing to support it. Too many identified her work with "hated feminism" and actively hindered her efforts.

Shortly after the Revolution, the Zhenodtel, the women's department of the Party, was organized within the Central Committee. Its tasks included the education, organization, and protection of women workers and peasants. Delegates of the Zhenodtel waged a literacy campaign throughout the vast reaches of Russia, intervened against foremen who abused women workers, established discussion and support networks, disseminated birth control information, and in every way sought to raise consciousness among women concerning personal health and economic independence. As the Commissar of Social Welfare, Kollontai campaigned for a law to legalize abortion, which was passed in 1922. She insisted that the concept of illegitimate children be ended, and she changed all maternity hospitals into homes for maternity and infant care. But like the Zhenodtel, Kollontai's programs were miserably underfunded, understaffed, and the target of frequent hostility. Her goals included equal rights for women in the labor force and as citizens; radical changes in household chores, maternal responsibilities, and family life generally. Her book *The New Morality and the Working Class* (1918) was bitterly criticized. She wrote that Soviet marriage laws were "not essentially more progressive" than those in other countries, and she called for the nationalization of maternity and infant care. This was distorted by her opponents, who declared that she had ordained that little girls of twelve were to become mothers and that she had called for the "nationalization of women."

Shortly after the Revolution, Lenin had seemed to support Kollontai's work. But the reality of Soviet finances and the protracted and vicious counterrevolution, spearheaded by the Allied intervention, all worked to wreck social and economic changes the new state had planned. In addition, Kollontai's model nursery and maternity care palace was burned to the ground. She was discouraged economically and officially. Her views on domestic drudgery and women's enslavement in the kitchen, an accepted aspect of Marxist theory (Engels considered household work unproductive, and the key prop to male domination), resulted in experiments with cooperative living, communal kitchens. But these, like the nurseries, were so poorly staffed and supported that Kollontai's work was rendered a mockery. Yet she persisted until she was dismissed.

While the greatest criticism against Kollontai was directed toward her views on women and the family, she was dismissed for her activities on behalf of the Workers' Opposition.[2] In February 1921, before the Tenth Party Congress, Kollontai publicly defended the Workers' Opposition. The entire Central Party Congress deplored this "divisive" movement that endangered party "unity" in the face of white terrorism, the Allied blockade, and civil war. It resembled *"anarchism," "bourgeois idealism," "syndicalism."* Trotsky called for an obedient, disciplined workers' state, in which each worker would feel "like a soldier of labour." The unions would enforce order. He envisioned "the militarisation of the working class." Lenin too considered the Workers' Opposition the "greatest danger to our continued existence."

The workers had called for the democratization of the work place, workers' input into Party decisions, the transfer of industrial management away from Party bureaucrats and into the hands of unions. At the factory level, control would be with factory committees; unions would ratify all appointments; there would be regular national congresses; local unions would elect local managers; an All-Russian Producers' Congress would be convened. Workers would thereby initiate, influence, eventually control the development of the economy.

Kollontai agreed that revolution could not be imposed by Party bureaucrats who were, to begin with, suspicious of and hostile to workers. Just as the Zhenotdel served the women, so unions "could now encourage workers to assert their independence and creativity." It was a period of starvation, unemployment, dislocation, corruption—led by highly paid bureaucrats particularly resented for their new roles in unions and soviets. Kollontai's defense of "The Workers' Opposition" was precise.

Fiercely, for fifty pages, she denounced the leadership—their priorities, compromises, and nonrevolutionary attitudes. She accused them of "adaptation and opportunism," and warned that their current road to revolution could lead away "from the future to the debris of the past," littered with an even more rigidified "abyss between the 'ups' and the 'downs'." The immediate reason for the Workers' Opposition, she pointed out, was the fact that "the economic situation of the working class . . . has not only not been improved," it became "unbearable":

> The Commissariat of Labour is the most stagnant institution of all the Commissariats. . . . The rank-and-file worker is observant. He sees that so far as the problems of hygiene, sanitation, improving conditions of labour in the shops . . . has occupied the last place in our policy. . . . To our shame, in the heart of the republic, in Moscow itself, working people are still living in filthy, overcrowded and unhygienic quarters, one visit to which makes one think that there has been no revolution at all.

Peasant conditions improved, specialists lived well, bureaucrats lived well, workers were still to be integrated into the workers' state. The task now, Kollontai insisted, was for the Party to heed the workers' call, "fearlessly to face the mistakes" of its path, and to correct "the activity of the Party by means of going back to democracy, freedom of opinion, and criticism inside the Party." The Party's task was not to control the workers, to dominate and supervise. "The Party task is to create the conditions—that is, give freedom to the working masses united by common industrial aims—so that workers can become worker-creators, find new impulses for work . . . and discover how to distribute workers in order to reconstruct society. . . . *Only workers can generate in their own minds new methods of organising labour as well as running industry.*" There was, for Kollontai, one simple Marxist truth: *"It is impossible to decree communism."* She considered "fear of criticism" ridiculous. There can be no self-activity without freedom of thought and opinion, for self-activity manifests itself not only in initiative, action, and work, but in independent thought as well.

Kollontai's defense of the Workers' Opposition coincided with the Kronstadt uprising. On February 28, 1921, the sailors at Kronstadt, in the Gulf of Finland, demanded a new soviet revolution and initiated a general strike. They called for the reelection of soviets by secret ballot, freedom of speech for all parties, the restoration of union freedoms, amnesty for all revolutionary political prisoners, an end to official propaganda, and an end to "the shooting of foragers." From March 2–17 the sailors prevailed and issued a daily paper. On March 6 Trotsky announced he planned to destroy the mutiny by military force. The Communist sailors of Kronstadt were decreed traitors. During "the battle at Kronstadt," 4,127 people were wounded, 527 were killed, and many others were drowned.

Throughout the spring and summer of 1921, Kollontai defended the Workers' Opposition. Her essay was translated and printed in Germany and the United States. The iww printed it with an introduction that praised Kollontai "for exposing the brutality of the Bolshevik dictatorship." During the June Comintern Congress, called to approve Lenin's New Economic Policy and condemn the Workers' Opposition, she again denounced the leadership and demanded the integration of the workers into full participation in the decision-making process of the new economy. Met with silence by the entire assembly, she was publicly rebuked the following day by Lenin, Trotsky, and Bukharin. She had been a Menshevik. She was "muddled," misinformed, and "over-emotional." She spoke for nobody but herself. Above all, she had no right to speak. She had breached Party discipline.

The New Economic Policy emphasized the value of the private sector and intensified the roles to be performed by bureaucrats and specialists. Unionists received none of their demands. The Zhenotdel was targeted for significant cutbacks and the number of staff was reduced by almost half. In August 1921 Kollontai was removed from the fray in Moscow and sent on assignment to Odessa. She was isolated, her work trivialized; the Zhenotdel workers, angry that her support for the Workers' Oppositon threatened the existence of the Women's Department, sought to disassociate themselves from her. In January 1922 Kollontai was recalled to Moscow by the Party's Central Committee and expelled as Director of the Zhenotdel. In March, during the Eleventh Party Congress, there was an effort to expel her and other "unrepentent oppositionists" from the Party for the crime of "factionalism." But a majority of the Congress, according to Trotsky, "in open defiance of Lenin's demand" refused to expel them.

Kollontai returned to Odessa. Without official work, she returned to her writings on women. She began a novel, a series of short stories, and articles on the new morality. These works *(Soon—or in 48 Years' Time, Love of Worker Bees,* and *Women on the Threshold of Change)* became the subjects of bitter controversy. But they sustained Kollontai, and she continued writing, publishing, and agitating for changes in the lives of women from exile as Ambassador to Oslo beginning in October 1922.

Opposition to her views on women intensified as violence and unspeakable brutality accompanied efforts to introduce the concept of an independent woman free from paternal or marital bondage. Moslem women in Zhenotdel clubs in Azerbaijan, Turkestan, the Crimea, and the Caucasus were willing to remove their veils and expose the cruelty of their lives—"Our husbands beat us with sticks . . . whenever they felt like it." But they did so at their peril. Men with wild dogs poured boiling water on women as they emerged from a women's club in Baku. Husbands killed their wives for removing the veil. A young daughter was hacked to death by her father and brothers for wearing a bathing suit. Men used the new laws against polygamy to cast out their older wives. In the city of Saratov, free love was interpreted as rape on demand: The city fathers made it a crime to "refuse a Communist." Between 1925 and 1927 a terror campaign against independent women ensued. In Uzbekistan over 200 women were kidnapped and raped; many were murdered. In 1929 Stalin halted the modernization campaign of women in Moslem Russia. He also disbanded the Zhenotdel in 1929, claiming that its work was so successful there was no longer a need for a women's commission. By 1929 in European Russia the concept of feminism was reduced to women's right to work. And Kollontai was blamed for many of the excesses that had occurred during the moment of potential change.

After all, she had introduced the concept of the "New Woman," and had described her fully in 1919: The New Woman was economically independent and undominated sexually. She was not fettered by husband or family. She "asserted her personality" and "protested the universal servitude of women to the state, the family, and society." She fought for her rights as a representative of her sex. She no longer accepted the old notion that the sexes are unequal even in the sphere of physical and emotional experience. The new woman was free, sometimes lonely, but always self-defined. She was different.

The feminine virtues on which she had been raised for centuries: passivity, devotion, submissiveness, gentleness, proved to be fully superfluous, futile and harmful. Harsh reality demands other characteristics from independent women: activity, resistance, determination, toughness, that is to say, characteristics which hitherto were viewed as the hallmark and privilege of men.

With these new characteristics, the New Woman refused to be her husband's servant, her lover's toy, her friend's possession. For her "love is only a stage, only a brief respite on life's path." Able to take for herself the age-old rights and privileges hitherto reserved only for men, "the aim of her life, its content, is the Party, the idea, agitation, and propaganda work." For Kollontai her work was her life. And since her work was time-consuming she insisted on her right to control her time.

Unpossessed, she had no interest in possession. Reminiscent of Emma Goldman's essays on love and jealousy, Kollontai wrote that disinterest in love as possession freed the new women to be comrades, to feel "a collectivity of comradeship in love." No longer jealous, she was free to fulfill herself, her own needs for work and creativity. "The woman of the past had been raised by her lord and master to adopt a negligent attitude toward herself, to accept a petty, wretched existence as a natural fate." But it was now clear that "Everywoman who exercises a profession, who serves any cause or idea needs independence and personal freedom." For the New Woman, in service to the social idea, science, or creativity, love cannot become servitude. In this she separated herself from the past when the dignity of women was measured only by standards of "property-based bourgeois morality," of "sexual purity." In the past (the very recent and rigid Russian past of arranged marriages) a woman who "sinned against the sexual moral code was never forgiven." But today the wife no longer stands beneath the shadow of the husband. Before us stands today "the personality, the woman as human being." This, Kollontai insisted, was one of the great tasks before the revolutionary working class and its Party: "to create healthier and more joyous relations between the sexes." "History has never seen such a variety of personal relationships." The Revolution required "a basic transformation" of the human psyche so that people will be able to "achieve relationships based on the unfamiliar ideas of complete freedom, equality and genuine friendship."

For Kollontai the Revolution was about emancipation, freedom, workers' control, fulfillment. It was about happiness. She believed in the power of love, the energy of love. And she believed in community, work, and purpose. But during the 1921–1922 effort to discredit her, her words were twisted, mocked. Bukharin wrote of her "purely physical" sexual views as "vulgar materialism." "Sex-conservationists" deplored the waste of sexual energy that might better be used to fuel the revolution. In 1925 when Kollontai returned briefly to Moscow to campaign against a reactionary marriage law that reintroduced alimony, but only for "registered" wives, Lenin's interview with Clara Zetkin, held five years earlier, was suddenly published. It was presumably printed to end once and for all Kollontai's influence. Her "ultra-leftist" rejection of women in the traditional role of wife and mother, chaste and virtuous, was forevermore to be depicted as "petty-bourgeois debauchery," damaging to the health of society. In 1923 she had published "Make Way for Winged Eros," in which she celebrated "multifaceted love." She wrote that the task "of proletarian ideology is not to drive Eros from social life," but to create informed sexual "relationships in the spirit of the great new psychological force of comradely solidarity." She insisted on a new respect for different love relationships among society's many differing people, who would be free to choose. Free love did not mean women on demand. For Kollontai it meant, very specifically, choice, options, understanding, and "respect for the right of the other's personality." This, like her other work, was egregiously distorted to give rise to the "glass of water theory," the theory that sex should be as easy and uncomplicated as drinking a glass of water.

In this long interview with Clara Zetkin, Lenin denounced the glass of water theory:

> To be sure, thirst has to be quenched. But would a normal person normally lie down in the gutter and drink from a puddle? Or even from a glass whose edge has been greased by many lips?
>
> . . . . The drinking of water is really an individual matter. But it takes two people to make love, and a third person, a new life, is likely to come into being. The deed has a social complexion and constitutes a duty to the community. . . .
>
> Not that I want my criticism to breed asceticism. . . . Communism should not bring asceticism, but joy and strength. . . .
>
> Be neither monk nor Don Juan, but not anything in between either, like a German philistine. . . . Promiscuity in sexual matters is bourgeois. It is a sign of degeneration. . . .
>
> You should not allow these questions to be handled in an un-Marxist way or to serve as the basis for disruptive deviations and intrigues.

Bourgeois "deviations" threatened Lenin's goal of proletarian purity, which depended on the male-centered family. While Lenin believed that traditional domesticity had reactionary aspects and he encouraged women to work, there were limits to revolutionary change. Lenin believed women wanted numerous children and considered birth control, for example, "bourgeois defeatism." Despite a brief moment of experimentation that involved communal living and cooperative kitchen and laundry arrangements, Lenin and his successors favored the traditional family, traditionally structured.

The rejection of Kollontai's vision of feminism and of all feminist concerns that involved experimentation, personal transformation, and familial alternatives resulted in the persistence of male dominant attitudes and a patriarchal social structure. Having rejected a marxist-feminist perspective, the Soviet leadership had only Engels to rely on for guidance on the "woman question." And Engels too championed marriage and tradition. In *The Origins of the Family, Private Property and the State,* Engels wrote: "The predominance of the man in marriage is simply a consequence of his economic predominance and will vanish with it automatically."

For Engels the traditional family unit was sacrosanct. Relations between men and women, under capitalism so distorted by commodity production, "will flourish on a higher plane under socialism so that monogamy, instead of collapsing [will] at last become a reality."

The liberation of women was thereby limited to women's entrance into the work force. As Crystal Eastman noted in 1923, that would be the easiest part. Men admire women with jobs, especially since the cost of living doubled. Feminism, the feminist consciousness of socialist women like Eastman and Kollontai, had little place here. Questions of domestic labor and its social role, once heatedly debated, were suspended; issues of personal freedom, emotional and sexual equality, were turned aside—or attacked. The New Woman and the new family were reduced to the true woman and the true family. The insistence on tradition in the male-ordered home resulted in the condemnation of all experimentation and difference as disruptive deviationism.

But the rigidification of this position did not occur immediately. Immediately after the Revolution, in fact, the opposite was true. The Family Code of October 1918, which Kollontai influenced above all, was a truly revolutionary document. All children were declared legitimate; wives and husbands were each to control their own earnings. Women, in or out of marriage, could retain their own names, establish their own residences. The hated tsarist passport system which had rendered women slaves in terms of travel and work of their fathers or husbands was abolished. Equal rights over children was granted. And women were officially expected to work and to study.

In the 1920s Dr. Grigorii Batkis, director of the Moscow Institute of

Social Hygiene, issued a pamphlet, *The Sexual Revolution in Russia.* That revolution, wrote Batkis, involved "the absolute non-interference of the state and society in sexual matters, so long as nobody is injured, and no one's interests are encroached upon." Regarding homosexuality specifically, Batkis wrote that all forms of "sexual gratification" are regarded as "natural" and "all forms of sexual intercourse are private matters." That situation did not change until 1934, when Stalin identified homosexuality with Nazism, and homosexual men faced criminal sentences of up to eight years at hard labor.

Today feminism and sexual freedom remain the most cruelly divisive issues. As we look around, it is easy to see in socialist countries and socialist parties, no less than in capitalist environments, a male-dominant and sexually repressive culture. There is nothing simple about that fact. While the right drapes itself in banners heralding family, faith, and flag, the left is in tatters over issues relating to women and sexuality—and workers' control. To understand precisely how that happened, given the reality of our socialist-feminist past, as envisioned by the many women like Eastman and Kollontai, promises to be a vast undertaking. Just to imagine what the Communist world might now look like if the input of the feminists had actually been integrated and absorbed instead of dismissed, denied, and finally buried for over fifty years makes the task clearly worthwhile. From the 1880s to the 1920s feminists insisted that questions of personal growth, personal transformation, and joy were inseparable from questions of economics and politics. During the last month of her life Kollontai imagined the future and concluded: "The world never stagnates, it is always stirring, new forms of life are always appearing." She looked forward to a "wonderful beautiful future" of "Happiness! Happiness for everyone!"

It has been a long hiatus, a costly and cruel hiatus that at once reenforced patriarchy and diminished the promise of socialism. But that was the first phase. Crystal Eastman and Alexandra Kollontai gave us the legacy of their lives, their vision, and their spirit. More than that, their experiences demonstrate the brutality that feminists have faced and will continue to face as men—and their male-identified associates—struggle to keep their power untouched and unlimited, whether in states called capitalist, communist, or socialist. When that power is transformed by feminists and feminist principles, we can begin to consider revolution. Equal rights. Equal opportunity. Work. Control over our own bodies. Pleasure. Power. Today feminists refuse to compromise or suspend those goals. And that is revolutionary.

Notes

1. The quotations from Crystal Eastman's essays are from Blanche Wiesen Cook's *Crystal Eastman On Women and Revolution* (Oxford University Press, 1978).

Much of Alexandra Kollontai's writings are now in print. I have benefited especially from her *Autobiography of a Sexually Emancipated Woman,* introduction by Germaine Greer (London, 1972) and the collection of her writings selected and translated by Alix Holt: *Selected Writings of Alexandra Kollontai* (Lawrence Hill & Company, 1977). Of the recent biographies of Kollontai, I have used especially Cathy Porter's *Alexandra Kollontai* (Virago, 1980)—the most detailed overview of her life and political situation. See also Barbara Evans Clements, *Bolshevik Feminist: The Life of Aleksandra Kollontai* (Indiana University Press, 1979); Beatrice Brodsky Farnsworth, "Bolshevism, the Woman Question, and Aleksandra Kollontai" (*American Historical Review,* April 1976): 292–316; and Anne Bobroff, "Alexandra Kollontai: Feminism, Workers' Democracy and Internationalism" (*Radical America,* November–December 1979): 51–75.

2. See Christine Fauré's article in this volume for further discussion of the reaction of the Soviet Union to Kollontai's role in the Workers' Opposition Movement and of the publication history of her pamphlet *The Workers' Opposition.*

THE UTOPIA OF THE NEW WOMAN IN THE WORK OF ALEXANDRA KOLLONTAI AND ITS IMPACT ON THE FRENCH FEMINIST AND COMMUNIST PRESS

Christine Fauré
Translated by Debra Irving

Alexandra Kollontai, Bolshevik revolutionary, exemplifies the New Woman. This image gains historical strength from the remarkable role she played in the Soviet Union during the early years of that new society. Interested in the emancipation of women from the very beginning, she stressed the needs of members of her sex while she served as People's Commissar for Social Welfare of the young Soviet Republic and then as the government's respected representative and ambassador. Her vision of the future for women took on utopian dimensions. But we must keep in mind that only a minority, indeed a fringe group, shared her political convictions. Although she had access to political decision-making circles, she declined to fulfill many of the collective responsibilities of a regime which had, in her eyes, become bureaucratized too quickly. All too soon, she would be isolated from those who wielded authority.

In the early 1970s, France suddenly rediscovered the utopian ideas of Alexandra Kollontai. They had been neglected by many publishers since the 1920s.[1] There are a number of reasons for this renewed interest, some of which relate to the local political situation in France and others, more broadly, to the intellectual history of Western industrial society. The most obvious political event which helped rescue Kollontai's work from oblivion was the women's liberation movement. Many of the women who came to feminism were initially motivated by their disapproval of the traditional leftist parties (Communist and Socialist) and of those of the extreme left (Maoist and Trotskyite groups). Through demonstrations, slogans, a newspaper,[2] and other writings, the women's movement was inspired by a new libertarian approach to politics, one which adopted and expanded the spirit and forms of political action which had grown out of the events of May 1968. At this point, Kollontai emerged from the political obscurity to which the Soviet regime had condemned her with the republication of her pamphlet *The Workers' Opposition.*

But as we emphasize the importance of the French feminist movement and the events of 1968, we should not forget how the French intellectual left was influenced earlier by the spontaneous revolts of working-class organizations in Central and Eastern Europe (the Hungarian revolt of 1956) which fought against Soviet bureaucratic oppression.

Kollontai prepared the original text for a speech she gave in 1921 at the Tenth Party Congress, where she spoke as the leader of the Workers' Opposition Movement. In the author's own words, the distribution of the text was sabotaged, because the speech deviated sharply from the official Party line. Nevertheless, it was translated into English and appeared in Sylvia Pankhurst's *Worker's Dreadnought,* but we have no date.[3] The translation was reprinted in 1962 by the English political group Solidarity;[4] it was then retranslated into French by the periodical *Socialisme ou Barbarie* in 1964.[5] In 1973, Pierre Pascal uncovered a copy of the French translation he had made at the time the speech was delivered. It too has been published recently.[6]

The publication history of this manuscript serves as an important case study of the fate of works that chose to criticize totalitarianism by making the Soviet Revolution and the subsequent development of Soviet bureaucracy the focus of such a reflection. As a result, it places the discussion of the reemergence of interest in Kollontai into a wider perspective, requiring us to look beyond contemporary French politics to the political and intellectual debates occurring at the present time.

The renewed fascination with Alexandra Kollontai's writings and political career was sparked by the same developments that gave rise to the sudden popularity in the 1970s of the ideas Wilhelm Reich had advanced some forty years earlier. Perhaps only after the thaw initiated by Khruschev at the Twentieth Party Congress (1956) and the transformation of the policies and strategies in the East and in the West could the works of such unorthodox Communists come into their own. Through them, intellectuals on the left have sought to understand the various events that have brought forth repressive regimes such as Nazism and Stalinism.

The influence of the work of Herbert Marcuse has also contributed to creating a receptive audience for Kollontai's politically loaded texts. Marcuse argued that with the growth of industrialization, both in the West and in the Soviet Union, the differences between capitalism and socialism were fast disappearing. He saw instead the evolution of a "global society" which was capable of stifling liberation struggles. In response, new forms of struggle have been emerging which can resist the forces of social integration.[7]

As a spokesman for students in the 1960s and 1970s, Marcuse proclaimed the importance of the pleasure principle and proposed theories about spontaneous outbursts which challenged the future growth of industrial society. According to him, the success of the women's movement was a confirmation of his hypotheses.[8] Against this intellectual background, the notion of a "social utopia" was legitimized. The strength of the imagination was seen as a real weapon against forms of domination and repression.

Despite the contemporaneity of the issues discussed in Kollontai's texts, her writings remain very much part of her own period. The way we ask questions today makes the ones she raised seem foreign. But Kollontai was concerned with similar problems, with the role of sexuality and whether women needed to restructure society entirely in order to make a place for themselves. She simply tried to answer these questions within her own cultural context and as somebody who had been privileged to witness one of the greatest social upheavals in modern history.

The Work of Alexandra Kollontai

For the sake of argument, we might distinguish three stages in Kollontai's work. The first found expression in her earliest book on women, *Social Foundations of Women's Issues*, which she wrote in 1909. Recognized in its day as the most important study on the subject ever made by a Russian woman, the book relied heavily on the approaches of the German Social Democratic movement.

Auguste Bebel's *Women and Socialism* (1879) was the main source for Kollontai, and she quoted from it liberally at the All-Russian Women's Congress of 1908, convened by the "bourgeois feminists," and in the book she subsequently published the following year. Kollontai wrote up her ideas so that they might serve as the basis for theoretical discussion within the workers' delegation.

In *The Social Foundations of Women's Issues,* Kollontai analyzed the crisis of the family which, as a result of the development of capitalism, was no longer performing its old functions. The problems of marriage and prostitution were treated as social phenomena that had to be transformed by working women who would take control of their own situation. While Auguste Bebel set himself the goal of raising the consciousness of the general public regarding the social and political liberation of women, Alexandra Kollontai, following Clara Zetkin's example, spoke directly to working women in order to rally them to the socialist cause and, along the way, to the feminist cause. Following the new standards which were emerging within the working class, she saw communal models which would bring about the disintegration of the family, that outmoded institution of women's repression, and she launched into a polemic with the so-called "bourgeois" feminists on the very subject. While in 1909 Kollontai had acknowledged the Social Democratic Party's effective role in the women's liberation struggle, by 1912 she was criticizing the Party mercilessly, denouncing its bureaucratization and castigating its approach to the woman's question. Furthermore, she attacked local Party leaders for refusing to take her seriously when she came to give speeches on the subject and for their attempts to keep their wives from attending the meetings.

In the second stage, Kollontai's work centered on her social and political role which, after October 1917, was no longer confined to propaganda activities. For five months (October 1917 to March 1918) she held the post of People's Commissar for Social Welfare. During this time, the first Family Code of the Soviet Union was adopted (1918). And it was Kollontai who was primarily responsible for legalizing marriage by civil ceremony, divorce upon demand, and free abortion, among other things. But these measures, each having a different impact, were simply not in line with the prevailing ideology and mentality of a country in which serfdom had been abolished only in 1861.

The third stage began after Kollontai's "ministerial" duties had been fulfilled. Now her writings were characterized by an all-encompassing, deep-rooted desire for innovation on a grand scale. They described a society, utopian in its capacity to generate new social units, yet they did not underestimate the radical nature of the proposed transformations. Most of the following discussion will focus on this third stage.

The twenty-five pages of *The Family and the Communist State* (1919) are devoted to clearing up the remaining ambiguities in the analysis of that outmoded institution the family. Taking up Engels's theory that the reallocation of the means of production entails a radical change in the status of women,[9] Alexandra Kollontai banished from the field all those irrational elements which militate against the coming of the new society, such as class prejudice and uncertainty about how to apply the new forms of social organization. "What was the family's strength in times past? First, that the husband and father supported the family; then, that the parents educated the children. What remains of this today? As we have just pointed out, the husband is no longer the family's sole breadwinner. In this respect, the working woman has become man's equal."[10] The fact that times have changed enables her to conclude that the old world has been left behind and that the march toward a contented society has begun. "In the name of equality, liberty and free love, we call upon workers and peasants, both male and female, bravely and confidently to take up the task of reconstructing human society to make it more perfect, more just and better able to give the individual the happiness he deserves."[11]

In order to understand why such flights of fancy characterize utopian thinking (Kollontai goes on to describe the advent of Paradise on Earth), we must recall what the Revolution meant in material improvements for the entire population, in spite of the civil war and the country's disorganized economy. "The average lifespan increased by 14.8 years during the revolution, from 31.9 to 46.7 . . . the 25% drop in the mortality rate was a precious result, in the demographic sphere, of the Russian revolution."[12] Contemporary prescriptions for bringing about the socialist utopia abound: Alexandra Kollontai's thinking was fed at the communal wellspring of socialist and Communist millenarianism. But to take a new historical view of the situation of women and of such universals as marriage and prostitution was to delve into an unexplored area of utopian thought by bringing to light the feminine component which has not been given political expression in our societies.

At first, the Soviet Republic found itself at odds with women workers and peasants. In a text from 1920 (*Women Workers and Peasants in the Soviet Republic*), she tells us of the difficulties the young state encountered because of women's perennial ignorance.

> In response to the Minister for Social Welfare's attempt, in January 1918, to take over the huge Alexander Nevsky Monastery, which was underinhabited, and turn it into a communal home for invalids, women and priests organized a protest march through the streets of Petrograd, carrying icons and singing religious songs. Women were the

locus of the discontent and unrest of backward social strata. . . . The doors of the Communist Party were wide open to working-class women; by law, they had every opportunity to take part in the work of the Soviets and, through them, to change and improve their material conditions. But instead, women workers and peasants turned away in fear from Communist women and the power of the Soviets, seeing in them only disrupters of the familiar order and traditions, heretics who had separated Church from State, heartless beings who sought to tear children from their mothers to be raised by the State.[13]

Women became the repository of all of society's religious thinking. The fundamental social units had to be reformed in order to counteract this influence. It was through disciplinary measures that Kollontai thought to win out over the masses who were resisting the new regime. "We had to find an original means of reconciliation with the most impoverished women workers and peasants so we could develop special methods of working with women which would force them to recognize their place in society." And she was not afraid to speak of dragooning women as an extreme means of achieving this reshuffling of the social roles. Although the civil war and Communism lent a sense of urgency to this approach, the end of women's oppression was still seen as residing in their strict adaptation to the political and strategic imperatives of the new state; yet the forcible integration of women into the country's social and political life conflicted with these women's own desires.

The indiscriminate nature of this project, which claims to reconcile the social contradictions between the sexes through a new deployment of productive forces, melds in a single destiny the classical individual-collective dichotomy. In this sense, Kollontai interpreted an end to the oppression of women as an end to a particular type of behavior, to a certain situation. In setting up a lay society (separating Church and State), the Bolshevik Party was looking at religion as a force which competed with its government and which was allied with the most conservative social classes. In an activity which paralleled her "planning" efforts, Kollontai had to propose models for new forms of self-expression, which the banning of religious observance had necessitated. Sixty years after the development of the "archetype" of the New Woman, we are witnessing in the Soviet Union a revival of the link between feminine experience and religiosity.[14]

The New Morality and the Working Class (1919), which appeared in French as *La Femme nouvelle et la classe ouvrière*,[15] takes literary examples as the basis for an analysis of the behavior of the New Woman. The "model" is not really literary, however: the new living conditions are its source. Single, no longer enslaved by her emotions, the New

Woman channels all her creative forces into work to benefit society. The importance women traditionally attach to their love lives had been displaced, and social action becomes their main means of self-expression. In defining this new life-style, Kollontai stresses the novelty of behavior in which the external expression of private life ultimately mingles with the work of society. She explains the abolition of individual self-expression by analogy with the control of the means of production by individuals, the sexual possession of women by men, and the image of love relations which women then form in imitation of the initial usurpation. With regard to morality, she handles the contrast between public and private order in much the same way that the Bolsheviks handle economic problems. She represents the importance of the New Woman's sexual liberation as the product of the redirection of all the individual's forces toward social action. It is noteworthy that Kollontai's theories about free love are offshoots of the efforts to define a new or "proletarian" culture, following a trend set by Bogdanov in his *Tectology* (1913–1915): "All of mankind's tasks can be reduced to the transformation of the world through its organization to achieve perfect harmony, and progress will derive from the 'richness and growing intensity of the use of the conscience'." These views would lead Bogdanov to see "revolution less as the transfer of the means of production to the proletariat than as the development of a proletarian culture."[16] And the idea of a proletarian culture involved "the extension of the class struggle" to morality and the arts. That culture, independent of economics and politics, would be the foundation of the coming socialist society.[17] Lenin was probably thinking of Alexandra Kollontai when he so categorically rejected the water-glass theory in an interview with Clara Zetkin.[18] The problem of sex was relatively insignificant in his view, compared with the mammoth efforts required of the proletariat worldwide. Two of Alexandra Kollontai's articles, which appeared simultaneously in Nos. 2 and 3 (1923) of the periodical *Molodaya Gvardia*, one on the poetess Anna Akhmatova and the other entitled "Make Way for Winged Eros,"[19] reaffirm the author's belief in the transformation of society through an uninhibited proletarian culture. "The task of proletarian ideology is not to drive Eros out of sexual relations, but merely to refill his quiver with a new type of arrow, to inform love between the sexes with the spirit of the great new psychic forces: solidarity and comradeship." Alexandra Kollontai's thinking is derived from those Bolshevik heretics who were called God-builders and condemned by Lenin in 1909, in his lengthy work entitled *Materialism and Empiriocriticism*.

In her pamphlet *The Workers' Opposition*, which has wrongly been isolated from her works on women, she voiced a position which broke with the main Party line. In his speech to the Tenth Party Congress, Lenin had described a situation which jeopardized the future of the young government. The growing discontent of the masses called for the implementation of a new economic policy.

Against this background, the demands of the Workers' Opposition, which primarily involved complaints about the diminishing role of the workers in industrial management, emerge as an outgrowth of the struggle for influence within the Party. "Why didn't Comrade Shliapnikov, when he was People's Commissar, and Comrade Kollontai, when she was, teach us how to fight bureaucracy?"[20] Indeed, as expressed in the last stand which Alexandra Kollontai's pamphlet represented, the theories advanced by the Workers' Opposition pursued the ideal of a worker's democracy as the Russian workers had understood it in 1917, when they had created bodies through which they themselves would govern society. These theories opposed politically clear-cut principles to the politicization of the Bolsheviks, who had already taken control of political institutions and were engaged in gaining complete dominance of the production process. Political utopia? Did workers' control make it impossible to adjust to political and social reality, as the Bolsheviks so often argued? Was Alexandra Kollontai deeply committed to the idea of workers' control over production? We are justified in asking these questions in view of the great discretion with which her works handle this commitment which, we must not forget, was the reason for her withdrawal from politics.[21] Whatever the answers to these questions, this militant, who had already rallied to the "left Communists" during the debate over the peace of Brest-Litovsk, losing her place on the Central Committee in the process, showed unflinching political courage in the Party's conflict with the Workers' Opposition. She was one of the twenty-two members of the Workers' Opposition who protested to the Communist International, and the Central Committee tried to bar her from the Eleventh Party Congress of March 1922. In her bravery and rebelliousness, she belonged to the intelligentsia which, on the basis of its liberal beliefs, had led the struggle against the tsar's tyranny since the start in the previous century. Alexandra Kollontai's feeling that the role of proletarian ideology was crucial and her equally deep belief, demonstrated through the Workers' Opposition, in "democratic" means of production management, place her works within the intellectual and cultural mainstream of the Russian intelligentsia, despite her undeniable commitment to Marxist thought and to German Social Democratic theories about women.[22]

In a recent work, an American historian, Richard Stites, has analyzed the components of the various political movements, from the Decembrists to the Revolution, which paved the way for the discussion of women's liberation in Russia.[23] The significance of the nihilist response to the question of women's liberation is self-evident. Chernyschevsky and Dobrolyubov, to whom Kollontai had devoted her first published study, had taken a hard look at sluggish Russian society and concluded that the writer and his art must serve human progress.

"Literature itself is a force which can be used in propaganda." Does not Alexandra Kollontai's work bear out these words of the prematurely silenced nihilist?

References in the French Feminist and Communist Press to the Writings and Activities of Alexandra Kollontai

In 1919, no French traveler had yet been exposed to a stay in the country of the Soviets. After 1920–1921, friends of the new Russia—for the most part Communists recognized by Moscow—sallied forth. It is therefore not surprising that only muted echoes of the upheaval that ended the tsarist regime appear in the militant press prior to 1920. One must recall the slowness and limitations of the means of communication at the time. There is another barrier to our study of women's issues: the feminist press was, on the whole, silent regarding the changes which had taken place in Russia because it was preoccupied with the fruitless effort to break down the obstacles to French women's suffrage. One had to be involved fairly deeply in the socialist movement to be interested in what was happening in such a far-off land. We will therefore draw our examples from the feminist-socialist press, in the broad sense of the term.

In the feminist periodical *La Voix des femmes*[24] we find a number of articles[25] concerning the status of women in Soviet Russia which preceded the accounts of Madeleine Pelletier's[26] 1921 trip as a special correspondent for the publication. These articles, which are favorable to the new government, are generally vague. A revealing example of this disparity between the tone of political support and that of personal observation is the article which Pelletier wrote before her departure, "The Future Family," which reflects her whole-hearted commitment to the socialist ideal: it reads like a profession of faith.

> The Russian Revolution frees women from every aspect of their servitude by industrializing domestic tasks. Teams of professionals clean the house; clothes, undergarments and shoes are taken out to repair shops which refurbish them; home cooking has been abolished, every-

one eats at restaurants, and no one is the worse for it. . . . One could say that in France, only the grande bourgeoisie has friends; the middle class, and even more so the working class, are restricted to the close circle of the family, which is itself restricted to the couple and their children. In the future society, entertaining will no longer be a luxury, and life will be enhanced and more joyous for it.

The tone of her first impressions, published in *La Voix des femmes* upon her return from Russia, is completely different.

Can a feminist declare herself "entirely" satisfied with the status of women in Russia? I love Communist Russia and ardently hope that it will triumph, but truth, which must come first, obliges me to answer, "No!" . . . There can be no objection from the legal point of view: women have the same rights as men, the same powers and almost the same duties. . . . But in practice, things are altogether different, and women actually perform only subsidiary tasks. . . . They fed me the old French clichés there: women are inferior, they have a special role, a vocation to charm, etc., and my heart sank as I thought of how I had travelled several thousand kilometers under horrible conditions to hear a new version of old Western prejudices.

This article on the status of women in Communist Russia comprises excerpts from Pelletier's book, cleverly put together in order not to have an unduly demoralizing effect on readers while giving them first-hand information.[27] Subsequently, regular accounts, again comprising excerpts from the author's book, continued to inject their note of reality. Pelletier takes a shrewd look at Russia, despite all the linguistic and bureaucratic barriers she has to cross. Her writings about Kollontai aptly summarize the political climate of the period:

Although I've seen her several times, she seems reluctant to talk politics, because someone is always there. All I've learned from her is that the Bolsheviks were wrong not to place more faith in the working class. . . . She tells me that the left Communists are gaining more and more supporters. At present, she is concentrating on feminist propaganda, which she directs. She has written a book: the women around her think it actually too advanced and have advised me not to promote it in France. I think, on the contrary, that it should be promoted: it calls for absolute sexual freedom with, as a corollary, legal abortion and state responsibility for raising children. There is only one thing about which I do not agree with this Communist leader: she makes the sexual act a moral obligation.

Pelletier's stay in the Soviet Union was punctuated by frequently comical episodes that reflected the militant feminist's inability to accept the militarized, already bureaucratized, world of Russia at that time.

Not many women journalists undertook the voyage to the country of the Soviets to report on the extent of the social upheaval. Louise Weiss took the plunge at the same time as Madeleine Pelletier, and in the same solitary manner. Her account, "Five Weeks in Moscow,"[28] is a lively portrait of Kollontai's personality. She seems to have seen the radicality of ideas about the transformation of the status of women as being linked to widespread poverty and views the role of Alexandra Kollontai, whom she considers a first-class revolutionary, as having been overwhelmingly important.

"Nothing but abject poverty is behind this law [the decree on legal abortion]. Women can no longer feed their children, the community is still unable to bring them up, and so what is to be done? It's better to authorize, provisionally, what we cannot prevent." Weiss's account of this dialogue between the two women seems to conform more to the laws of French journalism than to the bold claims of the Bolsheviks at that time. Louise Weiss was playing to a public that would respond to an account of Russia's woes and titillating its interest gradually and carefully. Her 1921 speech on the situation in Russia made no reference to Communist ideas about women's liberation.

The Socialist and Communist press was generally discrete regarding women's liberation. Under pressure from the Communist International, *L'Humanité* (the French Communist newspaper) announced that the French Communist Party would take a new approach to women's problems: it would establish a secretariat for women and launch a Communist women's newspaper. In the meantime, the "Women Workers' column in *L'Humanité* must gather information affecting women and publish it once a week." With very little space assigned to them, throughout 1921–1922 these columns never mentioned the work of Alexandra Kollontai, with one exception: *L'Humanité* of Nobember 28, 1921, published a communiqué from the International Secretariat of Women Communists written by its Secretary—Kollontai.

In *L'Ouvrière*, the Communist weekly for women established in March 1922, there was no such sponsorship, deliberate or otherwise. It frequently referred to two works by Kollontai: *The Family and the Communist State* and *Women Workers and Peasants in the Soviet Republic*. Add to this the in-depth articles on the status of women in Soviet Russia: Marguerite Rosmer's enthusiastic account (September 16, 1922) of the fundamental change in attitudes and the lyrical letter to Kollontai by the Dutch marxist Henriette Roland-Holst, who was also a great poet: "You and I understand each other as two women who have a place for one another in our hearts and feel that we have much in common." Nor did Kollontai's downfall prevent her writings from being printed. Such was her authority on women's questions that it was impossible to reduce its effect at that time. Finally, however, in 1923 two articles by Trotsky in *L'Ouvrière* urged the need for a new family structure.[29] The moderation of his words undercut the radical optimism of Kollontai's positions. In these articles, he implicitly criticized the best-known theses of the author of *The New Morality and the Working Class.*

Did Trotsky's prestigious name have to be deployed to oppose Kollontai's authority? Were his articles part of the war which was already raging among the founders of the Bolshevik Party and which would become even more virulent under Stalin?[30] Perhaps. Whatever the reason for publishing Trotsky's articles, we do know that Kollontai was subsequently silenced. She would not be read again widely in France for another forty years.

Notes

1. French editions of the works of Alexandra Kollontai (in chronological order):

> *La Famille et l'Etat communiste,* Paris, 1920
> *L'Ouvrière et la paysanne dans la République soviétique,* Paris, 1921
> *La Femme nouvelle et la classe ouvrière,* Cahiers de l'Eglantine, Paris-Bruxelles, 1932
> "L'Opposition ouvrière," in *Socialisme ou Barbarie,* Janvier–Mars, 1964 (based on the English translation published in *The Worker's Dreadnought,* no date, London). Introduction by P. Cardan
> *Anthologie Alexandra Kollontai: marxisme et révolution sexuelle* par Judith Stora-Sandor. Ed. Maspéro. Paris, 1973, 1977
> *L'Opposition ouvrière,* traduction intégrale exéouté en 1921 d'après la brochure originale non mise dans le commerce par Pierre Pascal, Ed. du Seuil. Paris, 1974. Préface d'Anne Valh.
> Alexandra Kollontai, "Des gentilshommes repentants aux apparitchiki: féminisme et révolution."
> *Anthologie. Autobiographie suivie du roman "les amours des abeilles travailleuses."* Préface Christine Fauré. Ed. Berg-Belibaste. Paris, 1976
> *Conférences sur la libération des femmes: Alexandra Kollontai* (introduction J. Heinen) Ed. La Brèche. Paris, 1978
> A very complete bibliography on A. Kollontai has been published by Henryk Lenczyc. *Cahiers du Monde russe et soviétique.* Vol. XIV. 1–2 (Janvier–Juin 1973)

2. *Le Torchon brûle,* 6 issues, 1971-1973.
3. The original 1921 text by Kollontai was never published. As a result, the

sources for the American, German, and English versions mentioned by Blanche Cook in her article in this volume and myself are of questionable authenticity.

4. Solidarity: an ultraleft English political group formed in 1960 which characterized Eastern countries as exploitative societies and the bureaucracy as the new dominant class.

5. *Socialisme ou Barbarie*, 1949–1965.

6. Pierre Pascal went to Russia in 1916 as a delegate to the Russian military staff. The events of 1917 were to win him over to the cause of the Bolsheviks.

7. Herbert Marcuse, *The One Dimensional Man* (Boston: Beacon Press, 1964).

8. Herbert Marcuse, *Actuels: Echec de la nouvelle gauche, Marxisme et féminisme, Théorie et pratique* (Recueil de conférences) (Galilée, 1976).

9. "With the transfer of the means of production into common ownership, the single family ceases to be the economic unit of society. Private housekeeping is transformed into a social industry. The care and education of the children becomes a public affair." Friedrich Engels, *The Origin of The Family, Private Property, and the State*, edited and with an introduction by Eleanor Burke Leacock (New York: International Publishers, 1981), 139.

10. *The Family and the Communist State*, 1919.

11. Ibid.

12. S. N. Prokopovicz, *Histoire économique de l'URSS*, translated by M. Body (Le Portulan, 1952).

13. Ibid.

14. "In a society where everything sacred is trampled underfoot and crushed, where human energies and faculties are perverted, human nature itself is deformed. The gross lack of spirituality which characterizes the prevailing values creates a one-dimensional human being without intrinsic value—an asexual 'homo sovieticus'." From "Délivrée des larmes d'Eve, réjouis-toi!" Tatiana Goritcheva, *Femmes et Russie* (Editions des Femmes, 1980).

15. "La Femme nouvelle et la classe ouvrière," *Les Cahiers de l'églantine*, No. XII (Paris-Brussels, 1932).

16. Pierre Pascal, *Les Grands courants de la pensée russe contemporaine* (L'Age d'homme, 1971).

17. See Kendall E. Bailes, "Alexandra Kollontai et la nouvelle morale," *Cahiers du monde russe et soviétique* No. 4 (1965).

18. During a famous interview with Clara Zetkin in late 1920, Lenin branded the promulgation of the theory of sexual revolution, and the theory itself, as contrary to the interests of Communism: "You must be familiar with the famous theory that in a Communist society, the fulfillment of sexual instincts and love needs would be as easy, and have as many consequences, as 'drinking a glass of water'. As a Communist, I have no sympathy whatsoever for the 'water glass' theory, even when it bears the attractive label of 'free love'. Incidentally, this liberation of love is neither new nor Communist. . . . In my opinion, the sexual hypertrophism which we see so often nowadays does not increase vitality or dynamism, but merely diminishes them. At the current stage of the Revolution, this is very, very disturbing." Excerpts from *Souvenirs de Lénine* (Berlin, 1957). See B. W. Cook's article for a long quote from Lenin's interview with Clara Zetkin about the "water-glass" theory.

19. Concerning "The Dragon and the White Bird": "Bourgeois culture has fed and fortified the 'dragon' in man, while it has killed the 'white bird' in woman. The culture of working humanity will create the necessary conditions

for the disappearance, not only of the voluntary humiliation of women, but of the age-old problem of antagonism between the sexes. The 'dragon' will disappear, and the winner will be the 'white bird'—the creative work of each individual, male and female, within the collective." Judith Stora-Sandor, *Alexandra Kollontai: Marxisme et révolution sexuelle* (Maspéro, 1973).

20. Tenth Congress of the C.P.S.U., 1921.

21. Her autobiographies are silent on this point, perhaps because of repression. Marcel Body, who had been part of the French mission to Russia in 1916 and worked as a diplomat in Norway with Alexandra Kollontai, tells us that, despite the pressing demands of the Workers' Opposition, she subsequently declined to come out on their behalf. *Preuves* No. 14 (April 1952).

22. Her speeches in the spring of 1921 at Sverdlo University, Leningrad, barely touch on the subjects she dealt with in *The New Woman and the Working Class* (sexuality and family problems) and are confined to an analysis centering on the role of economics, sticking close to the Bolshevik Party's majority line.

23. Richard Stites, *The Women's Liberation Movement in Russia* (Princeton University Press, 1978).

24. The newspaper was founded by Colette Reynaud in 1917 for pacifist feminists.

25. A listing of these *La Voix des Femmes* articles, in chronological order:

> *April 24, 1919: "Les courants féministes en Russie," by E. Despreaux*
> *July 24, 1919: (Untitled), by Monnette Thomas*
> *August 7, 1919: "L'oeuvre d'Alexandra Kollontai," by Boris Souvarine*
> *September 9, 1920: "La famille et l'Etat communiste," by A. Chareau (summary of a study by A. Kollontai)*
> *October 14, 1920: "La révolution et les femmes," by M. Bigot*
> *November 18, 1920: "La condition des ouvrières dan la Russie des Soviets," by C. Jeannet*
> *July 7, 1921: "Conférence des femmes communistes et la Troisième Internationale," by A. Kollontai*
> *July 28, 1921: "Pour la Russie"*
> *August 11, 1921: "Vera Zassoulitch," by Charles Rappoport. "Le code bolchevik du mariage"*
> *August 25, 1921: "La famille future," by M. Pelletier*
> *October 27, 1921: "La condition des femmes dans la Russie communiste," by M. Pelletier (after her trip)*

26. Madeleine Pelletier (1874–1939) was the head of the feminist group "La Solidarité des femmes" from 1906 on.

27. Madeleine Pelletier, *Mon Voyage adventureux en Russie communiste* (Girard, 1922).

28. *L'Europe Nouvelle*, No. 51, December 17, 1921.

29. *L'Ouvrière*, September 13, 1923: "En Russie soviétique, de l'ancienne famille à la famille nouvelle, éveil de la personalité. Crise causée par les évènements," and September 22, 1923: "En Russie soviétique, de l'ancienne famille à la nouvelle. La révolution des moeurs retarde sur la révolution économique et politique," Trotsky.

30. See Marcel Body, *Un Piano en bouleau de Carélie, mes années de Russie, 1917–1927* (Hachette, 1981).

CONTRIBUTORS

MIEKE AERTS is Assistant Professor of Women's Studies in the Social Science Department of the University of Amsterdam. She is co-author of *Naar natuurlijk bestel*, a history of Dutch women's organizations in the 1930s. Her articles on feminist theory and on the ideologies of women's organizations have appeared in such Dutch journals as *Tijdschrift voor Vrouwenstudies* (which she co-founded) and *Jaarboek voor vrouwengeschiedenis*. She was a co-organizer of the first Dutch National Women's Studies Conference (1981) and of the first international conference on the history of same-sex relations "Among Men, Among Women" (1983).

FRANÇOISE BASCH is Professor of Civilization at the Institute of English, Charles V of the University of Paris VII. She is author of *Relative Creatures: Victorian Women in Society and the Novel* and editor of Theresa Malkiel's *Diary of a Shirtwaist Striker*, entitled *Journal d'une gréviste*. Her articles on English and American women of the nineteenth and early twentieth centuries have appeared in P. Grimal, editor, *Histoire mondiale de la femme* and in such journals as *Etudes anglaises, Romantisme,* les *Cahiers Charles V,* le *Mouvement social* and *La Quinzaine littéraire*. She is one of the founders of the Groupe d'Etudes Féministes (G.E.F.) at the University of Paris and has served on the editorial board of *Nouvelles Questions Féministes*.

GISELA BOCK is Privatdozentin at the Historical Institute of the Technical University in Berlin and Associate Professor of European History at the European University Institute in Florence. She is author of *Thomas Campanella, Die "andere" Arbeiterbewegung in den USA, 1905–1922: The Industrial Workers of the World,* and *Zwangssterilisation im Nationalsozialismus: Studien zür Rassenpolitik und Frauenpolitik,* an analysis of racism and sexism through a study of compulsory sterilization in Nazi Germany.

MARIE-JO BONNET is a historian and writer. She is author of *Un Choix sans équivoque,* a historical study of love relations between women from the sixteenth to the twentieth century, and *Subversions: Epopée de la conscience,* a book about her own experience with the contemporary women's liberation movement in France. Her articles have appeared in such journals as *Vlasta, Profil,* and *Neuf.*

BLANCHE WIESEN COOK is Professor of History at John Jay College of Criminal Justice (City University of New York). She is editor of *Crystal Eastman on Women and Revolution* and author of *The Declassified Eisenhower: A Divided Legacy of Peace and Political Warfare.* Her articles on twentieth-century American political and military history and on women's political and social history have appeared in several anthologies and in such journals as *Signs, Ikon, The American Historical Review, Heresies, Radical Historical Review* and *Ms.*

FRANÇOISE DUCROCQ is Maître de Conférences of English Civilization at the Institut d'Anglais Charles V, of the University of Paris VII. Her articles on British nineteenth-century working-class and feminist history have appeared in such journals as *Critique, La Révue d'Enface, Pénélope* (in France), and *Feminist Studies* (in the United States). Ducrocq was one of the organizers of the first national conference on Women's Studies in France, which took place in Toulouse in 1982.

YASMINE ERGAS is a sociologist, a former consultant to O.E.C.D., UNESCO, and WHO, and now a Staff Associate at the Social Science Research Council in New York. She is author of *La Maglie della politica: feminismo ed istitzioni nell Italia degli anni settanta*, a book of essays on contemporary feminism. Her articles on present-day social movements, including feminism, and on Western political systems have appeared in several Italian journals and in *Comparative Politics* in the U.S.

CHRISTINE FAURÉ is Chargé de Recherche in Sociology at the Centre National de Recherche Scientifique (C.N.R.S.) in Paris. She is author of *Terre, Terreur, Liberté*, a book about Russian Populism, and *La Démocratie sans les femmes*, about the place of women in French liberal theory. In France her articles have appeared in *Cultures* (UNESCO), *Les Temps Modernes, Le Bulletin du C.R.I.F., Change International*, and *Corpus*. In the U.S. she has been published in *Signs*.

GENEVIÈVE FRAISSE is a researcher in philosophy at the Centre National de Recherche Scientifique in Paris and is responsible for a seminar at the Collège International de Philosophie. She is author of *Femmes toutes mains, essai sur le service domestique* and *Clémence Royer, philosophe et femme de sciences*. Her articles have appeared in a number of anthologies and in such journals as *Les Temps modernes, Raison présente, M/F*, and *Corpus*. Fraisse also helped found the following journals *Les Révoltes logiques* and *Pénélope*.

JUDITH FRIEDLANDER is Associate Professor of Anthropology at the State University of New York, College at Purchase. She is author of *Being Indian in Hueyapan: A Study of Forced Identity in Contemporary Mexico*, and her articles on feminist theory and ethnicity have appeared in such journals as *Latin American Research Review, Dialectical Anthropology, Judaism, Heresies, Nouvelles Questions Féministes*, and *Revue française d'études américaines*.

DIANA GITTINS was Lecturer in Sociology at the University of Essex and Plymouth Polytechnic. She is author of *Fair Sex: Family Size and Structure 1900–1939* and *Family in Question: Changing Households and Familiar Ideologies*. Her articles have appeared in such journals as *Victorian Studies, Oral History*, and *Feminist Review* and in the anthologies *The Interview Method in Social Science* and *Labour and Love*. Presently she is a free-lance writer.

ATINA GROSSMANN is Assistant Professor of History at Mount Holyoke College. She is co-editor and contributor to *When Biology Became Destiny: Women in Weimar and Nazi Germany*. Her articles on the Sex Reform Movement and the New Woman in Weimar Germany have appeared in the books *Powers of Desire: The Politics of Sexuality* and *Towards the Holocaust: The Social and Economic Collapse of the Weimar Republic* as well as in various German publications.

ALICE KESSLER-HARRIS is Professor of History at Hofstra University, where she co-directs the Center for the Study of Work and Leisure. She is author of *Out to Work: A History of Wage-Earning Women in the United States* and *Women Have Always Worked: A Historical Overview*. She has published widely in such journals as *Signs, Feminist Studies*, and *Labor History*, and her articles on women workers and on women in the labor movement have appeared in many anthologies, most recently in *Women, Work and Protest: A Century of U.S. Women's Labor History.*

CLAUDIA KOONZ is Associate Professor of History at the College of the Holy Cross in Massachusetts. She is co-editor, with Renate Bridenthal, and contributor to *Becoming Visible: Women in European History* and author of *Mothers in the Fatherland: Women's Responses to Nazism.* Koonz's articles on women in Nazi Germany have appeared as well in *When Biology Became Destiny: Women in Weimar and Nazi Germany* and in history and feminist journals.

ELINOR LERNER is Associate Professor of Sociology at Stockton State College, New Jersey. Her articles on the response of different ethnic groups in New York City to the women's suffrage movement have appeared in the anthologies *From the World of the Other: Papers From the Fifth Berkshire Conference on the History of Women* and *Encounter of Jew and Gentile in America* and in such journals as *American Jewish History, Heuristics,* and *The Insurgent Sociologist.*

MARCELLE MARINI is Maître de Conférences at the University of Paris VII in the Faculty of Sciences des Textes et des Documents. She is author of *Territoires du féminin avec Marguerite Duras* and of articles in *Littérature, Critique, Pénélope, Cahiers Renaud/Barrault,* and *Cahiers du G.R.I.F.* (Brussels). Marini also works closely with the Centre de Recherches et d'Information Féministes (le C.R.I.F.).

MARIE-CLAIRE PASQUIER is Maître de Conférences in the Department of English and American Studies at the University of Paris X. She is co-author of *Le Nouveau théâtre anglais* and author of *Le Théâtre américain d'aujourd'hui.* She has translated Edward Bond's play *Lear* (with Simone Benmussa), Gertrude Stein's play *Doctor Faustus Lights the Lights,* and William Kennedy's novel *Ironweed.* Her articles have appeared in *Les Temps Modernes, Théâtre/public, Modern Drama, Comédie-Française,* and *Delta* and her short fiction in *Sorcières.*

FRANÇOISE PICQ is Assistante (Assistant Professor) of Political Science at the University of Paris IX, Dauphine. She is author of *On the Theory of Mother Right: Anthropological and Socialist Discourses* (thesis), and her work on feminism and socialism in nineteenth- and twentieth-century France has appeared in *Les Temps Modernes, Pénélope,* and *Revue d'en face.* Picq was one of the organizers of the first national conference on Women Studies in France (Toulouse, 1982) and the founder of the Feminist Studies Association in Paris.

RAYNA RAPP is Associate Professor and Chair of Anthropology at the Graduate Faculty of the New School for Social Research. She is editor of *Toward an Anthropology of Women,* and her articles on feminist theory and French social anthropology have appeared in the anthologies *Powers of Desire: The Politics of Sexuality* and *Rethinking the Family* and in such journals as *Feminist Studies, Signs, Comparative Studies in Society and History,* and *Anthropological Quarterly.*

ELLEN ROSS is Associate Professor of Women's Studies at Ramapo College in New Jersey. She has written on women and the family in nineteenth- and twentieth-century England and the U.S. Her articles have appeared in the anthology *Powers of Desire: The Politics of Sexuality* and in the journals *Feminist Studies, History Workshop, Signs,* and *Comparative Studies in Society and History.*

GUDRUN SCHWARZ is Wissenschaftlich Mitarbeiterin (Assistant Professor) of Sociology and Women's Studies at the Free University of Berlin. Her doctoral research is on the changes in sexual morality in Germany between 1850 and

1933, with particular focus given to ideas about female homosexuality. Her articles have appeared in *Frauen suchen ihre Geschichte, Among Men, Among Women: Sociological and Historical Recognition of Homosexual Arrangements*, and *Die ungeschriebene Geschichte: Historische Frauenforschung*.

CARROLL SMITH-ROSENBERG is Professor of History and Psychiatry at the University of Pennsylvania and Director of the women's studies program. She is author of *Religion and the Rise of the American City* and *Disorderly Conduct: Visions of Gender in Victorian America*. Her articles have appeared in the anthologies *A Heritage of Her Own* and *The Signs Reader* and in the journals *Signs, Journal of Contemporary History, American Quarterly, Feminist Studies*, and *Social Research*.

ANNE-MARIE SOHN is Assistante (Assistant Professor) of History at the University of Paris I. Her research on feminism and syndicalism among teachers in France and on French feminist leaders and the role of French women at the turn of the century has appeared in thesis form *(Féminisme et syndicalisme)* and in the journals *Mouvement Social* and *Revue d'histoire moderne et contemporaine*.

CATHARINE R. STIMPSON, Professor of English and Director of the Institute for Research on Women at Rutgers University, the State University of New Jersey, was the founding editor of *Signs: Journal of Women in Culture and Society*. She has written a novel, *Class Notes*, edited six books, and published over 75 monographs, short stories, essays, and reviews. She is an active lecturer and the member of several boards. She serves as Chair of the New York State Council for the Humanities, of the *Ms.* magazine Board of Scholars, and of the National Council for Research on Women.

CAROLE BEEBE TARANTELLI is Associate Professor of English Literature at the University of Rome, Faculty of Letters and Philosophy, and a practicing psychoanalyst. She is author of *Ritratto de ignoto: l'operario nell romanzo vittoriano* and has edited and written an introduction to the Italian version of the autobiography of Fredrick Douglass. Tarantelli was among the founders and editors of the Italian literary journal *Calibano*, and her articles on feminist literary criticism and Victorian Studies have appeared in the journals *Studi inglesi, Calibano*, and *Nuova Corrente*.

ANNEMARIE TRÖGER teaches sociology and social history at the University of Hannover (Germany). She is co-author of *Mutterkreuz und Arbeitsbuch*, a book on the history of women in the Weimar Republic and under National Socialism. Her articles on women and fascism have appeared in such anthologies as *Frauen und Wissenschaft, Frauen in der Geschichte II*, and *When Biology Became Destiny*. Articles have also appeared in such American journals as *Radical America, Quest*, and *New German Critique*. Tröger is co-founder and an editor of the German women's studies journal *Feministische Studien*.

MARTHA VICINUS is Professor of English and Women's Studies at the University of Michigan. She was a founder of the Women's Studies Program at Indiana University and has directed the Women's Studies Program at the University of Michigan. She has published widely on Victorian popular culture and working-class culture, and Victorian women and the history of sexuality in *Signs, Feminist Studies, New Literary History, Style* and *College English*. She is author of *The Industrial Muse: Nineteenth-Century Working-Class Literature, Independent Women: Work and Community for Single Women*, and editor of *Suffer and Be Still: Women in the Victorian Age* and *A Widening Sphere: Changing Roles of Victorian Women*.